THE NEWSPAPER AXIS

THE NEWSPAPER AXIS

Six Press Barons Who Enabled Hitler

KATHRYN S. OLMSTED

Yale

UNIVERSITY PRESS

New Haven and London

Yale University Press books may be purchased in quantity for
educational, business, or promotional use. For information, please
e-mail sales.press@yale.edu (U.S. office) or sales@yaleup.co.uk
(U.K. office).

Set in Janson type by IDS Infotech Ltd.
Printed in the United States of America.

Library of Congress Control Number: 2021942672
ISBN 978-0-300-25642-0 (hardcover : alk. paper)

A catalogue record for this book is available from the
British Library.

This paper meets the requirements of ANSI/NISO Z39.48-1992
(Permanence of Paper).

10 9 8 7 6 5 4 3 2 1

For Eric

Contents

Acknowledgments

I AM GRATEFUL TO THE many archivists and librarians who helped me with this project, with special thanks to archivists Virginia Lewick at the Franklin D. Roosevelt Presidential Library, Spencer Howard and Craig Wright at the Herbert Hoover Presidential Library, Eric Gillespie at Cantigny Park, and Anne Thomason at the Lake Forest College Archives for providing exceptional assistance. I also thank Davor Mondom at Syracuse University for photographing documents for me. I conducted the initial research for this book while enjoying fellowships at Clare Hall and at the Centre for Research in the Arts, Social Sciences, and Humanities at the University of Cambridge.

Here at UC Davis, Daniel Goldstein at Shields Library agreed to buy twelve years of microfilm of the *San Francisco Examiner*, and Brian Scheu, Jeremiah Daniel-Padgett, Sarah Ainsworth, and Isabella Ainsworth trawled through those reels to help locate articles. Isabella also found and photographed documents for me and read the entire manuscript with care and precision. Jason Newborn assisted me by obtaining microfilm of the *Washington Times-Herald* and other texts through interlibrary loan. I also appreciate the support of the Academic Senate Committee on Research.

I benefited greatly from colleagues who provided insights. Todd Bennett was kind enough to read chapter 10 and helped clarify my understanding of the role of visual media in the intervention debate. Matthew Pressman, Andrew Johnstone, and Christopher McKnight

Nichols alerted me to key documents and works. I also received helpful advice from colleagues who heard me present parts of this project at conferences. I am grateful to Mark Brilliant, Caitlyn Rosenthal, Nils Gilman, Robin Einhorn, and Brooke Blower for providing helpful feedback on the first draft of my proposal for this book at the Greater Bay Area Modern American Political Economy Seminar. I am especially indebted to Brooke, who gave astute advice each time she heard me present a different iteration of the project. I also appreciate the comments I received after presentations at the Organization of American Historians annual conference and two conferences of the Boston-California-London political history group. Special thanks to Jennifer Burns, Jim Campbell, John Huntington, Bruce Schulman, and David Astin Walsh for their comments at these venues. Here at UC Davis, Ari Kelman generously read an entire draft and provided constructive suggestions for the manuscript.

Thanks also go to my agent, Lisa Adams, who expertly guided me through the publication process, and my editor at Yale University Press, Bill Frucht, who helped sharpen the arguments and the text. Robin DuBlanc was a superb copyeditor.

I am, as always, most grateful to my husband and colleague, Eric Rauchway, who not only traveled to archives with me and photographed documents for me, but also shared his many insights on the New Deal.

Introduction

ON CHRISTMAS EVE 1934, Lord Harold Rothermere, owner of the London *Daily Mail*, filed a story from Munich about a magnetic national leader who had "given Germany a new soul." As Rothermere explained to his millions of readers, young Germans were now full of vigor and "zest for work." They were nothing like the oppressed people of fifteen years earlier, when their nation was reeling from its defeat in World War I and the vengeful peace treaty that followed. Germany was "on her feet again."

What was responsible for this marvelous transformation? "By what force has this land been lifted from a despondent, discouraged, disregarded condition to its old place in the front rank of the Great Powers?" Rothermere asked his readers rhetorically. "*HITLER*. That is the whole answer." In less than two years in power, Rothermere wrote, the Nazi chancellor had fulfilled a "predestined task" by assuming all of Germany's "forces and energies," now placed in the hands of one strong leader. Rothermere went on to assure his readers that accounts of the Nazis' persecution of Jews were untrue. In German restaurants and hotels during the Christmas season, he frequently saw "merry and festive parties of German Jews who showed no symptoms of insecurity or suffering."[1]

While Rothermere praised Hitler's "rekindling of the German soul," the Nazi government had ousted Jews from most professions and public positions, banned opposition political parties, and arrested and killed political opponents. It had also established a network of concentration camps. Although not yet mass-extermination factories, these camps imprisoned tens of thousands of Jews, communists, and others the Third Reich considered inferior or dangerous.[2]

Rothermere was extreme in his enthusiasm for Hitler, but not unique. For years, he and his fellow press barons in the United States and the United Kingdom pressured their nations' leaders to ignore the menace of fascism. As a result, these publishers helped give the aggressor nations the opportunity to seize valuable territory and resources. The press lords' insistence that their governments should not confront the fascist dictators made a war against fascism both more likely and more difficult to win.

The six most powerful media moguls in the United States and the United Kingdom—Rothermere, Lord Max Beaverbrook, William Randolph Hearst, Robert McCormick, and Joseph and Cissy Patterson—all dismissed the fascist threat. These five men and one woman owned and directed the best-selling newspapers in their countries, reaching up to 16 million Britons and 50 million Americans in the late 1930s—and more during the war.[3] Their xenophobic, nationalist, imperialist, and anti-Semitic views made it harder for anti-fascists in their governments to challenge the Nazis earlier.

These six publishers were among the most influential and controversial political players of their day. Lashing out at the administration's critics, one Roosevelt official called them "the newspaper axis." British prime minister Stanley Baldwin publicly denounced Rothermere and Beaverbrook for exercising "power without responsibility."[4] Ernest Bevin, a Labour leader, claimed that Beaverbrook and the rest of the British press, known collectively as Fleet Street, after the thoroughfare in London where most had their headquarters, wielded more authority than the people's elected representatives. "I object to this country being ruled from Fleet Street, however big the circulation, instead of from Parliament," he said in 1945.[5] In the United States, readers boycotted the press lords and burned copies of their papers. Some proprietors welcomed this image of themselves as master manipulators. Beaverbrook once boasted that he ran his newspapers "purely for the purpose of making propaganda."[6]

The mass-circulation newspaper publishers helped develop a new style of journalism that gave them power to mold the political opinions of their fellow citizens. Nineteenth-century newspapers had been subsidized by political parties, but modern mass-market newspapers relied on funding from advertisers. To increase profits, therefore, they required more readers. They quickly discovered that they could attract these readers by selling outrage and scandal. William Randolph Hearst, the most successful media entrepreneur of them all, described his ideal newspaper this way: "You looked at the first page and said, O GOSH!—and at the second page and said GEE WHIZ!—and at the third page and said HOLY MOSES!"[7] And once they had the attention of their readers, these press lords could try to sell them policy positions as well as consumer goods.

These modern newspapers favored spectacle over substance, celebrity over leadership, and polemics over sober debate.[8] The most successful publishers discovered that they could attract readers by highlighting race, nation, and empire—themes that their advertisers could also support. They could make money and gain political power by selling an exclusionary vision of their nations—"us" versus "them." The new journalism was not always reactionary, but its emphasis on individuals, personality, strength, and ethno-nationalism could help promote authoritarian politics.

Though these newspapers catered to the average reader, their publishers made their own outrageously consumerist lifestyles and outsized personalities part of their brand. They sold themselves by writing front-page editorials, launching campaigns for political causes, and carefully curating the coverage of their personal images in their papers. They did not just sell the news: they sold "the news," a product they constructed, sometimes by reporting on events that had not happened—in other words, by lying.

These media moguls, who trafficked in populist slogans but lived like kings, were part of a transnational movement to boost white supremacy and discourage resistance to fascism. They did not shrink from all British or American military interventions abroad. Rather, they opposed American or British intervention against the Nazis specifically. They fought public officials' attempts to challenge Hitler, whose goals, as they saw them—order, anti-communism, "racial purity," and Anglo-Saxon domination—they generally supported even as they condemned his methods.

Some of these publishers, untethered from local parties, cooperated across the Atlantic to promote their shared values and policies. At a very dangerous moment in world history, as Hitler built up his military and invaded his neighbors, these press lords worked together to pressure their respective governments to dismiss and ignore the fascist threat. In the process, they helped create a discourse of right-wing grievance and ethno-nationalism that still animates British and American politics today.

•

Lord Rothermere was the most notorious of these press barons because of his blatantly pro-fascist views. In news articles that he wrote himself, the publisher praised Benito Mussolini's Italy and Hitler's Germany as the "best-governed nations in Europe today." He rhapsodized about the "immense benefits" the Nazis had brought to Germany, claiming that Hitler had "saved his country from the ineffectual leadership of hesitating, half-hearted politicians." While conceding that the Nazis might have committed some "minor misdeeds," Rothermere argued that they needed to control the "alien elements" and "Israelites of international attachments" who were "insinuating themselves" into the German state.[9] He also cheered the British Union of Fascists ("Hurrah for the Blackshirts!" read one infamous headline) because he believed Britain needed a right-wing party to take over national affairs "with the same directness of purpose and energy of method as Mussolini and Hitler have displayed."[10]

By contrast, Lord Max Beaverbrook, owner of the London *Daily Express*, *Sunday Express*, and *Evening Standard*, was no Nazi apologist. But he did encourage readers and British policy makers to dismiss or appease Hitler throughout the 1930s. He believed in "splendid isolation": protecting the British Empire while ignoring conflicts on the European continent. "The policy for Britain is plain: no more truck with the foreigners," he wrote in 1933. "No more European trammels on our freedom. Backs to the Continent and faces to the Empire!"[11] He repeatedly assured his readers that Britain need not bother itself about Hitler's anti-Semitism or his threats to neighboring countries. The publisher also tried to prevent his readers from hearing alternative viewpoints. Because Beaverbrook regarded his longtime friend, the Tory MP and anti-Nazi Winston Churchill, as a warmonger and an enemy of the empire, he fired Churchill as his columnist in 1938. Beaverbrook insisted until the last possible moment that Hitler posed no threat to Britain. As late as August 1939, he assured his millions of readers there would be "no war this year."[12] Just three weeks later, the Nazis invaded Poland and World War II began in Europe.

Across the Atlantic, William Randolph Hearst, one of the most dominant figures in American media history, owned the largest newspaper chain in the world. At his peak, he published twenty-eight newspapers. One in four Americans read his Sunday papers. He also owned thirteen magazines and a news syndication service that sent news, photos, and features around the world. A pioneer in new media, he produced feature films, serials, and newsreels.

Hearst's critics at the time called him a fascist, though the articles he himself wrote were never overtly pro-Nazi. He did, however, do business with the Third Reich, and his critics believed that the Nazis had bribed him in return for favorable coverage.[13] In private, Hearst praised Hitler's "enormous energy, intense enthusiasm ... and great organizing ability"; in public, he predicted that the Nazis would soon turn away from anti-Semitism.[14] His admiration for fascists extended to Mussolini, whom he called "a marvelous man."[15] Hearst hired Mussolini, Hitler, and other top fascist officials to write self-serving articles for the Hearst press.

Like Beaverbrook and Rothermere, Hearst worried that the "white race" would be eclipsed and destroyed by "savage races" if European nations fought one another. He was not a pacifist. He had warned his readers against the "yellow peril" for decades and frequently demanded that his government prepare for war against Asian nations; he also argued for various U.S. invasions in Latin America. But he maintained that the United States should not intervene in Europe in either world war. Even after America joined World War II, Hearst told his readers that the war in Europe had begun much like the Continent's previous conflicts: "a tribal squabble" over "trivial commercial advantages or inconsequential territorial tracts," characterized by "hatred and jealousy of this European nation for that or the other European nation."[16] The "vilest deed"

Nazi Germany had committed was to unite with Japan and turn an intra-race dispute into a world war by allying "against its own white race with the yellow peril."[17]

In addition to Hearst, America's most influential publishers included a trio of cousins: Robert McCormick of the *Chicago Tribune*, Joseph Medill Patterson of the *New York Daily News*, and Eleanor "Cissy" Medill Patterson of the *Washington Times-Herald*. Grandchildren of Joseph Medill, an early owner of the *Chicago Tribune* and a founder of the Republican Party, the cousins built on their inheritance to acquire a media empire second only to Hearst's. And like Hearst, they used their papers to proselytize for nationalism, appeasement, and isolation.

McCormick enjoyed a reputation as the most reactionary major publisher in the United States—the "greatest mind of the fourteenth century," one critic called him.[18] He viewed Franklin Roosevelt's New Deal as not merely wrongheaded but a plot to destroy the Constitution, the republic, and the liberties of the American people. He singled out Roosevelt's Jewish advisers, such as Supreme Court Justice Felix Frankfurter, as members of a foreign-directed conspiracy against America.[19]

Like Hearst, McCormick was a hemispheric imperialist who supported U.S. invasions of Latin America while warning against the dangers of confronting Hitler. He never wrote pro-Nazi stories or editorials or made business deals with the Nazi government. But he did allow a pro-Nazi reporter to cover European news for the *Tribune*, even after it became clear that the reporter was unreliable and biased. (He became a Nazi propagandist during the war.) McCormick told his readers that neither Germany nor Japan threatened the United States. When the United States joined the war, McCormick insisted that the struggle was pointless, that Roosevelt was incompetent in directing it, and that the president might have conspired to enter it so that he could become a totalitarian dictator and create a one-world "superstate."

Known as "the colonel," his rank in the U.S. Army in World War I, McCormick was an ultra-nationalist who questioned the patriotism of his American political enemies and even the legitimacy of their laws. McCormick went so far as to defy national security laws by printing two stories based on secret information. One, published before the United States entered the conflict, exposed the military's secret war plans; and the second, printed during the war, could have revealed to the Japanese that American cryptographers had broken their codes.

McCormick's cousin Joseph Medill ("Joe") Patterson also vehemently opposed American entry into World War II. Like Hearst, he worried that a war in Europe would lead to the "passing of the great race" and allow "yellow hordes" to invade America.[20] To avoid this racial catastrophe, he urged his government to appease Germany and, after 1940, Japan. His newspaper covered anti-Semites so sympathetically that Jewish groups organized boycotts against it.

Joe's sister, Cissy Patterson, ran the largest newspaper in Washington, D.C., and was the first female publisher of a major U.S. metropolitan daily in the twentieth century. She did not have strong political opinions or write many editorials. But she printed her brother's editorials in her newspaper almost every day beginning in 1941, putting them in the hands of national policy makers. She also published stories by the Patterson/McCormick reporters, who slanted the news in favor of isolationism.

These proprietors published the most popular newspapers in their countries, and indeed the world. In 1930, Rothermere's *Daily Mail* sold more copies, 1,845,000, than any other daily in Britain; after a few years of decline, it still enjoyed sales of 1,580,000 in 1937. The *Daily Express* increased its daily sales from 1,693,000 in 1930 to 2,329,000 in 1937 to claim the title of the world's best-selling daily newspaper. By contrast, the staid, respectable, pro-appeasement *Daily Telegraph* sold 637,000 copies a day and the London *Times* just 192,000.[21]

In the United States as well, the papers that earned the least respect sold the most copies. In 1937, the distinguished and interventionist *New York Times* reported 472,000 daily sales and 712,000 on Sundays; the *New York Herald Tribune*, another high-end, internationalist publication, sold 327,000 daily papers and 476,000 on Sundays. (Unlike in Britain, Sunday newspapers were not separate publications with distinct staff, but rather weekend editions of the daily newspaper.) These might seem like impressive numbers, but they were just a fraction of the circulation of the most popular isolationist papers. The tabloid *Daily News*, the nation's best-selling newspaper, sold more than 1,600,000 daily copies and 2,800,000 Sunday copies. The *Chicago Tribune*, America's most popular broadsheet, boasted 800,000 daily sales and more than 1,000,000 on Sundays; and the Hearst chain had more than 6,889,000 daily and 7,364,000 Sunday sales.[22]

Estimating four readers per copy, it is likely that the McCormick/Patterson press reached more than 12 million Americans daily and 20 million on Sundays. Hearst had 30 million readers, and the *Mail* and the *Express* together counted about 16 million British readers. As tensions in Europe reached crisis levels in the late 1930s, more than 60 million people in both countries got their news from these isolationist newspapers.

These publishers did not always agree on domestic political issues. Rothermere, Hearst, and McCormick were on the far right in the 1930s; they consistently opposed government spending, high taxes on the rich, and labor unions, and they believed that liberals and leftists in their countries were stooges for the Bolsheviks. They fabricated stories to draw false connections between the New Dealers or Labour Party members and the Soviets. Beaverbrook and Joe Patterson, on the other hand, never showed much concern about the dangers of communism, either at home or abroad. They appeared to be sincere believers in democracy, at least in the Anglo-American world. Patterson was a genuine liberal who endorsed Franklin Roosevelt for the presidency three times and was an ebullient promoter of the New Deal's policy revolution.

But they all shared the same assumption about foreign policy. It would be disastrous, they believed, for their nations to endanger their own interests by confronting the Nazis.

∎

This is the first book to analyze how British and American press lords worked together to delay and undermine the Anglo-American alliance against Hitler. A transnational approach, as opposed to a focus on a single nation, reveals common arguments, beliefs, and language in the debate about resisting Nazism. An Anglo-American analysis can help us better understand where "isolationism" comes from, how the term was used, and what it meant.

In the United States, some opponents of intervention in Europe disavowed the term *isolationism* because they believed that it lacked nuance, and scholars have expressed reservations about it in the years since. Many different groups in Britain and America opposed a confrontational policy with Hitler: imperialists as well as pacifists, Socialists and fascists, Democrats and Republicans, Tories and Labour Party members. Given the breadth of this coalition, some historians have argued that "isolationist" and "isolationism" should be used with skepticism, if not completely retired.[23]

A transnational study, however, can help uncover the origins and meaning of the term. Since the Victorian era, British public officials had used the phrase "splendid isolation" to describe a system of imperial preference and protection. "This policy of splendid isolation," as Beaverbrook said in 1933, "is the traditional policy of the Conservative Party. It was the policy of Disraeli, of Salisbury, and of Joe Chamberlain," he continued, referring to past Tory prime ministers.[24] Once Hitler came to power and Beaverbrook worried that his nation might become involved in the affairs of Europe, the *Express* publisher frequently used "isolationism" and "isolationist" to describe his insistence that Britain should remain aloof from the repression and pogroms in Nazi Germany. By 1934, he believed that he was making headway in persuading other Britons in the media as well as those in government to adopt his policies. "We are all Isolationists now," he crowed in one editorial.[25] Rothermere also used "isolation" and "isolationism" to describe his preferred foreign policy, though he was not as much as an evangelist for the terms as Beaverbrook.[26]

Beaverbrook did not confine his enthusiasm for isolationism to Britain: he also worked to promote the language and substance of isolationism in the United States. In April 1935, for example, he wrote a piece for the Hearst press explaining the ideology of "the section of opinion to which I belong—the Isolationists." He argued, "Britain should make no alliances except with the United States, that we should incur no obligations, no responsibilities, no liabilities to any nation outside the Empire except in relation to the Anglo-Saxon race." It was through splendid isolation, he said, that Britain could gain "freedom of will and action" and avoid "Continental intrigues and maneuvers."[27]

Joe Patterson, who worked with Beaverbrook to promote isolation on both sides of the Atlantic, also eagerly embraced the term

isolationist. As early as 1925, in an obituary for Senator Medill Mc-
Cormick of Illinois, Patterson's cousin, the *Daily News* described the
anti–League of Nations lawmaker as "an isolationist."[28] Patterson
called himself, his sister, and his cousin Robert McCormick "the isolationist furies," and referred to his allies in Britain, both Beaverbrook and Prime Minister Neville Chamberlain, as isolationists as
well.[29] He angrily rebutted the interventionists' attempts to make
the term an epithet. "We've been accused by some readers of being
an isolationist paper. You bet we're an isolationist paper," the *News*
stated in 1938.[30] In 1944, during the war, Patterson wrote an editorial proclaiming himself an isolationist, even though the "world-
savers" had tried to make the term a "brand of infamy."[31]

Hearst was not as enthusiastic about the term *isolationist*, and
McCormick explicitly disavowed it. But they both argued for similar policies even as they used different language. Hearst preferred
the phrase "America First"—the slogan some of his newspapers
wore on their front-page nameplates from 1919 into the 1960s. But
for Hearst, "America First" and "isolationism" meant essentially the
same thing: a refusal to participate in "squabbles" among Europeans. "Your columnist is an isolationist, yes," he wrote in his front-
page column in November 1941, shortly before U.S. entry into the
war.[32] McCormick described himself as a "nationalist," but he allowed his reporters to use "isolationist" in their news stories.[33]

When they spoke of "isolation" or "isolationism," the mass-
circulation publishers did not mean that they wanted to cut off all
contact with other nations. For Rothermere and Beaverbrook,
"splendid isolation" meant defending the British Empire, imposing
high tariffs on nonimperial products, and refusing formal alliances
with other nations. Beaverbrook explained his meaning: "isolation
for Britain, isolation splendid and secure through our closer relations with the Empire."[34] It might seem strange to us today, but in
the 1930s British imperialists believed they could best defend the
empire through what they called isolationism.

The U.S. press lords practiced an American version of splendid
isolation. They opposed the League of Nations and what they called
"entangling alliances," echoing George Washington; they supported
tariffs on imported goods, strict immigration controls, and a military strong enough to dominate Latin America and project U.S.

power into the Pacific. They argued that isolationism meant opposing any "meddling" in European affairs.

Though these publishers did not want to isolate America or Britain from the world, they did want their governments to work in isolation from other major powers, especially those in continental Europe. Far from being neutralist, noninterventionist, or antimilitarist, they were committed to military interventions in their formal (British) or informal (American) empires; they believed, in effect, in a kind of autarkic imperialism.

These British and American press barons opposed resisting Hitler because they either sympathized with the Nazis (in Rothermere's case) or failed to sympathize with the Nazis' victims. They worried that challenging the Nazis would endanger what they most cared about: the imperial power of their respective nations.

∎

The most conservative of these press lords did not always achieve their domestic goals, at least in the short term. Franklin Roosevelt won reelection to the presidency in 1936, 1940, and 1944, despite the overwhelming opposition of the mainstream media. In Britain, after Prime Minister Baldwin proved that a canny leader could outflank the publishers, Rothermere and Beaverbrook never again wielded as much power over Conservative Party politics.

Given their limited success in domestic politics, how do we know that the newspaper owners played a major role in shaping public views on foreign policy? It can be difficult to assess the relative influence of newspapers on public opinion as opposed to other sources of information. We do know, though, that leaders of both nations believed that the isolationist publishers wielded enormous influence on perceptions of foreign policy.

Prime Minister Neville Chamberlain and his cabinet read the national newspapers closely to discern the public mood. Scientific polling did not come to Britain until 1937, and policy makers paid little attention to the polls before 1939. "The lack of faith in the emerging science of opinion polling," explains historian Daniel Hucker, "ensured that the press remained the principal means of gauging opinion."[35] If the press supported appeasement, Chamberlain believed, then the public must as well. At least one poll suggests that he was correct. In a 1938 survey on the possibility of war, a plurality of Britons—35 percent—said they based their opinions on what they read in the newspapers.[36]

As in England, newspapers in the United States helped mold the public's views on national and foreign affairs. Eighty-two percent of Americans read a daily newspaper regularly, and 57 percent said they got most of their news—and, presumably, many of their opinions—from the papers.[37] As a result, leaders of both parties monitored and tried to influence print coverage. Former president Herbert Hoover, desperate to return to a leadership role in the Republican Party, read thirty papers a day, and he assiduously courted their publishers and editors.[38] Anti-interventionist senators like Burton Wheeler of Montana and Robert Reynolds of North Carolina routinely entered the Patterson/McCormick editorials into the *Congressional Record.*[39] Archibald MacLeish, the director of the Office of Facts and Figures, expressed the views of many Roosevelt advisers when he declared that the press "played a larger part than any other instrument," including government, in "shaping the public . . . mind."[40] President Roosevelt complained to his aides that the right-wing press barons made it difficult for him to convince Americans to take more forceful action against aggression abroad. "It's a terrible thing," he once told an adviser, "to look over your shoulder when you are trying to lead—and to find no one there."[41]

To keep tabs on the news and opinion in the mass-circulation dailies, Roosevelt read eleven papers each morning, including a Hearst paper and two Patterson/McCormick dailies, and received editorial summaries of other newspapers from his staff. He also realized the value of opinion polling much sooner than Chamberlain did. He hired pollsters and directed them to keep him informed of the public's shifting views on neutrality.[42]

After the war in Europe began, Roosevelt set up several different information and propaganda agencies to survey the press and devise strategies to combat the publishers' isolationist views.[43] When they continued to question the value of the war after the United States joined it, he criticized the press lords directly, insisting in one Fireside Chat, for instance, that the war effort must not be impeded by "a few bogus patriots who use the sacred freedom of the press to echo the sentiments of the propagandists in Tokyo and Berlin."[44]

Roosevelt attacked the press barons not out of personal pique but as a political necessity. He understood that their pro-appeasement, anti-interventionist, and even pro-Nazi press coverage and editorials made it harder for ordinary Americans and Britons to understand the threat Nazi Germany posed. Moreover, once their countries joined the war, the policies the press lords had advocated for so long—and in some cases continued to promote—impeded their governments' efforts to win the war.

■

Scholars have found it challenging to evaluate the coverage of these newspapers because of the difficulty of accessing them. Despite the immense reach of the Hearst press and of the *New York Daily News*, for example, archivists only recently digitized these papers and added them to major databases. Some important papers, such as the *Washington Times-Herald*, are still available only on microfilm as of early 2021. Thus researchers have, quite understandably, focused more on the digitized *Washington Post* than the better-selling *Times-Herald*.[45]

Historians have also tended to dismiss the more popular papers because they were rowdier, angrier, and generally less respectable than their more sedate rivals. Because these publications were overtly anti-intellectual, it's easy to overlook them as key sources of ideas. "It would be ludicrous to devote as much space or attention to Lord Beaverbrook's or Lord Rothermere's few unsophisticated and obsessive ideas as to the development of important ideas and attitudes in the columns and offices of the quality newspapers," writes one historian of the British press.[46] In the United States, scholars of the right-wing media have mostly focused on the post–World War II period and on special-interest periodicals or broadcasters with a relatively small reach.[47] Yet in the 1930s and 1940s, media conservatism was not a fringe phenomenon: the mainstream media *was* the far-right media.[48]

Even at the time, opinion leaders underestimated these newspapers' influence because they were sensational rather than sober. Elite journalists' dismissal of his newspaper infuriated Joe Patterson. In 1938, when the *New York Times* reprinted a *New York Herald Tribune* editorial as part of a roundup of media opinion but did not print anything from his *Daily News*, Patterson fumed that "the

News currently has three times the circulation of the *Times* and five times that of the *Herald Tribune*. If the *Times* pretends to collect cross sections of press opinion on important national affairs and print them for its readers' full information, it ought to include the *News* opinion."[49]

He had a point. The *Times* should have acknowledged the *News*'s powerful influence, and so should we today. The more highbrow, quality newspapers may have influenced opinion leaders, but Rothermere, Beaverbrook, Hearst, McCormick, and the Pattersons shaped the views of millions of ordinary Americans and Britons. Their divisive politics and sometimes hateful messages had enduring appeal, as the recent resurrection of the phrases "America First" and "Britain First" show.[50]

The isolationist press lords trumpeted their love for their country, festooned their newspapers with waving flags and soaring eagles, and promoted war bonds. Yet they also tried desperately to undermine public officials' anti-fascist, interventionist policies before the war and, in the case of the American publishers, sought to contradict the nation's commander in chief during the war. They demonized liberals and internationalists, they invented and spread conspiracy theories, and they encouraged Americans and Britons to view everyone who did not think as they did as an "alien." In fighting against resistance to fascism, they helped lay the foundation for the nationalist, racist, and anti-Semitic Right that we live with today.

CHAPTER ONE

The Good Haters

I N LATE 1900, ALFRED HARMSWORTH, the innovative and some-what infamous proprietor of the London *Daily Mail*, arrived in New York on a mission to transform American journalism. Harmsworth had been invited by Joseph Pulitzer, the publisher of the *New York World*, to guest-edit the issue of January 1, 1901, the first newspaper of the twentieth century.

Given complete authority by Pulitzer to change the *World* for a day, Harmsworth printed the paper on half-size sheets, small enough to be read easily on a train, and filled it with short, snappy stories aimed at busy city dwellers. He called the new size "tabloid," after a British pharmaceutical company's term for a compact tablet. It sold out immediately, and Pulitzer printed one hundred thousand more to meet demand.[1]

Pulitzer admired the way that Harmsworth had shaken up the British newspaper industry and developed a new style of journalism. Harmsworth, soon to become Lord Northcliffe, believed that modern newspapers needed to throw off the traditions of the past. His London papers were marketed not to political or business elites but to the urban masses. To outcompete their rivals, publishers of mass-market papers often splashed catchy headlines or outrageous stories on their front pages in hopes of attracting the eyes and cash of passersby on urban streets—the Victorian version of click bait.

While twentieth-century newspapers, both tabloids and broadsheets, catered to ordinary readers, they also sometimes pandered to right-wing prejudices. Their owners discovered that the themes of nationalism, imperialism, and order resonated with lower-middle class readers. The modern papers, funded by advertising dollars and owned by very rich men, often became transmission belts for conservative, even fascist politics.

Alfred's younger brother Harold, ennobled as Lord Rothermere, would later take over the Harmsworth newspapers and continue to trumpet the same conservative, nationalist, and populist themes. Rothermere deployed his papers as propaganda weapons in political crusades to cut taxes and spending, to discredit the socialists, and to get rid of the Tory Party leaders he called "semi-Socialists." Above all, he used his papers to promote the continental and British fascists who, he believed, might be the only men strong enough to stop a communist takeover of Europe.

The Harmsworth brothers transformed not only the newspaper industry but also their nation's politics. They were the first Anglo-American media moguls to try to dictate their country's foreign policy, but others would soon follow their example.

■

Unlike the American press lords, who were born to wealth and privilege, the most significant British newspaper magnates worked their way up from the middle to the top. Alfred Harmsworth Jr., the son of a barrister, showed an early talent for journalism and for entrepreneurship. At age sixteen he dropped out of school to work as a freelance writer and editor. By his twenties he had saved enough money to start his own publishing business.

To help run his growing company, Alfred brought in his brother Harold, who resigned a civil service job to manage what grew into the family media empire. Alfred had more journalistic talent than his brother, but Harold was a business mastermind who figured out how to monetize his brother's creative genius.[2]

In 1894, the Harmsworth brothers bought their first daily newspaper, the *Evening News*, and two years later they launched the *Daily Mail*. The *Mail*'s founding marked a watershed moment in journalism history. Other editors credited Alfred Harmsworth with revolutionizing their craft. He was "a consummate journalist, who changed the whole course of English journalism," wrote Geoffrey Dawson, the longtime editor of the London *Times*.[3] A research group in the 1930s went so far as to declare that the first issue of the *Daily Mail* "may be taken as the beginning of modern journalism."[4]

That was a bit of an exaggeration. Britain's Sunday newspapers had used sensational techniques in their reporting for years, as had American publishers like Charles Dana and James Gordon Bennett. But Harmsworth's contribution, as historian Adrian Bingham has said, was to "transfer these populist techniques to the arena of the national morning newspaper."[5] London's morning dailies were dull gray broadsheets filled with transcripts of political speeches— reading matter "suitable," one report put it, "only for those who could retire to their clubs at four o'clock and spend two or three hours in digesting it."[6] The *Daily Mail* was aimed at the masses. It was, sniffed Lord Salisbury, a newspaper "written by office boys for office boys."[7] But there were millions of office boys and their equivalents, and the paper sold.

Alfred Harmsworth was not just inventive; he was also lucky. He entered journalism just as the field was changing quickly. Telegraphs and trains, and then telephones and automobiles, made it simpler to gather the news; rotating cylinder presses made it easier and cheaper to print it.[8] Embracing new mass-production and mass-distribution methods, the Harmsworths manufactured inexpensive papers and put them on trucks and trains to distribute throughout London and the nation.

The introduction of universal public schooling in Britain in 1870 created a huge market for these cheaper popular papers. Millions of new readers were looking to occupy their time as they traveled to their jobs in the nation's burgeoning cities, but they had little interest in the staid quality papers. The new public schools, Harmsworth told a friend, "are turning out hundreds of thousands of boys and girls annually who are anxious to read. They do not care for the ordinary newspaper. They have no interest in society, but they will read anything which is simple and is sufficiently interesting."[9]

The large retailers of the expanding consumer economy wanted to reach these new readers, and they paid high prices to place advertisements where their potential customers could see them. These ads in turn underwrote the cost of the newspapers and made them still cheaper for people of modest means. Readership continued to climb through the early decades of the twentieth century. By the late 1930s, circulation of national British dailies topped 10 million copies, or roughly one for every family.[10]

Because advertisers wanted to reach as many consumers as possible, the popular newspapers on both sides of the Atlantic experimented with innovative graphics and content to catch the eyes of commuters. Harmsworth learned about bold typography from Americans like Pulitzer, and American publishers adopted Harmsworth's circulation-boosting sales techniques such as beauty contests, guessing games, and gifts for new subscribers, including everything from insurance to household appliances.[11]

Above all, Harmsworth found that he could sell more newspapers by celebrating the British Empire and demonizing its critics. "The British people," he was quoted as saying, "relish a good hero and a good hate."[12] There were many opportunities to find heroes and hates in foreign conflicts. During the Boer War and the Boxer Rebellion, the *Mail*'s jingoistic coverage helped it become the first daily in Britain to sell a million copies.[13] Harmsworth did not reach this historic sales level through rigorous fact-checking. In one infamous example, the *Mail* reported that the Boxers, an ultranationalist Chinese secret society, had "completely wiped out" all the white people in the diplomatic quarter in Beijing, but not before they had "outraged English women and tortured children."[14] The massacre, it turned out, was entirely fictitious—an example of "faked news," as it was called at the time.[15] Other journalists began calling the *Daily Mail* the "Daily Liar."[16]

Despite the criticism from other journalists, readers kept buying the *Mail*, and Harmsworth's newspaper empire continued to expand. He founded the *Daily Mirror*, the first modern British tabloid, in 1903. He bought the *Observer*, *Times*, and *Sunday Times*, among other publications, over the next two decades. His growing power was recognized in 1904 when he became a baronet and then, the next year, Baron Northcliffe.

The "Napoleon of Fleet Street," as Northcliffe liked to be known, continued to sell newspapers by warning of potential dangers abroad. He stirred up so much hatred against the Germans that some critics accused him of causing World War I. "Next to the Kaiser," said one Liberal Party writer, "Lord Northcliffe has done more than any other living man to bring about the war."[17]

Northcliffe did not want to rule the country directly, though. Instead, he preferred to shape the policies of the men who did. "Heaven forbid that I should ever be in Downing Street," he wrote in a private letter. "I believe the independent newspaper to be one of the future forms of government."[18] He believed he and his fellow press barons were a kind of shadow government of the people—a government as legitimate as, or perhaps even more legitimate than, the one formed by elected representatives. His influence reached its peak during World War I, when he helped to topple Prime Minister H. H. Asquith.[19]

In building a power base outside the Tory Party, Northcliffe set the mold in Britain and America for a press lord who pulled the levers of power in national politics. Later press critics would coin the term *Northcliffe complex* to describe a media baron who wanted, as George Seldes explained, to "rule or to manipulate the strings of the stooges who rule."[20]

While critics like Seldes saw Northcliffe as a villain, some publishers admired his swagger. Keith Murdoch, an Australian editor, regarded Northcliffe with such affection and awe that other editors called him Lord Southcliffe. "You have been the biggest influence and the biggest force over me," he wrote Northcliffe.[21] Murdoch's son, Rupert, followed his father's example and became the most successful heir of the Northcliffe tradition.

The prime minister after Asquith, David Lloyd George, was more attuned than his unlucky predecessor to the power of the press barons. To secure their loyalty, he asked the king to bestow honors on the owners of the largest provincial and national papers, including Harold Harmsworth, who became Lord Rothermere in 1919. These press lords did not inherit their peerages; they were ennobled and given seats in the House of Lords by politicians grateful for their support. In America, the term *press lords* was metaphorical, but in Britain it was literal.

Yet Northcliffe wanted more than a title. As World War I ended, he demanded a seat at the treaty negotiations in Versailles and insisted that he needed to approve Lloyd George's choices for his cabinet. The prime minister responded by excoriating Northcliffe in Parliament, charging that he was trying divide the British from the French, and that not even his "diseased vanity" could justify "so black a crime."[22] Lloyd George meaningfully tapped his head when he said the words "diseased vanity," alluding to the rumors that Northcliffe was losing his mind to syphilis.[23] Northcliffe was indeed succumbing to dementia, though probably from a blood infection, not a sexually transmitted disease.[24] He died in 1922. Because he had no legitimate offspring—his four children had been born outside of marriage—his brother Harold stood ready to inherit Britain's most formidable media empire.

■

While Northcliffe inspired admiration as well as enmity, his younger brother had few defenders, even among his employees and his own family. A "lascivious, gluttonous, Hitler-grovelling, penny-pinching, power-mad, boring old sod," one of his editors, Hugh Cudlipp, later said of him.[25] His nephew Cecil Harmsworth King called him an "incredibly inept politician," a bad manager, "inarticulate and no administrator," and just plain sad and ugly.[26] Tall and heavy-set, with sagging features that reminded people of a bulldog, Rothermere in middle age struck observers as depressed, stubborn, and arrogant. "His face . . . conveyed the considerable judgement," Cudlipp wrote, "that everyone and everything had a price he could afford to pay."[27]

When two of Rothermere's sons died in the Great War that his papers had helped promote, he plunged into a deep depression and retreated from the business for nearly a year. His brother died shortly afterward. "I think in later life Rothermere had really nothing to live for," his nephew King speculated, "and took refuge in drink, very crude womanizing, and making money." Rothermere had affairs with innumerable women, King remembered, including a secretary who sported a ring he had given her with a diamond "the size of a pigeon's egg." He once told his nephew that "old mistresses were much more expensive than Old Masters, and he had plenty of experience of both."[28]

But he found comfort in the task of building his business and his fortune. By the mid-1930s he controlled fifteen dailies and two Sunday and six weekly papers, though he personally directed the coverage only at the *Daily Mail*.[29] As his media holdings grew, so did his bank accounts. His nephew estimated that he amassed a fortune of £26 million (well over a billion in today's money), which made him the third-richest man in Britain.[30]

He also seemed to discover some purpose in far-right political activism. Like his brother and all the press lords, Rothermere tried to become an independent force in politics by crusading for various causes. Right after World War I, he joined with his brother in a campaign to force the coalition government to end its "orgy of spending" and "appalling taxation."[31] He demanded that officials slash public spending, sell off state-owned shipyards and factories, and eliminate wartime regulations. When the government did not adopt these policies rapidly enough, he published articles against "Squandermania" and supported candidates for an "Anti-Waste League" in parliamentary by-elections. Rothermere would benefit personally from cuts in the tax rates, but he consistently framed his government-bashing editorials, or "leaders," as they were known in Britain, as an effort to defend the interests of the middle and working classes and to promote the public good. "For more than two years I have waged a rather lonely fight against Squandermania," he wrote in 1921. "I have done so in the national interest, and my only object is to serve my countrymen."[32] Rothermere succeeded in pressuring the government to privatize some state-held assets.

If "Squandermania" seemed a scandal to Rothermere, the Bolshevik Revolution was a catastrophe. He believed that the Reds would march out of the Soviet Union and sweep across Europe, seizing property, sparking riots, and wreaking havoc in the world's financial markets. In his view, British socialists in the Labour Party were aiding and abetting these foreign revolutionaries while contributing to "degeneracy" and dependence among the English working classes. "He was convinced," said one of his editors, Collin Brooks, "that Britain had entered a phase of decline, had lost her old militant virtues, and, in her softness, was lusting after strange idols of pacifism, nationalisation and everything which would continue to sap self-reliance."[33]

The formation of the first Labour government in 1924, under Ramsay Macdonald, convinced Rothermere that disaster would soon befall Britain. Loyal readers of his editorials in the *Mail* in the 1920s and 1930s received a daily dose of doom. Financial panic, chaos, revolution—all loomed on the horizon. Worse, the leaders of Rothermere's own party did not seem to grasp the extent of the peril. In his opinion, the head of the Conservative Party, Stanley Baldwin, was blind to the existential danger posed by the allegedly pro-Soviet policies of the Labour Party.

Rothermere seized the opportunity to demonstrate the Red peril to his readers with some fake news. Shortly before the election of 1924, with Labour's control over the government hanging in the balance, the *Mail* received a copy of an explosive letter, supposedly from a Soviet official in Moscow, Grigori Zinoviev, to his comrades in the British Communist Party, urging them to bore within the British military to prepare for revolution. The "Zinoviev letter" suggested that a trade deal with Soviet Russia—an agreement championed by the Labour Party—would help bring about that revolution.

Prime Minister MacDonald's government questioned the authenticity of the Zinoviev letter, with good reason. It was a fraud, possibly crafted by Russian "Whites" who opposed the Soviet regime. But the forgery was not proven until decades later.[34] Despite the government's skepticism, the *Mail* printed the letter four days before the election under a multi-tier headline: "MOSCOW ORDERS TO OUR REDS: GREAT PLOT DISCLOSED YESTERDAY; 'PARALYSE THE ARMY AND NAVY'; AND MR. MACDONALD WOULD LEND RUSSIA OUR MONEY!" The letter revealed, the *Mail* said, "a great Bolshevik plot to paralyse the British Army and Navy and to plunge the country into civil war."[35]

The Zinoviev letter, according to the *Mail*, proved that the communists were "the masters of Mr Ramsay MacDonald's Government." To fight back against the "murderous, alien despotism" seeking to destroy British "flesh and blood," the paper urged a vote for "*a Conservative Government which will know how to deal with treason.*"[36] The controversy did not seem to depress the Labour vote, but it polarized British politics and persuaded many formerly Liberal voters to defect to the Tories, hastening the eventual demise of the Liberal Party. Stanley Baldwin's Conservatives won a smashing victory in the election, and Rothermere believed he—the publisher who had revealed Labour's treachery—deserved the credit for tipping the vote to the Tories and depriving Labour of perhaps one hundred seats in Parliament.[37]

Because he thought he had won the election for the Tories, Rothermere felt betrayed by the moderate policies of the Conservative government he helped put in power. Women over age thirty and working-class men had just won the right to vote in 1918, and Baldwin tried to appeal to these newly enfranchised voters by moving the Conservative Party a bit to the left. The new premier decided to work with, not demonize, the leaders of the Labour Party; he favored giving India more autonomy; and though he raised tariffs, he refused to hike them as much as Rothermere wanted. Baldwin also supported expanding the franchise to give women twenty-one to thirty the right to vote. Rothermere was horrified by this proposal, largely because he believed younger women would vote Labour. He campaigned vigorously against the "Fatal Flapper-Vote Folly," claiming it would "bring down the British Empire in ruin."[38]

Rothermere argued that Baldwin proposed to beat Socialism with "semi-Socialism," a strategy doomed to fail. He resolved to oust Baldwin as Conservative leader. This political crusade—his most ambitious foray into domestic political combat—would unite him with another major press lord of his day, Max Beaverbrook. Though the two men would fail to reshape the Tory Party, each would play a key role in influencing British policy toward the Nazis.

Beaverbrook was Harold Rothermere's fiercest competitor and also his constant friend. The two became close during their service in the House of Lords in the 1910s; Beaverbrook said that Rothermere gave him his first tour of Parliament and taught him the rules. After the deaths of Rothermere's sons in the war, Beaverbrook invited his rival to his country home, providing a place for him to recover. Rothermere, who had few close chums, called Beaverbrook his "greatest friend"; Beaverbrook, who had many, regarded Rothermere as his best friend in newspapers.[39]

Rothermere and Beaverbrook agreed that the most important political issue in interwar Britain was the defense of the empire. And the best way to protect it, they believed, was to wall it off from the rest of the world. They extolled splendid isolation: free trade within the empire; high tariffs to discourage the importation of goods, including food, from the outside; and no alliances with other countries. They believed these metaphorical walls, both economic and diplomatic, would protect British dominions— including Canada, Australia, New Zealand, and South Africa—as well as British colonies.[40]

The press lords thought that under Baldwin's leadership, the Conservative Party was not doing enough to safeguard the empire. In 1930 they grew so disgusted with Baldwin that they tried to start their own political party, the United Empire Party, in hopes of re-placing Baldwin with someone—perhaps Beaverbrook—who shared their views on protecting the empire.[41] In a private letter, Rother-mere told Beaverbrook that control of the Tory Party was within their grasp: "If you, with my assistance can overthrow the Central Conservative organisation, the Conservative Party is ours."[42]

But Baldwin countered with a furious and clever attack on the press barons, calling their papers "engines of propaganda for the constantly changing policies, desires, personal wishes, personal likes and dislikes of two men." These men, he said, printed "direct false-hood, misrepresentation, half-truths." The prime minister continued his assault with a widely quoted statement: "What the proprietor-ship of these papers is aiming at is power, and power without re-sponsibility—the prerogative of the harlot throughout the ages."[43]

Rothermere and Beaverbrook were strong enough to force the leader of their party and their country to criticize them personally, but not powerful enough to beat him. After the Beaverbrook-Rothermere candidate lost a crucial by-election, Baldwin confirmed his hold on the Tory Party and negotiated a deal with Beaverbrook, who agreed to drop the press lords' challenge to the party leadership in return for some concessions on trade policy. The publishers would not attempt again to destroy Baldwin's career or to reshape the nation's domestic politics. But they would continue to try to mold its foreign policy, es-pecially toward Germany. In Rothermere's case, this meant praising the Nazis and advocating a British alliance with them.

■

Some British and American citizens who had experience with Nazi Germany understood from the start the menace posed by Adolf Hitler. Sir Robert Vansittart, the head of the British diplomatic service, warned his colleagues of the dangers of Nazism as early as 1930, and his concerns grew once Hitler gained power three years later. "Hitlerism *is* exceedingly dangerous," he wrote in 1933. "I do not think that anything but evil and danger for the rest of the world can come out of Hitlerism."[44] Britain's ambassador in Berlin, Sir Horace Rumbold, reported to his government on the Nazis' establishment of the first concentration camp in 1933 and explained that hatred of the Jews was central to Hitler's worldview and policies. It would be a mistake to assume, Rumbold wrote, that anti-Semitism was "the policy of his wilder men whom he has difficulty in controlling."[45] The leaders of the Labour Party, though divided at first over how to oppose Hitler, decided by the mid-1930s to support British rearmament and collective security through the League of Nations.[46] A few Conservative MPs, most notably Winston Churchill, also began to warn of the dangers of Hitlerism.

Yet many other Britons viewed Hitler as the inevitable product of the unfair Treaty of Versailles. British politicians and journalists had come to see the postwar settlement, which had fixed the blame for the conflict on Germany and forced it to yield territory and pay reparations, as punitive and vengeful. Rothermere agreed, writing extensively about the failures of Versailles as well as those of the Treaty of Trianon, which had ended the Allies' war with Hungary.

Rothermere's views of these treaties were shaped in part by a mysterious princess who, according to British intelligence, later became a spy for Hitler. In Monte Carlo in 1927, Rothermere fell under the spell of an attractive, flirtatious Viennese-born woman, Stephanie Hohenlohe-Waldenburg-Schillingsfürst, who had once been married to a Hungarian prince. The princess persuaded the press lord that the Treaty of Trianon had oppressed Hungarians by forcing millions of them into the newly created country of Czechoslovakia and the expanded nation of Romania. Rothermere took up the cause of border revision with great enthusiasm, writing several editorials about the injustices of the postwar settlements.[47] Some influential Hungarians, thrilled that the English publisher favored them with his editorial attention, named squares and streets after him, hung his picture in public buildings, and even invited him to be their king. (He declined but suggested his son instead.)

Although many Britons felt guilty about the postwar treaties, Rothermere's opinion of the fascist leaders in Italy and Germany went beyond sympathy. He approved of the fascists' ideas, especially their opposition to Bolshevism. He also liked their style, which he described as strong, vigorous, and manly. Scholars of fascism highlight its "extreme stress on the masculine principle and male dominance," as Stanley Payne has said, as well as its anti-communism, anti-liberalism, and militarism, all of which appealed to Rothermere. His esteem for its ideas and tactics led him to promote fascism throughout Europe, first in Italy, then in Germany, and finally in his home country. Because of his power in the media, he helped legitimize and normalize fascism in the national discourse.[48]

When Benito Mussolini became the first major European leader to establish a fascist dictatorship, he earned the *Daily Mail*'s deep respect. In 1923, a year after Mussolini's rise to power, Rothermere extolled the Italian dictator for rescuing civilization: "In saving Italy," he wrote, Mussolini had "stopped the inroads of Bolshevism which would have left Europe in ruins. . . . In my judgment he saved the whole Western world."[49] Over the years, as Mussolini banned opposition parties, ordered the murder of his leading political opponents, and used his black-shirted thugs to assault and terrorize dissidents, Rothermere praised his "exalted motives" and "courageous and intelligent leadership," qualities that had brought justice and "disciplined liberty" to Italy.[50] He was, Rothermere concluded in 1928, "the greatest figure of our age. . . . Mussolini will probably dominate the history of the twentieth century as Napoleon dominated that of the early nineteenth."[51]

But Adolf Hitler soon surpassed Mussolini in Rothermere's estimation. The press lord first wrote about Hitler on September 24, 1930, when he traveled to Germany "to examine at close range" what he saw as a momentous historical occasion: the Nazis' remarkable showing in a recent election, when they increased their number of seats in Parliament from 12 to 107, making them the second-strongest party in the Reichstag. The headline of his story predicted the dawning of a new historical era:

GERMANY AND INEVITABILITY
A NATION REBORN
YOUTH ASSERTING ITS POWER
NEW CHAPTER IN EUROPE'S HISTORY

Rothermere correctly assessed the historical significance of the Nazi surge to power. "To underestimate the importance of these events would be folly," he wrote, "and in my belief to overestimate it would be difficult."

Rather than foreseeing danger in the Nazi victory, however, Rothermere saw hope. He praised Hitler and his supporters for confronting Communism with a manly vitality that put the democratic parties to shame. He hoped that the Germans would establish some sort of "great national combination under German hegemony" in central Europe so that there would be "a strong, sane government to set against the pressure of Soviet lunaticism."[52] In other words, the Nazis should redraw the map of Europe and place much of it under their control.

When writers for other newspapers expressed astonishment at Rothermere's embrace of Hitler's party, he hit back against his critics. Using the gendered language common to many of his articles about fascism, he made fun of "the old women of three countries—France, Germany, and our own." His opponents, he claimed, were losing readers and relevance because they did not appreciate the boldness of Hitler's vision. "A new idea invariably produces this effect upon the pompous pundits who pontificate in our weekly reviews and those old-fashioned morning newspapers whose sales and influence alike sink steadily month by month towards vanishing-point."[53]

In response to his critics, Rothermere directly addressed the Nazis' anti-Semitism—something his first article on Hitler had not mentioned. He agreed with Hitler that "the Jewish race" had "shown conspicuous political unwisdom" over the years. "Tactlessness," he wrote, "has always been one of the outstanding defects of the children of Israel." But he believed "Jew-baiting" was "a stupid survival of medieval prejudice," and the Nazis should appear more tolerant if they wanted international support.[54]

Rothermere seemed to object to Jew-baiting for instrumental reasons. He generally empathized with his "blood-kindred," as he called the Germans, in their efforts to strip Jews of citizenship and civil rights.[55] But he worried that violent attacks on Jews might alienate world opinion. He did not seem to grasp that the Nazi Party's anti-Semitism was not a tactic but a central reason for its existence.

Hitler saw the *Daily Mail* and its proprietor as useful allies, and he did all he could to flatter the British press lord. In a special interview granted to a *Mail* reporter shortly after Rothermere's long tribute to Nazism, he praised Rothermere's unparalleled ability to understand the essence of Nazism, particularly the party's "life and energy." "To have seized upon this outstanding fact," he told the *Daily Mail* correspondent, "shows that Lord Rothermere possesses the true gift of intuitive statesmanship."[56]

Over the next two years, as the Nazi Party gained seats in the Reichstag, the *Daily Mail* continued to extol its leader's virtues. In a 1932 article headlined "Hitler's Triumphal Tour of East Prussia: Received Like a Prophet; 400 Miles of Cheers," the *Mail's* reporter touted Hitler as "the man who has revived Germany's faith in herself." The ranks of unsmiling, brown-shirted Nazis, their right hands raised as they marched past Hitler's car, inspired the reporter to write: "They filled me with respect."[57]

The *Mail* boosted Hitler even as the Nazis used terrorist tactics against their political enemies. In the German national elections of 1932, the Nazis won a plurality of the vote. President Paul von Hindenburg, thinking he could control Hitler, appointed him chancellor in January 1933. When the Reichstag building was torched by a mad anarchist in February, Hindenburg issued an emergency order that suspended civil rights and due process. The Nazi government began to arrest its political opponents, hold them without trial and, starting in March 1933, only two months after Hitler came to power, put them in the first concentration camp, Dachau. Nazi Germany became a police state with no protections for individual rights. The Sturmabteilung (SA), or Storm Troopers, also known as the Brownshirts, assaulted their political and cultural enemies with no legal consequences.

Now that he controlled the state and its police powers, Hitler called a new election. When the Nazi vote share rose to 44 percent, British and American reporters in Berlin deplored what they saw as the death of German democracy. As many observers noted, the election was tainted by the daily terror meted out by the Storm Troopers. One British magazine correspondent portrayed the "brutal beatings, killings, suicides of dismissed intellectuals, the lacerated backs, cripplings and ruined existences which have marked the triumph of Hitlerism."[58]

But the *Daily Mail* saw a "relaxation of tension" in Germany. "Herr Hitler has won his majority cleverly. If he uses it prudently and peacefully," the *Mail* editorialized, "no one here will shed any tears over the disappearance of German democracy."[59]

Not only the *Daily Mail's* editorials but its news stories betrayed a pro-Nazi bias. Rothermere's reporters understood that their boss's sympathies lay with Hitler. Some, like the *Mail's* correspondent in Berlin, Rothay Reynolds, censored themselves to align their stories with Rothermere's views.[60] Others had no need of self-censorship. Rothermere's star European correspondent, G. Ward Price, eagerly embraced the *Daily Mail* policy on the Nazi regime. In a 1938 book, he described Hitler as a gentle soul who loved children and dogs and had a soldier's "aversion" to war.[61]

But his employer outdid even Price in his support for the Nazi regime. In his most famous, or infamous, commentary on Hitler and the Nazi Party, Rothermere journeyed to "somewhere in Naziland," as his dateline put it, in July 1933 to see the Nazis in action for himself. In an article headlined "YOUTH TRIUMPHANT," Rothermere wrote: "Something far more significant than a new Government has arisen among the Germans. There has been a sudden expansion of their national spirit like that which took place in England under Queen Elizabeth. *Youth has taken command.*"

Rothermere dismissed those who pointed to the Nazis' use of terror to maintain order. He had no patience, he reiterated, with "the old women of both sexes" who filled British newspapers with reports of "Nazi atrocities." The Nazis needed to act with determination to control the "alien elements" within Germany: "In the last days of the pre-Hitler regime there were twenty times as many Jewish Government officials in Germany as had existed before the war. Israelites of international attachments were insinuating themselves into key positions in the German administrative machine." Hitler, he concluded, had "saved his country from the ineffectual leadership of hesitating, half-hearted politicians."[62]

The Nazis later used Rothermere's "Youth Triumphant" article as propaganda.[63] Hitler himself believed Rothermere was "one of the very greatest of all Englishmen" and that the *Mail* was "doing an immense amount of good. I have the greatest admiration for him."[64]

Harold Rothermere possessed "the true gift of intuitive statesmanship," Adolf Hitler said, because the *Daily Mail* publisher appreciated the Nazi Party's "life and energy." The two men met several times, including on this occasion in 1934. (Süddeutsche Zeitung Photo / Alamy Stock Photo)

Rothermere's cheerleading for the Nazis continued over the next several years. In early 1934, he argued that the African colonies taken from Germany after World War I should be returned to the Nazis. "We cannot expect a nation of 'he-men' like the Germans," he wrote, "to sit forever with folded arms under the provocations and stupidities of the Treaty of Versailles."[65] A few months later, after the Night of the Long Knives, when Hitler ordered the arrest and execution of dozens of Storm Troopers who he claimed were plotting against him, the *Daily Mail* praised him for heroic and speedy action against treachery. "Herr Adolf Hitler, the German Chancellor, has saved his country," read the lede of the *Daily Mail* news story.[66]

Rothermere enjoyed Hitler's hospitality in December 1934, when the dictator invited him to a dinner party in his official residence in Berlin. The press baron, assisted by his friend Princess Stephanie, reciprocated by hosting Hitler at a grand dinner at the Hotel Adlon, the finest hotel in Germany. During the dinner, Hitler launched into an interminable monologue and prevented anyone else from talking, but Rothermere came away impressed.[67] Never before, he told his readers, had the chances for Anglo-German friendship been better. "Their interests, our own, and those of the entire civilised world will be best served by close and friendly co-operation between us."[68]

■

Rothermere's admiration for fascism was not limited to the Continent. For a time, he was also the most significant booster of the British Blackshirts. By publicizing and promoting Oswald Mosley's fascists, he hoped to legitimize the most racist, anti-Semitic, and violent social movement in 1930s Britain.

A British aristocrat soon to inherit his family's baronetcy, Mosley was a war veteran and a charismatic speaker. He had served as a Tory member of Parliament, then defected to Labour, and finally started (and quickly dissolved) an independent political party called the New Party. In 1932 he formed the organization for which he would become infamous: the British Union of Fascists (BUF), popularly known by the nickname inspired by its uniforms, the Blackshirts.[69]

The BUF tried to emphasize its patriotism by putting "British" in its name and placing the Union Jack emblem on its jackets. But the movement clearly owed much to European fascism—from its uniforms, modeled on those of the Italian fascists, to its anti-foreign, anti-Semitic policies. Like the continental fascists, the BUF stressed the need for racial purity and called for the end of all immigration. Jews, who were part of the "alien menace," had to put "Britain First" or risk deportation.[70] Regardless of any apparent loyalty to Britain, all Jews in a fascist Britain would be regarded as foreigners and denied citizenship and civil rights.[71] Mosley also proposed establishing an authoritarian state with dictatorial powers. Parliament would still exist, but it would be organized along corporatist lines, with representatives for occupations and industries rather than localities.

Mosley maintained that the Conservative Party was failing to conserve Britain's racial hierarchies and to stop its slide into economic depression, Communism, and degeneracy. "The function of modern Conservatism," he wrote, "is merely to fit a weak brake on the runaway machine of liberal-Socialist ideas. Blackshirt policy scraps the whole machine and substitutes a new engine of modern design."[72]

In emulation of Mussolini's Blackshirts and Hitler's Brownshirts, Mosley established a paramilitary squad to brutalize political opponents. Called the Fascist Defence Force, the private army comprised a few hundred men, mostly veterans, who were trained to intimidate and harass political enemies.

Rothermere saw in Mosley the same virtues he perceived in the Nazis: the youth, vitality, and strength he believed were necessary to defeat communism. Unlike the Conservative "semi-Socialists," Mosley proposed to meet the Red threat with force and, if necessary, brutality. In January 1934, in a news article he wrote and headlined "Hurrah for the Blackshirts!" Rothermere proclaimed that the British Union of Fascists was breaking the "stranglehold which senile politicians have so long maintained on our public affairs." Though the movement was distinctly British, he insisted, its tenets resembled those of the fascists in Italy and Germany, "beyond all doubt the best-governed nations in Europe to-day." The article ended by giving the mailing address of the BUF in London for the benefit of the young men who wanted to join. These potential recruits should remember that black shirts did "not cover Faint Hearts!"[73]

The Rothermere press cheered on the Blackshirts for several more months. His *Sunday Dispatch* ran so many articles praising them that one historian has called it "a house journal for the BUF." The paper offered cash prizes every week for the best letter from a reader on "Why I Like the Blackshirts" and gave away free tickets to Blackshirt rallies.[74] Reporters at the *Daily Mail* began wearing black shirts to work to show solidarity with their boss's politics.[75]

Rothermere could continue to praise Hitler in print because his advertisers raised no serious objection, but his support for fascists closer to home soon lost him readers and advertising money, especially after the Blackshirts' thuggish tactics became clear for all to see. In June 1934, when the BUF staged a huge rally at Olympia, an event hall in West Kensington, the evening did not go as planned. Socialists, communists, and other anti-fascists had infiltrated the gathering. When they began booing, the fascists turned in fury on the interlopers. According to one newspaper account, "Blackshirts began stumbling and leaping over chairs to get at the source of the noise. There was a wild scrummage, women screamed, black-shirted arms rose and fell, blows were dealt." The BUF's paramilitary forces began beating the protesters and dragging their limp bodies from the building, whereupon they beat them some more.[76]

The *Daily Mail* tried to justify the violence. G. Ward Price called the victims "Red hooligans" who "got what they deserved."[77] But some Conservative members of Parliament—and, more critically for Rothermere, many of the *Daily Mail*'s advertisers—denounced the Blackshirts' assaults on their fellow Britons. According to Mosley's memoir, Rothermere approached him privately a few weeks after the Olympia riot to confide that department store owners had pressured him to end his support for the BUF.[78] The *Daily Mail* and its sister papers stopped overtly promoting the BUF after July 1934, though they still provided plentiful coverage of the movement.[79]

In domestic matters, Rothermere found himself constrained by his advertisers and his pocketbook. But he would discover that he had much more freedom to influence foreign policy. Advertisers had forced him to drop the British fascists. It would take a world war to persuade him to distance himself from the German kind.

■

Rothermere did have a patriotic explanation for his praise of the Nazi government. At the same time that his paper acclaimed Hitler as the savior of Germany, he told British leaders privately that he was stroking the dictator's ego as part of his plan to protect Britain.

Rothermere wrote Winston Churchill in a private letter that the British should use "the language of butter" with Hitler because it was prudent to flatter dictators who lived in "an atmosphere of adulation and awestruck reverence."[80] He claimed to other acquaintances that he needed to make friends with Hitler to keep open an avenue for diplomacy should British and German relations deteriorate, telling one correspondent, "I think when the emergency comes this relationship might be of great value to this country."[81]

He also argued that his government needed to spend more money on defense, particularly on airplanes, in case the Germans eventually turned on Britain. He wrote many editorials calling for a massive expansion of airplane production and even paid for the design and construction of a bomber called the "Britain First" (the slogan of the British fascists), which later became the prototype for the RAF's Blenheim Bomber. Years later, as the Nazi regime went to war with his beloved England, the publisher defended himself by pointing to his consistent support of British rearmament.[82]

Rothermere's decision to praise the Nazis while calling for more arms to defend Britain against them struck many observers as contradictory and bizarre. In August 1934, Churchill, who was friends with Rothermere and who earned huge sums by writing articles for his papers, wrote to his wife that he was "disgusted" by the *Daily Mail* coverage of Hitler. Rothermere, he said, wanted the British to be very "strongly armed and frightfully obsequious at the same time." Nevertheless, Churchill concluded, it was "a more practical attitude than our socialist politicians. They wish us to remain disarmed and exceedingly abusive."[83]

Rothermere's defenders credit his argument that he had hidden reasons for flattering Hitler and maintain that he worked consistently for his country's best interests.[84] But his affection for the Nazis went far beyond any self-appointed mission to help the British government. His praise for Hitler predated the Nazis' rise to power; his first rapturous article on the Nazis appeared in 1930, years before any but the most optimistic Nazi sympathizers believed Hitler would rule Germany or could threaten the British. Moreover, Rothermere showed his esteem for fascism in many ways, not just in his stories about Hitler. A longtime fan of the Italian and Hungarian fascists, he did more than anyone else to give credibility to Mosley, the would-be Hitler of Great Britain.

The *Daily Mail* was unsurpassed among British and American mainstream papers in its consistent enthusiasm for the Nazi government. But even when other newspaper publishers were not actively pro-Nazi, their support of isolation had consequences that were just as grave.

CHAPTER TWO

The Celebrity Strongman

I N 1897, AS CUBAN rebels battled Spanish colonialists, William Randolph Hearst asked Frederic Remington, the renowned painter and sculptor, to go to Cuba to draw pictures of the conflict for his New York newspaper, the *Journal*. According to legend, after arriving, Remington complained to Hearst that he could not find any battles to record: "Everything is quiet. There is no trouble here. There will be no war. I wish to return." Hearst responded: "Please remain. You furnish the pictures, and I'll furnish the war."[1]

Though historians doubt the veracity of this famous anecdote, the exchange captures Hearst's attitude toward journalism. Hearst molded the news into a product to sell, initially during the Spanish-American War, when he made himself part of the story through his reporting, and again during his crusades for domestic policies. He used his newspapers first to fight for progressive reforms and later against the president he called "Stalin Delano Roosevelt."

While Hearst failed to remove Roosevelt from office, the publisher's campaign for an isolationist foreign policy was more successful. He would lobby for a strong, nondiscretionary Neutrality Act to prevent President Roosevelt from intervening in European crises. He would also give German leaders an opportunity to spread their propaganda to his 30 million readers. He used his control over

information to furnish not a war but a distorted version of reality—
an alternate universe where New Dealers were communist, Italian
fascists were admirable, and Nazis were only slightly anti-Semitic.

■

From the start, Hearst had a reputation as an unprincipled and undisciplined rich boy, but not necessarily a man of the Right. The
oldest of the World War II press lords, he was born in San Francisco in 1863, just a few years after his father had made a mining
fortune in the gold rush. The only child of doting parents with
great wealth, young Will spent much of his youth touring Europe
and New England. By his late teens, he was known as a playboy,
wastrel, and general mischief maker. He attended Harvard, where,
in the words of his authorized biographer, he "majored in jokes,
pranks and sociability" before getting expelled.[2] In 1887, at age
twenty-four, Hearst returned to his home state and asked his father
to let him manage one of his recent acquisitions, the *San Francisco
Examiner.*

Hearst took a small paper in the sleepy Pacific Coast media
market and transformed it into an innovative, entertaining, and prof-
itable daily that drew attention throughout the United States. He
recruited a crew of talented journalists, including the short story
writer Ambrose Bierce, and hired "sob sister" reporters like Win-
ifred Black to write feature stories so touching they reduced their
readers to tears. At the same time, he made the front page more vi-
sually appealing by reducing the number of stories, banishing advertisements to inside the paper, blowing up the size of the headlines
and, in an age before it was economical to publish photographs in
daily papers, hiring artists to draw images to illustrate the news.

In short order, his *Examiner* drew even in sales with its major
rival, the *San Francisco Chronicle*, and Hearst discovered that he
liked running a newspaper. He decided to move into the most exciting and competitive market in the United States. In 1895, he
bought the *New York Journal* and started a circulation war with the
other great American press baron of the day, Joseph Pulitzer, and
his *New York World.*

Hearst used his enormous fortune to improve his papers and
win more readers. He made publishing history with his trailblazing
Sunday comics supplement and his innovations in printing photo-

graphs. He also hired the best editors and writers and paid them extravagant salaries. In his biggest coup, he poached from Pulitzer the artist Richard Outcault, whose Yellow Kid comic character in the *World*'s color Sunday supplement was phenomenally popular. As the *World* and the *Journal* tried to outdo each other with colorful comics, enormous headlines, and sensational coverage of war and crime, their critics coined a term to describe the Hearst and Pulitzer reportorial strategies: "yellow journalism," a sensationalist variant of the "new journalism"—or mass-market journalism—being practiced on both sides of the Atlantic.

Like Northcliffe, Hearst discovered that many readers craved a steady diet of nationalism and anti-elitism in their political coverage. To win a larger audience, the Hearst papers decried Wall Street and "the interests" while championing America and Americanism. Hearst also emulated Northcliffe by fashioning a persona to sell himself along with his newspapers. To his employees he was "the chief." To his readers he was the publisher who signed his own front-page editorials; and sometimes he was the story himself—the successful businessman, fabulously wealthy investor, adventurer, celebrity journalist, and friend of the little people. Above all, he was a patriot who always put America first.

Hearst first showed his ultra-nationalism and his desire to insert himself in his stories during the Spanish-American War. The *Journal* treated the conflict like a morality play, with the Cubans cast as heroic underdogs opposing the powerful Spanish villains. When the USS *Maine* exploded in Havana Harbor, probably because of a faulty boiler, the *Journal* immediately judged the Spanish guilty of murdering hundreds of U.S. sailors and called for vengeance. After another newspaper blamed Hearst for starting the war, he responded by taunting his critics and claiming credit for American intervention. "How do you like the *Journal*'s war?" he asked his readers two weeks after Congress officially declared hostilities.[3]

Once the war began, Hearst personally reported on the fighting and even joined it. He hired a ship to transport him and *Journal* artists and correspondents to Cuba. He captured some beleaguered Spanish sailors on a beach and called them prisoners of war. One of his reporters, James Creelman, joined a charge on a Spanish fort and was shot in the arm. As he lay on the grass, his boss, with a straw hat on his head, revolver at his waist, and pencil and notepad in hand, eagerly took down his story. "I'm sorry you're hurt, but wasn't it a splendid fight?" Hearst said to him. "We must beat every paper in the world!"[4]

Hearst sought more than to beat every paper in the world: he also wanted to build the largest media empire in history. He created a wire service for international stories, the International News Service, to which hundreds of newspapers around the country subscribed; bought several mass-circulation magazines; and started a feature film studio and a newsreel company. He acquired papers in almost every major media market, including Los Angeles, Chicago, Boston, and Washington, D.C., and expanded the number of his New York papers to three. Though each Hearst paper ran its own local stories, they shared national and foreign news as well as editorials. The Hearst chain became the closest American equivalent to Britain's national newspapers.

As he built his media kingdom, Hearst fashioned a new identity: a man of business who was rich enough to buy anything in the world. He obsessively acquired European art: armor and altars; Rembrandts and van Dycks; Italian fountains and Egyptian mummies; even a Spanish monastery broken into ten thousand pieces for transport— all manner of treasures made their way from the Old World to the New at Hearst's behest.[5] He displayed his art in his many palatial homes, including an eight-hundred-year-old castle in Wales, a faux-Bavarian village in northern California, a sprawling retreat on the beach in Santa Monica, and the largest apartment in New York City. But above all there was San Simeon, known as Hearst Castle, his 115-room estate on the California coast, complete with a private zoo, where he and his girlfriend, actress Marion Davies, would entertain visiting dignitaries and Hollywood stars at elaborate masquerade balls and other weekend fetes. The image of Hearst's lavish lifestyle did not please everyone. Disgusted by the tycoon's conspicuous consumption during the Depression, his critics would organize protests and boycotts, write venomous biographies, and, in one celebrated case, make one of the greatest American films, *Citizen Kane*.

Hearst, in short, was more than the most formidable media mogul in America. He was also a celebrity strongman, building his brand by embodying his readers' idea of what it meant to be rich, powerful, and ostentatious. He did not merely report on Cuba: he fought in the war and captured prisoners. He did not just amass wealth: he spent it on zebras and giraffes for the backyard of his California "castle." His image gave him pleasure, but it also helped him brand and sell his products. Moreover, his attraction to that particular image—the strong, charismatic man of the people—might explain his interest in fascist leaders like Benito Mussolini and Adolf Hitler.

■

Hearst's editorial pages argued for his preferred policies in a hectoring style that might remind present-day Americans of former President Trump, especially the undisciplined use of capital letters. "The first session of the Seventy-fourth Congress," he wrote in a typical screed, "was the dividing line between the INDIVIDUALISTIC-DEMOCRATIC-CONSTITUTIONAL America of Jefferson, Madison and Lincoln and the PREDATORY SOCIALISTIC America of Roosevelt, Wallace, Tugwell, and Frankfurter."[6] College journalists parodied his style in a 1936 editorial that called Hearst a "REAL RED-BLOODED AMERICAN" who "has more REAL RED JEFFERSONIAN CORPUSCLES IN HIS BLOOD THAN ANY MAN NOW LIVING."[7]

In addition to overseeing the editorials, Hearst influenced the coverage in his newspapers by directing his editors and reporters to slant the news. In this practice he resembled Northcliffe and Rothermere but differed from many U.S. newspaper publishers. In the early twentieth century, American reporters began aspiring to an ideal of journalistic objectivity, or what Walter Lippmann called a search for "a common intellectual method and a common area of valid fact."[8] Borrowing terminology and ideas from the social sciences, reporters strove to professionalize their craft by replacing the hyper-partisan journalism of the past with consistent methods of verifying and communicating information.[9] The American Society of Newspaper Editors formally adopted the doctrine of objectivity in its statement of principles in 1923: "Sound practice makes clear distinction between news reports and expressions of opinion. News reports should be free from opinion or bias of any kind."[10] Content analyses of newspaper stories from 1850 to 1950 have shown that the new norms did change journalism: the use of charged language declined noticeably over that time.[11]

Many U.S. newspaper publishers at the time honored the bright line between their news and editorial pages. Roy Howard, who controlled America's second-largest chain, Scripps-Howard, was a die-hard noninterventionist until the middle of 1941, but his papers' coverage of the European crisis was relatively free of bias. Frank Gannett, a New Yorker who owned the third-largest U.S. newspaper chain, also despised Roosevelt and even sought the Republican nomination against him in the presidential campaign of 1940. But Gannett seldom interfered with his news reporters and editors.

Hearst did not embrace the new professional norms. Throughout his career, he would order his reporters and editors to select, write, and place their stories in ways that reflected his own political opinions. He saw newspapers as a means to an end. He wanted to gain political power—first for progressive causes, and later for increasingly conservative and corporate-friendly ones.

Surprisingly, considering his later reputation as a reactionary, Hearst was known in his youth and early middle age as a populist who enthusiastically backed unions, government regulation, and trust busting. He ran for office several times as a progressive Democrat: in two successful campaigns for Congress as well as failed attempts to become the Democratic nominee for the presidency (1904), New York City's mayor (1905 and 1909), and New York's governor (1906). His early admirers, who included the socialist authors Lincoln Steffens and Upton Sinclair, praised him for trying to redress the imbalance of power between the people and the corporations.

But Hearst shifted to the right after the Bolsheviks took power in Russia in 1917. He saw the revolution as a world-shattering event that threatened not just his pocketbook but all of civilization. In the 1920s he began to adopt conservative positions on domestic issues and to endorse Republican presidential candidates. He was a particular fan of conservative Republicans like President Calvin Coolidge and Treasury Secretary Andrew Mellon, whose trickle-down economic theories helped those who, like Hearst, were already on top.

Though his ideas on domestic politics changed dramatically during his lifetime, Hearst's foreign policy views remained consistent: he wanted the United States to stay out of Europe, fight the

William Randolph Hearst, pictured here in 1904,
made journalism history with his jingoistic stories about the
Spanish-American War. But in the 1930s he opposed U.S. intervention
in Europe against fascism and argued for a policy of "America First."
(Historic Collection / Alamy Stock Photo)

"yellow peril" in Asia, and control Latin America by force. His landholdings south of the border help explain his hemispheric imperialism. Scholars have estimated that he owned up to 7.5 million acres of land in Mexico alone as well as ranches and mining operations throughout Latin America. As the journalist Ferdinand Lundberg documented in his 1936 book *Imperial Hearst*, the publisher used his media companies to promote policies that would benefit his other businesses, including raids into Mexico to protect his own and other American landholders' property.[12] He went so far in 1927 as to publish forged documents that purported to disclose a worldwide Bolshevik conspiracy centered in Mexico (thus requiring an American invasion to quash it). When his paper alleged—again based on false documents—that four U.S. senators had taken bribes from these plotters, one of the accused lawmakers denounced the Hearst press as "the sewer system of American journalism."[13]

Hearst advocated for an aggressive interventionist policy toward Asia as well. Like many white Californians, he was violently anti-Asian. In 1916, his film studio produced a serial called *Patria* that featured brave Americans defeating a Japanese plan to use Mexican peasants to invade the United States. The movie was so offensive to Asians that President Woodrow Wilson, a devoted racist himself, nevertheless asked Hearst to pull it from distribution. The publisher refused, but he did agree to some edits.

Hearst published countless editorials urging white people to unite against what he called the yellow menace. "The white races are blinded by the fury of their internecine strife," he warned in March 1918. "They are so crazed by jealousy of each other that they cannot see the real danger which threatens their civilization and their world domination."[14] Because Asians were "the racial enemies of the white peoples," he wrote in another editorial, members of the "white race" needed to stop fighting each other and pull together for the sake of civilization and democracy.[15]

Hearst's racist views—his fears of the Japanese and his sense of kinship with other people of white "blood"—explain his opposition to American involvement in wars in Europe. The media tycoon who urged war against Latin Americans and Asians could see no reason his country should fight the Kaiser or Hitler. Before U.S. entry into the Great War in 1917, he insisted that the nation had no security interests at stake in a war he saw as pointless.

After the Allied victory, Hearst demanded that the U.S. Senate reject the Treaty of Versailles and refuse to join the League of Nations. The League covenant committed its members to a collective defense of other members if they were attacked. It also called for all member nations to begin reducing their stockpiles of arms. In short, the League represented everything Hearst and other isolationists despised: internationalism over nationalism, disarmament over rear-mament, and collective security over unilateral action. President Wilson touted the organization as a way to maintain peace, but in Hearst's view, it was not "a league to keep us out of war but a league to get us into war."[16]

Hearst considered the Senate's rejection of the treaty one of the greatest accomplishments of his life. "If it had not been for my papers, this country might, through the League of Nations, have become involved in war," he said proudly in 1936.[17] The fight over the treaty and the League are what led the *Examiner*, in 1919, to embed a new slogan in its front-page nameplate: "America First."

Just as Woodrow Wilson's multilateral diplomacy drove Hearst from the Democratic Party, the Republicans' internationalism—or Hearst's perception of it—led him back to the Democratic fold in 1932. He had endorsed the Republican presidential nominee, Herbert Hoover, in 1928, but grew increasingly disenchanted with Hoover as president. He broke with his fellow Californian for good after Hoover agreed to allow Britain and France a one-year pause in the repayment of their World War I debts to the United States. Hearst later came to see Hoover as the "hired man of privileged in-terests" and the "most conspicuous failure in American history."[18]

Disgusted by the Republicans, Hearst began to search for an ap-propriate Democratic candidate to support. After surveying the field, he found the man he believed could rescue America from the Great Depression: John Nance Garner, a congressman from Texas and the Speaker of the House. Hearst complained that the front-runner for the nomination, Governor Franklin Roosevelt of New York, was too internationalist. Roosevelt had served in the Wilson administration, supported the League of Nations in 1920, and failed to say the word *American* often enough in his speeches. Garner, by contrast, was a "loyal American" whose "heart is with his own people."[19]

To win Hearst's approval, Roosevelt tried to disavow his earlier support of the League of Nations. In a February 1932 campaign speech designed specifically to placate the newspaper baron, Roos-evelt said he had backed the League in 1920 because he believed the United States would join it and make it a force for world peace. Since the United States had never joined the League, Roosevelt explained, he no longer supported it.[20]

This renunciation of the League did not satisfy Hearst, who continued to favor Garner until that summer's Democratic convention. In that era, a candidate needed the approval of two-thirds of the delegates at the convention in order to become the nominee. As Roosevelt struggled to achieve that many votes, he struck a deal with Garner's supporters: if they would allow the delegates from California and Texas to support him, he would name Garner as his running mate.[21] They agreed, and in November 1932, Roosevelt won an overwhelming mandate to implement what he called a "New Deal for the American people."

Even with Hearst on board, Roosevelt won the endorsements of just 41 percent of America's daily newspapers in 1932—and that was the peak of his popularity with the press. Fewer and fewer papers endorsed him with each subsequent election.[22] He and his aides recognized that most of the wealthy men who owned the nation's largest newspapers would never support his progressive policies. As Interior Secretary Harold Ickes wrote in his 1939 book, *America's House of Lords*, the newspaper owners were "more interested in private profits than in public welfare."[23]

In this hostile media landscape, Roosevelt understood that he could not afford to lose the backing of the nation's most powerful media mogul, and he did what he could to conciliate and flatter Hearst. He wrote effusive letters to "W. R." and invited him for luncheons, dinners, and even overnight visits to the White House.[24]

Hearst praised Roosevelt's vigor and boldness when he took office in March 1933. The publisher was so impressed by Roosevelt's early accomplishments that he proposed that the nation celebrate a "President's Day" in April to show its gratitude.[25] In the same month, Hearst's studio released a movie, *Gabriel over the White House*, about a fictional president who takes on dictatorial authority to get the United States out of a depression. Hearst's fantasy president adopts an isolationist foreign policy, authorizes the summary execution of gangsters, and accepts Congress's decision to adjourn and cede its powers to him. Hearst clearly had no problem with the prospect of Roosevelt becoming a dictator—as long as the president followed the press lord's policies.[26]

But Hearst, who worried that unionized workers could endanger profit and property, grew increasingly disappointed with Roosevelt's pro-labor policies. He hated Roosevelt's National Industrial Recovery Act of 1933, which created the National Recovery Administration (NRA) and gave protection to industrial workers who wished to organize. Condemning the NRA with his customary intemperance, Hearst said its letters spelled out "No Recovery Allowed" or even "Nonsensical, Ridiculous, Asinine interference with national and legitimate industrial development."[27] He fumed that the law aimed to undermine democracy and would negate the results of the election by turning the United States into a communist dictatorship: "The people approved the well considered proposals of the Democratic platform, not the theories of Karl Marx and the policies of Stalin."[28]

Hearst's worst fears were confirmed, he believed, when the labor provisions of the National Industrial Recovery Act helped encourage a surge of unionization across the country, including in newspaper city rooms. Seeing empowered workers as the shock troops of a coming communist takeover, he ordered his editors to start running articles on the Red plot "to overthrow the government and establish a Soviet regime in the United States," as one story reported in 1934.[29] He was particularly worried about left-wing professors who, in his view, spewed hate and had too much power to mold young minds. Almost two decades before Senator Joe McCarthy began his Red hunts, Hearst ordered "that names, pictures and activities of disloyal professors and others should be printed continually and commented upon" in his papers.[30]

The San Francisco general strike, called by labor leaders in July 1934 after deadly police attempts to break a longshoremen's strike, confirmed Hearst's view that the Russians were coming— and that some of Roosevelt's advisers, if not the president himself, would welcome them. "The revolution in California against stable government and established order," he wrote in a signed editorial, "would never have occurred except for the sympathy and encouragement which the fomenters of revolution were receiving or believed they were receiving from those high in the counsel of the Federal Administration." The "fires of sedition," he concluded, "had been lit by these visionary and voluble politicians."[31]

Progressives fought back against the Hearst Red-baiting campaign. A Popular Front alliance of students, radicals, liberals, and civil libertarians picketed Hearst buildings in various cities and organized a boycott of his papers. Edmond Coblentz, the editor of the *New York American,* reported to Hearst that there was "no doubt that the boycott, which is becoming more intense and widespread every day, is hurting our circulation."[32] Hearst's opponents distributed millions of lapel buttons saying "DON'T READ HEARST" and forced hundreds of movie theaters to stop showing Hearst newsreels."[33]

Jewish groups, who charged that Hearst's news pages included coded anti-Semitic slurs, joined the protests. Some prominent Jews met with Hearst's general manager, Tom White, to complain about anti-Semitism in the Hearst press. Hearst responded by accusing the visitors of clannishness and hypersensitivity. "I can tell these gentlemen how to avoid prejudice," he lectured White, "and that is . . . by not protecting on pure racial grounds an individual who deserves criticism, and by not attacking for purely racial reasons a good friend simply because he is also a good American and is doing what they admit is good for the country."[34]

Despite the boycotts and protests, Hearst refused to drop his crusade against supposed Reds or their enablers in Washington. In April 1935, he decided it was time, as he told Coblentz, to "settle down to a consistent policy of opposition to this Administration." The New Deal was corrupting "the whole spirit of America," he wrote, by creating "a dependent class insisting on being supported." He had no doubt whom to blame for this catastrophe: "It is not the motley crowd of clowns and mountebanks with which Roosevelt has surrounded himself that are responsible. It is the man who placed those mountebanks in positions of power and authority where they could exploit their ridiculous and disastrous policies."[35]

Roosevelt still tried to placate the nation's most important publisher. He explained to one of his closest aides, Harold Ickes, that he could not afford to lose any more press support before his reelection campaign. "The president," Ickes wrote in his diary, "remarked that, outside of Hearst and one or two other strings of newspapers, all the balance of the press of the country would be against him and naturally he wants all the support he can get. Therefore, he wants to watch his step on the Hearst matter."[36]

But Roosevelt's 1935 plan to raise income taxes on millionaires like Hearst made rapprochement impossible. The president tried his best to defuse an inevitable Hearst explosion by inviting Coblentz,

Hearst's lieutenant and editor, to the White House for a private explanation of the reasons behind the tax increase. At the four-hour
discussion, at which Vincent Astor, one of the richest men in the
country, was also present, Roosevelt defended his tax plan as a necessary response to pressure from the Left. Senator Huey Long of
Louisiana, who proposed a confiscatory tax on the highest incomes
and a radical redistribution of wealth, was then at the peak of his
popularity, with millions listening to his radio show every week.
Roosevelt argued that he needed to co-opt Long's message and reassure his followers that the government could reform itself. "I want
to save our system, the capitalistic system," Roosevelt explained. To
do so, he needed to raise the marginal tax rate on incomes over
$1 million—a proposal, he clarified, that would apply to fewer than
four dozen Americans. "It may be necessary," he said, "to throw the
46 men who are reported to have incomes in excess of $1,000,000 a
year to the wolves."[37]

Hearst, who was one of those forty-six men, was not convinced
by Roosevelt's explanation. The next month, when the president
presented his tax plan to Congress, Hearst fired off an incensed
message to his editorial writers. The president's proposal "divides a
harmonious and homogeneous nation into classes," he wrote, "and
stimulates class distinction, class discrimination, class division, class
resentment, and class antagonism." The plan was "essentially communism," the product of "a composite personality which might be
labelled Stalin Delano Roosevelt."[38] Hearst opposed tax increases
for ideological reasons: he thought they stifled investment and business expansion. But the proposed hike would also hurt him personally. He asked his general manager to help rearrange his accounts to
keep down his earnings. "If it goes over a million dollars," he wrote,
"they will practically confiscate the income."[39]

Though Roosevelt called the revenue act the "soak the rich"
tax, Hearst directed his editors to use instead the phrases "soak the
thrifty," "soak the saving," or "soak the prosperous" in news stories.[40] Two months later, he ordered them to stop referring to the
"New Deal"—henceforth, the Hearst press would call it the "Raw
Deal."[41] White House aides got a copy of this directive and triumphantly disseminated it to the rest of the press, along with a presidential comment that cited the "Raw Deal" memo as proof that "a

minority of owners and editors" refused to cover the news objectively and instead engaged in the "deliberate coloring of so-called news stories."[42]

This attempt to humiliate Hearst did not work. The very next day the Hearst press ran the headline "Soak-Successful Tax Bill Jammed through Senate." The first paragraph said the administration needed the levy to finance the "Raw Deal."[43]

From that point on, the president and the nation's most prominent publisher fought in open warfare. The Hearst papers' editorials, columns, op-eds, and sometimes even news stories predicted the imminent collapse of the republic. "This band of revolutionary radicals propose to OVERTHROW THE GOVERNMENT," read a news article in fall 1935, "AND THEY ARE DOING IT."[44]

Some Roosevelt backers worried that Hearst's attacks would erode the president's support. One of Eleanor Roosevelt's friends in the media, George Allen of the Columbia Syndicate, told her that he had traveled around the middle of the country and "found but one force effectively combating the Administration; namely, the Hearst papers." Eleanor routed the letter to her husband and wrote in the margin: "F.D.R.: I'm *sure* this is true."[45] But Roosevelt refused to believe that the publisher retained much influence over his readers' political views. There was "no question," he wrote to another concerned supporter, "that the political influence of these papers has been infinitely reduced during the past few years."[46]

Hearst did not just denounce Roosevelt in his papers; he intended to choose the next president. He first hunted for a Democrat to oust Roosevelt from office, then suggested forming a third party, and finally resolved that he would "depend on the Republican Party to rescue the country from experimental Socialism, and restore it to sound and stable Americanism."[47] For the nominee, he settled on Kansas governor Alf Landon, one of the few Republicans to win office in the great Democratic sweep of 1934.

After Landon won the GOP presidential nomination, Hearst put his entire media empire—twenty-eight newspapers with 30 million readers, thirteen magazines, eight radio stations, and a newsreel company—at the service of his campaign.[48] Hearst also personally directed his papers' news coverage, from ordering a series of articles on New Dealers' corruption or radicalism—"I WANT THE ARTICLES TO

BE IN GOOD BIG TYPE WITH PLENTY OF PARAGRAPHS"—to demanding stories on the "national scandal" of voter fraud, complete with cash rewards for the arrest and conviction of fraudulent voters.[49]

The Hearst papers had company in opposing Roosevelt's reelection. Nationwide, about 60 percent of newspapers backed Landon. Yet the president won the greatest reelection victory since James Monroe had run essentially unopposed in 1820. "Never have the newspapers, in my recollection, conducted a more mendacious and venomous campaign against a candidate for President," wrote Harold Ickes in his diary, "and never have they been of so little influence."[50]

■

Ickes was correct: the conservative American publishers had demonstrated little influence on domestic politics up to this point. Hearst tried to kick Roosevelt out of the White House, and he failed. He worked to stop the expansion of labor rights and the increase in taxes on the wealthy, but neither Congress nor the voters heeded him.

Like Rothermere, however, Hearst would discover that he could wield much more power over foreign policy. In the mid-1930s, he intervened in the debate over the proper U.S. response to the rise of fascism in two key ways: by backing a strong, unconditional Neutrality Act to keep America out of European conflicts, and by serving as a conduit for propaganda for fascist dictators.

In the view of Hearst and other isolationists, Congress needed to pass a strict Neutrality Act to prevent the sale of U.S. arms to nations at war. The Senate Foreign Relations Committee began debating such a proposal in the summer of 1935. President Roosevelt, who worried that neutrality legislation would tie his hands and make it hard to respond to aggression abroad, first tried to kill the measure, then attempted to amend it so that he could choose the countries to which it should apply. Back in March 1933, during the first days of his presidency, he had supported a similar flexible embargo, but it had died in the Senate. At the time, Hearst had called it an "un-American provocative and dangerous proposal" and an "attempt to lure the United States into a war-breeding alliance with foreign powers."[51] The publisher was no more disposed to it now.

Roosevelt's request for discretion in applying an arms embargo amounted "absolutely to the power to declare war," Hearst concluded. "The President in his immense and unreasonable and wholly unwarrantable egotism desires this added power to the immeasurable ones already bestowed upon him. This is the last thing to make him completely a dictator."[52] In the end, Congress passed the Neutrality Act as originally written and as Hearst demanded—a mandatory ban on arms sales to all countries involved in a formally declared war. Hearst also won the battle against the president's proposal that the United States join the World Court. He called this victory the one example in the congressional session "wherein Congress rose against un-American executive dictatorship."[53]

Yet even as he condemned Roosevelt as a dictator, Hearst praised the strongmen of Europe, going so far as to devote space to their propaganda. The Hearst newspapers gave Benito Mussolini fawning coverage from his early years in office, a decade before the beginning of the New Deal, and continued to promote him years later. In 1930, Hearst's wife, Millicent, published a front-page story on the Italian premier in which she pronounced him "simple, kindly, courteous" and a "true leader of men" who had earned "a high place in history and the hearts of his people."[54]

Hearst also paid Mussolini, Hitler, and several top Nazis to write for his papers at very high rates—$1 a word in Mussolini's case, or $1,500 per story (more than $20,000 today).[55] To be sure, he also hired other world leaders to write for him. David Lloyd George and Winston Churchill were frequent contributors. But by giving fascist dictators direct access to the American public and allowing them to present themselves as peace-loving, tolerant champions of order, Hearst helped to normalize them for his 30 million readers.

The Nazi columns in the Hearst press emphasized Hitler's talking points. The Germans, victimized by the Treaty of Versailles, wanted only to be left alone to pursue peace, but they would defend themselves if necessary. One typical story by Hermann Göring, the Nazi air minister and second-in-command to Hitler, sported the headline: "Nazi Germany Stands for Maintenance of Legal Security, Declares Göring: But Enemies of Our People Will Be Relentlessly Pursued."[56] Hitler himself, before he came to power, received prominent placement in the Hearst papers to decry "the enslavement of an entire nation" by the victors at Versailles and the "forced transfusion of their own lifeblood from Germany to France, England, and America."[57]

Like Rothermere, Hearst also provided enthusiastic personal reviews of the Nazis' regime. He finally got the opportunity to meet Hitler and several of his aides in September 1934, at the end of the publisher's annual tour of Europe. The Hearst entourage, including his mistress, his sons and their wives, some aides and associates, and valets, maids, and chauffeurs, traveled through several European countries. Always on the lookout for art to purchase for his many homes, Hearst visited palaces, cathedrals, and castles. He also stayed alert for news events to cover for his papers, including a Mussolini rally in Rome. But what he really wanted, he told reporters before he embarked on the trip, was to see Hitler.

In Germany, Hearst consented to an interview by Ernst Hanfstaengl, Hitler's press agent, which was published in a Nazi newspaper, distributed by the official government news agency, and picked up by American media outlets. In the interview, Hearst praised the Nazi leader's recent victory in a plebiscite that confirmed him as German president and chancellor. The vote was "a unanimous expression of the popular will," Hearst said, that would "open up a new chapter in modern history." If Hitler gave the German people peace, order, and the opportunity for "ethical development," the entire world would benefit. All "liberty-loving peoples," he concluded, viewed the German struggle for liberation from the unjust Treaty of Versailles with "understanding and sympathy."[58]

After the interview, Hearst and his party traveled to Nuremberg, where the Nazi Party was holding its annual conference—the political pageant immortalized by Nazi filmmaker Leni Riefenstahl in *Triumph of the Will*. Riefenstahl's propaganda piece shows what Hearst might have seen in Nuremberg: the streets lined with tens of thousands of cheering Germans, their hands flying up to salute the Führer as his motorcade made its way through the medieval city. It is unclear whether Hearst personally attended the giant rallies in the city's arenas and heard the crowds thunder their approval during the many speeches about German greatness and the need for racial purity. But Nazi newspapers reported that his eldest son,

George, attended some of them, and the Hearst group occupied ten rooms in the same hotel as top Nazi officials, along with another foreign press lord known for his Nazi sympathies, Rothermere.[59]

Hearst and his party continued to the spa town of Bad Nauheim, where the publisher consented to another interview—this one with Dr. Alfred Rosenberg, known as the foremost "Nazi intellectual," who engaged Hearst in a discussion of racial theory and persuaded him to share his ideas about racial hierarchies. It was clear, Hearst said, that Europeans were different from "Asiatics," and that a war between the two "races" would involve "conflicts of habits and customs, of law and religion, of living standards, of moral standards, of social and political ideals, of basic civilizations." Europeans were all the same race, even if they came from different tribes, and it would be "the most sinful thing in the world" for them to fight one another and thus "endanger Occidental civilization and supremacy" just to change the national borders within Europe. Instead, Hearst concluded, Europeans should unite against "Oriental invasion." He did not explain how Jews fit into his racial framework.[60]

While in Bad Nauheim, Hearst learned that his request to meet Hitler had been approved: he could fly to Berlin for a personal interview. Hearst's secretary, Harry Crocker, wrote an extended account of the meeting. An official black limousine whisked Hearst, Crocker, and Hanfstaengl to the Chancellery, a gray stone building guarded by Storm Troopers in brown shirts, SS troops in black shirts, and soldiers from the regular army. As the group waited in a long, narrow room, suddenly they heard "a barrage of heel clicks" and the doors swung open. Hitler entered the room to a chorus of "Heil Hitler!" and immediately set out to show his dominance over the other men. "In rapid succession," Crocker remembered, "he seized each of us by the hand. One quick forward jerk pulled each of us off balance. A second quick reverse movement thrust each back on his heels, nearly toppling him over backwards. It was enough to disconcert anyone."[61]

In his one-hour interview with Hearst, Hitler complained that the American press had misrepresented him. When Hearst explained that Americans distrusted him because they valued democracy, Hitler responded that he was a "product of democracy" and had been elected to office. Hearst then suggested that "a very large and influential and respected element in the United States" resented the Nazi treatment of their German relatives. "And this element," he continued, "has the sincere sympathy of practically all other elements of the American public." He apparently never uttered the word *Jew* in the conversation. Hitler assured the Americans that Germany's anti-Semitic laws were temporary and "will soon entirely disappear."[62]

Hearst gave exuberant reports of the conversation to other journalists. He emphasized Hitler's popularity within Germany, his restoration of "character and courage" and "hope and confidence," and his intent to moderate the anti-Jewish laws. "The whole policy of such an anti-Semitism is such an obvious mistake that I am sure it must soon be abandoned," Hearst exclaimed in September 1934. "In fact, I think it is already well on the way to abandonment."[63] He later claimed he had gone to meet Hitler on the advice of MGM studio head Louis B. Mayer who, as a Jew, hoped that Hearst could talk Hitler out of some of his most extreme anti-Semitic policies. There is no contemporary evidence of this, and Mayer never confirmed it.[64]

Hearst thought the interview went well and that he had been "able to do some good."[65] To his aide Joseph Willicombe, Hearst wrote that Hitler was "an extraordinary man" whom Americans underestimated. "He has enormous energy, intense enthusiasm, a marvelous faculty for dramatic oratory, and great organizing ability."[66]

Hearst had other reasons to feel positive about his trip, for he had concluded some important business deals with the Nazi regime. His newsreel company, Hearst Metrotone News, made a secret agreement with the largest film company in Germany, Ufa, to share news footage. Ufa would show parts of Hearst newsreels in Germany, and in return, Hearst agreed to place selections of Nazi propaganda films in his newsreels in the United States. No money changed hands; it was simply a film-swapping agreement.[67] The contract was similar to one Hearst made with a British company. However, as Louis Pizzitola has emphasized, in the German case, Hearst had agreed to incorporate "unfiltered propaganda into American newsreels."[68] Hearst Metrotone coverage of some of the most significant events of the 1930s—Hitler's visit to the Sudetenland after the

Munich agreement, the signing of the "pact of steel" with the Italians, and even the start of the war in Poland—originated as official Nazi footage.[69] Other rumors of Hearst's entanglement with the German regime flourished among American reporters, including allegations—never proved—that the Nazis had secretly paid him $400,000 for rights to his wire service as a quid pro quo for favorable newspaper coverage.[70]

As the gossip about his real and possible Nazi connections reached the United States, Hearst's enemies began calling him "Hitler's man in America."[71] The journalist who began his long career as a champion of progressive policies found himself, near the end, labeled an American fascist.

■

These whispers about secret Nazi influence were fueled by public facts, including Hearst's enthusiasm for Nazism. He did not write extended pro-Nazi articles like Rothermere's "Germany on Her Feet Again," and he never promoted domestic fascists, but he helped legitimize fascism by giving prominent Nazis a platform—in his newspapers and his newsreels—to spread their propaganda in America.

If Hearst had been the only major American publisher who crusaded for isolationism, his impact on the nation's foreign policy might have been less significant. But he had company.

CHAPTER THREE

The World's Greatest Publisher

RITICS USED MANY ADJECTIVES to describe the *Chicago Tribune* during the New Deal—including "unscrupulous," "reactionary," "dishonest," and "unspeakable." "I wonder," said one columnist, "if that rag ever prints a word of truth except racing and baseball results."[1] Its publisher, Robert McCormick, was too strident even for his chief rival in editorial intemperance. In 1938, William Randolph Hearst explained privately that he wanted to be "strategic" in his anti–New Deal coverage, because "if we are violent, we will only do [what] . . . the *Tribune* is doing—help those we are trying to oppose."[2]

Press analysts saw McCormick as the worst offender among the right-wing publishers. One such critic, John Tebbel, noted in 1947 "with shame" that many newspapers printed "outright lies" to smear labor unions and the New Deal, but that "few were more unabashed in their apparent lying than the *Tribune*."[3] Liberal journalist George Seldes wrote a 1938 book about the ways newspaper owners twisted the news and concluded that McCormick and the *Tribune* were the most dishonest of all. "I know of no newspaper," he wrote, "which is so stupid and vicious in its attacks on labor, no paper so consistent in its Red-baiting, and no paper [that] in my opinion is such a great enemy of the American people."[4]

Like Rothermere and Hearst, McCormick believed that the liberal intellectuals and public officials of his country were stooges —perhaps unwitting, perhaps not—of communist revolutionaries. He even published fake news stories to expose what he saw as a real plot against the Constitution by President Franklin Roosevelt.

Unlike Hearst and Rothermere, though, the colonel did not personally meet with Hitler or praise him in print (in fact, he wrote some anti-Nazi articles early on). McCormick was a far-right activist who believed the United States had no security interests in Europe and should not take measures to confront or resist Hitler. He consistently argued that German aggression was understandable because of the injustices of the Treaty of Versailles, and that the Nazis' territorial ambitions were not much different from British imperialism.

McCormick identified himself as an American nationalist—by which he meant a white Protestant American nationalist—fighting against "internationalists" (often code for Jews) who would draw the United States into unnecessary struggles. Like Hearst and Rothermere, he failed in his early domestic political crusades but would find success in shaping the nation's foreign policy.

■

While the *Daily Mail* and the Hearst papers inaugurated a new tradition of sensationalist journalism, the *Tribune* modified an old one: the newspaper as partisan organ. In the nineteenth century, newspapers tended to identify expressly with a political party and serve unabashedly as its voice. The *Tribune* was Republican from the days of Abraham Lincoln, and it remained so under McCormick.

Joseph Medill, McCormick's grandfather, bought into the *Tribune*'s ownership before the Civil War and was an early booster of Lincoln as well as a founder of the Republican Party. He became majority owner after the war and turned the paper into a leading mouthpiece of Republicanism in the Midwest. Medill's *Tribune* argued for hard-line, far-right policies, especially against unions, urging police to shoot strikers and mobs to lynch labor leaders. Medill made no attempt to keep his editorial opinions out of the news pages. In its news stories and headlines, for example, the *Tribune* referred to labor leader and Socialist Eugene V. Debs as "Dictator Debs."[5]

Medill's two surviving children helped consolidate their family's wealth and journalistic legacy through their marriages: Katharine (Kate) wed Robert Sanderson McCormick, a nephew of the harvester king Cyrus McCormick; and Elinor (Nellie) married Robert Patterson, the *Tribune*'s Washington correspondent. When Medill died in 1899, he left his fortune to his daughters and his journalistic inheritance to Patterson, who took over the paper.

All four of Medill's surviving grandchildren would follow his example and use the *Tribune* to fatten their bank accounts and increase their political influence. One, Medill McCormick, served in the U.S. Senate until his death by suicide in 1925. The other three grandchildren chose to exercise power through the media.

Robert Rutherford McCormick, the most conservative Medill grandchild, ultimately took charge of the family newspaper and turned it into the most popular broadsheet in the country. Born in 1880, McCormick learned in childhood to revere the political and economic system that brought wealth and power to men like himself. A more traditional conservative than Hearst, or indeed than his cousin Joe Patterson, McCormick never dabbled in mass politics. He believed in hierarchies of race, class, and gender and opposed any political movement that threatened them.[6]

McCormick disliked many individuals and classes of people, but he nursed a special hatred for the British. He first encountered the English at age nine, when his father, thanks to his family connections, received a posting as a diplomatic attaché with the U.S. embassy in London. His mother sent Bertie, as they called him, to a boarding school in Hampshire, where the young American adopted a lifelong enthusiasm for London tailors, cricket, polo, and riding to hounds. He seemed to love all things British except the people, whom he saw as arrogant and condescending. "It has long been a habit of the English," he wrote years later, "to berate and abuse Americans."[7]

McCormick responded to what he saw as British arrogance by developing a fierce sense of nationalism. He and his brother Medill tried to ward off any tendency toward Anglicization by reading vernacular American novels like *Tom Sawyer* and *Huckleberry Finn*.[8] He was disgusted by the red-coated, high-stepping guards at Buckingham Palace and the adoring throngs that greeted Queen Victoria's carriage. To emphasize his distinctiveness (and superiority), Bertie draped an American flag over his bed.[9] Throughout his life he expressed contempt for Americans who, in their weakness and insecurity, desperately sought approval from English aristocrats.[10]

When it came time for prep school, McCormick's parents sent him to Groton, where Franklin Roosevelt was a year behind him, though the two boys did not know each other well. Already an Anglophobe, Bertie learned from his time in Connecticut to despise New Englanders as well. He once again found himself patronized. His father suggested a cutting line to use in response to his classmates' condescension: "Tell them they are descendants of Boston tradesmen and you are descended from Virginia gentlemen."[11] Though Bertie continued to resent New Englanders' snobbery, he decided to attend Yale along with his brother Medill and cousin Joe. He later remembered aspects of his college years with great fondness, especially the gatherings where he and his classmates would belt out, "For God, For Country, and For Yale."[12]

In 1910, after his uncle Robert Patterson's suicide, McCormick seized the opportunity to take over his grandfather's greatest legacy, the *Tribune*. He and his cousin Joe convinced their mothers and the other stockholders to let them run the paper. Drawing lessons from Hearst and Pulitzer, the cousins worked together to turn the old-fashioned daily into a lively journal that could hold its own against Hearst's Chicago morning paper, the *Examiner*. The *Tribune* grabbed commuters' attention with eight-column bold headlines, while its features, funnies, Hollywood gossip, and advice columns helped to build reader loyalty. Joe Patterson showed a talent for choosing and developing popular comic strips, including, in later years, *Little Orphan Annie* and *Dick Tracy*. Soon after the cousins took over, the *Tribune* embedded a new slogan, "The World's Greatest Newspaper," in its nameplate on the front page.[13]

Though they admired and respected each other's business sense, the cousins clashed over editorial policy. Patterson favored reforms to help the working classes, while McCormick opposed progressive taxation and union rights. They hit on the idea of alternating control of the editorial page each month.[14] Even at the time, however, they knew this compromise could not work as a long-term strategy.

Four years after the cousins took over management of the newspaper, the outbreak of the Great War in Europe provided opportunities for journalistic adventure and, for McCormick, tests of his "manliness" and leadership skills. He covered the early years of the conflict as the *Tribune*'s correspondent and grew fascinated with war, especially the subject of male courage on the battlefield. "I have tasted the wine of death, and its flavor will be forever in my throat," he wrote in a 1915 book on his experiences as a war correspondent.[15] After returning to Chicago, he jumped at the chance to participate in a North American war. In 1916, McCormick joined a cavalry regiment of the Illinois National Guard in hopes of taking part in an American invasion of Mexico. Rebel leader Pancho Villa had led raids on U.S. territory, including an attack on the town of Columbus, New Mexico, that killed more than a dozen Americans. In response, President Wilson sent U.S. soldiers into Mexico in search of Villa and mobilized one hundred thousand additional troops at the border. Wilson stopped short, though, of the full-scale invasion demanded by McCormick and his newspaper. McCormick stayed in Texas throughout the confrontation, and eventually headed back to Chicago, disappointed that there would be no war.[16]

In 1917, U.S. entry into the Great War finally gave McCormick the opportunity to experience war as a soldier, not just as a journalist. McCormick joined the army as a commissioned major and later earned a promotion to colonel. He served on General Pershing's staff in France, went into the field as an artillery commander, and fought in the battle of Cantigny.

McCormick's wartime service was the most exciting period of his life, in part because war provided what he viewed as a "male mission."[17] Women were working in many different industries by the 1910s, and his own paper employed several as reporters and features editors. Yet the battlefield continued to exclude women and thus gave each soldier a chance to be "exalted in the sense of his manhood."[18] McCormick revered this male space. "Here men stand alone," he wrote, "the preservers, the admired of women. Here they glory in their masculinity and resent any suggestion that the males of another race can excel them."[19] Proving his masculinity would remain a lifelong concern, and slurring political opponents in gendered terms such

Colonel Robert McCormick's service in World War I helped define
him. "I have tasted the wine of death, and its flavor will be forever in
my throat," wrote the colonel, who was buried in his army uniform.
But despite his enthusiasm for the military, McCormick opposed U.S.
intervention in Europe in the 1930s. (Archive PL / Alamy Stock Photo)

as "hysterical effeminates" would become one of his favorite editorial
techniques.[20]

Forever changed by his wartime experiences, and intrigued by
the ways that battle tested men, McCormick came home to study
and write books about past wars and generals. For the rest of his
life, he made his staff call him "Colonel," and he renamed his
country estate after the battle in which he had fought, Cantigny.
After his death, he was buried in his World War I uniform, while

his estate was transformed into a military museum, the Cantigny War Memorial of the First Division. He would emerge as one of the most significant opponents of American participation in the next European war, but not because he hated militarism.

McCormick returned from the Great War determined to make good on his newspaper's slogan: the *Tribune* would become, truly, the world's greatest newspaper, inspiring awe around the globe. The paper's new headquarters, Tribune Tower, expressed the colonel's dominion over his hometown. After sponsoring an international competition for the design of the "most beautiful office building in the world," McCormick and Patterson chose a thirty-six-story plan for a hulking neo-Gothic fortress, complete with flying buttresses and gargoyles looming over Michigan Avenue. Its outer walls were embedded with stones acquired (often pilfered) from historic locations around the world, including European cathedrals, the Parthenon, the Great Wall of China, and the Taj Mahal.[21] Inside the palatial lobby, the Hall of Inscriptions featured quotations on the importance of a free press from Thomas Jefferson, Lord Macaulay, and the colonel himself.

The publisher directed his media empire from the twenty-fourth floor, surrounded by armed guards, working at a desk made of red and white Italian marble next to a Gothic window, plotting to spread his influence throughout the area he dubbed "Chicagoland": Illinois, Indiana, Iowa, Michigan, and Wisconsin.[22] By the 1930s, the *Tribune* was the best-selling full-size paper in the country. The colonel was justifiably proud of his paper's reach. "With our circulation averaging one million and counting little children," he boasted, "you can say just about everybody in Chicagoland reads the *Tribune*."[23]

McCormick also reached millions of Americans through his radio station. He bought the station WDAP in 1924 and changed its call letters to WGN, for World's Greatest Newspaper. The station brought some of the greatest events of the era into American homes: the Scopes "monkey" trial, the Kentucky Derby, the World Series, and party conventions. For decades, McCormick hosted his own show on WGN, which gave him another medium for telling Americans how to think about politics.

McCormick built a vast media empire not because he needed acclamation or affection but because he wanted to wield power.

His broadcasting career notwithstanding, he was an intensely shy man who took little pleasure in parties or society functions.[24] But he did demand respect, if not love, from his publishing peers. He insisted, for example, that other newspapers could not call themselves the world's greatest newspaper, which both the *Daily Express* and the London *Times* had the temerity to do during the 1930s. "It does not become these small overseas papers in London," he wrote, "either to steal our stuff or to put themselves in our class."[25]

McCormick's imperious eccentricities were legend among *Tribune* reporters. He would ring for a servant to retrieve a pencil that was just inches beyond his reach; he seldom house-trained his pet dogs, because he relied on servants to clean up their messes.[26] In his early days at the paper, he would dress in breeches, spurs, and an officer's cap, go to the roof of the Tribune building and clamber onto a mechanical horse, from which he would practice his polo shots while lecturing his underlings. These unlucky employees feared to contradict him, or to display some ignorance that might get them sacked. "I imagine perhaps you are right," drama critic Burton Rascoe would murmur at appropriate intervals whenever the colonel wanted to discuss military history with him.[27]

McCormick used his physical height and his luxurious lifestyle to impress and intimidate. At six foot four, he towered over most of his employees and carried himself like a soldier, projecting confidence and taking command. In the 1930s, in his middle age, he had bushy gray eyebrows and a matching mustache, thinning hair, a long nose, and a seemingly permanent look of distaste. His clothes completed his look: formal, well tailored, expensive. Though he did not own actual or pretend castles like Hearst, he did live very well. He bought a forty-foot boat, an amphibious plane, a mansion with a mile of coastline in Palm Beach, and a townhouse on Chicago's tony Astor Street. East of the city, his estate at Cantigny included hundreds of acres of woods for his private hunts.[28]

Though the colonel supported some ideas that would later be called "anti-statist" or "libertarian," he did not—at least before the New Deal—oppose a strong federal government in principle. He believed the U.S. government should put down labor unrest, squeeze European countries to repay their war debts, use military force to protect U.S. investors' capital in Latin America, and enforce draconian immigration restrictions that kept the country "homogeneous." McCormick dissented from other conservatives in one area: he opposed the federal ban on alcohol, partly because he saw how Prohibition had fueled the Chicago gang wars. Mostly, though, he advocated for a strong federal government that would protect private property and strengthen white Protestant supremacy. Only with the New Deal, when Franklin Roosevelt wanted to use federal powers to help unions and curb excessive wealth, did the colonel become an anti-statist.

McCormick also assumed that the United States should rule the rest of the Americas. Like Hearst, he was a hemispheric imperialist. He cared little about Europe or Asia; in fact, he pulled the *Tribune* correspondent from China in 1937 on the grounds that Americans were not interested in Chinese news.[29] But he thought the United States should dominate the Western Hemisphere. He despised what he called "little Americans"—those who called for the United States to shut itself off from the Americas as well as Europe and Asia—and he advocated for more U.S. interventions in Latin America.[30]

The colonel insisted that the United States had never invaded its southern neighbors to "degrade the inhabitants, to exploit them, to gain territory merely for imperial expansion, to extinguish liberties or destroy self-government." Instead, Americans strove to "extend order, attack the source of diseases, raise the standard of living, increase capacity for self-government, widen the boundaries of competent, productive life." The United States was not a "despoiler and tyrant" in Cuba, Haiti, Puerto Rico, Santo Domingo, or Nicaragua; it was "the health officer, the school teacher, the fiscal administrator, the policeman."[31] In 1930, as the United States continued to occupy Haiti, the *Tribune* argued that imperialism helped the Haitians. "So far as the protection of the obscure from the concrete evils of their lives is concerned—disease, poverty, stagnation and oppression—imperialism is their better friend and doctrinaire liberalism too often a false guide and futile guardian."[32] Given his enthusiasm for imperialism throughout the Americas, it is not surprising that another of McCormick's favorite presidents was Theodore Roosevelt.

In McCormick's opinion, Herbert Hoover was no Theodore Roosevelt. Upon reading Hoover's inaugural address in March 1929,

McCormick cabled his Washington bureau, "THIS MAN WON'T DO."[33] Hoover had called for stronger enforcement of Prohibition and praised the World Court. He could not have chosen policy positions more calculated to anger the colonel.

"On domestic matters he is ruled by the Anti-Saloon League," the publisher wrote of the president, "and in international matters by the English."[34] Hoover's support for Prohibition only proved his eagerness to pander to philistines. He was a captive of the "dry bigots," McCormick wrote.[35] Moreover, like Hearst, McCormick thought Hoover's proposal to pause the repayment of European war debts in 1931 showed that he had been captured by English interests.

McCormick also disagreed with Hoover on the causes of the Great Depression, and therefore how to end it. Hoover thought the Depression originated in European policies after World War I. McCormick argued that it began at home: "government extravagance and wild taxation" were to blame, and to restore prosperity, the government needed to cut taxes and spending to the bone.[36] When in March 1932 the House passed a revenue bill that boosted the top income tax rate to 63 percent, McCormick called the tax increase "the greatest crisis since Lincoln's assassination."[37] Hoover's decision to sign the bill confirmed McCormick's earlier vow not to endorse the president for reelection in 1932 even if he received the Republican nomination.[38]

But then the Democrats nominated Franklin Roosevelt, and McCormick began to reassess Hoover's relative failings. When the president attacked Roosevelt as a dangerous revolutionary—in whose proposals he smelled the "fumes of the witch's caldron which boiled in Russia and in its attenuated flavor spread over the whole of Europe"—McCormick recognized Hoover as a fellow archconservative, albeit late to the cause.[39] A few days before the election, the *Tribune* grudgingly supported the incumbent. Its endorsement was hardly unqualified: the editorial began with five paragraphs about how Hoover had failed the country. But McCormick concluded that Hoover had recently become "the only person in Washington willing or able to put himself openly and firmly against the radicalism which is using the American bureaucracy and American economic misfortunes to make a permanent change in the character of the American government." Hoover had joined the fight against too much government, and those on the far right had no choice but to vote for him. "We see no other place for conservatives in this election," the *Tribune* explained.[40]

After the election, McCormick briefly withheld judgment on President-Elect Roosevelt. The publisher looked forward to the end of Prohibition under the New Deal, and he applauded the president's stated intention to balance the federal budget—though he apparently did not notice that Roosevelt promised only to balance the ordinary budget of the federal government while increasing emergency spending to combat the Depression. McCormick even met briefly with FDR, his old schoolmate, and exchanged pleasant notes with him.[41]

But he instructed his editorial writers to make it clear that the government's role was to cut taxes and spending, not to come up with new policies for recovery. "I want to keep on reiterating," he wrote them on March 9, just five days after Roosevelt took office, "that this situation was brought on us by government expenditures, and never admit that government is a mere rescuer of the country from itself."[42] Since Roosevelt firmly believed that government—or collective action expressed through democratic institutions—was needed to rescue the country, the two men were clearly headed for a fight.

During the first one hundred days of the Roosevelt administration, McCormick greeted almost every New Deal policy with skepticism or contempt. The Tennessee Valley Authority, a major flood control and public power project, was a waste of money. Why did taxpayers need to pay for dams? "Floods are normal to rivers," he sniffed, "and people who take advantage of the richness of river bottoms can expect to pay for their luxury." He had "misgivings" about the Agricultural Adjustment Act, which was hugely popular in Chicagoland: "We hope it may do some good," he wrote, "but . . . there is opportunity for almost unlimited ill."[43] The National Industrial Recovery Act was far worse. "Is not the Industrial Law fascism?" McCormick asked one of his editorial writers.[44] The *Tribune* did praise the president for ending Prohibition, seizing the opportunity to show that the colonel's paper did not oppose all his actions. "Here is a chance, as it were," McCormick told one of his editors, "to say something nice about Roosevelt."[45] But such occasions became vanishingly rare. By the summer of 1933, McCormick was convinced that Roosevelt took advice only from his most leftist advisers. "Indications are for the present," he wrote in July, "that he is going to take the radical side of every division in his organization."[46]

That fall, Roosevelt committed what McCormick considered an even worse sin than raising taxes: he recognized the Soviet Union. Like Hearst and Rothermere, McCormick believed Bolshevism presented an existential threat. From that point on, McCormick saw catastrophe in every Roosevelt proposal. "Never," he wrote in 1934, "has the country been in greater peril."[47] The New Deal would transform the country "from a Republic to a dictatorship," destroy the Constitution, and confiscate Americans' wealth.[48] The only difference between Roosevelt and Louisiana senator Huey Long, McCormick told an editorial writer, "is between a Harvard accent and nigger talk."[49]

In McCormick's mind, shadowy operatives in the New Deal agencies were plotting to destroy the liberties of the American people. He particularly worried about the immigrants who advised the president. "A band of conspirators," he said in 1936, "including our Felix Frankfurter, who like Adolf Hitler was born in Austria, impregnated in the historic doctrine of Austrian absolutism, plans to inflict this Oriental atrocity upon our republican people." Franklin Roosevelt merely provided a "smiling mask" for conspirators working "to bring the end of self-government in the world."[50]

Some of these plotters, including Frankfurter, were Jews. McCormick embraced and helped fund several individuals and groups who promoted anti-Semitic conspiracy theories, such as Harry Jung and his American Vigilant Intelligence Federation, the Sentinels of the Republic, and Elizabeth Dilling, the compiler of the blacklist known as the *Red Network*. He provided office space for Jung's group throughout the 1930s and 1940s and wrote an endorsement for Dilling's book.[51] She and Jung did not see Judaism as a religion; instead, Jews were a separate, cunning race that aimed to destroy Western civilization.

Many observers accused the *Tribune* of trafficking in anti-Semitic conspiracy theories. Even one of McCormick's editorial writers,

Leon Stolz, who was Jewish, criticized the paper for coded anti-Semitism: referring to "international bankers," for example, or reminding readers that prominent Jews had Anglicized their names.[52] McCormick did try to hide his anti-Semitism. In April 1934 he suggested to Arthur Henning, his Washington editor, that Henning might investigate whether the "Christian radicals" or the "Jew radicals" in the Roosevelt administration advocated more extreme reforms. The phrase "Jew radicals" might be "somewhat difficult to handle" in print, he conceded, but Henning could use code words to signal certain individuals' Jewishness. "You can say," McCormick suggested, " 'the group of radicals headed by Judge Brandeis'—then name them—and tell about their headquarters in Georgetown."[53] The *Tribune*'s readers would know what that meant.

As he grew more worried about the menace posed by the New Deal, McCormick, like Hearst and Rothermere, directed his reporters to shape their coverage to fit his editorial line. Even before Hearst proclaimed the era of the "Raw Deal," McCormick told his White House correspondent to report New Deal work relief expenditures as "government easy money."[54] He pelted his reporters with dozens of directives each day, sometimes berating them for proposing a favorable story about a Roosevelt program, at other times spiking articles that made the New Deal look good or ordering reporters to slant their stories against the president. In July 1933, he told an Associated Press editor that he had killed an AP story after it had run in the first edition "because it seemed to me to be principally propaganda of the kind that Washington is always trying to get into the newspapers."[55] On another occasion, a *Tribune* editor wired the paper's Washington bureau chief that he had cut a story to just five hundred words after McCormick complained that the paper was giving "too much space to 'Roosevelt handouts.' "[56]

As he tried to reduce or eliminate positive coverage of the New Deal, McCormick also urged his staff to dig up negative stories about Roosevelt's programs. When the paper's Washington reporters protested that they could find little evidence of graft in New Deal agencies, the Chicago editors pressed them. "It is close to Colonel McCormick's heart," an editor wrote to the paper's Washington bureau. "Again I wish to emphasize that this is thought by

Colonel McCormick to be of extreme importance. He is very anxious to print it if the facts will permit."[57]

Yet his memos to reporters show that McCormick was not always concerned about what the facts would permit. Like Hearst and Rothermere, McCormick sometimes printed "news" articles on events that had not happened. In October 1936, during Roosevelt's reelection campaign, the *Tribune* published a photograph that purported to show a rag picker sifting through Roosevelt buttons that had been flung into the street by disgusted Chicagoans. "Apparently the buttons were tossed aside by pedestrians to whom they were handed by women members of the Young Democrats of Cook County, who made wholesale distribution," the caption read.[58] But the *Chicago Times*, the city's lone liberal paper, reported that the rag picker had been paid to pose for the picture after the *Tribune* photographer had thrown the buttons in the street.[59] The *Tribune* also repeated false Republican claims that the Roosevelt administration was planning to require all American workers to wear dog tags embossed with their Social Security numbers. A staged photo of a man wearing mock-ups of the "proposed" dog tags accompanied the article.[60]

The most consequential fake news story of the 1936 presidential campaign came from the *Tribune*'s eastern European correspondent, Donald Day. One of the most notorious American reporters of his age, Day's long tenure with the *Tribune* explains much of the paper's reputation for untruthful reporting. At various times during his nearly two decades of covering eastern Europe for the *Tribune*, Day was accused by the Polish, Soviet, and U.S. governments of faking and distorting his stories. McCormick, who knew that Day's reporting was unreliable, came close to firing him in 1934 and again in 1937. During World War II, Day became a Nazi propagandist and made radio broadcasts for the Nazis from inside Germany. But as his former *Tribune* colleague George Seldes explained, Day's decision to join the fascists was less influential and historically significant than his biased reporting. "The important fact," Seldes wrote, "is that Donald Day faked the news for more than 20 years and that Colonel McCormick knew that Day lied and printed his lies because he liked those lies."[61]

In 1936, McCormick asked Day to survey the Soviet press to find evidence that the Russians hoped for Roosevelt's reelection. In midsummer, Day reported triumphantly that he had found the proof he sought: the Kremlin's "official journal" had ordered American Communists to support the president's campaign.[62] Exuberant, McCormick notified the Republican nominee for president, Alf Landon, of Day's scoop: "I have coming over in the mails," he wrote, "a copy of the official Communist publication, calling upon American communists to vote for Roosevelt. . . . This may help us with the large Polish votes in certain cities and certainly with the American vote everywhere."[63]

But "Moscow's endorsement" was not what it seemed, or at least not what Day claimed it was. A Soviet periodical—not the official Kremlin organ—had printed a Russian translation of a speech that American Communist leader Earl Browder had given several months earlier in Chicago. Browder had called on U.S. Communists to defeat the "reactionary Republican Party" but also said that the party would not support Roosevelt—in other words, the opposite of what Day had written. Other papers at the time had covered Browder's speech, which was broadcast on the radio.[64]

In short, Day's story was completely wrong—about its source and what it said—and not even news. The *Chicago Times* gleefully denounced the article as a hoax and offered to donate $5,000 to the Freedom of the Press Committee of the American Newspaper Publishers Association if anyone could prove it was true.[65] Privately, Day conceded to his editor that he had "made a mess of the story."[66] But the *Tribune* doubled down on its mistake and ran an ad trumpeting Day's alleged scoop. McCormick followed up the article with a front-page editorial headlined "Soviets Take an Active Hand in U.S. Election."[67]

The "Moscow endorses Roosevelt" story reached millions more readers when the Hearst papers followed up on the *Tribune's* discredited article and contended that they had acquired "UNCONTRADICTABLE DOCUMENTARY PROOF" of Russian interference in the election.[68] As with the original story, the "uncontradictable proof" was soon contradicted, at least to the satisfaction of reporters outside the McCormick/Hearst universe.

McCormick supplemented his faked and slanted news stories with daily warnings to voters. Starting on March 11, 1936, McCormick's editorial page counted down the number of days until the presidential election and reminded readers, "Only 238 more days remain in which to save your country. What are you doing to save it?"[69] Telephone receptionists at the *Tribune* greeted callers with the same refrain. Starting in August, McCormick put the warning in a box, added anti-Roosevelt quotes or news items, and moved it to the front page.

Throughout the 1936 election, the *Tribune* staff, like the Hearst reporters, functioned as press agents for the Republican presidential candidate. Landon's campaign even asked McCormick's editorial writers to write material for the candidate's final speeches. "What they want is some fresh, vigorous language," one of the colonel's editors told his boss. Landon's top aides feared that they had "gone a bit stale in their verbiage" and their "supreme admiration" for the *Tribune*'s editorials prompted them to ask for McCormick's help.[70] The publisher responded by urging the candidate to "challenge Roosevelt on every particular of his program." *Tribune* reporters then extolled Landon for his "thrilling" campaign speeches and chided Roosevelt for failing to answer the questions that *Tribune* writers had inserted into those speeches.[71]

Roosevelt's supporters understood that McCormick and Hearst were trying to hurt the president, and they sometimes retaliated. When Roosevelt came to Chicago to campaign in October 1936, marchers threw eggs at the Hearst building and burned copies of the *Tribune* in front of Tribune Tower. The night of the election, crowds again gathered at Tribune Tower, to curse McCormick, hurl eggs at his fortress, and set his newspapers afire in the streets.[72]

Yet McCormick was no more successful than Hearst in achieving his domestic political goals during Roosevelt's first term. He could not defeat the president or block his most ambitious reform measures. But he could help shape the nation's foreign policy.

■

McCormick's contempt for Europe did not keep him from paying for bureaus and full-time foreign correspondents to be stationed there throughout the 1930s. The *Tribune* was one of just seven U.S. newspapers with a foreign news service, a very costly enterprise.[73] McCormick regarded the foreign desk as his "pet project," correspondent William Shirer remembered, and personally directed (and hectored) his reporters. "He ran it himself," Shirer wrote, "rarely informing either his managing editor or his foreign editor of the Napoleonic orders he sometimes peppered us with or his cryptic criticisms scrawled on the margin of our dispatches which came almost daily."[74]

McCormick's European correspondents helped inform his foreign policy views. The publisher required his foreign reporters to send him weekly unpublished letters on their regions. As he struggled to understand Hitler and the Nazis in the early 1930s, he received diametrically different analyses from his Berlin bureau chief, who was a committed anti-fascist, and from his eastern European correspondent, a future Nazi agent.

The *Tribune*'s Berlin bureau chief, who shaped the paper's anti-Nazi coverage until 1934, was also its sole female foreign correspondent. Chicago-born Sigrid Schultz, the daughter of a prominent Norwegian artist, had moved to Paris when she was seven years old and attended school and university in Europe. Fluent in five languages, she began serving as a translator and an assistant for *Tribune* correspondents after World War I. In 1926, McCormick hired her to run the paper's Berlin bureau, making her the only female European bureau chief for an American newspaper at the time.[75] As a woman holding a "man's job," Schultz worked hard to prove her skills as a reporter. She particularly impressed McCormick with her smart coverage of military issues. "You are a veritable Brunhilde," he told her in 1932, comparing her to the female warrior of Germanic myth. "Not only is your article on artillery the best I have received from Europe but I have sent it to men correspondents as a model for them to follow."[76] Years later, even after he had disagreed with her coverage of European tensions, he told one of his editors, "Schultz is our best correspondent."[77]

Schultz understood from the start that Hitler posed a menace to Europe and the world. In February 1933, as the Nazi leader consolidated his power, she wrote McCormick that Hitler's appeal, though "incomprehensible" to her, was undeniably widespread in Germany. "He seems like a cheap hysterical actor to me and most Americans in Berlin," she said, "but one can't be blind to the fact that millions of Germans fall for him and will do whatever he says."[78] The next month, she warned her boss that the Nazis were using terror to control their enemies. "A terrific wave of denunciations, recriminations, and suspicions is going over Germany," she wrote.[79] One scholar has found that Schultz, along with her *Tribune* colleague in Paris, Edmond Taylor, provided the most extensive coverage of the Nazi terror of any American reporters in the first few months of Hitler's reign.[80]

The Gestapo regarded Schultz as a political enemy and watched her carefully. Nazi agents bugged her apartment and paid her maid and her neighbor's valet to file reports on her movements. One day, she came home to discover that the Gestapo had planted anti-fascist propaganda in her home. She had burned the documents by the time agents arrived to "find" the materials and arrest her.[81] But unlike many other anti-fascist reporters, Schultz was never expelled from Germany—quite possibly because of the Nazis' high regard for McCormick.

Schultz influenced McCormick's views on the Nazis during the first year of Hitler's dictatorship. The *Tribune* ran most of her stories without major changes, and McCormick himself wrote some anti-Hitler articles after he saw her in Berlin in the summer of 1933. During her boss's visit, Schultz began to worry that the colonel, who loved military pageantry, would be impressed by the Nazi parades. To inoculate him against Nazi propaganda, she shrewdly told him about rumors that Ernst Roehm, the head of the Storm Troopers, was gay.[82] Horrified that Hitler had allowed a gay man into his inner circle, the colonel proceeded to publish several anti-Nazi stories under his own byline. In one, he told his readers that Roehm "was guilty of that crime that no man can live down."[83]

But in June 1934, the colonel's attitude changed when Hitler ordered the execution of Roehm and dozens of other Nazi leaders in the Night of the Long Knives. According to Schultz, McCormick from that point forward saw the Nazis as "regular military-minded people who were anti-communist," rather than the "gangsters" he had condemned in 1933.[84]

By 1935, the *Tribune*'s editorial and news pages consistently justified the Nazis' threats to their neighbors as understandable responses to the unfairness of the Treaty of Versailles.[85] The victors of World War I, the *Tribune* argued in a 1936 editorial, had deprived Germany of "sovereignty over its national territory" by demilitarizing the Rhineland. "It was their folly in imposing a needlessly harsh and humiliating treaty on the German nation which gave Germany its dictatorship, and dictatorships can be expected to produce wars." Hitler was "the natural flowering of the Versailles Treaty."[86]

In addition to his relief that the Nazis were not harboring homosexuals, it is possible that McCormick decided to moderate his paper's anti-Hitler views after he began to worry that a strong stand against Nazi aggression might lead to U.S. involvement in another European war.[87] The Continent, the *Tribune* warned, was headed toward "the end of an epoch in white civilization," and the United States should do its best to avoid the inevitable cataclysm. There was no need for America to help "the unfortunate people who cannot stop their progress toward ruin."[88]

McCormick might have softened his views on the Nazis for another reason: the anti-Semitic reports he received from Donald Day. At the same time that Schultz was warning McCormick of the Nazi terror, Day reassured his boss that the Nazis were rational people who were mainly concerned about the declining birth rate among Germans. Hitler had no intention of starting a war, he told McCormick; it was only the Jews who were "shrieking" about war. "Who is going to fight 'THEIR WAR' they don't know," he wrote, "but they are certainly eager for one."[89] In Day's view, "Jews" were synonymous with "Bolsheviks." He insisted that the real danger to America came not from Nazis but from Jews, who had "begun another campaign to nullify our immigration law. They are now making a big fuss about America throwing open her doors for Jewish refugees from Germany." Their communist activities had caused Germany and other European countries to kick them out, and now they were headed to the United States, where they would add to the circle of Red advisers around Roosevelt. "They have made Europe too hot to hold them," he concluded. "What they will do in America is already indicated in Washington."[90]

McCormick seemed to find Day's views of the Nazis more persuasive than Schultz's alarmist reports. In May 1933, as Schultz sent weekly letters expressing horror at the Nazis' treatment of Jews, her boss scolded her for not appreciating the valid reasons for Nazi anti-Semitism. The Germans, he explained, viewed their country in terms of race, not nation; and it made sense that they would not want other "races" to have power in their state. "In this country," he told her, "a Jew obviously has as much right as a person of any other race or religion, . . . but I can see the difference of point of view in Germany."[91] McCormick said that he did not hate Jews, but neither did he want the United States to protest German anti-Semitism—and he warned that American Jews would provoke a backlash if they continued to demand that their government oppose the Nazis. He told one of his editorial writers, "I feel, of course, a very great sense of duty to protect the Jews in this country, but not abroad."[92]

■

McCormick presented a different model of the right-wing isolationist press lord. Unlike Hearst and Rothermere, he never praised fascists or showed any interest in fascism as an ideology. But he was, like Rothermere and Hearst, extremely anti-communist and conservative on domestic and foreign issues. Moreover, he retained as one of his key European correspondents a man who sent weekly private letters revealing his hatred for Jews and his sympathy for Nazis. In the end, McCormick agreed with his fellow right-wing publishers that those who wanted to resist the European dictators posed a greater danger to their own country than the fascist leaders themselves. By the time Roosevelt won his second term, the colonel from Chicago was poised, along with Hearst and, ironically, his much more liberal cousin Joe, to oppose any efforts to challenge fascist aggression.

CHAPTER FOUR

The Ordinary Joe

I N HIS YOUTH, JOE PATTERSON would shock Chicago society by arriving at the opera in tattered tails and a flannel shirt. Later, as the publisher of the biggest newspaper in New York, he would sometimes take the afternoon off and ride the subway to Coney Island.[1] Unlike the other British and American press barons, Patterson did not live or dress like an aristocrat. He wanted to blend in with the masses that he tried to serve and to avoid attracting attention to his wealth or his power. "I think a newspaper-man should be heard and not seen," he wrote once. "That is, that he should remain as anonymous as possible from the general public."[2]

Patterson's image fit his liberal politics. From 1933 to 1940, the *New York Daily News* publisher was one of the most important advocates in the press for the New Deal. In an age when most media outlets showed conservative bias, Franklin Roosevelt valued Patterson's support.

But Patterson's foreign policy views were another matter. Believing strongly in the racial superiority of Anglo-Saxons, he worried that any attempt to confront the Nazis in Europe could undermine white rule throughout the world. He showed little empathy for Hitler's victims and saw no reason for his country to involve itself in Europe's expanding conflicts. He believed in social democracy, but only in the Anglosphere. The rest of the world, he seemed to think, was not ready for democratic institutions. His racism made him comfortable with fascism existing elsewhere even if, unlike William Randolph Hearst or Harold Rothermere, he showed no personal enthusiasm for authoritarian politics.

Patterson's publishing career demonstrates that isolationist publishers could be liberals who opposed both fascism and resisting fascism. The most powerful Anglo-American media barons viewed the crisis in Europe very differently, but they agreed on one core principle: their country must—as the *Daily News* said countless times—*stay out of it.*

■

Unlike Rothermere, Joseph Medill Patterson was born into the elite, and unlike Hearst and Robert McCormick, he felt guilty about his privilege. One of four grandchildren of Joseph Medill, the founder of the *Chicago Tribune,* Joe—like his sister Cissy and his cousins Robert and Medill McCormick—grew up with immense wealth. He attended Groton and then Yale, where his six-foot frame and broad shoulders helped him win a spot on the rowing team, before he returned to Chicago to marry an heiress.

But as a young reporter for the *Tribune,* Patterson clashed with his editors and his father, the paper's publisher, over their conservative politics and conventional journalism. He left the paper to work in city government, where a brief stint as Chicago's commissioner of public works convinced him that American workers suffered terribly because of capitalists like those in his family.[3]

In the early years of the twentieth century, Patterson moved to a farm outside Chicago and began churning out socialist novels and tracts. In *Confessions of a Drone,* an article he wrote for a socialist newspaper and then published as a pamphlet, he blasted the economic system that forced other people to support him in wealthy indolence. "The work of the working people and nothing else," he wrote, "produces the wealth, which by some hocus-pocus arrangement is transferred to me, leaving them bare."[4] He also wrote novels and plays that attacked various social ills: alcoholism (a recurrent curse in the Medill family), the immorality and ennui of the upper classes, racism, lynching, and restrictions on divorce. The works received mixed reviews ("distinctly amateurish," sniffed the *New York Times* of one novel) but sold well.[5] Literary success prompted Patterson to modify his political views. According to a later *New Yorker* profile, his "sampling of the delights of capitalism as a money-making writer had convinced him that the profit motive . . . was really the thing that made people work."[6]

In 1910, his father's suicide brought Patterson back into the family publishing business. He and his ultra-conservative cousin, Robert McCormick, took over the *Chicago Tribune*. Four years later, Patterson jumped at the chance to become a war correspondent, covering the European conflict for the *Tribune* from Belgium after the German takeover, and the U.S. occupation of the port of Veracruz during the Mexican Revolution.

In 1916, Patterson, like his cousin, joined the Illinois National Guard and traveled to the southern U.S. border. His flirtation with Socialism notwithstanding, he eagerly sought to bear arms to protect U.S. property. Enlisting as a private, he refused friends' offers to get him commissioned as an officer.

Like McCormick, Patterson eventually left Texas without invading Mexico. But the next year he would witness and participate in a much bigger conflict. After the United States joined the Great War, he enlisted in the American Expeditionary Force. He served in five major battles, survived German gas and machine-gun fire, and rose to the rank of captain in the artillery.

During the Great War, Patterson discovered a new kind of journalism. He began reading and admiring the London papers, particularly Lord Northcliffe's tabloid, the *Daily Mirror*. No American had yet tried to copy the *Mirror*'s model of a half-size, sensationalistic newspaper aimed at urban commuters. Patterson traveled to London on furlough to see Northcliffe. The English press baron said he thought a New York tabloid was such a good idea that if Patterson did not start one, he would do it himself.

Back in France, Patterson met with McCormick, his cousin and co-publisher, at a farm near the front. As they sat on a pile of cow dung and watched the German shells light up the night sky, Patterson asked for permission to use the family company to start a tabloid in New York.[7] His new enterprise would be linked financially with the *Tribune*, but the two papers would maintain separate newsrooms and editorial policies. McCormick sensed a good business opportunity. "I'm with you," he said, and the two toasted the family's new venture.[8]

The first issue of the *Daily News*, "New York's new pictorial newspaper," hit the streets in June 1919, offering a $10,000 prize for its first beauty contest and promising pictures of beautiful girls along with "sport news, fashion news, society news, theatrical news, household hints, editorials, humor" and, almost as an afterthought, coverage of local, foreign, and national news.[9] In its inaugural editorial, the *News* explained that it was "going to be your newspaper. Its interests will be your interests. ... It will be aggressively for America and for the people of New York." The paper assured its readers that it would have no "entangling alliance with any class whatever."[10]

Other journalists regarded Patterson's experiment as a joke, and it seemed at first that he might have made a mistake. New York's crowded newspaper market, with seventeen major dailies, was saturated. The *News*'s circulation fell to just twenty-six thousand daily sales. But New Yorkers began to warm to the paper's lively coverage of love nests, gangster shootouts, and runaway heiresses. After two years it was New York's second-best-selling paper, behind Hearst's *Journal*; a few years after that, the *News* passed the *Journal* and became the top-selling paper not only in New York but in the entire United States. Soon it would become the most popular newspaper in American history in numbers of copies sold, then or since.

Patterson adopted some of the English tabloids' proven methods for boosting circulation and invented new ones. Under his leadership, the *News* sponsored races and games that drew tens of thousands of participants.[11] He also paid attention to the comics page, knowing that a good selection of strips could drive sales. Finally, he gave his readers a sense of ownership of the paper through his expanded and highly entertaining letters pages. "Voice of the People" attracted more than forty-six thousand contributions a year.[12]

The *Daily News* reflected the excitement of living in an American city in the era of skyscrapers, jazz, flappers, speakeasies, gun molls, and new moral standards. As one *News* editor explained, "The things people were most interested in were, and in order, (1) Love or Sex, (2) Money, (3) Murder. They were especially interested in any situation which involved all three."[13] The *News* could not keep its middle-class audience if it covered sex explicitly, but its editors were skilled at deploying euphemisms. As *Time* wrote, "Constant readers of the *News* always read erotic for exotic, philanderer for dilettante, lesbianism for bizarre friendship, kept for showered with gifts, sexual intercourse for kiss."[14] But though the mores of the era required the *News* to be discreet in its stories about sex, there were no such restrictions on its coverage of crime and punishment. Patterson's paper published what *Time* called "the most sensational newspicture of the decade" when its photographer sneaked a camera into the execution viewing chamber at Sing Sing and snapped a shot of the famous murderess Ruth Snyder at the moment of her death in the electric chair. "DEAD!" screamed the headline over the page 1 photo. The *News* printed more than a million extra copies of the picture to meet public demand.[15]

The *News* showed an unerring instinct for understanding its readers and refused to talk down to them. *News* reporters and editors "are not supercilious of the masses they cater to," *Editor & Publisher* reported in 1934. "They like to think that they are a part of the crowd, that they share its likes and dislikes, its passions and prejudices, its predilection for a good belly laugh and a wistful sentimental tear." The article reported that other journalists dismissed the *News* for aiming at fourteen-year-olds rather than grownups. But the paper's general manager, Roy C. Holliss, found that criticism "academic" and irrelevant. "A part of everyone's mind is 14 years old, or 8 years old," he responded. "We try to edit the *News* to meet the varied requirements of the average person's mental equipment."[16]

Patterson wanted his paper to appeal to "Sweeney," an imaginary working-class New Yorker who liked his news simple and entertaining. The paper's slogan was "Tell It to Sweeney! The Stuyvesants Will Take Care of Themselves!" By "Sweeney," the *News* staff meant an ordinary New Yorker, working class or lower middle class, who worked hard, raised a family, and hoped for a better life for his children. A *News* promotional item for advertisers explained the slogan this way: "Sweeney and Mrs. Sweeney are ambitious and expectant of Life. They believe in God, the United States and life insurance. They respect education, and want the kids to have plenty of it. . . . And remember, when you talk to Sweeney, the people of bluer blood and more money who read The News will understand; whereas if you talk to the Stuyvesants, the Sweeneys won't listen. You can't lose by saying it so Sweeney understands."[17]

"Sweeney" apparently wanted his editorials to have the same breezy, cheeky style as his news stories. The *Daily News*, unlike most papers, was popular in part because of its editorials, not in spite of them. A Gallup poll found that 28 percent of men and 15 percent of women who bought big-city newspapers read the editorials. But according to an internal survey, *News* editorials had much higher readership: 60 percent of men and 41 percent of women.[18] The *News* appealed to New Yorkers by presenting clear, forceful arguments in straightforward, often colloquial language. The editorial page called its opponents "saps"; told lying politicians "no dice"; and did not hesitate to say "GOSH!" in response to amazing events. In 1936, when a *News* headline asked if the United States might be called to "Fight for France Again??," the paper had a quick retort: "There is but one American answer that we know of to that talk; and that answer is: 'Nuts.' "[19]

Patterson's personal mailbag was full of letters expressing admiration for the *News*'s unique style. "I believe that your editorials are the best-written editorials in the country," read one typical missive, this one from Chester Bowles, an advertising man who later became a diplomat, governor, and congressman. "They are simple and vivid and keyed to the hopes and beliefs of the great majority of people who make up the United States."[20]

Though he did not write the editorials himself, Patterson took responsibility for their content and style. He met with his chief writer, Reuben Maury, each morning to discuss the day's editorial. Patterson did not want Maury to come up with his own ideas but, as a *New Yorker* profile of Maury explained, to "put the Patterson ideas into words." The *New Yorker* writer compared them to ventriloquist Edgar Bergen and his dummy, Charlie McCarthy. The partnership clearly worked. Over the years they wrote more than ten thousand editorials, and Maury won the 1941 Pulitzer Prize for editorial writing.[21]

In 1930, Patterson signaled the *Daily News*'s importance to New York by commissioning Raymond Hood, the celebrated architect who designed the Tribune Tower in Chicago and later the Rockefeller Center in New York, to build a $10 million, thirty-six-story headquarters for the paper on East Forty-Second Street. Around the exterior entranceway, a massive frieze depicted workers, businessmen, and craftsmen all living in harmony; above the tableau, Patterson immortalized an oft-quoted (and possibly misattributed) line of Abraham Lincoln (a statesman who had won office partly through the efforts of the publisher's grandfather). "God must have loved the common man, because HE MADE SO MANY OF THEM." The words honored the common people filing through the entrance below.

The building captured Patterson's aspirations for his newspaper: bold and theatrical, it compelled attention and respect; yet it was also, as its letters pages proclaimed, the voice of the people. The *News* gave the people what they wanted and made sure their voices were heard.

After the stock market crash of 1929, Patterson decided that the people wanted fewer sensational murder stories and more news about the hardships they faced every day. "We're off on the wrong foot," he announced one day in the newsroom. "The people's major interest is no longer in the playboy, Broadway and divorces, but in how they're going to eat, and from this time forward we'll pay attention to the struggle for existence."[22]

In 1932, after three years of Depression, Patterson decided that Franklin Roosevelt was the best presidential candidate to help the people on the front lines of this struggle. Unlike Hearst, who fantasized a New Deal that would serve his own interests, Patterson seemed to grasp the essentials of the president's domestic policy as well as Roosevelt's call for "bold, persistent experimentation." The *Daily News* publisher not only endorsed Roosevelt for president in 1932 but stated in an Inauguration Day editorial that the paper would support him for at least a year, to give the new chief executive the time and flexibility he needed to embark on audacious reforms.[23]

The *Daily News* showed its affection for Roosevelt by launching a campaign to raise money to build a swimming pool at the White House, knowing that swimming was the president's preferred form of exercise because of his weakened legs. Shortly after taking office, the president thanked Patterson sincerely for the gesture and the support it represented: "The thought that this campaign was initiated voluntarily, without my knowledge or sanction, and subscribed to so generously means as much, if not more, than the pool itself."[24]

Patterson's editorial policy, in short, differed dramatically from that of his cousin. Robert McCormick once reassured a correspondent that though the cousins jointly owned the *Chicago Tribune* and the *Daily News*, they had agreed to give each other complete autonomy to run their respective newspapers. "On many subjects we are in agreement," McCormick wrote, "but . . . on the New Deal, our views are as far apart as the poles."[25]

Patterson's support for collective solutions to the nation's problems made him an unusual newspaper publisher. In the 1930s, there was no such thing as what critics today call "the liberal media."[26] Americans and Britons who complained about bias in the media typically talked about the "conservative press." As A. J. Liebling famously said, "Freedom of the press is guaranteed only to those who own one," and the owners of big-city newspapers, which sold millions of copies and dominated the media landscape, were rich men who had the resources to invest the vast sums needed for modern production and distribution.[27]

Patterson backed Roosevelt in some of the most significant domestic policy fights of the 1930s. Almost alone among news barons, he wanted to abolish child labor even though the ban would mean newspapers could no longer hire young boys to distribute their copies. The *News* also strongly endorsed the Social Security Act and hired "trained attendants" to help confused citizens fill out their first Social Security forms. More than twelve hundred New Yorkers showed up to the first day of the *News*'s information clinic on the new program. Anna Rosenberg, the regional director of the Social Security Board, thanked Patterson personally for providing the clinic and for running a series of articles aimed at calming the fears of Americans who were concerned about the registration process.[28] Unlike Hearst, Patterson also endorsed the "general aim" of Roosevelt's proposals for higher taxes on the rich and union rights for workers, though he found fault with some of the details.[29]

Patterson was happy to help an administration headed by a man he considered "one of the most admirable and courageous and high-hearted citizens this country ever produced, as well as . . . one of our greatest Presidents."[30] In late 1933, after nine months of the Roosevelt administration, he pledged $5,000 to the Democratic Party, explaining that he could see for himself the positive effects of the New Deal. "I believe it is largely due to the policies of President Roosevelt that we have come a long way out of the slump," he wrote in a private letter. "At all events, our business is considerably better than it was last year." The *News* had added 165 employees and, Patterson said, was making "more money net," as were all other New York newspapers and their large advertisers. "We indeed have something to be thankful for this Christmas."[31]

Patterson would become one of the Democrats' top donors. He contributed to key Democratic races around the country and gave $25,000 to the Democratic National Committee—and arranged to launder the contribution so that he would not have to pay taxes on it.[32] In total, Patterson donated $28,100 to the DNC and Democratic candidates during Roosevelt's first term (more than $500,000 in today's money), making him the party's fifth-largest donor.[33]

Roosevelt valued Patterson's editorial support even more than his monetary contributions. More than 60 percent of dailies nationwide opposed the president's bid for a second term, yet the *Daily News* cheered his every move and gave him almost sole credit for the economic recovery. "Our only mistake," the *News* argued right before the election, "seems to have been that we didn't have a New Deal soon enough."[34] One pro-Roosevelt publisher, J. David Stern of the *Philadelphia Recorder*, called Patterson's editorials "the best and strongest in the country. I wish they received even wider publication than your great newspaper gives them."[35] Roosevelt's advisers agreed. Jim Farley, the head of the Democratic National Committee, praised Patterson in February 1936 for the *News*'s editorials. "You are certainly doing a splendid job and I want you to know I appreciate it very, very much," he wrote.[36]

Keenly aware of the value of their support, Roosevelt cultivated friendships with the few media moguls who supported him. Over the next several years, Patterson and his wife dined at the White House, at Roosevelt's family home in Hyde Park, and on the presidential yacht.[37] Perhaps the warmth of their early alliance helps explain the bitterness of their later feud.

■

Joe Patterson, the publisher of the first American tabloid and the best-selling paper in American history, the *New York Daily News*, called himself, his cousin, and his sister "the isolationist furies." Patterson's *Daily News* editorials worried that European wars would lead to "the passing of the great race," as eugenicist Madison Grant had predicted. (George Moffet, Moffet Studio, Chicago, *Digital Collections—Lake Forest College*, http://lakeforestcollege.edu/items/show/3964)

Throughout Roosevelt's first term, Patterson agreed not only with the president's domestic reforms but also, surprisingly, with his foreign policy. He thought the president was appropriately tough on what the *News* called the "ferocious" Japanese nation.[38] At the same time, he thought—incorrectly, it turned out—that the president shared his belief that the United States should ignore aggressive actions by the fascist dictators in Europe.

Unlike Hearst and McCormick, Patterson had no fear that Roosevelt wanted to amass dictatorial power. In 1935, when Congress debated a bill designed to keep the United States out of foreign wars, the *News* advocated more presidential authority, not less. The proposed Neutrality Act, written by Senate isolationists, banned the sale of "arms, ammunition, and implements of war" to any foreign country involved in a war. Patterson supported neutrality, but unlike Hearst, he thought the president should determine when to use the law. "It seems to us," said a *News* editorial, "that the best way to safeguard our neutrality would be to leave the job of safeguarding it to the President. He should be given the power to embargo arms shipments in any way he might see fit; not commanded to embargo them all over the map."[39]

Patterson was also an avid booster of Roosevelt's efforts to expand the U.S. Navy in the Pacific. Almost every Monday during 1934 and 1935, the *News* ran an editorial headlined "Two Ships for One," urging the U.S. military to "build two fighting ships for every fighting ship Japan builds."[40] Like Hearst, Patterson believed Japan posed a great danger to the United States and that a war between the two powers might be inevitable. But unlike Hearst, Patterson trusted the president to manage U.S.-Japanese tensions. He heaped scorn on peace activists who thought an expansion of the U.S. Navy might provoke Japan, and he applauded Roosevelt for ignoring "pacifist bunk."[41] Fortunately, the *News* explained, Roosevelt understood the Japanese menace: "We hope and believe the President will continue this policy of looking out for American safety first, even though some of us stay asleep to what is fermenting on the other side of the Pacific."[42]

Patterson believed the United States must take a firm stand against the Japanese, whom he saw as a wily and savage people. "We cannot afford to take any chances with such a nation of fighting cocks," the *News* editorialized in 1935. "Give them an inch and they take a mile, as they have been doing in Asia for the last four years."[43] The *News* speculated frequently on the strategies Japan might use to attack the United States. In its most imaginative scenario, the paper suggested that the Japanese would conquer Baja

California and use it as a base to launch Viking-style raids on West Coast cities, which they would then hold hostage until they received tribute from the U.S. government.[44] In 1934, the *News* congratulated Treasury Secretary Henry Morgenthau Jr. for removing millions of dollars of gold from the San Francisco mint, where the editorial writers thought it was vulnerable to a Japanese heist, and relocating it to Denver.[45]

The *News* published its most extreme anti-Japanese views in the "Voice of the People" section—in letters that some critics thought were written by the paper's staff. These ordinary voices warned white Americans of the yellow peril and of the dangers of dividing the "white race" by meddling in Europe. "Wake up, dear white people, or you will be laid to rest forever," wrote a correspondent identified only by his initials in 1936. "Don't you know the yellow race is becoming stronger on this earth each and every day? Catastrophe is inevitable, unless the white race patches up its insane internal difficulties and forms a united front."[46]

In contrast to his truculence toward Japan, Patterson seemed indifferent to the brutalities of Hitler's regime. In the early days, the *News* seemed uninterested or even amused by the Nazis. In March 1933, as Storm Troopers terrorized and imprisoned hundreds of Jews, homosexuals, socialists and other political opponents, and as the Nazi regime opened its first concentration camp, the *Daily News* thanked the Nazis for closing nudist colonies. "When we saw pictures of some nudists in the raw, an anti-nudism crusade by anybody on any grounds seemed more than justified," the *News* joked. "Hitler has shown himself to be a true friend of all us true esthetes."[47]

As the Nazi oppression of Jews continued, *News* editorials dropped their jocular tone but still argued that the events in Germany had nothing to do with Americans. In 1935, the *News* worried that a U.S. boycott of the Olympic games the next year in Berlin might lead to conflict. Americans could consider joining a boycott, the *News* said, but the United States "shouldn't go any further than that in expressing our disapproval of Hitler's maltreatment of the Jews." Hitler had done nothing to justify a military or diplomatic response or even economic sanctions. "Just because you wouldn't invite some man to your house for dinner, you aren't obligated to fight him. Nor are you obligated to refuse to do business with him to your own profit."[48]

Patterson's insistence on dismissing and ignoring Hitler's brutal treatment of Jews in Germany posed a potential obstacle to his friendship with the president. For years, Roosevelt had believed that Hitler threatened democracy and civilization. He had written in his copy of *Mein Kampf* that the English edition minimized the dangers of Nazism. "This translation is so expurgated as to give a wholly false view of what Hitler really is or says—The German original would make a different story."[49] He understood that anti-Semitism was central to the Nazis' ideology and not, as the press barons thought, a peripheral strategy that they could be persuaded to abandon. Like Winston Churchill, writes the historian William Kinsella, Roosevelt showed an "intuitive prescience" about the evils of German fascism.[50]

But in his first term, the president focused on domestic issues and paid little public heed to Nazi persecution. It was only later that Patterson's and Roosevelt's differences on the proper response to German anti-Semitism would divide them. During the 1936 presidential campaign, the *Daily News* repeatedly stated that Democrats were far more likely than Republicans to isolate the country from the developing crises in Europe. When the president declared, "I hate war!" in a campaign speech, the *News* noted that he had "voiced the present feelings of the vast majority of us" and praised his determination to preserve American neutrality.[51] On another occasion, the *News* lauded Roosevelt's foreign policies and called Alf Landon, the Republican nominee, a "Meddlesome Mattie" who might involve the United States in a European war. "The best way to stay out," the *News* concluded, "is with a President who has given us a strong national defense and kept on good terms with the rest of the world."[52]

Patterson supported Roosevelt's foreign policy throughout his first term. He believed the president would safeguard the United States from European conflicts, though he did worry that other "meddlesome" officials—mostly Republicans—might create problems by trying to resist Hitler. It was in this context that he teamed up with a London publisher to persuade the citizens of Britain and America to embrace "splendid isolation."

CHAPTER FIVE

The Empire Crusader

IN SPRING 1935, AS BUSY London commuters purchased their daily papers, news agents would thrust an extra leaflet into customers' hands. The pamphlet's title, "From across the Atlantic," heralded an important message, and beneath its bold green headline, a British lion crouched at the feet of the Statue of Liberty. The text featured a quotation from Joseph Medill Patterson, the publisher of "the most influential newspaper in the New World" and the largest circulation paper in the United States, the *New York Daily News*. Patterson's message was so "tremendous," the flyer informed readers, that it deserved publication in the London *Daily Express* and its sister publications, as well as distribution in pamphlet form to every household in Britain.[1]

In the leaflet, Patterson voiced full-throated support for "Splendid Isolation." Whatever happened in Europe, Patterson told readers, should not involve America or Britain. "If those fools on the continent wish to destroy themselves that is certainly no reason for Great Britain to do likewise," he wrote. "I think your country and ours ought to stand alongside of each other in this crazy world."[2]

The flyer was the first of many collaborations between Lord Max Beaverbrook of the *Daily Express* and Joe Patterson of the *Daily News*, men who proudly called themselves isolationists and tried to pressure their respective governments to ignore or minimize Nazi aggression. They sought to use their top-selling newspapers to amplify their common message: the benefits of an Anglo-American partnership in splendid isolation. As Beaverbrook explained, the United States could be a "companion" with Britain in keeping apart from the rest of the world. "We should stand," he wrote in 1934, "in the closest relations of friendship with the United States, the watchtower of the Western world, united to us by the bonds of common race and language."[3] He and Patterson hoped to build a transnational movement of ultra-nationalists.

Beaverbrook and Patterson shared many convictions. Neither found any appeal in fascism, and they had little concern for the dangers posed by Communism, either abroad or at home—views that set them apart from Rothermere, Hearst, and McCormick. Finally, like Patterson, Beaverbrook was not on the far right of his country's political spectrum. But though neither was a right-wing extremist, they cared deeply about maintaining white rule throughout the world and worried that resisting European fascists could endanger Anglo-American hegemony.

The two men worked together to persuade their nations to avoid alliances outside the Anglo-American world. During several crises in 1935 and 1936—in Ethiopia, the Rhineland, and Spain—they jointly urged their governments to ignore emergencies precipitated by fascist aggression and to remain aloof from Europe. Ultimately they failed to keep their countries out of war, but not before the disastrous policies they backed allowed the Nazis to build up their military and industrial might.

■

Though he would become one of the most important figures in mid-twentieth-century Britain, Beaverbrook began his career in London as an immigrant and a middle-class outsider to English society, journalism, and politics. Max Aitken was born in 1879 in Ontario at a time when Canada was a self-governing dominion of the British Empire. One of ten children born to a farmer's daughter and a Presbyterian pastor, Aitken decided early on that he would never be poor like his father. "I resolved, on account of his penury," he wrote later, "that I would have money in my pocket and more money in the bank."[4] After growing up in New Brunswick, he attained a position as an aide to a businessman in Halifax and soon impressed his boss with his genius for sales and investing. He made a huge fortune by engineering the consolidation of the cement industry, but one of his business associates accused him of malfeasance and misappropriation of funds. Though he vehemently denied the allegations, Aitken decided to emigrate to the mother country. He was never formally charged with crimes, but the "cloud of suspicion," as one investigator termed it, followed him throughout his career.[5]

At age thirty-one, Aitken—a Presbyterian Canadian of modest birth who had never finished university—arrived in a country where a distinguished family tree, Anglican baptism, and Oxbridge degree often seemed essential to political and social success. Yet, thanks to his money, charm, and talent for manipulating others, he managed to join the English ruling class and eventually to captivate many of its members. He entered Tory Party politics and in 1910 won a seat in the House of Commons, where he soon developed a reputation as a ruthless and devious political infighter. Snidely labeled "a little Canadian adventurer" by a fellow Tory, he proved as adept at political gamesmanship as he had been at mergers and acquisitions, and managed to maneuver his friend (and fellow Canadian Presbyterian) Andrew Bonar Law into the Conservative Party leadership.[6] In 1917, Prime Minister David Lloyd George—whom Beaverbrook helped elevate to the premiership, only to connive to depose him several years later—recognized Aitken's growing prominence in British politics and society by convincing the king to give him a peerage. Aitken chose the name Lord Beaverbrook after a small community in New Brunswick. Near the end of the war, he served Lloyd George as minister of information.

While in Parliament, Aitken invested in a failing newspaper, the London *Daily Express*, but kept his involvement quiet. By remaining a secret investor, he could place stories that flattered himself in the paper without leaving any fingerprints. He could also remain a player in the Conservative Party, whose leaders disdained the popular press. In 1916, he gained control of the *Express*, though his ownership remained secret until the next year.[7]

Discovering a passion for political journalism, Beaverbrook began acquiring more newspapers, including the *Sunday Express*, the *Evening Standard*, and two Scottish dailies. He plunged into the battle for circulation supremacy with the other press lords. In what became known as the free insurance war, when Northcliffe's *Daily Mail* offered a £1,000 accident insurance policy to every subscriber, the *Daily Express* countered with a £2,000 policy. Soon both were dangling £10,000 policies before new subscribers and losing vast sums. The *Daily Express* would continue to offer freebies—from radios to can openers—until it was the top-selling newspaper in the world.[8]

Beaverbrook, one reporter noted, made enemies by the dozen and friends by the hundred.[9] The enemies included Prime Minister Stanley Baldwin, who complained that the publishers had waged a "personal vendetta" against him and compared Beaverbrook and Rothermere to prostitutes. Among his friends Beaverbrook counted several American press barons, including Roy Howard and Frank Gannett as well as Joe Patterson, and many British government officials. His most consequential friendship turned out to be with Winston Churchill, his whisky-guzzling, card-playing, history-writing chum who would rescue Beaverbrook's reputation in 1940 by appointing him minister of aircraft production. Beaverbrook helped Churchill stay politically relevant and financially solvent during the latter's years out of power by hiring him to write newspaper columns.[10]

Beaverbrook had many admirers who quarreled with his politics but appreciated his conviviality. They also enjoyed the way they lived when they visited him. He threw memorable parties at his two luxurious homes, Stornoway House in London and Cherkley Court in Surrey. He invited large groups of friends to travel with him on chartered planes as they hopped from one party spot to another throughout southern Europe. Though he was something of a dilettante—hobbies like horse racing would come and go—he never wavered in his commitment to having fun, whether he was sailing, gambling, drinking, or romancing other men's wives. He was not physically imposing: of medium height and slight build, he had a receding hairline, broad forehead, wide nose, and "the face of a sad goblin," as *Life* magazine described him.[11] But his infectious enthusiasm endeared him to scheming prime ministers and competitive press lords alike. "He had a gift for making you feel when you were with him that you were the most important person in the

Lord Max Beaverbrook had already acquired a reputation as a devious political infighter at the time of this photo, 1926. Stanley Baldwin, the Tory prime minister, would later denounce him and Lord Rothermere for exercising "power without responsibility," and Clement Attlee, the Labour Party leader, would call Beaverbrook the public figure "who is most widely distrusted by decent men of all parties." (Süddeutsche Zeitung Photo / Alamy Stock Photo)

world," remembered his biographer, the Oxford historian A.J. P. Taylor. "Of course I knew he forgot about me the moment I left the room but it was magical all the same. Max Beaverbrook well knew how to steal the hearts of men. He certainly stole mine."[12]

Not everyone found him endearing. He could be a very demanding boss. Beaverbrook insisted on installing telephones in nearly every room of his two mansions as well as in their gardens, so that he could call his reporters and editors at any moment. He barked his daily editorials into a Dictaphone machine. Though he gave the staff at his evening paper, the *Evening Standard*, and his Sunday paper, the *Sunday Express*, a little more freedom, he exercised tight control over the *Daily Express*, especially over its political coverage. As his chief editor, Arthur Christiansen, explained, "I was a journalist, not a political animal; my proprietor was a journalist *and* a political animal. The policies were Lord Beaverbrook's job, the presentation mine."[13]

Beaverbrook's policies were generally those of the Conservative Party, though with a populist twist. Unlike the twentieth-century American press, British newspapers in the 1930s often backed one political party and served one social class. The elite read the Conservative *Times* or the *Telegraph*, while industrial workers preferred the *Daily Herald*, which supported Labour. The middle classes tended to buy Rothermere's Conservative *Daily Mail*, the Liberal *News-Chronicle*, and Beaverbrook's "independent Conservative" *Daily Express*.[14] The *Express*'s proprietor showed his support for his customers by leading crusades for higher wages for railway workers, postal workers, and clerks, who had been hard hit by the Depression. Beaverbrook assured his loyal readers that he could be their champion because he was not beholden to their employers. "I have leisure and enough money to live on. I am independent. I am indifferent to the hostility of vested interests." He was, he insisted, a wealthy man who generously put his media empire at the service of his struggling subscribers.[15]

It was his commitment to public service, Beaverbrook argued, not a desire for profits, that drove him to become a publisher. Like many of the press lords, he claimed he did not go into the newspaper business to become rich. When he took over the *Daily Express*, it was his intention "to run a newspaper for the purpose of advocating a political policy," he wrote in an editorial in 1936. The paper was a financial success: it had grown to be "the biggest newspaper in the whole history of journalism." Yet, he said, he felt a "deep disappointment" because he had failed in his propagandist's purpose of achieving his political goals.[16] After the war, he famously testified to a royal commission that he had acquired his media empire "purely for the purpose of making propaganda and with no other object."[17]

Beaverbrook particularly loved "making propaganda" for the cause of splendid isolation, which he believed would strengthen the bonds of empire. "Isolation for Britain," he proclaimed, was "isolation splendid and secure through our closer relations with the Empire."[18] In this formulation, the British Empire was no longer an expansive project; instead, its existing territory needed to be consolidated and protected. Moreover, Beaverbrook focused his attention and praise on the white dominions like his birthplace of Canada, as well as Australia, New Zealand, and South Africa. He believed that white British people had the right to extract labor and resources from imperial colonies like India in return for the empire's protection. As a Canadian, he could identify as "British" by emphasizing the unity of the empire and the white dominions' equal standing with the home islands.

Beaverbrook showed his enthusiasm for empire in his choice of symbols for the *Daily Express* masthead. The media moguls of the 1930s liked to brand their newspapers by placing slogans and symbols next to the nameplate on the front page. Hearst used the mottos "America First" and "An American Paper for the American People." McCormick claimed the *Chicago Tribune* was "The World's Greatest Newspaper"—and later "An American Paper for Americans." In 1930, as Beaverbrook made a brief and abortive attempt with Rothermere to form a new "United Empire" Party, he added an icon to the masthead of the *Daily Express*. Printed in red ink and placed to the right of the paper's name, a medieval knight, clad in a helmet and chain mail, brandished a sword and carried a shield emblazoned with the cross of St. George.[19] This "Empire Crusader" would remain on the *Express* masthead for decades: throughout the brief life of the United Empire Party, during World War II and Beaverbrook's postwar campaign against European integration, and into the 2010s, when the *Express* led the charge for Britain to leave the European Union. Britain saw momentous changes over those decades, but the goal of the Empire Crusader remained the same: national defense through isolation.

Beaverbrook's conception of empire assumed Anglo-Saxon racial superiority and control. Like the American nativists, the *Express* publisher believed in a racial hierarchy with northern Europeans at the top. He spoke in terms of "race" or "blood" when advocating continued imperial domination of the "natives" in British colonies. "The British Empire," he wrote, "exists for the British Race. It is our heritage. Let us cultivate it, defend it, cherish it, and make it great, rich and strong in righteousness, an example and an object-lesson to the rest of mankind."[20]

Because he saw Britain as a self-contained empire and not part of the European continent, Beaverbrook showed little concern about Hitler's rise to power. After returning from a visit to Germany in March 1933, he told one of his editors that the "stories of Jewish persecution are exaggerated." He directed the man to write a column about the comic amateurishness of the Storm Troopers. "He said, or made me say," the editor wrote in his diary, "that the cavalry leader could not sit on his horse, that the bands were bad, and that the men, mostly ill-formed lads and dissipated old boys, gave no appearance of a disciplined body."[21]

Well into the decade, Beaverbrook continued to believe that the Nazis presented little danger to Britain, though he changed his mind several times about the threat they posed to their own citizens. At times the *Daily Express* seemed sympathetic to the German regime. In 1936, for example, it published an embarrassingly positive op-ed about Hitler by David Lloyd George. The former prime minister described Hitler as the "George Washington of Germany" and praised him, as Rothermere had done for years, as the savior of his country and responsible for "a marvelous transformation in the spirit of the people, in their attitude towards each other, and in their social and economic outlook."[22] In private, however, Beaverbrook told Lloyd George that he disagreed with the column and disliked "the regimentation of opinion" under the Nazi regime.[23] On another occasion, after the *Express* ran a short anti-Nazi editorial, Beaverbrook apologized profusely to the German ambassador to Britain, Joachim von Ribbentrop. "I have been trying to reach you by telephone," he wrote anxiously, "to say that I disapprove of the leader in *Express* of Friday which I did not see before publication."[24] Beaverbrook remained friendly with Ribbentrop over the next several years. The two men sometimes dined together and exchanged chatty letters.[25]

Beaverbrook revised his opinion of Hitler so frequently that he required his staff to write and rewrite various obituaries for the dictator, who he thought might soon be assassinated. After the 1934 Night of the Long Knives purge, he "turned solidly, fanatically, anti-Hitler," one of his editors reported; he compared the dictator to Al Capone and the Nazis to gangsters. At that point he forced his underling to rewrite an earlier favorable obituary. "I expect in four months' time I shall have to do another Hitler 'obit'—perhaps several!" the editor exclaimed.[26] But though Beaverbrook's views of Hitler fluctuated, he remained a consistent isolationist and appeaser.

In the mid-1930s, Beaverbrook believed that the League of Nations posed a greater threat to the empire than Germany. While Hearst, McCormick, Patterson, and other American isolationists had helped keep their country out of the League, Beaverbrook faced the challenge of opposing the international organization even as Britain remained one of its leading members. The League nations committed themselves to collective security: article 16 of the Covenant declared that an assault against any League member was an attack on all. Beaverbrook worried that the League would force Britain to protect members whose defense was not in the empire's interest.

In 1934, a nationwide survey known as the "Peace Ballot" heightened Beaverbrook's concern that League membership would commit Britain to an unnecessary war. The survey, conducted by the League of Nations Union, a private advocacy group, canvassed the British people on their support for collective solutions to international crises. The ballot asked Britons if they backed the League and collective security, if they wanted mutual disarmament, and if they believed in imposing economic and military sanctions on aggressors. Hundreds of thousands of volunteers fanned out across the country to deliver the ballots to every British household. More than 11 million Britons participated. In June 1935, the organizers announced that 95 percent of voters favored British membership in the League, 89 percent supported economic sanctions against aggressors, and 59 percent backed "military measures" against aggression—in other words, waging war against the dictators.[27]

The Peace Ballot was far from scientific, and its results could be interpreted in many ways. But Beaverbrook thought the campaign could have disastrous consequences. Calling the survey "the Ballot of Blood," he told readers that following such a policy would "drag you and your children" into a war ginned up by the "ambitious and unscrupulous powers" in the League of Nations.[28] "Tear up the ballot paper," he wrote. "Throw the pieces in the waste paper basket. Turn away from Europe. Stand by the Empire and Splendid Isolation."[29]

Beaverbrook worried that the ballot would have one particular destructive effect: it might persuade British leaders to resist Italian aggression against Ethiopia. Fascist Italy began to threaten that independent African nation in the fall of 1934, ostensibly because of a border dispute with the colony of Italian Somaliland, but really because Mussolini wanted to fight and win a war. The conflict created a crisis for the League of Nations and its two most powerful members, Britain and France. Ethiopia appealed to the League for assistance. If the League refused to come to its defense, the organization would lose credibility and aggressors would know they did not need to worry that the Western democracies might try to stop their belligerent actions.

In March 1935, in the midst of his fight against the "Ballot of Blood" and his concerns about war in Ethiopia, Beaverbrook received a short letter from Patterson in New York. The British press baron realized that he could work with the American publisher to promote their mutual cause of Anglo-American isolation.

■

The correspondence between the two press lords began with a routine business inquiry. Beaverbrook asked Patterson for more information about a *Daily News* program to build reader loyalty. Beaverbrook's *Express* was selling almost 2 million copies a day in 1935, but its owner wanted to know more about the contests and services that the *Daily News* had used to build its circulation to a level that rivaled that of the *Express*.[30] Patterson answered with the requested information and then pivoted to world politics. "We are all very much alarmed here about the prospect of war in Europe."[31]

With League of Nations officials still dithering over how to respond to Mussolini's threats against Ethiopia, Patterson assured Beaverbrook that the U.S. government and the nation's people wanted no part of any confrontation with the fascist dictators, and he hoped the British would follow the Americans' lead. "If war comes, it certainly will be the determination of every American to whom I have talked that we shall stay out of this one," he wrote. "I sincerely hope that England may find it possible to do the same thing."[32]

Beaverbrook responded swiftly. He asked for and received permission to print the last few lines of Patterson's letter on the front page of the *Express*, and then published editorials in his London papers extolling Patterson's views. To ensure that every person in Britain heard about them, he printed "From across the Atlantic," which quoted and praised both the original letter and the editorials about it.

The pamphlet celebrated the bonds that linked "the peoples of the Empire to those of the States"—peoples who allegedly had a common religion, language, and race. "The pioneers who tamed the wilderness of North America were men of British birth and Christian faith," the flyer claimed, overlooking the many people of different birthplaces, faiths, and even languages in both the United States and the British Empire. Yet what distinguished Americans and Britons above all was "the determination . . . to dwell in peace." Now the Americans, these Christian pioneers of British blood, were asking their cousins to "abandon the policy of association with countries whose outlook and methods have no contact with our own, whose policies expose us to the constant peril of embroilment in quarrels which do not concern us," and instead stand with "our own kith and kind, with men of peace and good will."

Besides folding the pamphlet into copies of the *Express*, Beaverbrook also hired a bus to transport some twenty volunteers around London to press it into the hands of as many people as possible. Then he arranged a meeting in a London suburb where three members of Parliament spoke about the importance of Patterson's message. But saturating London was not enough: he paid to distribute

10 million copies of the flyer throughout the whole nation, or roughly one per household.[33]

Beaverbrook hoped to demonstrate that Americans opposed both the League and the concept of collective security. Once British officials understood that most Americans favored splendid isolation, he thought the British government would refuse to get involved in Ethiopia or any future crisis involving European nations. One journalist described Beaverbrook's goal this way: "If the two countries get together on a firm basis, they can tell the rest of the world to go fly a kite."[34]

Patterson must have been surprised at the tremendous campaign his letter inspired, but he was also flattered. He responded by writing an editorial in the *Daily News* praising the British for trying to stay out of European conflicts. The United States, he wrote, needed to "stand with Britain for the protection of both of us against our would-be conquerors of various races."[35] Dozens of Britons wrote to say they were thrilled by his "stirring message," and he printed many of their letters in the *Daily News*'s Voice of the People section. "If the American people and our own could keep clear of all foreign entanglements, working together for our mutual benefit and 'hang the foreigner,' we should both be much better off," a reader in Sheffield wrote. A correspondent from Inverness thanked the *Daily News* for backing the policies of the *Daily Express*: "I write to tell you that the policy of 'splendid isolation,' pioneered by Lord Beaverbrook in this country, is gaining much public favor because of the New York *Daily News* support of it across the Atlantic." The *Daily Express* ran a story about how the *Daily News* was printing letters from *Express* readers about the *Express* stories about the *Daily News*. The two publishers created a transatlantic isolationist media echo chamber.[36]

Beaverbrook continued his isolationist crusade in other print venues as well. In April 1935, he wrote a piece for the Hearst press explaining the ideology of "the Isolationists." He argued that "the policy of collective security is only a policy of fear—fear and hatred of war." By contrast, he said, "those who follow the path of Isolation" believed that Germany would never threaten a strongly defended Britain, and therefore they offered "hope for Britain, hope for Europe, hope for the world."[37]

Like Patterson, Beaverbrook was a jingoist who consciously decided to describe himself as an "isolationist" to emphasize his insistence on staying out of European conflicts while maintaining control of the British Empire. He realized that not everyone shared his enthusiasm for the terms *isolationist, isolationism,* or even his personal favorite, *splendid isolation.* In editorials in the *Express* that spring, he conceded that the British government wished to avoid his chosen terms, even as it practiced his policies. "They will call it 'Detachment,' but the 'Daily Express' does not mind that," he insisted.[38]

Over the next few months, Patterson and Beaverbrook consulted each other on policy proposals, exchanged friendly notes, and agreed to campaign together for British and American isolation on a joint trip to Europe. In July 1935, Patterson accepted Beaverbrook's invitation to accompany him on one of his regular jaunts to the Continent—in Beaverbrook's words, to join his "high-powered, high-geared 'circus,' " in this case, a pleasure trip with some foreign policy goals.[39] Beaverbrook chartered a four-engine plane to take a party of eleven people, including Patterson and two of his daughters, on a mission of personal shuttle diplomacy. The group stopped in Rome, where the publishers were delighted to secure a three-hour interview with Mussolini. They had hoped to fly to Berlin to meet with Hitler, but the Nazi leader refused to see them. (Hitler gave few interviews to the Western press, and apparently Beaverbrook and Patterson were not of the caliber of Rothermere and Hearst.) Disappointed, the party continued to Warsaw and Belgrade, where Patterson's daughter Alicia remembered "endless dinners ... given by important people."[40] Beaverbrook's excursions were famous for their copious supplies of excellent wine and spirits, for which Patterson, on his way home, expressed somewhat rueful appreciation.[41]

■

Beaverbrook and Patterson found it easy to cooperate because they shared many political views. Both were intensely nationalistic; both believed they needed to defend their "race"; and both worried that their respective countries risked power, money, and civilization itself by intervening in European affairs. Their isolationist commitments undergirded their views on foreign crises in the mid-1930s, from the Italian invasion of Ethiopia to the German reoccupation of the Rhineland to the Spanish Civil War.

In each case, the American publisher and the British press baron had the same message for their government: "STAY OUT," as the *Daily News* repeatedly said in its editorials. Their similar coverage and analysis of European crises shows how democratic, non-fascist media elites promoted the same message of isolation and appeasement.

During the Ethiopian crisis of 1935, British elite opinion spanned the gamut from support of fascist aggression to pleas for collective security and multilateral defense of Ethiopia. Pro-fascists like Rothermere cheered Italy for "firmly upholding" the "cause of the white races," as the *Daily Mail* declared.[42] At the other extreme, British interventionists argued for invoking article 16 against Italy.

Beaverbrook took a middle position. He did not celebrate the fascist aggression, nor did he think the League members should do anything to stop it. In September 1935, as the League debated whether to impose sanctions on Italy, the publisher wrote a front-page editorial urging Stanley Baldwin's government to stay out of the conflict. "We cannot, we will not, we must not police the world alone," he insisted.[43] He worried that anti-fascist Britons would stampede the government into using the military to enforce the League's decisions. "Do not be led into warlike courses by hatred of dictators," he wrote. "There have been countless dictators in history. They have all come to a bad end. Let the people who are misgoverned rid themselves of their autocrats."[44]

When Mussolini's forces launched an air and land attack on Ethiopia in October 1935, the League responded by embargoing the trade of some materials, but not coal or oil. Beaverbrook continued to insist that the British government should do no more. Shortly after the Italian invasion, he reasoned in a signed article that Britons should protect the peoples of the empire, not those in Ethiopia. "Am I my brother's keeper?" he asked. "Well, of course. We have a responsibility. But here God has given us a special duty, a particular task. In our charge there are the countless races of the British Empire. That is where our immediate duty lies. That is a burden which we must bear, and we alone." Britain had an obligation to "teach those peoples and to tend them," to "raise their conditions of living and guide them towards higher standards." If the British turned their backs on the empire by intervening in European quarrels, he argued, their imperial subjects might "fall into the hands of evil people." Britain needed to protect its wards from the "sorrow and grief and death" that might come from a foreign war.[45]

For Patterson, the events in Ethiopia were a test of racial solidarity, not of collective security. He feared that a League decision to stop Mussolini's invasion would lead to a "world race war." Europeans, he wrote, should not go to war against a white nation because it had decided to invade an African one. Otherwise, the *News* claimed—in a dubious leap of logic—Japan might take advantage of the intra-European squabble and try to unify all people of color against Europeans and European Americans. "With the white race split up into warring factions, and all the colored races increasingly resentful of the whites' long world dominance, Japan's chances of making itself the spearhead of a world-wide anti-white military movement would be even better than they are now."[46]

The folly of opposing aggressive moves by other white nations would remain a theme of *Daily News* editorials—and of all the isolationist publishers' editorials—throughout the 1930s and early 1940s. McCormick dismissed Ethiopia as "a semi-barbaric country the like of which has always been regarded by occidentals as their natural prey," while Hearst declared it was the "divine decree" for white people to "reclaim the waste places of Africa" and rescue the "savage races" of the world.[47] Their views were similar to those of Hitler, who, in a private letter to Rothermere in 1935, bemoaned the British failure to understand that the Germans shared their goal of ensuring white supremacy throughout the world. "When, at last," he wrote, "will reason step in and tear the White race away from a development which otherwise inevitably must spell its doom?"[48]

Instead of confronting the Italians, Patterson urged the British to appease them. "Why march out to save Ethiopia," the *News* asked, "when it may cost you your empire and certainly will cost you a lot of valuable English soldiers and English pounds?"[49] In any event, whatever Britain and the League did, the course for the United States was clear: "The main object is to STAY OUT OF IT." Echoing Beaverbrook, the *News* insisted that the United States was not "the world's policeman," and Americans were "not under any obligation to stop any international outrage that doesn't affect us. We don't even belong to the League of Nations, a club of self-appointed world policemen who have yet to do a Grade A job of policing anywhere."[50]

Britain and the United States did stay out, of course. Unhindered by the League, Mussolini conquered the Ethiopian capital. The Ethiopian emperor, Haile Selassie, begged the League to impose stronger sanctions, but instead the League voted to lift them all. The Italo-Ethiopian War ended with Ethiopia conquered, the League discredited, and the fascist dictators emboldened by the democracies' unwillingness to enforce collective security.

The next test of British resolve came in March 1936, when Hitler sent German troops to reoccupy the Rhineland. The area, which borders France, Belgium, and the Netherlands, had been demilitarized by the Treaty of Versailles, and the German government had agreed to make the demilitarization permanent when it signed the Locarno Treaty of 1925. Hitler's blatant defiance of the two pacts put pressure on the British and the French governments: Would they do anything to defend the treaties and the principle of collective security?

Both France and Britain decided not to try to expel the Wehrmacht. In France, the general staff feared that they could not win a war against the Germans at that time. In Britain, public opinion was firmly against risking a wider conflict merely over the Rhineland. And British public opinion was, of course, partly shaped by one of Britain's best-selling newspapers, the *Daily Express*. "The Germans have reoccupied the Rhineland. What does that mean TO US?" the *Express* asked its readers. "The question is: WILL BRITAIN BE INVOLVED IN WAR? The answer is NO!"[51]

Across the Atlantic, the *Daily News* applauded appeasement and minimized the significance of the Nazi decision to unilaterally abrogate the postwar treaties. "After all," the *News* pronounced, "Hitler is occupying his own territory; he isn't invading anyone else's." Patterson lent his support to his friend Beaverbrook and others in Britain who urged their government to leave Hitler alone. Luckily, the *News* said, the British were quite sane and wise. They would "hardly be sap enough to go in with France in a war against Hitler over the Rhineland."[52]

Once again, the leading European democracies squandered an opportunity to stop the advance of the fascist dictators. With German troops in the region, France would find it much more difficult to come to the aid of the eastern European countries whose borders it had guaranteed, including Czechoslovakia and Poland. A fascist strongman had again defied the authority of the League and ignored the postwar treaties, and the League had done nothing.

Europe faced yet another crisis with the start of the Spanish Civil War in July 1936, when right-wing Nationalists under the command of General Francisco Franco mounted a coup to overthrow the elected center-left Republican government. An alliance of twenty-seven nations, including Germany, Italy, the Soviet Union, France, and Britain, pledged not to intervene in the war. But despite their public promises, the fascist states began to help Franco by sending arms, ammunition, and troops, while the Soviets aided the Republicans.

For many Americans and Europeans, the Spanish Civil War came to symbolize much more than a local conflict. It was a battle between democracy and autocracy, socialism and fascism. Thousands of ordinary men volunteered to fight for the Republic in the International Brigades. In Britain, liberals clamored for the government to help the Spanish Republicans, while Rothermere's *Daily Mail* propagandized for the fascists and spread real and imagined stories of communist plots and atrocities.[53]

The isolationists, led by the *Daily Express*, just wanted Britain to stay out. Beaverbrook compared British help for the Spanish Republicans with British assistance to anti-communists in the Russian Civil War more than a decade before. That earlier intervention, he wrote, "cost us some thousands of British soldiers' lives, £100,000,000 in cash, and the bitter enmity of the Russian government for the next ten years . . . and the intervention failed anyway." Britain had "backed a loser," he wrote, "and the mark of a 'mug' is to go on backing the same loser."[54] In comparing the Spanish democrats to the Russian czarists, Beaverbrook dismissed the ideological roots of the Spanish conflict. To his mind, all European conflicts, regardless of the issues under dispute or the various sides' political positions, were essentially the same, and the British should avoid them.

Over in New York, Patterson applied what was becoming a *Daily News* catchphrase: "STAY OUT OF IT." The United States should ignore the Spanish Republicans' entreaties for help, the *News* wrote in September 1936, "no matter whether we hate Communism or whether we hate Fascism or whether we love democracy. Stay out of it BECAUSE we love democracy. The best way we can show our love for democracy is to keep our country strong, prosperous and peaceful."[55] Two months later, in an editorial headlined "We're All Americans First," the *News* again advised the United States not to repeat its mistaken intervention in the Great War. "We can't settle Europe's world-old hates and dislocations, as we proved in 1917–18. Dabble with them again, and we shall get our fingers burnt, and we may get an arm chewed off. Stay out of it, and we may make this country the last refuge in the modern world of civilization, democracy and hopes of progress."[56]

■

It's obvious why Beaverbrook and Patterson formed their strategic partnership. They believed in the same principles and worked for the same goals. They had no interest in promoting fascism, yet they did not see the point of risking what they valued—the "race," the nation, the empire—by trying to stop fascist aggression. They also agreed on the ultimate purpose of their profession. As Beaverbrook said, they were not out to make money but to make propaganda. They hoped to influence readers—and, through their readers, governments.

Their odds of success increased dramatically when Joe Patterson's editorials began appearing in Washington, D.C.

CHAPTER SIX

The Lady Newspaperman

O N A HUMID SUMMER day in 1930, America's first female editor in chief of a modern metropolitan newspaper started her new job in style. Tall, slender, red-haired, and striking, Cissy Patterson arrived at the *Washington Herald*, William Randolph Hearst's morning newspaper in the nation's capital. She glided into the grimy newsroom and surveyed the crowd of bemused and disgruntled newsmen who had assembled to greet her, all clad in sports coats. "I suppose you think this is just a stunt," she told them. "Even if you do, let's all try to put it over. And you don't need to wear coats when I'm around, either."[1] And with that, Eleanor Patterson Gizycka Schlesinger, better known by her childhood name Cissy, a former countess who had never in her life held a real job before, became Eleanor Medill Patterson, a "newspaperman," as she called herself, at the age of forty-eight. When she took over the *Herald*, the youngest Medill grandchild was already famous for her marriages, her affairs, and her dinner parties. Now she would become known for her gleeful embrace of sensationalistic journalism and for her vehement, uncompromising isolationism.

Cissy Patterson is an underappreciated figure in media history. The *Encyclopedia of American Journalism* has no entry for her, though it does cover her brother, her cousin, and dozens of arguably less important editors and publishers. Yet she played key roles in the history of the 1930s and 1940s—first as a pioneering woman editor, then as a subtle saboteur of the anti–New Deal politics of her boss, William Randolph Hearst, and eventually as the Washington end of what critics called "the McCormick/Patterson newspaper axis."[2]

Newsroom culture in the 1930s was noisy, crude, and masculine —much like the discourse of the tabloid newspapers. To reinvent herself as a "lady newspaperman," Cissy Patterson needed to learn how to navigate that world. At the same time, she wanted to become a player in Washington power politics. First in the Hearst chain and then within the Patterson/McCormick system, she adapted to the role of a hard-boiled publisher and helped her relatives and her good friend Hearst spread the message of America First.

▪

Eleanor Medill Patterson so adored her older brother that she chose to use his childhood nickname for her even as she rose to be the most influential female newspaper publisher in the country. At age two, Joe found it hard to say "Elinor," as his new baby sister was christened, so he called her Cissy. She would later change the spelling of her formal Christian name and marry twice, changing her surname from Patterson to Gizycka to Schlesinger and back to Patterson. But she always retained the pet name that identified her as Joe's little sister.[3]

Though she was a grandchild of Joseph Medill, Cissy Patterson was a girl, and therefore not expected to take up the family publishing business. Her parents sent her to finishing school and then presented her to society in lavish debutante balls. The heiress was lively and attractive, though not conventionally pretty: "Her face was not the best part of her," wrote one of her friends, "but her figure was divine."[4]

After her debut, Patterson divided her time between her mother's Italian-style palazzo on Astor Street in Chicago and her equally extravagant mansion on Dupont Circle in Washington, D.C., both designed by the renowned architect Stanford White. She quickly rose to the top of Washington society and befriended the richest and most connected capital elites, including Alice Roosevelt, President Theodore Roosevelt's mischievous daughter.

As a young socialite, Patterson competed with Alice Roosevelt for the attentions of several prominent Washington politicians and international playboys. Alice married Nicholas Longworth, a handsome Republican congressman who later became Speaker of the House, but Patterson found an even more desirable partner—at least superficially—in Josef Gizycki, a dashing Polish count. But Gizycki turned out to be a greedy, brutal thug who had married Patterson for her money. After their wedding, he took her to his "estate" in Russian Poland, which, she discovered, was actually a dank, squalid ruin. As he and his wife began to quarrel frequently, he started to beat her.

Patterson's escape from her marriage was every bit as dramatic as a story in a Hearst or Patterson/McCormick tabloid. After their daughter, Felicia, was born, Patterson took the child and fled to London. Gizycki tracked them down, kidnapped Felicia, and demanded a huge ransom for her return.[5] It took several years and help from President William Howard Taft and the Russian czar before Patterson retrieved her daughter and won a divorce.

Single again, Patterson moved back to Washington and began a life as a society matron. In her house on Dupont Circle, which her mother deeded to her, Patterson entertained the city's most famous public officials (many of whom, her biographers believe, had affairs with the hostess). She divided her time among Washington, Paris, New York, and Jackson Hole, Wyoming, where she bought a ranch and enjoyed a years-long romance with a cowboy. Like her cousin Robert McCormick, Patterson loved foxhunts, but she also tracked sheep, goats, and elk on her western estate, decorating her mansions with their stuffed heads.

In addition to hunting, drinking, and partying, Patterson was legendary for her wardrobe, which took up two rooms of her Washington home and included dozens of gowns, furs, and bathing suits, as well as three hundred pairs of lounging pajamas. She liked to wear her brocaded "hostess pajamas" and her stunning array of diamonds and pearls to her dinner parties, where her guests knew they would be served the finest champagne.

In middle age, Patterson discovered a talent for writing. She had never attended college or had much instruction in literature or any other discipline. But she was happy to learn—and there were powerful men eager to showcase her distinguished family name as a byline in their publications. The first of Patterson's editorial mentors was Walter Howey, the hard-living, wisecracking news-man who would serve as the model for the Walter Burns character in Ben Hecht and Charles MacArthur's play *The Front Page*. Howey had worked for Joe Patterson at the *Chicago Tribune* but resigned after quarrelling with him. According to legend, as Howey stalked out of the *Tribune* city room, declaring his intention to work for a rival publication, he shouted to Patterson, "And what's more, I'm going to seduce your sister!"[6] A gloating William Randolph Hearst hired Howey for his Chicago paper; the two men then conspired to hire Cissy Patterson as a reporter (with a note identifying her as "Sister of the editor of the *Chicago Tribune*").[7] Howey made good on his threat to Joe and romanced Cissy, as well as tutoring her in reporting and writing.

After dabbling in journalism, Cissy Patterson decided to follow her brother's example and try her hand at fiction writing. In the mid-1920s, she published two romans à clef. The first, *Glass Houses*, inspired Washington politicos to try to identify its thinly disguised characters, including a vicious society belle (believed to be Alice Roosevelt Longworth) and a feckless western senator (apparently Idaho's William Borah). As the *New York Times* commented, the book was full of sexual gossip and "clever thrusts below the belt by an insider against other insiders in the game of politics."[8] Her sec-ond novel, *Fall Flight*, features a sad but stunningly beautiful rich girl from Chicago who grows up to marry an attractive but loath-some Russian prince, who beats her brutally until she escapes with her new lover. With their gorgeous heroines and irredeemable vil-lains, all of whom were punished for their crimes, Patterson's books served the dual purpose of wish fulfillment and revenge fan-tasy. She would use her newspaper in the same way.

In 1925, Cissy rebelled against her family's anti-Semitism by marrying a wealthy New York Jew, the lawyer Elmer Schlesinger. Like Patterson, Schlesinger had a mercurial temperament, and the newlyweds quarreled often and sometimes in public. He died of a sudden heart attack just four years after their wedding.

Some of Patterson's relatives contended that despite her mar-riage to Schlesinger, Cissy despised and distrusted Jews. Her daugh-ter, who fought bitterly with her mother for years and broke all ties with her in 1945, explained that Patterson never overcame her

"One can't be a good reporter and a lady at the same time,"
said Cissy Patterson, pictured here in the late 1920s. "I'd rather
be a reporter." Patterson showed a flair for the dramatic in her novels,
her style of dress, her private life, and her newspaper, the *Washington
Times-Herald*. (Collection of the Jackson Hole Historical
Society and Museum, 1958.3134.001)

prejudices and that her anti-Semitism was one of many reasons her marriage to Schlesinger seemed headed for disaster. "He was Jewish and she hated that and said so, often," Felicia told an interviewer after her mother's death.[9] According to Robert McCormick's second wife, Maryland, Cissy Patterson once embarrassed the family by verbally assailing a Jewish guest at a luncheon. "I know about Jews," she told him. "I was married to one." Maryland tried to stop Cissy from saying anything else, "but you couldn't shut Cissy up unless she wanted to be shut up."[10] In another incident, when she lost a court battle with the *Washington Post* over rights to comics, Patterson sent a hunk of raw meat—literally a pound of flesh, à la Shylock —to Eugene Meyer, the *Post*'s Jewish publisher.[11]

Schlesinger's fortune made Patterson richer than ever. Her share of his estate amounted to $750,000, or more than $11 million today. Meanwhile, her yearly income from the family newspaper business was $800,000 (or $12 million in today's money). Documents from her lawyer's office show that in 1941 her net worth was around $20 million, or about $360 million today.[12]

In 1928, in her mid-forties, after enjoying modest success as a reporter and novelist, Patterson decided she wanted to use her fortune to become a newspaper publisher like her brother and cousin. After trying and failing to purchase the *Washington Post*, she asked Hearst to sell her his morning paper, the *Washington Herald*, a stodgy, money-losing daily with a circulation of about fifty thousand copies, fifth among the capital's six dailies. Hearst already owned another Washington paper, the afternoon *Times*, and Patterson hoped he would want to unload a property that was costing him money. Both her cousin and her brother advised against the purchase. "It might be losing a vast sum of money," Joe cautioned her, "which would consume your income, or much of it."[13] Cissy Patterson was not dissuaded and continued to plead with Hearst—her friend and frequent party guest—to let her buy the paper.

But Hearst, who resisted parting with any of his newspapers, refused to sell or even lease the *Herald* to her, though his chief lieutenant, Arthur Brisbane, urged him to do so. Finally, in 1930, after more entreaties from Cissy, Hearst hit upon a solution. "If she wants to go into the newspaper business in Washington," he told Brisbane, "tell her I'll give her a job." Brisbane hired Patterson as the editor of the *Herald*. ("The 'hiring' is rather a formality," he explained, "since each trip to see Mr. Hearst in California in her private [railroad] car costs her as much as she earns in a year.")[14] On Brisbane's advice, Eleanor Josephine Patterson Gizycka Schlesinger changed her name to Eleanor Medill Patterson.[15] As she started a career in newspaper publishing, it would not hurt to remind everyone of her connection to a royal family of American journalism.

Patterson signaled that she planned to use the paper, as she had used her novels, to settle personal scores. On her fourth day on the job, in a front-page, signed editorial, the new editor titillated the capital city by taking a random and gratuitous swipe at Alice Roosevelt Longworth, depicting her old friend as vain and self-important.[16] The feud was grist for the Washington gossip mills. Newspapers around the country snickered about the editorial ("Amazonian War Livens Capital," the *Los Angeles Times* reported).[17] Throughout her tenure at the *Herald* (and later the *Times-Herald*), Patterson would take great pleasure in wielding her newspaper as a weapon to attack political and personal enemies. "The trouble with me," she once said, "is that I am a vindictive old shanty-Irish bitch."[18]

On the editorial page, Patterson toed the Hearst corporate line. She had little choice: the chief dictated his papers' editorial policy. But she had no desire to change the *Herald*'s policy even if she could. As she told her readers in one of her first editorials, she and her family shared Hearst's opinions (and, apparently, his fondness for capital letters). "The other newspapers with which my family has for so long been associated stand today with the Hearst papers on nearly all of the major issues. AGAINST prohibition. AGAINST the League of Nations. AGAINST the World Court. AGAINST the recent naval treaty. FOR an adequate defense and FOR the general debunking of our foreign relations."[19]

Notably, except for Prohibition, all the "major issues" on Patterson's list involved foreign policy. Proud of her family's isolationist reputation, the new *Herald* editor counted several anti-interventionist senators among her closest friends in Washington. She would change her opinions on domestic policies, but—like her boss, her brother, and her cousin—she never wavered on foreign policy.

In the 1932 election, Patterson followed Hearst's lead and supported Franklin Roosevelt for president. Beyond her obligations as a Hearst editor, she personally liked Roosevelt. She found herself charmed when she visited the candidate at his home in Hyde Park before the election, and at his summer home in Warm Springs, Georgia, shortly after. "Surely," she wrote in the *Herald*, "there is a special radiance about this man which makes you feel better just to be around him."[20]

With Patterson at the helm, the *Herald* steadily increased its circulation and its advertising revenue. Hearst proclaimed that he did not think Cissy "could do any better if she were [a] man or that any man could do better than Mrs. Patterson."[21] By October 1931, a little more than a year after she had taken over the paper, the *Herald* surpassed the *Post* to become the best-selling morning newspaper in the nation's capital.[22] Hearst rewarded her by promoting her to be the *Herald*'s publisher as well as its editor. In 1937, auditors reported that the *Herald* sold 112,354 copies a day, more than twice as many as when Patterson had taken over the paper seven years earlier.[23]

More Washingtonians bought the *Herald* because Patterson made it a better, livelier paper. Its appearance improved dramatically after she hired Jackie Martin, an art and photography director, away from a rival paper. To win female subscribers, she expanded the *Herald*'s society coverage and soon had four to five columnists writing up Washington gossip.[24] "We have done our darndest to tie up our women readers to the *Herald*," she reported to Hearst in 1935. "In time I believe we should considerably enlarge this field. Response so far has been excellent."[25]

In hiring women reporters, Patterson was following an industry trend. The number of female journalists in the United States more than doubled from 1920 to 1930. By 1940, when only about 6 percent of doctors and 2 percent of lawyers were women, more than one in four reporters or editors was female. Almost one-third of journalists were women by 1950.[26]

But these women were reporters, not top editors or managers. As the first woman editor in chief of a big-city paper in the modern era, and as Hearst's first and only female publisher, Patterson needed to overcome the suspicion of the men she would oversee. Brisbane warned her that she would have to endure some masculine condescension. "You will get your training," he wrote her, "with more or less temperamental and incompetent men. You must take it all philosophically."[27]

To succeed, Patterson needed to learn the rules of a very masculine game. Most metropolitan papers in the 1930s put out several editions—each with a separate deadline—every day. The pace was frenetic. Reporters in the crowded newsrooms drank frequently, smoked, and swore incessantly. In these male spaces, women journalists, especially hard-news reporters, tried to prove that they were one of the boys. As historian Kathleen Cairns has written, front-page women journalists "had to demonstrate stereotypical male qualities, or at least the qualities that men liked to think they possessed."[28] Patterson certainly enjoyed fitting the model of the hard-bitten editor. She downed a few Scotches while at work, swore like a sailor, and did not hesitate to fire any man who disappointed or angered her. "They call her 'Cissy' Patterson, but she's an old-fashioned, two-fisted publisher who can stand up to any man in the rough-tough business of newspapering," wrote an admiring interviewer in 1940. Like many female journalists of the era, Patterson insisted that women could be good "newspapermen" only if they were willing to act like men. "One can't be a good reporter and a lady at the same time," she said. "I'd rather be a reporter."[29]

At the same time, Patterson liked to emphasize her difference from male editors and suggest that her gender made her more persuasive and empathetic. "I'm a red-haired woman editor," she explained once, "and I have something to say."[30] She wrote investigative pieces that exposed suffering in her city. For a story on the plight of the homeless, she dressed in rags, ate in a soup kitchen, slept in a Salvation Army shelter, and knocked on doors in a fruitless search for work.[31] Her articles exposed pollution problems in the Potomac, the dearth of hot lunches for the city's poor children, and the mistreatment of animals (one of her favorite crusades, undertaken after she repented her many years of hunting).[32]

Arthur Brisbane, like Walter Howey before him, edited her copy and gave writing tips to the woman he called "a natural born newspaper 'man.' "[33] He was pleased with her progress, describing her to President Roosevelt as "an unusually brilliant writer."[34] Patterson appreciated the tutorials and had no difficulty adopting the sensationalist tone of the Hearst press. She and Joe liked to say that the Medill family motto was "When your grandmother is raped, put it on the front page."[35]

Patterson also raised the *Herald*'s profile by hosting the most interesting and lavish dinner parties in town. These events usually took place at her house on Dupont Circle, but often she would direct her drivers to take guests to her estate in Maryland, Dower House, a seventeenth-century mansion originally owned by Lord Baltimore. Her closest friends would take the train to meet her in New York, where she relaxed some weekends at Harbor Acres, a large waterfront estate on Long Island that she had acquired when she was married to Schlesinger.

Political leaders, union officials, novelists, and business tycoons loved to attend her parties. In the summer at her Maryland estate, the weekend-long events, complete with swimming and tennis, included Securities and Exchange Commission chairman Joseph Kennedy, First Lady Eleanor Roosevelt, and other administration figures. She was also good friends with maverick U.S. senators like Burton Wheeler and William Borah, who would become Roosevelt's most vociferous opponents in the intervention debate. As *Town & Country* magazine noted in a piece on her "circle" in 1935, "Cissy attracts people who are news, people who make news and people behind the news. There is even a hearing for those ahead of the news, the prophets without honor in their own districts."[36] Patterson also hosted some of the nation's top journalists, including Drew Pearson, a syndicated columnist who was briefly married to her daughter and with whom Patterson often feuded.

She was even friends, for a time, with the man who would become the conservative publishers' most effective opponent, Harold Ickes. A progressive Republican from Chicago, Ickes joined Roosevelt's cabinet as interior secretary in 1933 and would serve in that position until after the president's death. Ickes also ran the Public Works Administration, the New Deal agency responsible for building the Triborough Bridge and Hoover Dam, among other achievements. After his wife was killed in a car crash in 1935, he began spending more time with Patterson. Impressed by what he described as her gentleness, kindness, and concern for his welfare, he frequently dined with her, either attending her famous parties or meeting with her alone. "I have come to be very fond indeed of her," he wrote in his diary. "I have found in her the best friend I have made in Washington."[37]

But Hearst's turn against the New Deal strained the friendship between Patterson and Ickes, especially after the interior secretary began to distinguish himself as the most combative member of the Roosevelt team. In one fiery speech in Detroit, Ickes denounced "the cruelly ruthless exploiting class" who opposed Roosevelt because they wanted "to grow even richer while the masses become poorer and poorer." These rich men tried to mislead the voters, Ickes said, by red-baiting the New Dealers: "Communism is merely a convenient bugaboo. It is the Fascist-minded men of America who are the real enemies of our institutions through their solidarity and their ability and willingness to turn the wealth of America against the welfare of America."[38] The next week, the Hearst press published a column by Benjamin De Casseres that proved Ickes's point. The interior secretary should "resign and take out a card in the Communist party," De Casseres concluded, because his rhetoric showed him to be a Red.[39] When Patterson noticed the column in the *Herald*'s first edition, she pulled it from subsequent ones and called Ickes to apologize. "She said the editorial was not only mean; it was stupid," Ickes reported in his diary.[40]

An ordinary Hearst editor could not have survived (and would not have attempted) such an insubordinate act. But Patterson was no ordinary Hearst employee. Her $10,000-a-year salary as editor was approximately 1 percent of her income. She could afford to lose her job, and her confidence enabled her to do things that other journalists would never dare.

Patterson continued to suffer from divided political loyalties through the 1936 election. Not only her close friends but also her brother strongly supported the president's reelection. She told Ickes she felt torn. "She isn't for Roosevelt, although she isn't strongly against him," he wrote in his diary. "She said that she was pulled both ways as between Hearst and her brother Joe."[41] To resolve the tension, Patterson tried to lease the *Herald* from Hearst when she heard that Eugene Meyer, the owner of the *Washington Post*, had offered Hearst a considerable sum for it. After she begged him to refuse Meyer's offer, Hearst initially agreed to negotiate a lease with Patterson instead. But then, as she explained a few months later, "the lawyers stepped in and by the time they all had their say, of course nothing came of it."[42]

That summer, while visiting Patterson at her Long Island estate, Ickes wrote a radio speech denouncing Hearst. He called it "Hearst over Topeka" and depicted Alf Landon, the Republican presidential nominee, as Hearst's puppet. The "Hearst publicity machine," Ickes charged, consistently praised Landon as "a man who had never made a mistake" while "venomously misrepresenting" Roosevelt's record. He condemned the conservative media for hiding behind the First Amendment to promote their partisan interests. "It would almost seem that to some the cherished right of freedom of the press, about which Mr. Hearst and Colonel McCormick can become so excited when there is no occasion for it," Ickes said, "is often merely freedom to distort news and to suppress news."[43] The interior secretary took secret pleasure in writing this screed in the house of one of Hearst's editors. "I did not tell Cissy that I was doing this in her home," he wrote, "but I chuckled to myself that I should be there polishing up an attack on her boss."[44] He would continue to attack her boss and other conservative press lords throughout Roosevelt's years in office.

In October 1936, at the height of the Hearst and McCormick denunciations of the president as a Soviet stooge, Patterson confided to Ickes that she planned to quit her job. The reason, she claimed, was business rather than ideology. She simply could not "sit idly by and see circulation and advertising falling off because of the way Hearst plays politics." Instead of working for Hearst, she would love to buy the *Herald* and run it herself. "I gave her enthusiastic cheers from my end of the telephone," Ickes recounted.[45]

As Hearst continued to dither about leasing the paper to her, Patterson did something quite audacious. Instead of the canned Hearst editorials, she began running some of Joe Patterson's pro–New Deal columns—sometimes without crediting the *Daily News*, which irritated her brother. (Running a credit line "is the custom of the trade," he lectured her.)[46]

Hearst was even more annoyed than her brother. But Cissy Patterson protested that her boss had approved the plan. "Don't you remember one night during the entre-acte at the play," she wrote him, "I asked you what you would think of a 'Sale' of the

Herald to me. . . . 'And,' I said, 'let's even turn the paper a shade
new-dealish. We could run some of Joe's editorials.' You certainly
appeared to be listening to me. You were looking right at me, and
two or three times you nodded your head in apparent agreement."
Patterson insisted that her brother's editorials helped the *Herald*
recover its political credibility "after the sock in the jaw we got
after [the] Election." The liberal editorials "struck a fresh note
(sometimes *very* fresh) on the editorial page," she continued, with
some understatement, and she had only printed those that ac-
corded with Hearst's policy, except for "one bad accident" that she
did not explain.[47]

Hearst reassured her promptly. "I am not mad at you at all or
in the least for ANY reason," he wrote back. But he did not want her
to "overdo" the *News* editorials. "I definitely am NOT a New Dealer
. . . I admire Joe and respect him as an OPPONENT."[48]

Hearst hated to let go of any of his papers, even to a friend, but
financial disaster forced him to change his mind. The Depression,
the boycotts, and Hearst's staggering personal spending had brought
his empire to the edge of bankruptcy. He paid himself the highest
salary in the country, $500,000 a year, while he owed more than
$126 million. To begin to cover his debts, he needed at least $50
million, and quickly. As short-term measures, he took a $1 million
loan from his girlfriend, Marion Davies, and agreed to lease the *Herald* to Patterson for an additional $1 million loan.[49]

Those loans were far from enough to pay off his creditors. After
trying and failing to reduce his personal and business expenses, the
nation's best-selling publisher conceded defeat and turned his businesses over to an independent trustee. Hearst still maintained editorial control over his papers, but the trustee had veto power over
their budgets.[50]

The "great Hearst retrenchment plan," as *Time* magazine called
it, became one of the most famous near-bankruptcies in American
history.[51] Two-thirds of his great art collection, worth $15 million,
went on the auction block. Suits of armor, choir stalls, tapestries,
paintings, sculptures, silverware, and jewelry—most went to other
millionaires at fire-sale prices.[52] At the trustee's insistence, Hearst
himself, rather than his corporation, began to pay the expenses at

his California mansion. The staff at Hearst Castle was reduced to a skeleton crew and the lavish parties there ended. The elephant, leopards, and bears were sent to new homes.[53] His other castle, the historic estate in Wales, went on the market.

The publisher also had to sell or close some of his money-losing newspapers. Over the next few years, his chain of twenty-eight papers would be reduced to nineteen. Other journalists were most surprised by his closure of the *New York American*. The *American* was, as *Time* described it, "the queen-pin of his domain, the paper that was called his journalistic 'love child,' on which he lavished money and affection and talent." With tough competition from the *Daily News*, the *American* had lost $1 million the year before, and Hearst was forced to consolidate it with the morning *Journal* and lay off many of its twenty-eight hundred employees. Reporters and editors all over the country began to fret about their jobs. As *Time* explained, the journalists wondered, "If Hearst would kill the *American*, where would he stop?"[54]

Hearst, like Cissy Patterson, seemed to realize that his strident anti-Roosevelt politics could be costing him readers and money. In addition to reorganizing his companies and reducing expenses, he tried to reconcile with the president. In June 1937, when Patterson reported to Hearst that the president had spoken kindly to her of the old press lord, Hearst's response betrayed an almost painful desperation to make amends. "Of course you know," he told her, "that I have the highest regard and esteem for him personally, and that I differed from him merely on certain principles." He claimed that he had hated working with Republicans. "I was a fish out of water. I had always been a progressive—a radical. I had nothing in common with reactionaries." With Roosevelt's huge reelection victory, Hearst realized that he had made some mistakes, and he hoped to meet and make up with the president soon. "If he wants me at any time I am at his command. If he does not, I am going to be a Democrat and not a Republican anyway, and I am NOT going 'to gang up against the President.' I have had my experience and hereafter I will gang up with my own kind of folk."[55] Patterson helped arrange a meeting between the publisher and the president. The entente, however, seemed destined to fail. In the same month as the meeting, Treasury Secretary Henry Morgenthau Jr., who had vowed to close some tax loopholes used by the very rich, issued a report on the country's leading tax dodgers. Hearst, who in the past two years had evaded $5 million in income taxes, was the first name on the list.[56]

That summer, Eugene Meyer approached Hearst again and increased his bid to buy the *Herald*, with the intention of shutting it down so that the *Post* would have a monopoly in the morning. Patterson responded by asking Hearst to lease her both of his Washington papers, with an option to buy after five years. Under pressure from his trustee and his creditors, Hearst agreed.

At last, after trying and failing for nine years to persuade Hearst to let her run a big-city newspaper on her own, Patterson managed not one but two major metropolitan dailies. In a public letter to Hearst, she gushed over the opportunities he had given her. The past seven years as the *Herald*'s editor, she wrote, had "passed like a dream—the grandest and most brilliant adventure of my life." The next few years would be even better as she struck out on her own. She praised her former boss effusively. "I cannot thank you adequately now for everything that you have done for me, or tell you how much your protection and friendship have meant to me. Please do not cut me loose entirely. For I will want to turn to you for help and counsel just the same in the future as in the past."[57]

Though she reassured her friend that she would continue to seek his advice, political observers understood that the transfer of editorial control of the *Times* and *Herald* would change Washington's media landscape. Patterson intended to improve the *Times* with brighter typography, livelier writers, and popular features. Eventually, in 1939, she would buy both papers, merge them, and produce a round-the-clock newspaper with ten editions a day.

Most important, Patterson no longer had to run Hearst's reactionary editorials on the front page, or at all. Washington insiders did not know what editorial policy to expect from her, but they were certain it would be very different from Hearst's. Patterson was "no political ax-grinder, either for or against the New Deal," *Time* magazine reported, "though personally she leans more toward the liberalism of her brother, Joe, than toward the Hearst policies."[58]

Ickes and Roosevelt's other advisers now had their wish. Two Washington newspapers would stop screaming about supposed treason in the New Deal and would instead feature Joe Patterson's liberal editorials. The sale of the *Times-Herald* could turn out to be a huge boon for Roosevelt, assuming Cissy and Joe Patterson continued to support him.

CHAPTER SEVEN

Undominated

THOUGH THE CONSERVATIVE BRITISH and American media titans had achieved little in their efforts to influence domestic politics before 1937, in the late 1930s the Nazis' territorial demands roused them to fight for their preferred foreign policy. In the United States, the isolationist press angrily attacked President Roosevelt after his "quarantine speech," delivered in the shadow of the Tribune Tower, in which he suggested that a more confrontational stance toward foreign dictators was not only morally correct but essential to the survival of democracy. In the United Kingdom, leaders who counseled resistance to Hitler, including Anthony Eden and Winston Churchill, found themselves marginalized and increasingly alone.

Throughout this time, as the isolationist press barons lauded Hitler's appeasers and ridiculed his resisters, Germany and Japan continued to grab territory, build up their industrial and military might, and prepare for war.

■

The transfer of two Washington dailies from the anti-administration Hearst to the more sympathetic Cissy Patterson was welcome news for the president. Apart from that, 1937 gave him little to cheer about, as he headed into his second term facing an increasingly hostile press.

On the domestic front, the president's missteps cost him valuable political capital. In a series of decisions, the Supreme Court had struck down the National Industrial Recovery Act, the Agricultural Adjustment Act, and other New Deal laws. Roosevelt confronted this problem by proposing to increase the number of justices—or, as his critics phrased it, to pack the high court.

The court reform scheme infuriated Roosevelt's critics in the press, many of whom saw the court as a fortress against the president's desire to become a dictator. Hearst and McCormick invoked the specter of dictatorship whenever Roosevelt threatened to pursue policies they opposed. Hearst insisted Roosevelt was trying to destroy "the bulwark of the American system," with grave implications for the republic's survival. "And when the Supreme Court . . . goes, all American systems based on constitutional liberty and equality will follow," the Hearst papers stated in an editorial.[1] McCormick called the proposal "the essence of dictatorship."[2]

The president also faced unexpected hostility to his court plan from two other press lords. Frank Gannett, a New York State–based media mogul who owned six radio stations and nineteen newspapers, the third-largest chain in the country, had begun the New Deal era as a Roosevelt fan, praising the president's "remarkable courage and wisdom" and "wonderful leadership."[3] But like Hearst, Gannett soon perceived Roosevelt's tax-the-rich proposals and pro-union policies as signs of collectivism, regimentation and, eventually, full-on assaults on the Constitution.

Gannett dreaded what might happen to the country if Roosevelt's court reform plan passed. "The President now dominates Congress," he wrote to a friend. "To have him also dominate the Supreme Court would give him complete control of the government. This means the end of our democracy and I am not exaggerating when I say this."[4] Gannett formed a pressure group to lobby against the court reform bill and used his newspapers to fight against that proposal and other New Deal reforms such as executive branch reorganization and a minimum wage and maximum hours bill.

Roosevelt suffered another blow when Roy Howard and his news chain defected from the New Deal coalition. The Scripps-Howard newspaper group sold 2 million daily copies and included two dozen papers, including large urban dailies like the *New York*

World-Telegram, the *Pittsburgh Press,* and the *Indianapolis News.* Howard, the chain's chief, had endorsed Roosevelt in 1932 and 1936. But when the president proposed the judicial reform bill, he pledged that his papers would "fight to the finish" to scuttle the plan. After meeting with the president in March, Howard grew convinced that Roosevelt suffered from "delusions of grandeur" and vowed to oppose his "developing greed for power."[5] The court reform plan died in committee, at that point a rare domestic failure for the president.[6]

In fall 1937, the president endured another setback when the stock market suddenly dropped and the economic recovery slowed. Up to that point in his presidency, recovery from the Depression had been rapid.[7] Then in 1937, Roosevelt abruptly cut back on government spending and tightened the money supply at the same time that Americans started to pay their first Social Security taxes. The GDP plunged as a result. The "Roosevelt Recession," as his critics termed it, turned out to be temporary.[8] But the reversal of fortune made Roosevelt vulnerable to attacks from his right.

Sensing Roosevelt's weakness, conservative Democrats in Congress began to rebel against his newest domestic reform proposals. When he called Congress into special session to consider a farm program, a wages-and-hours bill, more public power projects, and a government reorganization plan, it adjourned after passing only the farm bill.[9] A dispirited Harold Ickes feared that if the president did not go on the offensive against his critics soon, "we will very probably be engulfed in a reactionary wave and all of the benefits of the New Deal will be swept away."[10]

Quite abruptly, the advantage in the power struggle between the president and the conservative press had shifted away from Roosevelt, and Hearst and McCormick were now winning their fights against the domestic New Deal. In the context of the recession and the bitter struggle over the justices, their relentless assaults on the president as a would-be dictator and proto-communist had become more effective.

Emboldened by their victory in the court fight, the president's critics fought back when Roosevelt tried to take a more assertive stand on foreign policy. The Neutrality Act, first passed in 1935 and extended in 1936, came up for renewal early in 1937. The president sought to change the law to give him more discretion, but now too many members of Congress agreed with the Hearst, McCormick, Gannett, and Scripps-Howard press that he wanted too much power. Congress renewed the law, made it permanent, and implemented a "cash-and-carry" policy that allowed belligerent powers to buy non-military goods in the United States as long as they paid in cash and carried away the goods in their own ships.[11]

Because the cash-and-carry clause favored strong naval powers like Japan, Roosevelt faced a dilemma that summer when the simmering Sino-Japanese conflict flared into full-scale warfare. The undeclared war had begun back in 1931 when Japan seized Chinese Manchuria, prompting then secretary of war Henry Stimson to announce that the U.S. government would refuse to recognize any territory taken by force. President-elect Roosevelt and the League of Nations both endorsed the Stimson Doctrine. The Japanese, undeterred, left the League. In July 1937, their troops began to lay waste to coastal Chinese cities, killing thousands of civilians.[12]

Isolationists in the press wanted the president to respond to the East Asian conflict by invoking the Neutrality Act, including cash and carry, even though the war was undeclared. Roosevelt resisted because he knew that Japan could easily meet the act's provisions, while China had neither the money to buy supplies nor the ships to transport them.

Roosevelt decided that he needed to make a powerful statement about working with other nations to halt aggression. He gave this speech right in the heart of American isolationism: within view of the Tribune Tower and across the Chicago River from the *Tribune*'s newsprint warehouse.[13]

The ostensible occasion for the speech was the dedication of a Public Works Administration project, the Outer Drive Bridge, a limestone span that joined the northern and southern segments of Chicago's Lake Shore Drive. On October 5, 1937, an estimated half a million Chicagoans lined the streets to cheer the president in a ticker tape parade that ended at the speaker's platform on the new bridge. The president looked straight at the crowd assembled below him and did not seem to—or pretended not to—notice the sign that McCormick had ordered his workers to paint on the *Tribune* warehouse's wall in five-foot-high letters: UNDOMINATED: THE CHICAGO TRIBUNE: WORLD'S GREATEST NEWSPAPER.

Roosevelt quickly dispensed with the bridge dedication and moved on to his primary purpose. He told the crowd that "the very foundations of civilization" were threatened as belligerent nations "ruthlessly murdered" civilians in aerial bombing. "Innocent peoples, innocent nations are being cruelly sacrificed," he said, "to a greed for power and supremacy which is devoid of all sense of justice and humane considerations." If the aggressors were not stopped, "the storm will rage till every flower of culture is trampled and all human beings are leveled in a vast chaos." For the speech's most memorable language, Roosevelt used a metaphor suggested to him by Harold Ickes. "It seems to be unfortunately true that the epidemic of world lawlessness is spreading," he explained. "When an epidemic of physical disease starts to spread, the community approves and joins in a quarantine of the patients in order to protect the health of the community against the spread of the disease."[14]

Horrified by what became known as the quarantine speech, the *Tribune* and the Hearst press charged the president with scaremongering. The *Tribune*'s front-page news story on the speech contrasted the jubilant crowds who had gathered for the bridge celebration with the president's grim rhetoric. "President Roosevelt came to Chicago to bless the bridge that spans two delightful and peaceful park systems," read the story. "He talked war."[15] In a series of vituperative editorials, the *Tribune* accused the president of resurrecting the discredited policies of one of the isolationists' chief villains. "Mr. Roosevelt announced a new foreign policy for the United States," an editorial stated. "It would be more accurate to say that he readopted the foreign policy of Woodrow Wilson, the policy which brought the United States first into armed conflict with Mexico and then into the world war, the policy which was overwhelmingly rejected by the American people after the war."[16] The real danger to America, the *Tribune* concluded, came not from Japan but from the president. "America is told that it has enemies when none attacks. It is told that it has responsibilities where none exists. . . . We can keep out of war, but not by going out to meet it half way."[17]

Hearst agreed with McCormick that the president was following Woodrow Wilson's "fallacious reasoning." Instead of "assuring America of peace," Roosevelt was pursuing "the same ominous course TOWARD WAR we pursued in 1917." The best way to stay out of war was to continue "MINDING OUR OWN BUSINESS" and to "KEEP OUT OF FOREIGN ENTANGLEMENTS." If the American people listened to their president, they would be led "into the maelstrom, not away from it."[18]

Roosevelt had expected to draw McCormick's ire—he had deliberately chosen to give the address in Chicago, after all, to show that he would not be intimidated by the colonel and his newspaper. But the Hearst editorial surprised him. In an off-the-record outburst against "old man Hearst" at a press conference, he called the piece "perfectly terrible—awful" and "the silliest thing ever written." The editorial "says it means this is getting us into war and a lot of that," the president scoffed.[19]

The president reacted so strongly because he understood that Hearst wielded more influence than any other figure in media history. Even in near-bankruptcy, he commanded the attention of one in five American voters. The old press lord's opposition had not doomed the New Deal, but it could undermine the president's commitment to a multilateral foreign policy.

Hearst and McCormick continued to warn of the dangers of involvement in the Asian war as Japanese soldiers swept into China. The invaders raped, pillaged, bayoneted, and shot their way through Nanking, killing up to two hundred thousand civilians in a massacre that shocked much of the world. The conflict hit home for Americans in December, when Japanese planes bombed a clearly identified U.S. gunboat, the *Panay*, in China's Yangtze River, along with three Standard Oil tankers, and then strafed the survivors with machine-gun fire. Roosevelt sent a strong message of protest to the Japanese government and demanded compensation, along with guarantees that similar assaults would not happen again. He also considered imposing an embargo on Japan, freezing its assets, and even blockading the country. But when Japan offered money and an apology, Roosevelt agreed to accept it. Though most Americans sympathized with the Chinese, they were not ready to risk war.

The attacks on the quarantine speech by the congressional isolationists and their friends in the press forced the president to moderate his rhetoric. "As usual," Roosevelt wrote to an adviser, "we have been bombarded by Hearst and others who say that an

American search for peace means of necessity, war."[20] He warned
the British that his options were limited. He could not "afford to
be made, in popular opinion at home, a tail to the British kite, as
has been charged . . . by the Hearst press and others."[21]

Not all newspapers condemned Roosevelt as a warmonger.
Joe Patterson argued for a *more* confrontational response to Japan.
In an editorial headlined, "Shall We Take Them Now, or Try It
Later?" the *Daily News* urged Congress to repeal or revise its neutrality laws to help China. Otherwise, if the Japanese succeeded in
conquering China and setting up an East Asian empire, they might
move on to bombing San Francisco or Los Angeles, and the American people would pay in "blood, tribute, or national humiliation"
for their failure to listen to Roosevelt's warning.[22] But Patterson's
belligerent stance was rare in 1937.

Roosevelt knew that press opposition had helped defeat his Supreme Court plan; he realized that the conservative media had
worked with his opponents in Congress to halt many important
legislative reforms. Faced with the partisan commentary against his
quarantine speech, he decided to back away from interventionist
foreign policies. He was not deluded, or overly sensitive to criticism. He understood the power arrayed against him, and he would
wait and fight another day.

◾

In Britain as in the United States, the isolationist publishers' influence grew just as the argument over whether and how to resist Hitler reached a new intensity. Beaverbrook and Rothermere praised
those public officials who advocated appeasement of Hitler, while
they systematically marginalized or pilloried those who counseled
resistance—even, in one case, when these policies harmed the press
lords' longtime friendships.

None of the press barons' relationships was more strained than
the friendship between Max Beaverbrook and Winston Churchill.
The two had met in Parliament before the Great War and bonded
over their mutual love of good writing and better living. In later decades they argued furiously over the significant issues of the interwar
period, including whether to overthrow the Bolsheviks (Churchill
was in favor, Beaverbrook opposed) and abandon the gold standard
(Beaverbrook was for, Churchill against). They also endured the dis-

approval of Churchill's wife, Clementine, who did not want her husband spending time with the libertine publisher. Yet they managed to navigate these political and personal obstacles and continued to share vacations, card games, and many boozy evenings. That is, until 1938, when the love of good champagne and supple prose could not transcend their bitter clash over the proper response to the greatest challenge of the century.

As 1938 began, Adolf Hitler set his sights on invading his native country of Austria. A pan-German nationalist, Hitler had declared from the start of his political career his intention to unite Austria with Germany. Nazis had assassinated the chancellor in Vienna in 1934, but the Austrians managed to maintain their independence—for a few years. That autonomy ended on March 12, 1938, when German troops crossed the Austrian border. Austria ceased to exist as a separate nation and became a state within the Third Reich.

As Hitler motored into Austria, he claimed that "my whole country rushed to meet me without a shot being fired and without a single victim" because he had decided to "put an end to further oppression of my home country."[23] It was true that hundreds of thousands of Austrians celebrated the annexation. Jubilant crowds lined the highways between Germany and Vienna to cheer the Nazi invaders. *Daily Mail* reporter and fascist sympathizer G. Ward Price rode in the Nazi leadership convoy and reported that throngs of elated Austrians showered the Führer with flowers. "The whole population was on the roadside," he wrote in the *Mail*, "shouting 'Heil Hitler,' and that slogan which has settled the fate of Austria—'One folk, one State, one Leader.' "[24] Price reported that the Austrian people were delirious with joy as they greeted their new leader, whom he called their "national saviour."[25]

Yet the Anschluss, as the invasion was called, was hardly joyous for all Austrians. The first few weeks of the German occupation were "an orgy of sadism," according to *CBS News* reporter William Shirer, as the Nazis celebrated their victory by terrorizing Viennese Jews and other anti-fascists. The German soldiers and their Austrian collaborators smashed windows, looted houses, and imprisoned and shot resisters. Storm Troopers dragged Jews into the streets to scrub anti-Nazi graffiti off walls and sidewalks and clean public toilets. Thousands of Austrian Jews were sent to concentration camps.[26]

Several thousand more committed suicide rather than submit to Nazi rule.

Unlike their counterparts at the *Mail*, *Daily Express* reporters did tell their readers about the Vienna terror.[27] But Beaverbrook's editorials assured *Express* readers that they had no responsibility to prevent the pogroms described on the news pages. According to the *Express*, the proper course for Britain was clear: "Mind our own business!"[28] Even before the Anschluss, the *Express* had counseled the British government not to "infuriate" the Nazis by protesting a German annexation of Austria. "It is we who should get out and stay out," the *Express* proclaimed. "We have no business whatever to forbid the German peoples to unite. Our business is to unite our own peoples in our own commonwealth by a policy of Empire Free Trade and Splendid Isolation."[29]

The American isolationist newspapers echoed Beaverbrook's call to stay out of central European politics. The *Chicago Tribune* blamed Britain and France for Hitler's invasion because those nations had given him an imperialistic model to follow. Hearst signed a front-page editorial declaring that isolation had brought the United States a "hundred years of peace and prosperity" while "participation in world affairs" brought nothing but war.[30] The *Daily News* cautioned Britain and France against confronting Hitler over the murders of Viennese Jews, reasoning that a European war would be worse for the Jews than any Nazi pogrom.[31]

The *News* need not have worried. Prime Minister Neville Chamberlain, who had succeeded Stanley Baldwin in 1937, had no intention of confronting Hitler over the treatment of the Austrian Jews. He viewed the Anschluss with disappointment, but also with relief that it had taken place without a clash of armies.

Chamberlain's enthusiasm for appeasing the fascists opened a rupture within the ruling Conservative Party. Foreign Secretary Anthony Eden disagreed so sharply with Chamberlain on how to deal with the dictators that he got into a shouting match with the prime minister during negotiations with the Italian ambassador.[32] Eden also believed that Britain needed to rearm at a much faster pace. By late February 1938, the dispute between the foreign secretary and the prime minister led to Eden's resignation from the government.

He was replaced by Lord Halifax, who strongly backed Chamberlain on appeasement.

Beaverbrook found himself warming to the new prime minister, who earlier had failed to impress him.[33] After the Anschluss, the *Express* noted that Chamberlain was clearly against any intervention in Europe. "And as anybody who is not an interventionist is in a sense an Isolationist," the paper editorialized, "we give thanks for small mercies."[34] In a private letter, Beaverbrook went even further, calling Chamberlain "the best P.M. we've had in half a century."[35]

One of Beaverbrook's most prominent columnists disagreed emphatically. Winston Churchill had been out of the Tory leadership since 1931, when he resigned over the decision to support a gradual transition toward Indian independence, and he would remain out until 1939, when the start of the war in Europe would force Chamberlain to acknowledge that Churchill's warnings about the Nazis had been correct. During this period, his "wilderness years," Churchill earned money and stayed in the public eye by writing for several British and American newspapers, including Beaverbrook's most independent publication, the *Evening Standard*.[36] In contrast to his policy for the *Daily Express* and *Sunday Express*, Beaverbrook tolerated some ideological diversity on the *Standard*, which also published the cartoonist David Low, an inveterate antifascist. Still, a postwar study found that the *Standard* from 1936 to 1939 pursued "an absolutely consistent policy of isolation, and that it gave unqualified support to the Chamberlain policy of appeasement."[37] Even Beaverbrook's least predictable publication was, in the end, predictable.

Churchill believed Hitler posed an existential threat to the British Empire. In a frank talk with the Soviet ambassador to Britain, Ivan Maisky, he explained that Hitler's Germany endangered the British far more than did Stalin's Russia. "Today," he told Maisky, "the greatest menace to the British Empire is German Nazism, with its idea of Berlin's global hegemony. That is why, at the present time, I spare no effort in the struggle against Hitler." But if the fascist threat ever ended and the "communist menace" threatened the empire, then, he explained, "I would raise the banner of struggle against you once more."[38]

Churchill's strong stand against the Nazis appalled and concerned Beaverbrook. In February 1938, the *Express* accused Churchill of aiding "the most violent, foolish, and dangerous campaign to drive this country into war since he drove us into it himself against Russia in 1919." At the time of the Bolshevik Revolution, the *Express* said, Churchill and other anti-communists had wasted British and Allied lives and money on invading Russia because of their unjustified fear that communism would sweep across the globe. "Now," the *Express* continued, "Winston fears that Fascism will engulf our civilisation. It won't. There is no need to try to stamp it out. It is not our business to stamp it out."[39] In other words, the editorial voice of one Beaverbrook paper, the *Express*, condemned the columnist of another Beaverbrook paper, the *Standard*. The contradiction was not sustainable.

The break came the next month. In a dramatic speech in the House of Commons after the Anschluss, Churchill made clear his opposition to the appeasement policies of Chamberlain and Beaverbrook. He denounced the "rape of Austria" and called for a stronger alliance with France, a guarantee to Czechoslovakia, and rapid rearmament—only the last of which was supported by the prime minister and by the proprietor of the *Standard*. "If we do not stand up to the dictators now," Churchill declared, "we shall only prepare the day when we have to stand up to them in far more adverse conditions."[40]

For Beaverbrook, the "rape of Austria" speech was the final straw. On the day of the speech, the *Evening Standard*'s editor, R. J. Thompson, informed its famous columnist that the paper would no longer need his services. The *Standard*'s association with Churchill had "given our columns a rare lustre," Thompson conceded, but his "views on foreign affairs and the part which this country should play are entirely opposed to those held by us."[41]

Churchill quickly rebounded and signed a deal with the *Daily Telegraph*. But he remained angry over his old friend's decision to sack him. "I rather thought," he wrote to Thompson in response to his termination, "that Lord Beaverbrook prided himself upon forming a platform in the Evening Standard for various opinions including of course his own."[42]

Churchill did not know the full intensity of Beaverbrook's fury. At about the same time that he ordered his editor to fire Churchill,

Beaverbrook summoned one of his reporters, Patrick Campbell of the *Evening Standard*, to the press lord's mansion, Stornoway House. As the two men stood in a small garden attached to the house, Beaverbrook disparaged his longtime friend. "This man Churchill," he told the reporter, "is the enemy of the British Empire." Campbell was so startled by the outburst that he stepped backward into a muddy flowerbed. Beaverbrook told him that Churchill was a "warmonger" who was "turning the thoughts of the peoples of the British Empire to war." He asked Campbell to make a dossier of clippings of Churchill's speeches. Churchill "must be stopped," Beaverbrook concluded. "Go get him. . . . Do it now." He then noted with amusement that Campbell's shoe was coated with mud. "I see you're in it already," he chuckled. The reporter hurried off to collect warmongering quotes from the future prime minister. Campbell never knew what, if anything, Beaverbrook did with the information he gathered.[43]

■

After the Anschluss, anti-Nazi Europeans waited in dread for Germany's next move. Czechoslovakia, the lone surviving democracy in central and eastern Europe, was clearly Hitler's next target. Most of the country's 3.25 million Germans lived on the German and Austrian borders in the Sudetenland region. Hitler sought to enfold them within the Reich; perhaps more important, he wanted to seize the region's military fortifications, factories, and prime agricultural land. Both France and the Soviet Union had defensive treaties with Czechoslovakia. If Hitler wished to avoid a continental war, he would need to bully the French and the Soviets into reneging on their treaty obligations—and to do that, he needed British help, or at least acquiescence.

In a venomous speech in Nuremberg at the Nazi party conference in September, Hitler insisted that the Sudeten Germans were suffering "tortures and oppression" under Czech rule and pledged to liberate them.[44] He secretly directed the leaders of the Sudeten German fascist party to refuse any concessions from Prague for self-rule and to prepare for a German invasion.

The British had several options for responding to the threats. They could work with the French, the Soviets, and the League of Nations to organize collective resistance to the Nazis; they could offer to help France if it went to war against Germany over the Sudetenland; or they could do nothing.

The first two options might lead to war, but ignoring Hitler's aggression would also come at a cost. Beyond the humanitarian crisis that would result from allowing a fascist aggressor to dismember a democratic ally, an Anglo-French agreement to stand aside while Hitler took the Sudetenland would make him immeasurably stronger. The citizens of Czechoslovakia would lose more than eleven thousand square miles of land, as well as their most productive industries and their ability to defend themselves against German invasion. Czechoslovakia and the rest of central Europe would be at the Nazis' mercy. Churchill understood these terrible consequences at the time. "We seem to be very near the bleak choice between War and Shame," he wrote a friend in mid-September 1938. "My feeling is that we shall choose Shame, and then have War thrown in a little later on even more adverse terms than at present."[45]

Prime Minister Chamberlain thought otherwise. In his view, Hitler wanted only to unite all Germans into one country, and he would go no further. The prime minister refused to respond to Soviet overtures to build an alliance between the Western democracies and the USSR to fight Hitler on two fronts, and he made it clear to the French that Britain would not support them if they decided to honor their commitment to Czechoslovakia. In September 1938, he flew three times to Germany to meet personally with Hitler, each time offering concessions to the Nazi dictator.

Beaverbrook's *Daily Express* provided consistent and enthusiastic support for the prime minister's policies and his assessment of Hitler's fundamental rationality. On September 1, 1938, a front-page editorial signed by Beaverbrook himself carried the headline "THERE WILL BE NO WAR"—a headline the paper would repeat often over the next year, right up to the outbreak of war. The press lord argued that the Nazi dictator was simply too reasonable to opt for war at the moment. "Hitler has shown himself throughout his career to be a man of exceptional astuteness," Beaverbrook opined. The Nazis were not ready for a war, and the German public would not support one. It was absurd to think that Hitler would choose war under those circumstances.[46] Privately, Beaverbrook assured British government officials throughout the fall that he would place his publishing empire at their disposal. "My newspapers will do anything to help you in your difficult negotiations with these Central European countries," he wrote the foreign secretary. "Or indeed," he added, "*in any direction.* Besides, I am in agreement with your policy, and I can give you the strongest support."[47]

Harold Rothermere no longer controlled the *Daily Mail* at the time of the Sudeten crisis, but he did what he could to help the cause of appeasement. In April 1938, on the occasion of his seventieth birthday, he had turned the paper over to Esmond Harmsworth, his surviving son and heir. Harmsworth believed his father's political activism had hurt the *Mail*'s circulation. Readership had declined slightly in 1930, when Rothermere tried to depose Stanley Baldwin as Conservative Party leader; failed to regain any ground during the *Mail*'s pro-Mosley period; and started to slide in earnest in 1935, as Rothermere persisted in backing Hitler even as other British papers began to see him as a threat.[48]

But although Rothermere no longer directly managed the paper, he still wrote occasional pro-Nazi articles and editorials, and kept up a friendly correspondence with Hitler. In May 1938, he assured his readers that they could trust Hitler's word: "There is no man living whose promise given in regard to something of real moment I would sooner take." The German dictator was a gentleman with a "great sense of the sanctity of the family."[49] In addition to Rothermere's personal articles, moreover, the *Mail*'s editorial policy remained firmly in favor of appeasement. It vigorously backed the prime minister and maintained that the British should not impede Hitler's quest to unite his "race" under the swastika.[50]

The *Daily Express* and *Daily Mail* were far from alone in supporting Chamberlain and appeasement. The *Times* of London, owned by Lord Astor and edited by the pro-appeasement Geoffrey Dawson, rivaled the *Express* and the *Mail* in its support for the Nazi takeover of the Sudetenland. The national newspapers' backing for appeasement dismayed the career diplomats in the Foreign Office who wanted Chamberlain to take a harder line with Hitler. They believed that the isolationist press had failed to inform the British people of the Nazi threat. "Lord Beaverbrook and other 'peace at any price' publicists," one official wrote, "must bear a heavy share of the blame."[51]

Though many British newspapers endorsed appeasement in 1938, only Beaverbrook and Rothermere went so far as to ask the cabinet for more government control over the press—in effect, for the state to work harder to spin the news. "The newspapers are all anxious to help the Prime Minister and to help you," Beaverbrook wrote to the foreign secretary, Lord Halifax, on September 16, 1938. But they needed "guidance" from the cabinet. He urged Halifax to designate a minister "to guide the newspapers in their policy, to strike out errors and to crush rumours."[52] On the same day, he made a similar plea to the prime minister, recommending that Chamberlain ask Beaverbrook's good friend, Home Secretary Sam Hoare, to meet with journalists and steer their coverage.[53] Chamberlain agreed, and Hoare soon began conducting daily meetings with the nation's top editors. Rothermere sent his own plea to Halifax, asking the government to curb newspapers whose inflammatory "cartoons and comments" against Germany might provoke a war.[54]

Beaverbrook and Rothermere wanted the government to manage their rivals' newspapers, not their own, for their news stories and editorials already put an exceptionally positive spin on Chamberlain's policies. Beaverbrook's *Daily Express* in particular acted as the government's mouthpiece. On September 22, for example, while the prime minister was in Germany, Beaverbrook personally wrote a front-page editorial that could have come straight from Chamberlain. Under the headline "THIS IS THE TRUTH," he asserted that Britain had "no duty or responsibility whatsoever" to defend Czechoslovakia; moreover, it was "wicked and untrue" to accuse Britain "of selling [out] Czecho-Slovakia or of deserting France."[55]

Though Beaverbrook thought it "wicked" to say so, Britain had in fact decided to abandon the Czechs. Chamberlain did not want to risk war over the Sudetenland. And as it became clear that Britain would not resist the Nazi invasion, the French government's resolve collapsed. The Soviets, in turn, had no intention of defending the Czechs without French and British help. Britain and France worked together to pressure Czechoslovakia to arrange a gradual transfer of the Sudetenland to Germany.

Yet even this concession was not enough. Hitler's demand for the immediate, rather than gradual, cession of the Sudeten territories plunged Europe into a crisis. The British mobilized their navy, while the French and the Czech armies prepared for battle. On September 27, in a nationwide radio address, Chamberlain expressed amazement that the British might fight the Germans for the second time in a generation—this time to save a country in central Europe. "How horrible, fantastic, incredible it is that we should be digging trenches," he said, "because of a quarrel in a faraway country between people of whom we know nothing!"[56]

Then, as Chamberlain spoke to the House of Commons about the coming war, Hitler abruptly changed his mind. He sent a message to the British prime minister inviting him, along with French prime minister Edouard Daladier and Italy's Benito Mussolini, to a summit in Munich. It was Chamberlain's third meeting with Hitler that month. At the conference, the Nazi dictator agreed to wait ten days before occupying the Sudetenland; in return for French and British acquiescence, he promised not to take any more territory. The summit ended with Chamberlain and Hitler signing an agreement "symbolic of the desire of our two peoples never to go to war with one another again."[57] Thanks to Munich, there would be no more war.

The *Daily Express* announced its approval of the agreement with a one-word headline across five columns, set in the biggest type ever used by a British newspaper up to that time: "PEACE." The typesetters did not have large enough blocks and had to ask for help from the photography processing department.[58] Above the headline ran this emphatic sentence: "The *Daily Express* declares that Britain will not be involved in a European war this year, or next year either."[59] Londoners were eager to hear Beaverbrook's message. Two hundred people mobbed *Express* sellers at midnight in Piccadilly as they brought out the first copies of the day's edition.[60]

Chamberlain returned to London to cheering throngs—to Britons "aflame," as the *Express* said, with "enthusiasm for the ender of crises."[61] The crowds screamed their approval first at the airport, where the prime minister triumphantly held the agreement above his head, then at Buckingham Palace, where he and his wife waved at the crowds from the balcony, and finally at 10 Downing Street, where he leaned out of a window to proclaim that he had brought back "peace with honour. I believe it is peace for our time."[62]

The *Daily Express* edition of September 30, 1938, celebrated the Munich peace agreement with the biggest type ever used by a British newspaper. (John Frost Newspapers / Alamy Stock Photo)

In its lead news story, the *Express* echoed Chamberlain's declaration that the Munich agreement guaranteed that Germany and Britain would never go to war again. "You may sleep quietly—it is peace for our time," the newspaper assured its readers.[63] Hitler had a different view. He said privately to his irritated foreign minister, Joachim von Ribbentrop: "Oh, don't take it all so seriously. That piece of paper is of no significance whatsoever."[64]

The editorial writers of the British press were nearly unanimous in their enthusiasm for a prime minister they described as resolute, noble, and courageous.[65] American isolationists joined the chorus of praise. Joe Patterson's *Daily News* compared Chamberlain to Abraham Lincoln (the greatest American, in the view of the grandson of Joseph Medill, one of Lincoln's biggest boosters) and to Jesus Christ.[66]

Some Britons did castigate the prime minister for betraying the Czechs and failing to resist Hitler's demands. The leader of the opposition, Labour's Clement Attlee, called the agreement "a tremendous victory for Herr Hitler." Tory dissenter Churchill termed it "a total and unmitigated defeat" for Britain and predicted that the Reich would soon absorb the rest of Czechoslovakia.[67] In response, Beaverbrook snidely wrote to an American editor that Churchill's political career was over. "This man of brilliant talent, splendid abilities, magnificent power of speech, and fine stylist," he wrote, "has ceased to influence the British public."[68]

The Czech ambassador to Britain, Jan Masaryk, pronounced the most ominous judgment: "If you have sacrificed my nation to preserve the peace of the world, I will be the first to applaud you," he told Chamberlain and Halifax. "But if not, gentlemen, God help your souls."[69] Though three members of Chamberlain's cabinet considered resigning over the agreement, only one, Duff Cooper, actually did, saying that it was the prime minister's "peace with honor" speech that pushed him over the edge. If Chamberlain had "come back from Munich saying, 'peace with terrible, unmitigated, unparalleled dishonour,' perhaps I would have stayed," Cooper said. "But peace with *honour!*"[70]

Many British journalists abhorred the newspaper owners' policies. Two *Times* reporters quit in disgust over their paper's pro-Munich stance, and correspondents for Rothermere's *Daily Mail* and Beaverbrook's *Daily Express* seriously considered resigning as well.[71]

If Cooper, Churchill, and the other anti-appeasers had received the fawning press treatment Chamberlain enjoyed, they might have been able to turn public opinion against appeasement much earlier. The British public was deeply divided on the issue.[72] In the midst of the Czech crisis, on September 22, 1938, when Hitler suddenly increased his demands, 44 percent of Britons reported that they were "indignant," while only 18 percent said they strongly supported the prime minister.[73] After Munich, despite overwhelmingly favorable press coverage, a surprisingly large minority—39 percent—told pollsters that they were dissatisfied with the prime minister. Most notably, 93 percent stated they did not credit Hitler's promise not to take more territory.[74]

Beaverbrook and other appeasers among the press lords shaped public views of the Sudeten crisis and the Munich agreement. By lauding Chamberlain and ignoring or dismissing those like Cooper and Churchill who argued for resisting the Nazis, the newspaper proprietors eagerly served as propagandists for the appeasers in the British government. Public opinion at the time was divided and malleable; polls suggested that many Britons were skeptical of Chamberlain's policies. But the newspapers most Britons read every day—their main source of foreign news—assured them that Hitler was reasonable, that Churchill and other resisters were obtuse, and that Chamberlain was committed to peace and order.

Meanwhile, Chamberlain's temporizing gave Germany time to speed up its rearmament. The Munich agreement provided Germany with land, industries, and resources in central Europe. As Churchill had predicted, the war came anyway, but on worse terms for the democracies.[75]

Perhaps most important, Munich taught Hitler some valuable lessons. He learned that the Western democracies did not have the will to stop him. "Our enemies are small worms," he would say the next year as he prepared to invade Poland. "I saw them in Munich."[76]

■

The worms had decided to appease the Nazis in part because of the role played by the most powerful media lords on both sides of the Atlantic. In the United States, Roosevelt tried to challenge the isolationists in Chicago, their capital city, and the press barons beat him back; in the United Kingdom, the media moguls suppressed the loudest interventionist voice and abetted the policy of appeasement. The leaders who believed in the necessity of resisting fascism approached 1939 with less influence and great foreboding.

CHAPTER EIGHT

"Hitler Agrees with the
Daily Express"

A MONTH AFTER THE Munich pact, German mobs, abetted by Storm Troopers and police, smashed the windows of Jewish stores and looted them, dragged Jews from their homes, and beat them in the streets. The Nazis wrecked thousands of properties, killed hundreds, and burned or blew up more than a thousand synagogues. Using the assassination of a German diplomat in Paris as a pretext, Hitler's regime provoked and encouraged anti-Semitic violence throughout the Reich. The Gestapo rounded up thirty thousand Jews and sent them to concentration camps, where hundreds of them perished in the ensuing weeks. Because of the broken glass on the streets, the press termed the violence Kristallnacht.[1]

The attacks greatly disturbed the isolationist publishers—not because of the state-sanctioned murders and other atrocities but because they thought Jews in their own countries might drag them into war in an effort to prevent further outrages. They feared that sympathy for the victims could undermine public support for appeasement and isolation.

The press lords' reaction to the pogrom laid bare how much their determination to ignore or appease Hitler was informed by anti-Semitism. Through the rest of 1938 and 1939, the isolationist press barons in Britain and the United States repeatedly stated (in private letters) or implied (in their editorials and news stories) that Jews in media and government, who did not have their country's best interests at heart, were conspiring to draw their nations into war.

Despite the isolationists' worries, it was not Nazi violence against German Jews but Hitler's refusal to keep his promises that finally convinced many policy makers in Britain to begin to abandon appeasement. But not even those broken promises—not even the Nazi invasion of Prague or Warsaw—ended isolationism in the United States.

■

Hitler's regime followed the bloodshed of Kristallnacht by issuing more anti-Semitic laws. The Reich ousted Jews from schools and universities, banned them from sections of Berlin, confiscated their property and artworks, prohibited them from most jobs, and levied a $400 million fine on the Jewish community for allegedly provoking the assaults against them. Nazi officials used explicitly anti-Semitic language to justify both the laws and the mob attacks. Julius Streicher, a prominent Hitler adviser, claimed that the pogroms would rid the world of a "poisonous germ. ... God entrusted the German nation with the task of solving the Jewish problem. When this question is solved in Germany it will be solved in the world."[2]

Even some of the strongest advocates of appeasement in the British press were horrified by the riots and their aftermath. The *Daily Mail*, now edited by Esmond Harmsworth and "entirely in [his] hands," according to his father, struck a new note of disgust at the Nazis' brutality.[3] A *Mail* editorial explained that though life had been difficult for German Jews before, "now they are denied not only freedom of movement and opportunities for advancement but almost the right to live."[4] The London *Times*, another reliable instrument of the appeasers, also published a scathing editorial. "No foreign propagandist bent upon blackening Germany before the world," the *Times* declared, "could outdo the tale of burnings and beatings, of blackguardly assaults upon defenceless and innocent people, which disgraced that country yesterday."[5]

Yet Beaverbrook's *Express* initially downplayed German atrocities in its news stories and editorials, or else tried to fix blame on out-of-control mobs rather than Nazi leaders. "LOOTING MOBS DEFY GOEBBELS" read the headline on the first *Express* story about Kristallnacht, implying that German leaders were trying to stop the brutality rather than inciting it.[6] The paper's editorial that day blamed the riots on the seventeen-year-old Pole whose assassination of a Nazi official in Paris had provided the pretext for the pogrom ("He has furnished to the enemies of his people an occasion and a motive, but certainly not a justification, for persecution and spoliation of the race everywhere").[7] An editorial graphic the next day pointed out that "more than half the continent is anti-Semitic," suggesting that the Nazi actions were not unusual.[8]

The *Express* soon began to print stories that depicted, in vivid language, the horrors of Kristallnacht. But its editorials still repeatedly urged the British people to avoid "recriminations" that might antagonize the Germans. "Both sides"—the British and the Germans—deployed unjustified and inflated rhetoric, the *Express* argued, and each nation needed to let the other handle a "domestic issue" without interference.[9] The *Express* insisted that it had "the greatest sympathy with the Jews" and that it deplored their persecution. In the end, though, it was best for the British to avoid provoking the Nazis. "Take counsel," the newspaper told its readers, "in the age-old saying which has now indeed become a commonplace: 'Least said, soonest mended.' "[10] Beaverbrook and other isolationists showed little sympathy for the suffering of German Jews or concern for protecting universal human rights.

Even as he advised readers to avert their eyes, Beaverbrook fretted that British Jews' sympathy for the victims of Nazi persecution would pull their country into conflict with Germany. In December 1938, the month after Kristallnacht, he complained in a private letter to Frank Gannett, the American newspaper publisher, that Jews were "drawing us into war." Jews "have got a big position" in the British press, he wrote. "I estimate that one-third of the circulation of the *Daily Telegraph* is Jewish. The *Daily Mirror* may be owned by Jews. The *Daily Herald* is owned by Jews. And the *News-Chronicle* should really be the *Jews-Chronicle*." After the last sentence, he added an asterisk: "not on account of ownership but because of sympathy."[11] At the time, Jews comprised less than 1 percent of the British

population, and only one press baron, the *Daily Herald*'s Lord South-
wood, was Jewish.

After expressing his concerns to Gannett, Beaverbrook followed
with a public letter to Joe Patterson at the *Daily News* about various
groups' allegedly nefarious influence on British foreign policy. He
lamented the opposition of the "Jews to a man and a woman, the
Die-hard Tories, the Labour Party and the Communists" to Chamberlain's efforts to appease the Germans. These warmongers, he argued, could drag the British into a European conflict.[12]

Patterson published part of Beaverbrook's letter, which he attributed to a "friend in London," in a *Daily News* editorial, and proceeded to elaborate on its meaning. "The Jews have great financial
and social influence in Britain, what with the large number of busted
or bent British aristocrats who have found it feasible to get the old
ancestral halls repaired by marrying heiresses to Jewish fortunes,"
the *News* explained. These influential Jews could combine with Tory
imperialists and Communist traitors to defeat the appeasers. The
predictable lesson was that America should stay out of Europe. "Our
reaction to it all," the editorial concluded, "is that the United States
should use the greatest caution in its foreign policy in the months to
come—and that isolation should be the keynote of that policy."[13]

In its own editorials about Kristallnacht, the *News*, like the
Daily Express, suggested that the mobs were anarchic, not directed
by the German government. The riots proved "that Hitler can no
longer control his people; that he is losing his grip to the born-thief
element" who were looting Jewish stores because they were hungry
or greedy. The *News* even maintained that the mobs were not particularly anti-Semitic and would soon turn on Gentile stores, or
maybe attack Catholics.[14] Moreover, the violence on display during
Kristallnacht was not especially noteworthy: "Stalin has killed more
Jews in the last two years than Hitler has in five," an editorial alleged. Many governments throughout history had confiscated citizens' property, the newspaper contended; the U.S. government
itself had done so during the Civil War.[15]

The *News* concluded, as did the *Daily Express*, that American
protests against German violence would actually hurt the victims.
One editorial bizarrely compared American diplomatic relations

with Hitler to negotiating with someone with odd personal habits. "In a business deal, you don't call the man you're dealing with names if you hope to put over the deal," it argued. "You negotiate with him, treat him politely, regardless of what you may think of his private life, his manners, his morals or the way he wears his hair."[16] By equating lethal pogroms with unconventional hairstyles, Patterson signaled that the Nazis' anti-Semitism was rhetorical or strategic, not ideological, and thus easily changed.[17]

A month after Kristallnacht, the *Daily News* published the first of many stories that would earn it a reputation for anti-Semitism. The paper's Washington correspondents reported that Congress would investigate "a bold attempt to create anti-Semitic feeling"—charges by the American fascist William Pelley, the head of the Silver Legion, that 275 Jews in the Roosevelt administration secretly ran the country. While appearing to deplore the accusations, the *News* helped spread the misinformation by printing the entire list of names of the supposed secret rulers, with pictures of the most prominent.[18] In an editorial, the paper condemned the allegations, yet it also commented that "plenty of people just now are exercising their right to dislike the Jews." The "racial faults" of "Old World Jews" and the tendency of Jews to be "too slick" explained this hatred, the *News* contended, even as it urged Gentiles to be more tolerant.[19]

In much of the press, Kristallnacht had prompted sympathy and horror, but for Patterson and Beaverbrook, the pogrom inspired public and private concern than Jews had too much influence. Their arguments echoed the Nazi line: Jews were devious and domineering; they had insinuated themselves into key positions in the bureaucracy and the media; and they would use this power to manipulate their governments to support their racial kin in Germany, against the interests of the real Americans or "the British race."

∎

The *Daily News* began to write about supposed Jewish influence in the New Deal precisely when President Roosevelt began taking a stronger stance against German fascism. That was no coincidence. Unlike Beaverbrook, who, in backing appeasement, needed only to cheer on the appeasers on Downing Street, Patterson faced a much greater test. As 1939 began, he and other isolationists in the media confronted an increasingly vocal anti-fascist in the White House.

Kristallnacht horrified Roosevelt on a visceral level. Even though he had distrusted the Nazis for years, the pogrom against German and Austrian Jews marked a turning point for him. He counted Jews among his close friends and was genuinely appalled by the Nazis' brutality. He began to see Hitler as inherently irrational—a "wild man" who "believes himself to be a reincarnation of Julius Caesar and Jesus Christ," as he told a group of senators early in 1939—and therefore a leader who could not be appeased.[20] He also worried that the Nazi regime posed a genuine threat to democracy worldwide and to U.S. security. On November 14, less than a week after Kristallnacht, the president convened a secret meeting of military leaders and warned them that the United States needed to increase its airplane production capacity from twelve hundred to ten thousand planes per year to prepare to meet the Nazi threat.[21]

Publicly, at a press conference the next day, Roosevelt announced that Americans were "deeply shocked" by the pogroms and that he himself could "scarcely believe that such things could occur in the twentieth century of civilization."[22] He stunned the Germans by recalling the American ambassador, who would never return to his post in Nazi Germany. The appeasers in the British and French governments worried—correctly, as it turned out—that Roosevelt's response portended a new, more strongly anti-Nazi policy for the United States.[23]

In his State of the Union address of 1939, the president continued to speak about the menace of dictatorships abroad. He argued that Americans needed to "prepare to defend not their homes alone but the tenets of their faith and humanity on which their churches, their governments and their very civilization are founded." He asked Congress to appropriate an additional half-billion dollars for defense spending and to revise the Neutrality Act. Nothing less than the "defense of religion, of democracy, and of good faith among nations" was at stake. "To save one we must now make up our minds to save all."[24]

But Roosevelt's campaign to awaken the American public to the dangers of Nazi Germany faced a stiff challenge: American anti-Semitism, abetted by the popular press. American voters had to be convinced that resisting Hitler would not lead to a war to save Jews. As in Britain, deep prejudice prompted Americans to blame Jews for others' hatred of them. In April 1938, 58 percent of Americans told pollsters that the anti-Semitic persecution in Europe was wholly or partly the Jews' fault.[25]

A large majority of Americans did not even want to allow more Jewish refugees fleeing Nazi violence to immigrate to the United States. Congress had staunched the flow of immigrants in 1924 by passing the National Origins Act, a law with such explicitly racist conditions and results that Hitler envied it.[26] It banned most immigration from Asia and allotted quotas to European countries. A regulation promulgated by President Hoover in 1930 further reduced immigration by requiring all potential newcomers to prove they would not become a "public charge," meaning that they had to arrive with enough money to support themselves and their families for an indefinite period. Because Nazi Germany refused to allow Jews to take their money out of the country, very few refugees were admitted. U.S. immigration quotas allowed more than twenty-five thousand immigrants from Germany per year, but most of those slots went unfilled.[27]

In 1937 and 1938, President Roosevelt took some administrative steps to allow more Jews fleeing Hitler to enter the United States. He combined the German and Austrian quotas, extended the temporary visas of visiting Germans, and quietly ordered the State Department to relax its interpretation of the public charge provision. German and Austrian immigrants to the United States used all of their quota slots in 1939.[28]

But Roosevelt hesitated to do more. Only 5 percent of Americans in 1938 wanted to raise immigration quotas to admit more refugees, and two-thirds sought to keep out all refugees, even those allowed under the existing quotas.[29] The young did not escape discrimination. Two-thirds of Americans opposed a 1939 bill to allow ten thousand German refugee children—most of them Jewish—to come to the United States.[30]

The president worried that measures to help Jewish refugees might provoke an anti-Semitic backlash that would prevent him from achieving his overall goal of preparing Americans to resist

Nazism. Historian Robert Herzstein, in *Roosevelt and Hitler*, asks his readers to remember Roosevelt's entire record on Nazi anti-Semitism, not just his reluctance to revise immigration quotas. The president's "increasingly bold" anti-fascist policies, Herzstein contends, "would one day culminate in the isolation of the anti-Semitic right at home, and the destruction of the Nazi regime in Europe."[31] Allan Lichtman and Richard Breitman, in *FDR and the Jews*, come to a similar conclusion: "Oddly enough, he did more for the Jews than any other world figure, even if his efforts seem deficient in retrospect. He was a far better president for Jews than any of his political adversaries would have been."[32]

By early 1939, the isolationists recognized that Roosevelt was becoming an increasingly bold enemy of their cause. One of his most important supporters in the press, Joe Patterson, began to worry that the man he had called "one of our greatest presidents" was now, as he wrote to Beaverbrook, "acting contrary to the wishes of most of his followers in his present foreign policy." Roosevelt's anti-fascist tendencies made it all the more important for Britain to continue to appease, not resist, Hitler; otherwise, both Britain and America could get drawn into a conflagration. "Of course, in the event of war," Patterson added, "our sympathies would get aroused as they did before and in the end we too might be in it. That's what I'm afraid of."[33]

∎

Though Patterson worried about his country's sympathies leading to war, Beaverbrook was bullish about the prospects for isolation in Britain. In a front-page, signed editorial in the *Daily Express*, he assured his readers that neither Germany nor Italy would ever invade France. "Such an enterprise would be madness. And the dictators are not lunatics." Those who said differently were "counsellors of evil." He urged his readers to "reject with indignation the false and malicious tales of decadence and defeatism."[34] After Hitler gave a speech in January 1939 in which he threatened to annihilate the Jews of Europe, the *Daily Express* chose to interpret other parts of the speech as a Nazi pledge of peace: "Now we know that Hitler agrees with the Daily Express. He says that he expects there will be peace for a long time. . . . There will be no war involving Britain in 1939."[35] In a letter to Patterson, Beaverbrook explained that Hitler would be constrained by his people. "Dictators are just like other types of government," he wrote. "They rule within the limits which the population permits."[36]

But Beaverbrook's rosy view of the European future received a shock in March. In direct violation of the agreement he had made the previous September in Munich, Hitler sent German troops to take over the rest of Czechoslovakia. Chamberlain realized he had been betrayed. His government sped up rearmament and introduced the first peacetime draft in British history. Even more significant, fearing an immediate German strike on Poland, Chamberlain's government pledged to secure the Polish borders. Soon it would follow with guarantees for Romania, Greece, and Turkey.

To that point, many in Britain had assured themselves that Hitler only wanted to unite all German-speaking peoples, but the Czech coup destroyed that illusion. The *Daily Telegraph* editorialized that with the Czech invasion, Hitler had "dropped the mask"; the *Times* wrote that "no defence of any kind, no pretext of the slightest plausibility, can be offered for the violent extinction of Czech independence."[37] The German government acknowledged this transformation of mainstream British media opinion with a memorandum excoriating "the anti-German attitude of the British Press, prompted by the British Government."[38]

Even the *Daily Mail* under Esmond Harmsworth abandoned appeasement after Prague. The change in the *Mail*'s editorial line was dramatic. On March 11, shortly before the coup, the *Mail* had argued that a Nazi takeover in Czechoslovakia need not concern the British: "It is only a move in the map-making which we must expect to go on in Middle Europe for many years to come."[39] Right after the invasion, the *Mail*'s editorials on March 15 and 16 used the passive voice: Czechoslovakia "has fallen into its constituent parts," and its destruction was natural and inevitable and "due to internal disruption, not to external aggression."[40] In any event, the outcome was positive: "Another big mistake made at Versailles has been rectified. Europe should rejoice that more frontiers have been changed without resort to a big conflict."[41] But suddenly, two days later, the *Mail* editors seemed to realize the enormity of what had happened. The German invasion was no cause to rejoice; instead, the *Mail* condemned Hitler for the "ruthless crushing" of a "free and sovereign people" and asked what his next step would be. "The question of whether or not he has embarked on a policy of unlimited expansion," the *Mail* suggested, "is of crucial importance to Europe."[42]

The new tone of resistance in previously pro-appeasement newspapers helped change British policy makers' perceptions of public opinion. Historian Daniel Hucker has found that the British public had actually turned against appeasement months earlier, shortly after Munich. But British elites did not realize or acknowledge this shift until the Prague invasion caused newspapers to catch up with their readers.[43] Chamberlain wanted desperately to believe what he read in the *Daily Express*—that the British public still supported appeasement. But as the other conservative papers expressed outrage over Prague, the prime minister realized that his policies were not as popular as Beaverbrook told him they were.

Since Harold Rothermere was retired, Beaverbrook stood alone among the press lords in insisting that the conquest of Czechoslovakia could not "possibly be a matter of concern for Britain," as the *Express* contended in an editorial. "Those distant regions on the Danube lie quite outside our bailiwick. We cannot be expected to influence the course of events there."[44] Beaverbrook also refused to endorse Chamberlain's pledge to protect Poland, despite its popularity. "There is no discordant voice anywhere save only from this newspaper," an editorial claimed. "The Daily Express opposes the commitment to Poland."[45] Nonetheless, the *Express* did lobby the government to continue its rapid rearmament.

At the same time that swastikas were raised over Prague and his newspaper declared no interest in "distant regions on the Danube," Beaverbrook continued to court a top Nazi official, Joachim von Ribbentrop. The *Express* proprietor had been friends with Ribbentrop for several years and had offered him "the loyal support of my newspapers" after he became foreign minister in early 1938.[46]

Now, in the midst of the Nazi takeover of Czechoslovakia, the German foreign minister contacted Beaverbrook from the newly conquered territory. "I am writing to you from Prag, where I arrived with the Führer this evening, and I hope the Führer will settle the future relations between the German and the Czech peoples once and for ever and to the benefit of all." He invited the press lord to visit him in Berlin.[47] Beaverbrook thanked him for his "charming invitation" but never made the trip. He appeased the Germans while stopping short of endorsing their conquests.

■

After the German invasion of Czechoslovakia, Franklin Roosevelt renewed his campaign to encourage American aid to European democracies, hoping to help Britain and France rearm and therefore to deter further German aggression. He delivered his messages through Fireside Chats, reaching over the heads of the press lords to talk with Americans in their homes. He also tried to improve the public image of the British by hosting King George and Queen Elizabeth on the first state visit to the United States by reigning British monarchs. In June 1939, the royals motored up to Hyde Park, where they enjoyed a much-photographed hot dog picnic that was designed to show their likeability and democratic leanings.

At the same time, and more consequentially, Roosevelt worked hard behind the scenes to encourage Congress to revise—really, to transform—the Neutrality Act. The president agreed to keep the cash-and-carry provisions and the ban on loans. But he wanted to cut out the heart of the law: the embargo on selling arms to belligerent nations. He argued that the ban on American arm sales to Britain and France actually encouraged war because it allowed Hitler to believe he could invade European countries with impunity.

The *Chicago Tribune* and the Hearst newspapers led a frenzied campaign against ending the embargo, arguing that its repeal would make Roosevelt a dictator, drag America into war, and help the Soviet communists. The *Tribune* thundered that the "mad dogs" in the New Deal yearned for war in the hope of winning a third term for Roosevelt and furthering his "dictatorial ambitions."[48] The Hearst papers, which dubbed the revision proposal "the anti-neutrality bill" on their news pages as well as their editorials, made Colonel McCormick's remarks seem understated. Hearst instructed his editors to campaign against the bill "at full tilt."[49] As Congress deliberated, he ordered his newspapers to publish op-eds by isolationist senators and to run a daily reminder on the news pages urging readers to tell their representatives to vote against the bill. On a crucial day of debate in the Senate, the *San Francisco Examiner* devoted its entire editorial page to pictures of dead and wounded Americans from World War I and an exhortation to readers to demand that Congress reject the bill.[50] In a private letter, Hearst explained his goals: he wanted "first, to educate our readers to the dangers of specific objectionable legislation, then to ask them to bombard their representatives with letters and wires of protest." Half measures would not work. "I do not think they are much influenced by a smattering of letters and wires," he wrote. "It is the deluge that they respect."[51] Members of Congress showed their respect for the Hearst and McCormick press by entering their editorials into the *Congressional Record* and praising the newspapers that "consistently exposed the propaganda of the internationalists to involve us in foreign entanglements and war," as Representative Hamilton Fish said of the *Chicago Tribune*.[52]

In this hostile environment, the *Daily News* continued to stand out as a rare friend to Roosevelt. The *News* agreed with the president that repealing the arms embargo was the best way to avoid war. The current law, an editorial argued, "will work for one side and against the other if this possible war in Europe breaks out. And it is encouraging Germany and Italy to kick over the apple cart, because their leaders are well aware of the way this law has unexpectedly turned out to be framed in their favor."[53] The *News* suggested that congressional isolationists, along with McCormick and Hearst, were so obtuse that they did not understand how their policies encouraged the dictators "to go on with acts of aggression which may lead to a European war."[54]

But the anti-interventionists won the battle. The president could not get the votes to revise the Neutrality Act, and through the summer of 1939, as war clouds gathered over Europe, the arms embargo remained U.S. law.

■

Patterson endorsed the end of the arms embargo because he trusted Franklin Roosevelt. But a clever propaganda campaign led by none other than Max Beaverbrook also helped inform his views. Beaverbrook fought for appeasement and isolation; but like Roosevelt, he believed that American arm sales to Britain would actually help to prevent war. To this end, in June 1939, he invited Patterson to visit Britain to learn more about the crisis in Europe firsthand.

Beaverbrook hoped to fortify Patterson's support for revising the Neutrality Act because, as his private letters show, he viewed the *Daily News* proprietor as a prime mover of American public opinion. As he asked various British leaders to find time to meet with his guest, Beaverbrook assured them of the immense importance of the publisher's good opinion. "Patterson has always been a friend of this country," he wrote Foreign Secretary Halifax, "and my purpose is to strengthen him in his advocacy of the British cause in America. . . . I would not ask you to see Patterson if I did not know the results would be worth it. I assure you he is a better medium of propaganda than anybody else I can suggest."[55] Beaverbrook hosted dinner parties for Patterson with British policy makers and arranged meetings with Home Secretary Sam Hoare and with the prime minister himself. He explained in a private letter to Hoare that he had worked hard to maintain a friendship with Patterson "on public grounds" for his "propaganda value," and had always done everything he could to "cultivate his good opinion of this country, and also of the Prime Minister."[56]

Patterson understood that Beaverbrook's lavish hospitality and professions of friendship were strategic rather than heartfelt. In an article on his trip to England, he described Beaverbrook as a "Master of Propaganda" and the unofficial "Minister of Public Opinion," known for hosting generous dinners for visiting dignitaries and newspapermen. "In skillful ways and plausible ones, but without being too obvious about it," Patterson wrote, "he tries to make Americans see that there is an affinity both in blood and interest between the British Empire and the United States." He ended his article with a tongue-in-cheek suggestion that for his efforts, Beaverbrook should be promoted to the rank of duke.[57]

After he left England, Patterson traveled to Germany where, in a staggering failure of foresight, he reported that isolationists in Britain and America were correct about Hitler's intentions. There would be no war in Europe anytime soon, he declared on August 1, 1939, exactly one month before the war began. His signed article from Berlin, titled "REICH UNREADY: Peril of War in '39 Grows Less," reported that the chances "are more than 10 to 1 against a general European war before September and 4 or 5 to 1 against war this year."[58] In two subsequent articles, he hailed the Munich agreement as a triumph for Britain and styled Hitler as a somewhat bizarre and aloof "mystic." Like many Europeans, Patterson wrote, the Führer hated Jews, but the Nazis' violence against them had "generally ceased."[59]

The *Daily Express* ran all three of Patterson's *Daily News* articles, the first on its front page with an emphatic headline and a flattering byline: "10 to 1 against War in Europe. From JOSEPH MEDILL PATTERSON, proprietor of the New York Daily News, largest sale daily newspaper in the United States."[60] It also published most of Patterson's tribute to Beaverbrook, except for the final joke about the proposed dukedom.[61] As the summer of 1939 came to a close, Patterson and Beaverbrook continued to cheer one another on because they agreed on major points: the Germans would not start a war; the British would be foolish to respond if they did; and it would be prudent for Britain to deter the Germans by stockpiling American arms.

Despite Patterson's endorsement, Beaverbrook found himself increasingly isolated among the British press barons as the summer of 1939 wore on. Most noticeably, the *Daily Express* refused to join a renewed drive to pressure Prime Minister Chamberlain to bring Winston Churchill into his cabinet in hopes of sending Hitler a message of British determination and strength. The *Daily Mail* and most British newspapers enthusiastically endorsed the idea.[62] But the Beaverbrook press covered the campaign only to discredit it, warning that the movement to include Churchill in the cabinet was actually a stealthy bid to depose Chamberlain.[63]

Beaverbrook tried everything he could to reassure the Germans in the last months of peace. One after another, the *Daily Express* editorials in July and early August 1939 told readers that the paper had been right all along, and there was nothing to fear:

There was no war last year, and there will be no European war involving Britain this year either.

The Daily Express has said all along that there will be no European war involving Britain this year. We repeat it.

The Daily Express reaffirms its belief that there will be no European war this year.[64]

The most infamous *Daily Express* story appeared just weeks before the war began, under the headline "NO WAR THIS YEAR." This issue of the paper would come to represent appeasement at its most contemptible: three years later, in a direct slap at Beaverbrook, the British film *In Which We Serve* featured a shot of this *Express* front page floating in the slime of the Thames.[65] The "NO WAR" headline ran atop an August 7 article on a survey, undertaken at Beaverbrook's direction, of the paper's twelve European correspondents. The *Express* reporters were asked to predict whether war would come soon to Europe. Two hedged their bets, but the rest responded firmly in the negative. "The last idea in Hitler's mind," said one Berlin correspondent, "is to risk a clash with a Great Power."[66] Showing his confidence in the prospects for peace, Beaverbrook left for a holiday in North America, where he repeatedly reassured Canadians that those who worried about a coming war could not be more wrong.[67]

Before he departed, Beaverbrook told his editors that these "no war" prophecies were necessary to ensure that the Germans did not feel encircled by enemies—a fear that could prompt them to attack. "We've *got* to reduce the temperature," he told two chief editors. "If it keeps on going up there will be no hope at all. We've *got* to curb the war fever."[68]

His isolationist friend Rothermere went even further in his attempts to calm the Germans. Even though he no longer commanded the editorial page of a major British daily, Rothermere tried to leverage his status as a former press baron and longtime friend of the Nazis to reach out to German officials as they prepared for war. In late June, he penned a sycophantic letter to "my dear Führer": "I have watched with understanding and interest," he wrote, "the progress of your great and superhuman work in regenerating your country." The British people, he assured the Nazi leader, "regard the German people with admiration as valorous adversaries in the past. But I am sure that there is no problem between our two countries which cannot be settled by consultation and negotiation." He had always regarded Hitler as "one who hates war and desires peace." If Hitler arranged a peace conference, he would "go down to history as one of the greatest of all Europeans." A few days later, he wrote more "effusions," as the British secret service termed them, to Hitler and Ribbentrop. "Our two great Nordic countries," he told Ribbentrop, "should pursue resolutely a policy of appeasement for, whatever anyone may say, our two great countries should be the leaders of the world."[69]

Because Rothermere no longer led the *Daily Mail*, his personal beliefs on appeasement were not reflected in the paper's news coverage or editorials. Under Esmond Harmsworth's direction, the *Mail* joined with all the British newspapers not owned by Beaverbrook in championing resistance to Hitler. No compromise was possible, the *Mail*'s editors wrote, if Hitler insisted on controlling Poland: "If it is peace it must be a peace that is acceptable to Poland, and it must be a long-term peace."[70]

Yet standing against the media's turn toward resistance, Beaverbrook's *Express* continued throughout the summer of 1939 to question the value of Chamberlain's guarantee to Poland. "The Daily Express admits that there are some reasons in favour of an alliance with France," an editorial stated in early August. "But our alliances in Eastern Europe are another matter."[71] Rothermere agreed privately with Beaverbrook. "Why British foreign policy should be chained to the chariot wheels of Warsaw," he wrote, "baffles my comprehension."[72]

There was one more shock in store for British policy makers. On August 21, the official German news agency announced that the foreign minister, Beaverbrook's friendly correspondent Ribbentrop, was flying to Moscow to sign a nonaggression pact with the Soviet Union. Stalin, convinced that the British and French governments would betray him as they had abandoned the Czechs, had made a deal with Hitler, giving the Nazis a free hand in eastern Europe. If Hitler invaded Poland, he would not face opposition from the east.

Throughout the last week of August, Beaverbrook continued to cling to his hope that war might be avoided, though his papers' headlines suggested a darker future. "BRITAIN STANDS BY POLAND," reported the *Daily Express* of August 23; then, three days later: "HITLER: 'MY PATIENCE ALMOST EXHAUSTED,' " followed by "HITLER'S OFFER REFUSED," " 'I DEMAND DANZIG AND THE CORRIDOR,' " and "BRITAIN GIVES LAST WARNING." Hearing the dire news while still on holiday in Quebec, Beaverbrook decided to rush back to England.[73] On September 1, 1939, German troops swept into Poland.

Yet even as German bombs rained down on Polish cities, the *Express* believed Hitler might change his mind. Arthur Christiansen, editor of the *Daily Express*, called his office on Saturday, September 2, shortly before the *Sunday Express* went to press. Even though the *Daily Express* that morning had published a grim editorial about the inevitability of war, the editors of Beaverbrook's Sunday paper were still holding out hope for peace. "I gathered," he wrote later, "that the intention was to prophesy even at that time that war would be averted."[74] The *Sunday Express* heralded a possible last-minute peace plan proposed by Mussolini: "CONFERENCE STILL POSSIBLE," it predicted, "IF GERMANY WITHDRAWS HER TROOPS." But Germany, of course, did not withdraw her troops. The next day, the *Daily Express* simply informed its readers, "FLEET BEGINS THE BLOCKADE."[75]

The secondary headline in the *Express* that day told a different sort of story, about a remarkable political rebirth: "WINSTON BACK."[76] Churchill, his judgment vindicated, had returned to the cabinet as first lord of the admiralty. And as Britain entered the war, Beaverbrook, Churchill's onetime friend—the man who had hired him, fired him, and furiously disagreed with his policies and predictions—was the one on the outside.

■

Beaverbrook had spent the last year of peace blaming Jews for the escalating tensions and insisting, with growing desperation, on putting a bright face on Hitler's aggressive and brutal actions. Hitler agreed with the *Daily Express!* There would be no war!

Patterson's strategy had been more insidious and more successful: his anti-Semitism was coded, but he still helped undermine his president's anti-fascist measures by implying that the only Americans who wanted to fight Hitler were Jews. Now he, as well as his sister, his cousin, and Hearst, confronted a formidable challenge: with the British in the war, how could they keep their own country out?

CHAPTER NINE

Foreign Wars

THE START OF THE war in Europe triggered a crisis for the isolationist press barons. How should they respond, now that the war that they had fought so hard to avoid had finally begun?

For some American press lords, the period from September 1939 to November 1940 was a time to fight back with increasing fury. As Roosevelt and his aides launched an effective public relations campaign for aid to the Allies, Hearst and McCormick discovered that their power to shape public opinion on foreign policy was waning. The unprecedented third-term bid by a president they despised could bring their nation inching closer to war. And so they predicted, in ever more apocalyptic tones, that the election of 1940 might be the last democratic vote in American history. Joe Patterson, meanwhile, stayed loyal to his president by clinging to the hope that Roosevelt could keep the country out of war.

The British publishers greeted the start of the war with a mixture of sulky resignation and trepidation. Beaverbrook criticized the British war effort until suddenly, in a dramatic twist, he found himself in charge of producing enough airplanes to win it. Rothermere, meanwhile, faced the embarrassing prospect of becoming the subject of juicy tabloid articles when one of his former friends threatened to publish his private letters to his "dear führer" for the world to see.

■

Rothermere's troubles had begun in 1938 when he decided to fire Princess Stephanie Hohenlohe, his "political representative" on the European continent. Up to that point, the princess had enjoyed a substantial income as Rothermere's aide. A government agent reported in her MI5 file that the mysterious Viennese-born aristocrat, whom it labeled an "adventuress," had "wormed her way into society circles in London" and "exercised considerable influence" over Rothermere, who was twenty-three years her senior.[1] In 1932 he began paying her the considerable sum of £5,000 per year to introduce him to major European figures.[2] Over the next several years, he gave her more than £51,000, equivalent to about $3.5 million in today's money.[3] At the same time, British intelligence heard reports that she was a Nazi spy, and that Hitler had offered to pay her hundreds of thousands of pounds to influence Rothermere to promote the return of Polish land to Germany.[4]

Rothermere chose to end his attempts at European diplomacy in January 1938—he did "not wish to be considered an international busybody," he told Hohenlohe—and cut off her funds.[5] She angrily warned him that he needed her help to negotiate the political environment in Germany. When Rothermere refused to restore her salary, she threatened to sue him for breach of contract.

Hohenlohe claimed that she had letters from Rothermere that promised her an annual income. She did not. She did, however, possess letters that could seriously embarrass him if they came out during her lawsuit. The princess's cache of documents included cables and personal letters from Rothermere to Hitler in which the publisher flattered the dictator in embarrassingly sycophantic terms. In 1938, Rothermere wished Hitler good luck for "another successful year of Your wonderful regiem [*sic*]" and assured him that the English were impressed by the effectiveness of his methods: "Every day in England there is developing the opinion that parliamentarism is unable to meet the needs and so the problems which confront modern democracies."[6] When Austrians endorsed their country's annexation by the Reich in a rigged election, Rothermere congratulated the dictator for "your excellency's marvelous triumph in the plebiscite" and added that "your star is rising higher and higher but has not yet shone with its full effulgence."[7] A few months later, he expressed his "strong belief" that with his "wise statesmanship," Hitler would find a way to resolve the problems between England and Germany, "two branches of the same big Nordic stem."[8] After the Munich agreement, Rothermere compared Hitler to Frederick the Great of Prussia, who was highly regarded in Britain. "May not Adolf the Great become an equally popular figure? I salute your excellency's star which rises higher and higher."[9] Hohenlohe also possessed a memo in which Rothermere asked officials in Hungary to enthrone his son as their king, and some copies of Hitler's pleased responses to the publisher's praise.[10]

Rothermere had already transmitted copies of his Hitler correspondence to British officials as part of his apparently earnest campaign to improve relations between the two countries. But even considered as private diplomatic efforts to mediate between Britain and the Nazi regime, the letters were shamefully obsequious. Did he need to call Hitler, the man who had already sent tens of thousands to concentration camps, "Adolf the Great"? The princess secured copies of the letters from Berlin, probably with the aid of her lover, Fritz Wiedemann, a close adviser to Hitler until early 1939. Wiedemann sent Rothermere a not-so-subtly threatening letter expressing regret at the unpleasantness that would result if they were made public.[11] But Wiedemann and Hohenlohe miscalculated: bristling at the audacity of the blackmail attempt, Rothermere refused to pay. So Hohenlohe followed through on her threat and filed suit against him in an English court.

The British government learned about the princess's attempts to squeeze Rothermere in March 1939, when a Hungarian lawyer arrived at a border control post at Victoria station with a satchel full of incriminating correspondence. Under prodding from immigration officials, the attorney explained that he had come to London for his client, Hohenlohe, and he opened his briefcase to show them some documents, which he said were part of her breach-of-contract suit against Rothermere. The letters were "astonishing," a passport official reported; they included one in which Rothermere urged Hitler to invade Romania, and another praising the annexation of Czechoslovakia.[12]

The letters would have been embarrassing at the time that the border police found them. But by the time Hohenlohe got her day in court, they might have appeared treasonous. One of Rothermere's lawyers privately visited the Home Office shortly after the start of the war in September 1939 and asked the British government to expel the princess from the country as a Nazi spy and toss her suit out of court.[13] The government declined, and let the legal process run its course.

The trial began in November and garnered a lot of press attention, especially from American correspondents, many of whom portrayed Hohenlohe as a gold digger and a pathetic, middle-aged vamp.[14] It lasted just six days. Because she did not have evidence for her breach-of-contract claim, the judge ruled against her and ordered her to pay court costs.

The trial was embarrassing for Rothermere, who had to endure salacious stories in American publications about his "ludicrous" relationship with Hitler and his absurd desire to make his son king of Hungary.[15] But this discomfort was minor compared to what might have happened if the court had disclosed his letters to Hitler.

Possibly because the judge wanted to help the press lord dodge a scandal, or because Hohenlohe did not want to give up her one remaining trump card, the trial concluded with the public still unclear about what, exactly, the former *Daily Mail* publisher had said to the leader of Nazi Germany. The lawyers read some snippets into the record, but the correspondence remained under seal. The judge assured the onlookers that there was nothing untoward in them. "From first to last, there is nothing discreditable to Lord Rothermere, or to the writers of any of the letters in this bundle," he announced.[16] Notably, Hohenlohe's cache only included letters that dated from before her lawyer's furtive trip to London in March 1939. She did not have copies of the unctuous missives Rothermere had sent to Hitler and Ribbentrop that summer.

Rothermere was surprisingly generous to his blackmailer after the trial, perhaps because the letters remained secret. When she lost her suit, he covered her court costs—some £10,000—and offered to pay her to leave Britain and relocate to the Continent. Hohenlohe took the money for the court costs but refused to move to war-torn Europe. Instead, she came up with the cash for tickets for her mother and herself to go to America, where her lover, Wiedemann, was serving as German consul in San Francisco.[17] The stash of letters would remain private until after her death in 1972.

■

As Rothermere sought to hide his letters to Hitler, Max Beaverbrook struggled to figure out how to support the war—a conflict he did not want and had often argued would never happen. Though he publicly backed Neville Chamberlain's government, he remained, in the words of his reporter Michael Foot, "sulking in his appeaser's tent."[18] His newspapers relentlessly thrashed the government's attempts to prepare the country for a long war.

The start of the conflict, on September 1, was strangely anticlimactic for Britain. British and French citizens waited anxiously for several months through a period known in Britain as the "bore war" and in America as the "phony war." The Allies could do nothing to help Poland repulse the German invaders. They could not stop the Soviet Union from grabbing parts of eastern Poland. Nor could they do much to aid Finland in November after the Soviets invaded that country. Britons built bomb shelters, carried gas masks, and endured nighttime blackouts, waiting for German air raids that for several months did not arrive. Hitler bided his time.

Beaverbrook found the war regulations and preparations maddening and unnecessary—and possibly, he thought, the result of a bureaucratic conspiracy. In an editorial demanding the abolition of the Ministry of Food, the *Daily Express* insisted that government officials wanted food rationing because they had printed too many ration cards, not because they worried about keeping the public fed. "The cry for rationing and registering springs from a mad passion to regiment the public," the *Express* contended. "There is a desire to impose a bureaucratic order of government. It smacks strangely and smells strongly of a combination between Socialism and Fascism."[19] The wartime regulations, the *Express* said in another editorial, were the result of bureaucratic "schemes for bullying the public and bossing our industries."[20] Editorials also decried the government's efforts to increase the size of the army as the country waited for the inevitable German offensive. "The Government plan a mighty Army. Millions of men in khaki. What for?" the *Express* asked. "To please the French."[21] The *Express* became, in the words of Beaverbrook's sympathetic biographer A. J. P. Taylor, the "channel for every sort of grumble and grievance."[22]

Beaverbrook's campaign against preparedness alienated some readers and struck at least one observer, the journalist Hugh Cudlipp, as "seditious."[23] Perhaps more people would have used that term had they known of Beaverbrook's private efforts to promote a negotiated peace with the Germans. He secretly encouraged several political figures on both the right and the left who hoped to persuade their government to come to terms with Hitler. In January 1940, he met with the Duke of Windsor, the former Edward VIII, who had abdicated the throne four years earlier. The former king, who had moved to the Continent, was known for his Nazi sympathies. Beaverbrook encouraged him to return to England from exile to lobby for a peace deal. The duke rejected this idea, which one observer called "treason," in part because he learned that if he moved back he would have to pay British income taxes.[24] Beaverbrook also met with members of a pacifist offshoot of the Labour Party, the Independent Labour Party, in March 1940 and offered to support its efforts to press for a compromise peace. One of those present, John McGovern, reported that Beaverbrook "could not see any alternative at that time but to negotiate an honourable settlement, retire behind our Empire frontiers, arm ourselves to the teeth, leave the Continent to work out its own destiny and defend the Empire with all our strength."[25]

At the same time, Beaverbrook tried to forge an alliance with the United States. Shortly after the war began, he traveled to Washington, where he charmed Franklin Roosevelt and formed a friendship with the president that lasted throughout the war.[26] The publisher also continued to cultivate his many contacts among the press lords in America and encouraged them to use their publications to support Britain. He was "exactly the man," Rothermere told him in a private letter, to send to the United States on Britain's behalf. "You are much better known to the American public than any other English journalist and moreover you are extremely well-known and popular with the American journalists."[27]

Beaverbrook was full of ideas for persuading the Americans to give more aid to Britain, including a proposal to send a skilled propagandist to the United States to whip Scandinavian Americans into a frenzy over the brutalities of the Russo-Finnish winter war.[28]

The British foreign secretary, Lord Halifax, found this plan alarming and wrote to Beaverbrook that he worried about Americans' "phobia" of foreign propaganda. No matter how "deftly camouflaged," any British attempt to manipulate American sentiments on the war could easily backfire.[29] Still, Beaverbrook believed the Chamberlain cabinet was not taking the need for propaganda in America seriously enough. "The domestic situation in the United States," he wrote the next month to Halifax, "should not be left to chance."[30]

Roosevelt agreed that advocates for aid to the Allies needed to act quickly to reassure Americans that they could help the Western democracies while keeping out of the European conflict. At the start of the war, he told Americans in a Fireside Chat that he could not expect his constituents to remain neutral in thought, as President Wilson had insisted at the start of the last war. "Even a neutral," he told his listeners, "has a right to take account of facts. Even a neutral cannot be asked to close his mind or his conscience." At the same time, he pledged that he would do everything possible to keep out of war. "I hate war. I say that again and again. I hope the United States will keep out of this war. I believe that it will. And I give you assurance and reassurance that every effort of your Government will be directed toward that end."[31]

Roosevelt then called Congress into special session to modify the Neutrality Act to allow warring nations to buy munitions from the United States as long as they paid cash and carried them away in their own ships. He asked for the revisions, he said, not because he wanted to join the war but because he believed in keeping out of it. Because the revisions would require American citizens and ships to stay out of war zones, the new statute would actually help the United States to avoid war. "By the repeal of the embargo," he argued, "the United States will more probably remain at peace than if the law remains as it stands today."[32]

The request for an end to the arms embargo provoked a furious response from isolationists. Wisconsin Republican Robert La-Follette Jr. asserted that he and his fellow bitter-enders in the Senate would fight the repeal "from hell to breakfast."[33] Followers of Father Charles Coughlin, the anti-Semitic priest with millions of radio listeners, organized a "women's march" on Washington, in which about five hundred flag-waving women lined the Capitol rotunda and shouted slogans like "No blood money" and "No foreign entanglements" at passing senators.[34]

Aviation pioneer and national hero Charles Lindbergh, a leading spokesman for the anti-repeal forces, charged in a radio speech that the United States had no reason to take sides in a fight among "white" nations. "This is not a question of banding together to defend the white race against foreign invasion," he said. "This is simply one more of those age-old quarrels within our own family of nations—a quarrel arising from the errors of the last war—from the failure of the victors of that war to follow a consistent policy either of fairness or of force."[35]

As usual, President Roosevelt faced his greatest challenge in the influence of the isolationist press, particularly among the 30 million Americans reached by William Randolph Hearst. The California publisher responded to the president's request in a predictable fashion: he called him a liar. Ending the arms embargo, the Hearst papers editorialized, would make the United States more likely to join the war, not less. "Whatever else that is, that is NOT NEUTRALITY."[36] Also as usual, Hearst did not confine his views to his editorials. The Hearst news story on Roosevelt's call for repeal—a request the president explicitly framed as a way to stay out of war—categorically stated the opposite, reporting that repeal would force America to "draw closer to Europe's war." In any event, the Hearst papers asserted, few had been swayed by the president: "Talk Held Weakest of His Career" read the headline on the story about Roosevelt's speech to Congress. On the same (news) page, the Hearst papers included a boxed story urging readers to "Wire Congressmen to Keep out of War."[37]

When the Soviets invaded Poland, Hearst did briefly contemplate supporting the president's request to end the arms embargo. He had long predicted a Red conquest of Europe, and now it was coming to pass. "The greatest disaster to civilization of this European war, so far, is not the invasion of Poland by Hitler," the Hearst papers editorialized, "but the Communistic-Asiatic advances of Red Russia into Europe proper." Now the world could see the true purpose of the war: "Thus from behind the screen of Nazism emerges at last the real villain of this whole European drama: JOSEPH STALIN."

An editorial cartoon showed a giant ape labeled "Communism," accompanied by clouds of "Atheism" and "Destruction," marching across Poland en route to ravaging a cluster of terrified women and children.[38] Now that Stalin had revealed himself, in Hearst's view, as the instigator of the war, the publisher was momentarily uncertain whether his papers should support repeal of the arms embargo after all. On September 23, 1939, the chief ordered a moratorium on editorials "critical of the president in this war situation."[39]

But soon the Hearst papers reverted to form, telling readers of their news pages how an anti-interventionist senator's "Stirring Plea for Peace" had thrilled the Senate and organizing a pressure group, the Mothers of America, which lobbied Congress against repeal.[40]

Unlike Hearst, Robert McCormick never wavered from his conviction that repealing the arms embargo would lead to war, disaster, and dictatorship for the United States. In his editorials, McCormick declared that it was foolish to give any help to Britain and France, which the *Tribune* labeled "the so-called democracies of Europe."[41] Like the Hearst papers, the *Tribune* reflected its owner's political beliefs in its news coverage as well as its editorials. Its news pages suggested a moral equivalence between the French and the British on one hand and the Nazis and Soviets on the other. They routinely referred to the Allies as "empires," as in "Turks Sign with Empires" or "Empires Scorn Appeals by Hitler for Truce."[42]

The *Tribune*'s criticism of the Allies infuriated many of its correspondents. Edmond Taylor, who headed the paper's Paris bureau, grew increasingly angry about editorial interference with his copy. He wrote the colonel in December 1939 that the *Tribune* editors had done everything possible to impede his work, from questioning his facts to charging him personally for the transmission costs of filing one of his articles. He was forced to conclude that his newspaper no longer wanted him to file stories about the war.[43] Taylor quit the paper soon afterward and began giving public lectures about the colonel's "lamentable bias" and his determination to twist the news.[44]

McCormick's vehement stand against aid for the British stemmed in part from his Anglophobia. His disdain for Britain had only worsened with age. In his view, the British government was almost indistinguishable from the fascists except for the absence of "concentration camps, castor oil, and blood purges" (which some people might see as rather notable exceptions). In 1937, he had personally reported a story on the aftermath of Edward VIII's abdication and, in an interpretation as strained as it was unusual, concluded that the "Nazi government of England" had forced the monarch from the throne. "England has gone fascist," he told readers. The only source he cited was an anonymous banker who explained that Britain had embraced a "corporate state."[45]

Mostly, however, McCormick opposed aiding the Allies because he distrusted Franklin Roosevelt. The colonel had been spinning a conspiracy theory about the president and the European crisis for months before the war started. In an Independence Day speech in 1939, he used the words *conspirators* or *conspiracy* four times in one sentence to describe Roosevelt's alleged goal of dragging the United States into war: "And now we are in the middle of a conspiracy to throw this country into that war, and the conspirators are in partnership with a conspiracy far greater and far more dangerous to our national welfare—the conspiracy to scrap the Constitution of the United States and supplant it with the terrorism and communism of Russia."[46]

McCormick charged that the president thought a war would save the New Deal by boosting factory orders and taking men out of the labor supply—some permanently. "A war," the *Tribune* explained, "would save the faces of New Dealers, create the possibility of a third term, and at the same time further the New Deal's dictatorial ambitions."[47]

Colonel McCormick's cousins, Joe and Cissy Patterson, also remained proud isolationists, but with an important distinction: they continued to support Roosevelt throughout the fight over the repeal of the embargo. Cissy Patterson seemed to hold few political convictions, but she followed her brother's lead. In 1939, she exercised her option to buy both the *Times* and the *Herald*, merged them, and began regularly publishing her brother's editorials in the new *Times-Herald*.

The Pattersons' readers learned that the president was telling the truth when he said he wanted to end the embargo to stay out of the war. Unaided, the Allies would surely be defeated, putting

Hitler in a position to attack the United States. But with American help, the Allies might hold off Hitler. Thus, the president and his supporters reasoned, aid to the Allies would most probably render U.S. entry to the war less likely. The *Daily News* contended that the existing law benefited Germany, not the Allies. "We cannot afford to retain the entangling, danger-loaded encumbrance which the Neutrality Act has turned out to be," the *News* insisted in one of its many editorials in favor of repeal.[48]

The Pattersons contradicted every one of the points made by Hearst and by their cousin in Chicago. Roosevelt, the *News* said, was trustworthy and inspiring; his call to end the arms embargo was "one of the best speeches he has yet made during either of his terms as President."[49] The *News* also praised the British and the French, calling them "the Allies" or "the democracies" (as opposed to "empires"), and maintained that the United States clearly needed them to win: "Spiritually and ideologically, the United States is much closer akin to the democracies than to the dictatorships."[50] Still, the *Daily News* and the *Times-Herald* carried the flag for isolationism and argued that the United States must do all it could to stay out of the European war. But "on our Pacific exposure," the *News* noted, "the case is different. We have to keep our guard up there, because the hordes of Asia know what a wonderful country we have, and they would love to come swarming over here."[51]

The president finally won the fight in late November 1939 as Congress voted to overturn the arms embargo and allow belligerent nations to buy war supplies in the United States. Roosevelt hailed the vote as a great step toward keeping the United States out of war, but most isolationists remained convinced that he was lying.

■

The "bore war" on the western front ended abruptly in April 1940, when the Germans attacked Denmark and several ports in Norway. Hitler hoped to forestall an Allied occupation of Scandinavia and secure German access to iron ore in neutral Sweden. Denmark fell within hours, but Norway resisted the Nazi assault. The British sent an expeditionary force to help the Norwegians hold out. But they were forced to withdraw as the Germans' air superiority enabled them to take Norway and its valuable North Sea ports.

The German success in Norway triggered a political crisis in London and one of the most extraordinary debates in the history of Parliament. The Labour Party combined with Liberal MPs and some rebel Conservatives to force a division of the House—effectively, a vote of confidence in Chamberlain's government. Conservative MP Leo Amery quoted Oliver Cromwell's words to the Long Parliament centuries earlier: "You have sat too long here for any good you have been doing. Depart, I say, and let us have done with you. In the name of God, go."[52] The government won the vote, but Chamberlain's majority was severely reduced and his credibility shattered.[53] Yet he remained in office and attempted to consolidate power again.

Beaverbrook maintained his faith in Chamberlain and appeasement to the end. He refused pleas from friends to help topple the prime minister.[54] On May 6, two days before the confidence vote, he wrote a signed article in the *Express* casting doubt on the importance of the defeat in Norway. "What is the damage?" he asked, and then gave an answer: very little. "There can be no possible ground for the depression and gloom that exist over the course of events in Norway," he reassured his millions of readers.[55] Chamberlain was so pleased with the article that he wrote Beaverbrook to express his gratitude. "When so many are sounding the defeatist note over a minor setback, it is a relief to read such a courageous and inspiriting summons to a saner view."[56] Rothermere also praised the prime minister's leadership and encouraged him to remain in office. "Hold on and you will win," he wrote Chamberlain on May 7, the day before his disastrous vote in Parliament.[57] As historian Richard Cockett has argued, the undeserved support the prime minister received from Beaverbrook, Rothermere, and a few other press lords gave Chamberlain a distorted view of his policies' popularity and success, and helped persuade him to try to "cling to office" after he should have quit.[58]

But the new German offensive had sealed Chamberlain's fate. Having lost the confidence of his party, appeasement's great champion was forced to resign. Winston Churchill, who had spent much of the 1930s warning of the Nazi menace, became the new leader of the war effort. "I have nothing to offer but blood, toil, tears, and sweat," he told Parliament in his first speech as prime minister, on May 13. "You ask, what is our aim? I can answer in one word: It is victory, victory at all costs, victory in spite of all terror, victory, however long and hard the road may be."[59]

Churchill's ascension to the premiership signaled a dramatic change in British foreign policy; it also marked an astonishing turning point in Beaverbrook's career—the start of what he called "the most glittering, glorious, glamorous era of my whole life."[60] The *Daily Express* publisher had done all he could to undermine Churchill's efforts to awaken the country to the Nazi threat. He had fired Churchill as a columnist and asked an employee to gather a dossier of his speeches to use against him. Yet Beaverbrook controlled the biggest daily in the country, along with a major Sunday paper and a hugely popular evening one. And despite all the difficulties over the last few years—the fights, the policy differences, the firing—Churchill regarded him as his friend at a time when he had few others in high political circles.[61] He asked Beaverbrook to serve in his cabinet as minister of aircraft production.

Churchill had long recognized the need to build planes faster, particularly the fighters that would defend Britain against a potential Nazi blitz. Now that he was prime minister, he carved out of the Air Ministry a new agency specifically for production, and placed his friend in charge. Not everyone cheered the appointment. King George VI, who disliked Beaverbrook for, among other things, supporting his brother during the abdication crisis, asked Churchill to reconsider on the grounds that Beaverbrook was very unpopular in Canada.[62] But Churchill would not be swayed. "I needed his vital and vibrant energy, and I persisted in my view," he wrote in his memoirs.[63]

With his appointment to the cabinet, Beaverbrook achieved something that other isolationist publishers desired but never attained: a power base independent of party—and even independent of his newspapers. The press barons had all launched crusades to change government policies and command respect and authority. Hearst had served in Congress and run for governor, and Beaverbrook and Rothermere had tried to start their own party and depose the leader of the Tories. Yet none had won national leadership. Now Beaverbrook was part of the government, not just influencing it from outside. He had succeeded in winning real power—but ironically, it was power in service of the war he had fought to escape.

Beaverbrook took charge of producing airplanes just as his nation entered its "darkest hour," as Churchill memorably termed it. In late May, just weeks into Churchill's premiership, as the Germans relentlessly pushed into the Netherlands and France, more than three hundred thousand British, French, and other Allied soldiers retreated to the coast and found themselves trapped on the beaches of Dunkirk. Only the heroic efforts of hundreds of skippers, many piloting small boats, evacuated the soldiers across the English Channel and saved the men from capture by the Germans. The French could not hold out much longer, and in June 1940 they signed an armistice with Hitler that gave him control of most of the country, including the northern coast. The next month, Hitler launched a massive air assault against Britain to force its leaders to accept a compromise peace or face invasion. The Royal Air Force tenaciously fought the Luftwaffe in the Battle of Britain, at the expense of thousands of air crew killed or wounded, while more than fourteen thousand civilians died from the German bombs. The British fliers who defended their country included Max Aitken, Beaverbrook's eldest son.

Beaverbrook's legendary service as minister of aircraft production during the Battle of Britain helped save his nation from conquest by the Nazis. He worked eighteen hours a day, seven days a week, from his headquarters at his mansion overlooking Green Park, constantly demanding, hectoring, cajoling, and charming military men, workers, and businessmen into doing his bidding. Sir Hugh Dowding, air chief marshal and head of fighter command, credited Beaverbrook's "dramatic irruption into the field of aircraft production" with saving Britain. "We had the organization, we had the men, and we had the spirit which could bring us victory in the air, but we had not the supply of machines necessary to withstand the drain of continuous battle," he wrote in the London *Times* soon after the German surrender. "Lord Beaverbrook gave us those machines, and I do not believe that I exaggerate when I say that no other man in England could have done so."[64] Sir Archibald Rowlands, the permanent secretary to the Ministry of Aircraft Production, proclaimed that the Royal Air Force won the Battle of Britain, but it "would never have had the chance to do so but for the activities of one man—and that man was Lord Beaverbrook."[65]

Some historians believe these tributes are exaggerated. "There is the myth that Lord Beaverbrook waved a magic wand and lo! there were aircraft where none existed before," Richard Hough and Denis Richards have written.[66] They point out that aircraft production had already begun to increase the month before Beaverbrook became minister.[67] Still, though Beaverbrook did not single-handedly win the Battle of Britain, he clearly contributed to the victory. The number of aircraft produced from June through August 1940, the first three months of Beaverbrook's tenure, almost doubled the total from the previous three months, while the production of fighters—Hurricanes and Spitfires—almost tripled. Churchill said that Beaverbrook had "done miracles."[68]

Beaverbrook succeeded by conveying a sense of urgency, refusing to take no for an answer, and making key decisions about production and development—which kind of planes to build and which new models to pursue. He managed the ministry the way he ran his newspapers: with abundant energy and disdain for protocol. He could be petulant—he threatened to resign fourteen times in eleven months. But his approach worked. His talent for public relations made everyone "aircraft-production-conscious to an unprecedented degree," as one historian of the RAF has written; higher morale translated into more Britons working more shifts for longer hours for the good of the nation.[69] The official history of the RAF summed up his contribution this way: "In the long run his method—the reliance on personal inspiration and 'hunches,' the utter rejection not only of red tape but of all closely planned programmes—might lead to confusion or even loss of production. But just now it was not the long run which counted."[70]

Beaverbrook's historical reputation was saved not just by his performance during the Battle of Britain but by the efforts of three early historians of the war. As British troops evacuated from Dunkirk, three journalists on the *Evening Standard*—Beaverbrook's most independent paper—met to write a quick history of appeasement. They planned to denounce the men who had endangered the nation. Michael Foot, Frank Owen, and Peter Howard, all of them talented editors, collectively produced a short manuscript that told the "story of an Army doomed *before* they took the field"—ruined by the willfully myopic policies of a small group of national leaders.[71] The leftist publisher Victor Gollancz produced the 125-page book, *Guilty Men*, within a month, and it soon sold 250,000 copies. The authors published under the pseudonym "Cato," though many observers, including their employer, soon figured out who they were. The list of the guilty men included the obvious suspects: the three prime ministers of the 1930s, Chamberlain, Stanley Baldwin, and Ramsay MacDonald, as well as their top advisers. But one name was strangely absent.

The "guilty men" trope helped to frame Britons' understanding of the history of the 1930s, and the authors' decision to leave Beaverbrook off the list of the offenders—despite his considerable contribution to the false optimism of appeasement—helped save his reputation. Clearly, the personal affection the authors felt for their boss helps explain their reluctance to condemn him. But it is also true that, by the time of *Guilty Men*'s publication, Beaverbrook had repaired much of the damage he had done as an appeaser.

■

Another British press lord was also eager to erase the memory of his actions. The stress of winning his case against Princess Hohenlohe had worsened Harold Rothermere's health problems. In March 1940 he wrote Beaverbrook from Egypt that he worried about becoming a permanent invalid.[72] But the sudden ascendancy to power of his old friends Max and Winston briefly cheered him. "My dear Max," he cabled Beaverbrook from France, on his way back to England, "overjoyed at last some governmental use has been found at this critical juncture for you[r] glittering abilities."[73] He asked if he could serve his nation by encouraging American firms to produce more aircraft for Britain. "Am dying to help the country in this great crisis under your leadership; sure results may be quite extraordinary."[74] Beaverbrook agreed to give his friend a mission. "I will want your services in America and hope you will go there at once."[75]

Not everyone thought it was a good idea to send the proven Naziphile to North America as Britain struggled to secure U.S. aid. Foreign Secretary Halifax angrily complained to Beaverbrook that Rothermere was prophesying doom for Britain, and wanted him stopped from going to the United States.[76] In fact, it's possible that Rothermere inspired a defeatist editorial in the *Daily News*. On August 15, 1940, the *News* referred to "an observer just over from

England" who said that the British people "did not want to fight Hitler's army" and wondered if the war was worth fighting. This "observer" predicted that Churchill, "a born fire-eater and possibly the most enthusiastic hater Hitler has in the world," would be tossed from the cabinet and replaced by Beaverbrook, who would then sue for peace.[77] The identity of the source is unknown, but Rothermere was in North America at the time.

Beaverbrook responded to Halifax by claiming he did not know whether Rothermere had already arrived in the United States. "In any case he is an old man," Beaverbrook concluded.[78] Rothermere was gravely ill. After a few months surveying some Canadian and American factories, he traveled to Bermuda with his granddaughter and checked himself into a hospital, his heart failing. He died there in November 1940.

Beaverbrook wrote a generous note of condolence to the new Viscount Rothermere. "Your father," he said, "was a man of immense charm and endless kindness. . . . He conferred on me many benefits. I hope that I was not entirely the debtor, but so it seems to me at present."[79] He was being overly modest. According to Collin Brooks, an editor who accompanied Rothermere to North America, Beaverbrook and Esmond Harmsworth had invented the "mission" to America and contrived to send Rothermere away from Britain, possibly because they thought his pro-Hitler past might lead to his arrest if he stayed.[80]

■

The swift German victories in the spring of 1940 shook up American as well as British politics. Franklin Roosevelt had initially signaled his intention to honor the no-third-term tradition and retire to write his memoirs and set up his presidential library, but the German advances changed his mind. Although he refused to make a formal bid for the nomination, he allowed others to organize delegates for him, and he accepted his party's draft at the convention in July.

Besides forcing Roosevelt to delay his retirement, the Nazi conquests also disrupted the combinations in Congress that favored or opposed the president's policies. Before 1940, the New Deal had confronted a growing coalition of conservative Republicans and Southern Democrats who had wearied of Roosevelt's reforms and consistently voted against his initiatives. But the fall of France horrified some conservatives and prompted them to support the president's rearmament and foreign aid policies—though the domestic New Deal remained anathema to them. Roosevelt added two Republicans to his cabinet, Secretary of War Henry Stimson and Secretary of the Navy Frank Knox, to show his intent to pursue a bipartisan foreign policy. These appointments further embittered Colonel McCormick, who loathed both men, but especially Knox, the publisher of the *Chicago Daily News* and one of his chief rivals.

Like some leading Republicans, many of the nation's newspapers were changing their minds about Roosevelt's foreign policies, as White House staff discovered in a study of editorial opinion. At the direction of press secretary Steve Early, the Office of Government Reports surveyed newspapers throughout the nation in the spring and summer of 1940. Early's staff noted a new trend in "the steadily mounting number of papers which have come out editorially for immediate and unstinted aid to the Allies." In particular, they saw a shift among the anti–New Deal newspapers in the South. "It is significant to note," they reported, "that the Southern papers, usually not only conservative, but sectional rather than either national or international in their policies, have taken the lead in advocating aid for the Allies."[81]

Conservative newspapers in other regions also began to back the president. The *Los Angeles Times*, which saw the hand of Joseph Stalin behind just about every New Deal program, advocated for aid to the Allies as France fell under the Nazi boot.[82] The *New York Herald Tribune*, described by the government reports as "violently anti-Roosevelt," urged the United States to declare that "its neutrality in respect to the European war has come to an end."[83] The *Philadelphia Inquirer*, another longtime foe of the president, published a front-page editorial on June 2 headlined "America Must Help Allies to Beat Hitler." When, on June 10, Mussolini's Italy joined Germany in the war against the British and the swiftly collapsing French, even more anti–New Deal publishers decided it was time to abandon isolationism and cheer the president's foreign policy.

But the "dyed-in-the-wool isolationist papers," as the editorial opinion report called them, still opposed aid to the Allies.[84] For the first time, Joe Patterson's *Daily News* began to question Roosevelt's argument that helping Britain and France would enable the United

States to avoid war. "Soon it will be 500 planes that the Allies must have, then probably another 500, and so on," the *News* predicted. "It is now easy to foresee another A.E.F. going to another war to end war."[85]

At least Joe Patterson thought Roosevelt was well intentioned. His cousin at the *Chicago Tribune* believed the president was "hell-bent for war" and would use it to become a dictator. Even worse, the *Tribune* charged, he would not make a very effective one. Colonel McCormick employed his usual tactic of questioning the chief executive's manhood. "Mr. Roosevelt is a panty-waist Hitler," read a *Tribune* editorial, "who can be counted upon to fill his conscripts' minds not with iron but with mush."[86] McCormick thought Roosevelt would make "an atrociously bad war president" who would bring the "grandiose, contradictory, and impractical dreams" of the New Deal to wartime administration.[87]

The Nazi victories in Europe upended the Republican Party's selection of a presidential nominee in 1940, resulting in a choice that disturbed many isolationists. As the French surrendered much of their territory to German occupation, some GOP leaders began to worry that they would lose the election if the party chose a staunch anti-interventionist like Ohio senator Robert Taft or Michigan senator Arthur Vandenberg. Instead, in a dramatic surprise, the party convention that June nominated Wendell Willkie, a businessman with no history of public service but—unlike the front-runners—no isolationist past. Late in the campaign, Willkie did begin to attack Roosevelt as a warmonger, but for much of the summer he focused on his disagreements with the New Deal, not on Roosevelt's foreign policy.[88]

Because Willkie would not say much about the European war, Hearst chose to ignore signs that the candidate might favor intervention and instead concluded, somewhat illogically, that he must be a secret isolationist. His newspapers endorsed Willkie and his "solid, matter-of-fact, mind-your-own-business AMERICANISM." A Willkie victory, Hearst predicted, would help the American people "sweep the arrogant, plutocratic and autocratic and completely undemocratic and UN-AMERICAN New Deal politicians and bosses out of their path."[89]

But as Willkie sank in the polls, Hearst began to criticize the candidate for failing to distinguish his foreign policy views from the president's, or even to show any reason to vote for him at all. Always a performer, Hearst judged other public figures in part on their presentation skills. He had come to respect Roosevelt as a leader and communicator, but Willkie was far less satisfactory in those categories. "Every time Mr. Willkie speaks," Hearst wrote in a September 1940 column, "he says something—but it is generally something which Mr. Roosevelt has said before and said better."[90] Beginning in March 1940, Hearst published his own front-page column in his newspapers, called "In the News," which meant that he now had two chances almost every day—his editorial and his column—to state his views on political matters. As the election neared, he used those opportunities to show his displeasure with Willkie's internationalism and his general self-presentation.

The *Chicago Tribune* was initially suspicious of Willkie, a former Democrat, and supported him only once his nomination became official. McCormick deeply distrusted Republicans who backed Roosevelt's foreign policy; anyone who did so, the *Tribune* said, "is promoting the cause of dictatorship and is doing so either because he is emotionally unbalanced or because he is craftily seeking to undermine a form of government he does not like."[91] But as the election drew near and the colonel grew terrified that Roosevelt would win, he once again abandoned any pretense of objectivity and slanted his news coverage to favor the Republican. According to a survey by Harold Ickes, the *Tribune* devoted 96 percent of its presidential news coverage in October 1940 to Willkie and only 4 percent to Roosevelt.[92]

Joe Patterson, despite his growing misgivings, endorsed a third term for his hero. The contrast between the two major-party candidates on domestic issues was too stark for a progressive like Patterson to ignore. On one side, Willkie called for unfettered capitalism. As "an insider of the insiders himself," the *News* wrote, Willkie was naturally "against government control of business for the general welfare." On the other side stood Roosevelt, whom Patterson considered one of the best presidents in American history on economic policy. Yes, his pleas for aid to the Allies gave Patterson some concern. "As regards foreign policy, we've sometimes been unable to follow the President," the *News* confessed. "The President is what is called an interventionist."[93] But Patterson chose to take Roosevelt at his word that his policies would save the United States from another world war.

Patterson's strong support for Roosevelt even survived the shock of the September 1940 deal between the United States and the United Kingdom to trade naval bases for destroyers. Churchill wanted the U.S. ships to patrol the western approaches to Britain. Roosevelt hesitated to grant Churchill's request; he believed that he needed congressional approval for the transfer of the destroyers, and he knew he would not get it. In mid-August, however, he decided he could transfer fifty ships to Britain on his own authority. In return, the British would give the United States the right to construct air and navy facilities on British possessions in the Western Hemisphere.

The bases-destroyers deal—a "decidedly unneutral act," as Churchill put it in his memoirs—signaled the United States' commitment to the defense of Britain.[94] The transfer of the ships, Churchill said in a speech, showed that the "two great organisations of the English-speaking democracies, the British Empire and the United States, will have to be somewhat mixed up together in some of their affairs for mutual and general advantage."[95]

Outraged isolationists responded by forming a national anti-intervention group, the America First Committee (AFC). Headquartered in Chicago and strongly supported by McCormick, the group's platform asserted, "American democracy can be preserved only by keeping out of the European war."[96] The AFC was funded and run by wealthy businessmen like Sears Roebuck chairman Robert E. Wood, who served as the group's national head, and automaker Henry Ford. Notably, its eight hundred thousand members did not include Hearst. The leaders of America First had solicited his help, but he never responded, possibly because he was annoyed that they had not consulted him earlier. After all, he had been using the slogan for decades.[97]

Joe Patterson would soon become one of the biggest individual donors to America First, but in September 1940 he supported the bases-destroyers deal. "True, it was a high-handed act on the part of the President," the *Daily News* editorialized. "It may have been downright illegal." The nation's founders probably "twirled in their honored graves" on hearing the news. But the ends justified the means: "Legalities and technicalities aside, the fact remains that the President by this move has forged a chain of Atlantic defenses which this country badly needed."[98] Surprisingly, McCormick also praised the deal, which he viewed as the result of his frequent demands for more U.S. bases in the Caribbean. He even took credit for it, calling the acquisition of the bases "the greatest contribution of this newspaper to the country's history since the nomination of Lincoln."[99]

Hearst, though, believed that the deal portended the end of American neutrality and the death of democracy. "The deed is done—the die is cast—Mr. Roosevelt has his wish at last. His heart's desire has been to get us into war before the election, and apparently he has realized it," he wrote in his column. The bases-destroyers agreement, he argued, was "an act of aggression and participation—a vicarious onslaught upon the other combatants. . . . The only question now is what the retaliatory measures will be by those whom we elect to consider our enemies."[100]

As a first step, Hearst predicted, the agreement would drive Germany and Italy into an alliance with the Japanese. After that, he thought the war could come very soon, and California might be on the front line. "So the good people on the Pacific coast would better begin digging bomb-proof cellars," he advised, "because they may have Oriental visitors." He personally planned to move his valuables inland to protect them from Japanese bombers.[101]

Hearst's fears for his glassware might sound extreme, but his prediction of a German-Italian-Japanese alliance turned out to be correct. The Nazi conquests of France and the Netherlands emboldened the militarists in the Japanese government. They saw an opportunity to seize the colonial possessions of the now-defeated European powers, and they wanted to neutralize American opposition. At the same time, German leaders, worried by the bases-destroyers deal, realized the value of allying with a Pacific power.[102]

In late September 1940, Japan joined with Italy and Germany to sign the Tripartite Pact, an alliance clearly aimed at the United States. One article in the pact committed the three nations to "assist one another with all political, economic and military means when one of the three powers is attacked by a power at present not involved in the European war or in the Chinese-Japanese conflict."[103]

Fear of a Japanese-German wartime alliance prompted a remarkable turn in the Asian policy of the Hearst papers and the *Daily News*. Hearst and Patterson had been warning about the "yellow peril" for years. But now, as they came to worry that a confrontational stance toward Japan could suck the United States into a war in Europe, they changed their views.[104] In 1935, Patterson's *Daily News* had called Japan "one of the most ferocious nations in the history of the world."[105] Yet in June 1940, the paper reversed course and declared that Japan posed no threat: "It is physically impossible for Japan to come over here and invade and conquer the United States." Moreover, the Japanese were "the most nearly like us" of "all the Oriental peoples." The *News* counseled "soft-pedaling the moral indignation over Japan's aggressions in China for a while."[106]

Hearst, one of the most influential and vicious proponents of anti-Asian racism in American history, also changed his view of the Japanese. In an open letter to a Tokyo journalist in fall 1940, he claimed that "the government of Asia should be a matter for Asiatics to decide" and likened the Asian subjects of European colonial powers—and thus the Japanese who wished to overthrow those colonialists—to the American revolutionaries. Japanese imperial conquest, he wrote, was similar to the U.S. dispossession of the Indians (which he saw as a positive event). He denounced the Roosevelt administration's "carping, complaining, meddling, interfering attitude" and called for "restoring the good will and kindly spirit of respect and friendship" which, he said, had always existed between the two countries.[107] This was the same Hearst who, in 1918, had identified the "fundamental character of the Oriental" as despotic. "Wherever the yellow man's civilization advances," the Hearst papers had insisted then, "despotism is substituted for republicanism, tyranny for democracy."[108] Now that a firm stance against Japanese despotism might lead the United States into war with Germany, Hearst decided that Japan was the moral equivalent of America in 1776.

■

In the last weeks of the presidential campaign, Hearst and McCormick predicted calamitous consequences if Roosevelt won—nothing less than a "third-term dictatorship," to McCormick, and for Hearst, "the end of democracy."[109] Hearst speculated that if Roosevelt won a third term, he might never leave office. "The country has virtually ceased to be a 'democratic nation' for seven years," a Hearst editorial pronounced. "These United States will cease to be a democratic nation IN FACT if we re-elect President Roosevelt for four more years— which may mean, like Caesar Augustus, for the REST OF HIS LIFE."[110]

Roosevelt fought back with his clearest statement to date that he would keep America out of the European war. "I have said this before, but I shall say it again and again and again. Your boys are not going to be sent into any foreign wars," he pledged in a campaign speech in Boston on October 30.[111] He dropped his previous qualifier of "except in case of attack," reasoning that if the country were attacked, then "it's no longer a foreign war," as he told his speechwriter. He would put the phrase back in his subsequent speeches.[112] But he had given the isolationists a weapon to use against him: the "again and again and again" refrain would become his enemies' favorite taunt.

Joe Patterson, though, was still a Roosevelt man in November 1940. Talk of a third-term dictatorship was "complete bosh," the *Daily News* assured its readers.[113] When the president won decisively, with 54.7 percent of the popular vote and 449 electoral votes, the *News* again tried to reassure voters who "took overseriously" the charge that Roosevelt planned to "take a long step toward totalitarianism" and make himself dictator. "It doesn't look that way to us," the paper concluded.[114]

Roosevelt's multilateral foreign policy still worried Joe Patterson. But as long as the British had the dollar and gold reserves to pay for their arms purchases, and as long as they possessed a large enough fleet to carry those purchases away in their own ships, Patterson was willing to support the president, however grudgingly. It wasn't as if the United States was lending or leasing military equipment to the British, or using the U.S. Navy to convoy those arms. Roosevelt would never go that far.

CHAPTER TEN

The Dictator Bill

T HE STRUGGLE OVER MORE American aid to the British began abruptly on November 23, 1940, when Pan American Airways' Atlantic Clipper touched down at a New York airport and disgorged its fourteen passengers. A gaggle of reporters gathered on the tarmac to ask questions of one of the weary travelers. Would Lord Lothian, the British ambassador to the United States, please comment for the American press? As it happened, Lothian did indeed want to talk. He had grown impatient with his government's reluctance to explain Britain's dire financial situation to the American public and had persuaded Prime Minister Winston Churchill to write a detailed and emphatic request for help to President Roosevelt. But Churchill did not share Lothian's sense of urgency, and the letter was still undergoing rounds of revision by various British officials. The ambassador thought it was time to level with the American people. At the impromptu press conference, he startled the reporters with his candor. Britain's need for funds was "becoming urgent," he admitted. The coming year would be "difficult," he said; Britain would require planes, ships, ammunition—"and perhaps a little financial help." It could no longer pay cash for what it needed to fight the Nazis.[1]

"Envoy Lothian claims Britain is going broke," jeered the *Chicago Tribune*.[2] The ambassador seems to have used slightly more diplomatic language, though the *Tribune*'s more inflammatory account is the version in many history books.[3] Even with careful phrasing, the statement sent shock waves through Washington. Clearly, the British wanted—and needed—a radical change in U.S. neutrality policy, from cash and carry to credit and convoy. In response, President Roosevelt and his interventionist allies on two continents would launch a clever propaganda campaign, primarily using newer media like radio and movies. The president relied on the help of professional propagandists to help him maneuver around the isolationist publishers, including Joe Patterson, up to this point one of his best friends in the press.

■

Churchill was displeased by Lothian's unauthorized statement. "I do not think it was wise to touch on very serious matters to reporters on the landing stage," he wrote to his ambassador.[4] But the prime minister did finish his letter to Roosevelt—"one of the most important I ever wrote," he later said.[5] It laid out precisely what Britain needed and the consequences to the English-speaking democracies if those needs were not met.

The letter was not "an appeal for aid," Churchill told Roosevelt, but "a statement of the minimum action necessary to achieve our common purpose." Britain's most pressing problems stemmed from the cash-and-carry restrictions in the U.S. neutrality law. After months of U-boat attacks, the British did not have enough ships available to carry supplies across the ocean. They needed U.S. vessels to transport their war materiel, and they wanted the U.S. Navy to help escort these ships across the dangerous North Atlantic. Just as urgently, Churchill told the president, the British soon would "no longer be able to pay cash for shipping and other supplies." They required credit to continue fighting the Nazis.[6]

Roosevelt responded with a clever plan to help the British while avoiding a direct tussle with Congress over the Neutrality Act. At a press conference in December 1940, he told reporters that he saw no need to repeal either the Neutrality Act or the Johnson Act, a 1934 law that prohibited giving credit to nations at war. Instead, he said he would propose something wholly new: a plan to lend war equipment to the British during the crisis and   · later "get repaid sometime in kind, thereby leaving out the dollar mark." Using a compelling metaphor, he compared the program to lending his garden hose to a neighbor whose house was on fire. "I don't say to him . . . 'Neighbor, my garden hose cost me $15; you have to pay me $15 for it.' . . . I don't want $15—I want my garden hose back after the fire is over."[7] In a Fireside Chat on December 29, as the Germans conducted a devastating bombing raid that left vast swaths of London around St. Paul's Cathedral in rubble, Roosevelt argued that the British needed "the planes, the tanks, the guns, the freighters which will enable them to fight for their liberty and for our security." In another memorable metaphor, he urged Americans to make their country "the great arsenal of democracy."[8]

The next week, in his annual address to Congress, Roosevelt yoked American security to the British cause. "The safety of our country and of our democracy," he said, "are overwhelmingly involved in events far beyond our borders." Countering suggestions by isolationists that the British should negotiate a truce with Hitler, he insisted that the Allies needed to win a clear victory in the war against fascism. "We cannot, and we will not, tell them that they must surrender, merely because of present inability to pay for the weapons which we know they must have." He ended by setting forth his vision of a postwar order, "a world founded upon four essential human freedoms." This was not, contrary to the isolationists' warnings, a war to preserve the British Empire: it was a struggle for freedom of speech and religion; it was a fight to guarantee freedom from want and fear.[9]

Days after his Four Freedoms speech, Roosevelt's supporters in the House introduced a bill titled "An Act to Further Promote the Defense of the United States, and for Other Purposes," a name that isolationists found deliberately duplicitous ("It is, truthfully, 'for other purposes,' " the *Chicago Tribune* snarked).[10] Under the proposed law, the U.S. government could sell, exchange, lend, lease, or "otherwise dispose of" war materiel to "any country whose defense the President deems vital to the defense of the United States." The House parliamentarian gave the bill the number 1776—a clever way of signaling that the act would help safeguard American freedom and independence. Far from being an entangling alliance, the measure's backers argued that it guaranteed U.S. autonomy.[11] As it made its way through Congress, many observers referred to it as

H.R. 1776, while others began calling it "Lease-Lend" or the name that stuck, "Lend-Lease."

The Hearst, McCormick, and Patterson publications, though, often used a different term to describe the proposal: the president's dictatorship bill. To these publishers, the winter of 1941 marked the last chance to save American democracy and ensure the survival of the "white race."

Although many other newspaper barons opposed Lend-Lease in their editorials, only the Hearst/Patterson/McCormick publications presented biased news coverage of the congressional debate. The Scripps-Howard and Gannett newspapers, respectively the nation's second- and third-largest chains, stridently opposed the bill on their opinion pages, but their papers' news stories on Lend-Lease were relatively even-handed and free from inflammatory language.

That was not the case in the Hearst newspapers. The country's biggest chain gave prominent and extensive coverage on its news pages to speeches by anti-interventionist senators, whom it portrayed as brave resisters to the president and the "powerful war bloc" in Congress. The "weary opposition Senators, nerves whipped raw and voices hoarse from the long struggle, were no match for the Administration steamroller once it got going today," read a typical passage.[12] Readers learned that Roosevelt had asked for "absolute power to give away U.S. planes, guns, warships" and that Lend-Lease was a "blank check" bill, an "unlimited armament aid" bill, even a "dictator bill." That last was not set off in quotes but simply reported as if it were fact: "Senate Fight Opened to Beat Dictator Bill."[13]

Chicago Tribune reporters and editors also referred to H.R. 1776 as the president's dictator bill or the administration's dictatorship bill, without quotation marks, in their news stories and headlines. The bill's opponents received respectful and generous coverage, while its supporters popped up in *Tribune* stories primarily to express amazement at the president's "demands" for dictatorial powers, as in: "Administration supporters conceded that never in the history of the republic, not excluding the world war days under Woodrow Wilson or the so-called 'hundred days' of the first rubber stamp congress under Mr. Roosevelt, had an American President sought such an imperial grant of power."[14] (This news might have surprised faithful *Tribune* readers who had learned of many previous power grabs by Roosevelt, including his demands for various "dictator bills" to reorganize the government, increase farm aid, and curb war profits.)[15] Other *Tribune* stories suggested vast conspiracies involving leaders of both major political parties. The paper's Washington bureau chief, Arthur Sears Henning, reported that Wendell Willkie, who supported Lend-Lease, had only received the GOP presidential nomination the previous year because of behind-the-scenes plotting by prominent Democrats, including Roosevelt. "The President himself is suspected of being the brains of these manipulations," the *Tribune* reported in the front-page story.[16]

Before the Lend-Lease debate, most journalists regarded *Daily News* reporters as more reliable than those employed by Hearst or McCormick, but their coverage of the British aid bill soon undermined their reputation for objectivity. Like the *Tribune* reporters, the *News* and *Washington Times-Herald* correspondents sometimes identified H.R. 1776 as the "president's appeal for one-man dictatorial powers" and "Roosevelt's bid for war-dictator powers."[17] The *News*'s senior Washington correspondent, John O'Donnell, betrayed such an obvious bias against aid for the British that a pro-Roosevelt Philadelphia newspaper described him as a "Naziphile" who had "broadcast his sympathy with most of Hitler's aims" (an allegation that prompted O'Donnell to file a libel suit, which he ultimately won).[18]

Roosevelt acted quickly to counter some of the isolationists' most extreme arguments. When Montana senator and isolationist leader Burton Wheeler claimed that Lend-Lease would "plow under every fourth American boy," Roosevelt denounced the accusation the next day as "the most dastardly, unpatriotic thing that has ever been said."[19] Some historians have criticized Roosevelt for magnifying a charge that received scant press attention.[20] But though the *New York Times* and other elite dailies gave it little notice, the remark was on the front page of the Hearst and McCormick newspapers, and the president knew that he needed to answer it.[21]

If the Hearst/McCormick/Patterson news coverage of Lend-Lease was biased, their editorials were positively apocalyptic. According to Hearst, Americans could be enjoying their "very last hours of DEMOCRACY AND FREEDOM" if the Lend-Lease bill and its "sweeping provisions for dictatorship" became law. "Speak up, America! Let us make democracy work, but first let us KEEP DEMOCRACY," a Hearst editorial warned.[22] Hearst's front-page columns painted horrifying pictures of the future. If Lend-Lease passed, he asserted, American democracy would die, "enveloped in the flames of the holocaust. And out of the smoldering ruins of our social and political system will rise the scarlet woman of Communism."[23] McCormick's *Tribune* editorials sounded the same alarms. Roosevelt had "seized upon the war" to divide his opponents and distract attention from the failures of the domestic New Deal. Lend-Lease, the *Tribune* declared, "is a bill for the destruction of the American Republic. It is a bill for an unlimited dictatorship."[24]

The Lend-Lease bill was the breaking point for Joe Patterson, who abandoned the president and joined Hearst and McCormick in predicting tyranny and dictatorship if the arms bill passed. *Daily News* editorials, which also ran almost daily in the *Washington Times-Herald*, agreed that those who called the aid bill "Lend-Lease" or "Lease-Lend" were merely trying "to prettify it." Its proper name, the *News* insisted, was "A Bill to Set Up a Dictatorship in the United States With a View to Combating the Dictators of Germany, Italy and Japan." Its passage threatened to "write democracy's finish forever in the United States."[25] The *Daily News*'s Pulitzer Prize–winning editorial cartoonist, C. D. Batchelor, illustrated the editorials with often gruesome antiwar imagery. One cartoon in early 1941 portrayed Uncle Sam in an embrace with a ghoulish female figure labeled "War" with a skull for a face. Uncle Sam is toasting the woman—"Here's looking at you!"—while lifting a martini glass labeled "Dictatorship Bill." She raises hers in return and replies: "Cheerio, you bloody blighter!"[26] A few weeks later, the same couple appeared again, this time with caption identifying them as "Uncle Sap and his new girl friend."[27]

But though the *Daily News* editorials echoed the Hearst and McCormick themes, Patterson's arguments were subtler, more expertly crafted, and therefore more influential. His longtime support for Roosevelt—up to and including the election of 1940—gave him credibility that Hearst and McCormick did not possess. Moreover, his sister's newspaper, which by 1941 published ten editions a day, put his editorials in front of national political leaders and earned Patterson a devoted following among isolationist members of Congress. "I think you are one of America's greatest patriots," wrote one of his fans, North Carolina senator Robert Rice Reynolds, to Joe Patterson soon after the Lend-Lease fight ended.[28] Some *Times-Herald* readers questioned their paper's almost daily use of columns from New York, but Cissy Patterson defended the practice on her editorial page. "Now and then," she wrote in January 1941, "somebody asks why we publish the editorials of the New York Daily News in this column. Answer: Because they are always interesting, well written and express a thought with which we agree."[29]

Unlike Hearst and McCormick, Joe Patterson conceded the appeal of some interventionist arguments before labeling them absurd. To be sure, the *News* admitted, Franklin Roosevelt seemed genuinely concerned about the dangers of Hitlerism. "We think his motives are unimpeachable; that he sincerely believes he is wise and far-seeing enough to run our whole aid-Britain effort without a lot of time-killing talk from a lot of Senators and Representatives," one *Daily News* editorial explained. "But that is not the way a democracy operates."[30] The *News* used the same semantic techniques in arguing against aid to Britain. One headline avowed, "We're Not Anti-British." But the paper refused "to back up Great Britain every time she gets herself into a squabble over the decaying carcass that is Europe."[31]

News editors also claimed that they were not anti-Semitic, an argument few found convincing. The most insidious *News* editorials pretended to deplore anti-Semitic arguments while actually spreading them. The American Jewish Congress started keeping a file on the *Daily News*'s anti-Semitism in 1938, when the newspaper feigned horror at a list of hundreds of allegedly disloyal Jews in the New Deal.[32] In 1940, the *News* described a group of American Nazis, who had been arrested for plotting to overthrow the republic, kill all the country's Jews, and set up a Nazi government, as "nondescript and dreamy-eyed young men." It then used their arrests as an opportunity to blame the victims. "Anti-Semitism in this country," the paper argued, "is not due so much to the actions of the Jews here as to their natural sympathy for their persecuted racial kinfolk in Europe." As a result, non-Jewish Americans—like those dreamy-eyed Nazis—shared "an instinctive fear" that Jews' "pro-alien sympathies" might cause the United States to be "dragged into the war."[33] The editorial's language evoked anti-Semitic tropes of rootless cosmopolitans who could never be true Americans because of their alleged dual loyalties.

In 1941, during and after the Lend-Lease debate, the *News* continued to publicize anti-Semitic slurs while pretending to condemn them. It decried the "whispering campaign" that "the Jews are mainly to blame" for possible U.S. entry to the war. "After the war, when blame is being dealt around for the inevitable tragedies of it all, this legend will probably be dug up in this country, and anti-Semitism may have a flare-up."[34] This was a familiar isolationist argument: McCormick voiced similar "fears" in the *Chicago Tribune*, warning that "the American people" (a category that apparently excluded Jews) might assault minorities if the United States entered the war. "Given a terrible injury, the American people, we may fear, will yield to that instinct of intolerance for minorities that had bred a series of disasters throughout all history. The stage is being set by its inevitable victims."[35]

Patterson's biggest concern was that American Jews' "pro-alien" solidarity with Hitler's victims, if it drove the United States to war with Germany, would lead the "white race" to suicide. In February 1941, he fretted that the United States would join the "dance of death" that was entrancing "all the white nations." When that happened, "the yellow race will be the next logical rulers of the world."[36] Channeling the popular pseudo-scientific racist Madison Grant, the *News* predicted in March 1941 that the war would lead to the "passing of the great race" and end with Europe "so enfeebled that the yellow hordes of Asia will find it easy pickings. European racial suicide today may be paving the road for another Mongol invasion a few years hence."[37]

The news coverage and editorials of the Hearst/Patterson/McCormick press boosted the isolationist cause and its foremost organization, the America First Committee, though none of the isolationist publishers joined the group. Both McCormick and Joe Patterson declined invitations to support the committee on an official basis, because as Patterson said, "I have found it wise not to join committees which might commit not only me, but also, in a sense, the paper I edit, to details of action which I cannot now foresee."[38] But he and his cousin quietly helped bankroll America First.[39] On one occasion, while thanking Patterson profusely for a generous check, the secretary of the AFC's New York chapter noted that his editorial backing was even more important than his money: "I doubt if our activities could have continued successfully without the aid of your very powerful paper."[40]

•

Yet even the combined opposition of the Pattersons, McCormick, and Hearst, whose papers collectively reached about 30 percent of Americans, could not defeat Lend-Lease. Congress passed the bill by healthy margins, 260-165 in the House and 60-31 in the Senate. Eighteen months earlier, these publishers had succeeded in stopping Roosevelt from ending the arms embargo, but now they could not muster enough votes to kill a much more interventionist measure. Two things had changed: the international crisis had worsened, and the Roosevelt administration had grown more adept at combating the isolationists.

The president and his allies won the battle against anti-interventionist propaganda in the nation's best-selling newspapers by commencing a public relations campaign of their own, one even more formidable and effective than the combined power of the isolationist press. The interventionists created, as the *Chicago Tribune* said, a "propaganda organization reaching into every community in the country, the like of which the capital has never seen before."[41] McCormick was known for his conspiracy theories, but this time he was correct. Official administration sources, private interventionist groups, and British propagandists exploited the power of radio, newsreels, and movies to challenge and overwhelm the isolationist print media.

Many executive departments joined the official effort to encourage aid to the Allies. Every defense agency employed public relations specialists who put out press releases, radio broadcasts, pamphlets, and op-ed pieces to build morale and persuade the American people that they needed to help the British win the war. The Roosevelt White House also set up several information agencies, including the Division of Information in the Office of Emergency Management, the Office of Government Reports, and, in fall

1941, the Office of Facts and Figures, to convey war news and defense information to the American public.[42]

These government propaganda efforts, spread among many agencies, were often poorly coordinated. But Roosevelt in 1941 hesitated to create a centralized propaganda machine within the government while the United States was not at war.[43] Instead, he relied on unofficial, private groups to help boost the interventionist message. The most important of these was the Committee to Defend America by Aiding the Allies, founded in 1940 by Kansas newspaper editor William Allen White, which soon grew to three hundred chapters.[44] Called the "warmongers' principal propaganda agency" by the *Chicago Tribune*, the group organized letter-writing drives, published pro-intervention pamphlets, and produced a short film on a possible Nazi invasion.[45] After internal conflicts led to White's resignation, the committee faded in importance and more aggressive interventionist groups, such as the Fight for Freedom Committee, took the lead in advocating aid to Britain.

At the same time, skilled propagandists from across the Atlantic worked to shift Americans' views of the war. The isolationists were not wrong when they accused the British of manipulating American public opinion. British information specialists and intelligence officers carried out what one historian has called "one of the most diverse, extensive, and yet subtle propaganda campaigns ever directed by one sovereign state at another."[46] Public relations experts produced short films and radio programs designed to awaken American sympathy for the British people by showing the human suffering caused by the Blitz.[47]

The British needed to step up their propaganda campaign because the Germans were also active in trying to influence the American debate on aid. German agents countered the British by writing and planting pro-Nazi and anti-British propaganda in American newspapers. One German spy, George Sylvester Viereck, even secretly wrote speeches for isolationist members of Congress, who then arranged for copies to be sent to their constituents at no cost by using their franking privilege.[48]

In this contentious media environment, with all sides trying to shape public opinion, Roosevelt asked for help from a few interventionist allies in the print media. One important FDR backer entered the newspaper business specifically to help the president. Marshall Field III, the heir to an estimated $100 million fortune from his family's Chicago department store, had made his first foray into journalism in 1940 when he founded *PM*, a liberal New York tabloid. The next year, some Chicagoans asked if he might consider starting a morning paper in his native city to compete directly with the *Tribune*. The estimated start-up costs for a metropolitan newspaper in 1941 were around $5 million, but Field, a New Dealer and internationalist who insisted that he should "pay taxes cheerfully," was a rare deep-pocketed progressive. Liberals were thrilled that a wealthy interventionist "who actually looks upon publishing as a public service," as the *New Republic* put it, had agreed to challenge McCormick.[49] The first edition of Field's *Chicago Sun*, carrying the motto "An Honest Newspaper," debuted on December 4, 1941.

The president found another new ally in the media in 1941— ironically, one who had opposed him on just about every domestic policy but who shared his views on the need to counter enemies abroad. Henry Luce, the founding publisher of *Time* magazine, helped start the interventionist Council for Democracy and soon emerged as an important counterweight to the isolationist newspaper moguls. The child of American missionaries to China, Luce believed from an early age that Americans should bring Christianity and modernity to Asia and the world. Beginning in 1923 with *Time*, the nation's first weekly newsmagazine, he built a media empire that soon included *Fortune*, a business periodical, and *Life*, a glossy pictorial. In 1931, he added the *March of Time* radio show, and in 1935, the *March of Time* newsreels.

Luce was strongly Republican, anti–New Deal, and conservative —views that put him in the mainstream of American publishers. But he differed markedly from Hearst, McCormick, and the Pattersons on foreign policy, particularly regarding Europe. As he explained in a famous February 1941 essay in *Life*, "The American Century," Luce hoped the United States would "accept wholeheartedly our duty and our opportunity as the most powerful and vital nation in the world and in consequence to exert upon the world the full impact of our influence." Decrying the "virus of isolationist sterility" in the Republican Party, he called for "a truly *American* internationalism" that would help the United States serve and lead the entire world.[50] It is impossible to imagine a philosophy more anathema to his isolationist peers in the press.

Luce's magazines helped shape public opinion about America's role in the world, but his film documentaries were even more consequential. *Time*, *Life*, and *Fortune* collectively sold 3.2 million copies a week in 1940 (with *Life* accounting for 2.4 million); the *March of Time* newsreels were seen by more than 20 million Americans every month.[51]

More than simply news reports, the *March of Time* films were twenty- to thirty-minute documentaries about current events. Each month, the producers would take on a single contemporary issue—rising militarism in Japan, say—and craft a short film that interpreted events with a mixture of real footage and dramatic re-enactments. The series first took on Hitler in 1938, with a segment called "Inside Nazi Germany." The footage had been shot with Nazi approval and showed triumphant parades and celebrations. But the producers also filmed dramatic reenactments of Nazi harassment of political prisoners—including a scene with New York cleaning women, dressed in habits, presented as Catholic nuns imprisoned in a German jail—and knitted the clips together with a strongly anti-Nazi voice-over. The film ended with the narrator delivering a powerful message in the didactic, stentorian tones for which *March of Time* became famous: "Nazi Germany faces her destiny with one of the great war machines in history. And the inevitable destiny of the great war machines of the past has been to destroy the peace of the world, its people, and the governments of their time."[52]

The *March of Time* continued to produce anti-Nazi and pro-Allied films throughout the fight over American entry into the European war. An early 1941 issue, "Uncle Sam—The Non-Belligerent," which came out during the Lend-Lease debate in Congress, was so blatantly pro-British that Burton Wheeler denounced it as "warmongering propaganda."[53] And though Luce's films were the most strident advocates for intervention, by 1939 other newsreel companies —even the one owned by Hearst, who exercised less editorial control over his films than his print media—were also casting Germany as the villain.[54]

In addition to documentaries and newsreels, Americans in 1940 and 1941 could see and hear fictional stories about Nazi brutality or British pluck on their movie screens. The feature film studios were slower than the newsreel companies to produce anti-fascist or pro-Allied movies.[55] Throughout the 1930s, the major studios had been reluctant to make "message" films because they threatened profit margins. An overtly political movie could alienate domestic or foreign consumers or trigger more scrutiny from the industry's self-censorship board, the Production Code Authority. As producer Samuel Goldwyn never actually said, "If you have a message, call Western Union."[56]

But after the fall of France in 1940, the Hollywood studios started producing movies that made heroes of their brave English-speaking cousins across the Atlantic. The decision to make "message movies" about the war had many causes, both political and financial. Once the Nazi regime banned American films from all its territories, the studios no longer worried about offending German censors or consumers. Moreover, the Roosevelt administration may have secured a pledge of support for aiding the British from the chiefs of the seven major studios in return for settling an anti-trust suit against them. As the historian Todd Bennett explains, many observers believed that Roosevelt's aides had negotiated a deal with the film industry: the studios could keep their cinema chains, as long as they backed Roosevelt's policies.[57]

Some filmmakers eagerly seized the opportunity to make anti-Nazi films. Many studio heads were Jews who had hesitated to make movies about German brutality because they did not want to be smeared as un-American "internationalists." Once the political winds shifted toward intervention, these producers chose to celebrate the heroism of those who fought Nazism.[58] In 1940 and 1941, several studios produced hugely popular movies that portrayed the British as stalwart defenders of democracy and freedom. Some of the most effective, such as Alfred Hitchcock's *Foreign Correspondent* and Daryl Zanuck's *A Yank in the RAF*, told conversion stories about skeptical American characters who came to understand the dangers of German fascism.[59]

The most celebrated film of 1941—indeed, the best movie of all time, according to the American Film Institute—was not overtly interventionist, but it indirectly served the internationalist cause by attacking the nation's most prominent isolationist in the media. Orson Welles, the star, director, and co-writer of *Citizen Kane*, spent the 1930s immersed in the New York City culture of the Popular Front, a community that considered Hearst (as a book title put it) one of the "forerunners of American fascism."[60] In 1940, the young director, now under contract with RKO, began casting about for topics for his first feature films. After some conversations with Herman Mankiewicz, a California screenwriter and journalist (and the child of Jewish immigrants), Welles decided to focus on Hearst as a fascinating case study of toxic nationalism. He and Mankiewicz co-wrote the screenplay.[61]

The film, originally called *The American*—a name that evoked Hearst newspapers, many of which had "American" in their titles— told the story of a newspaper chain owner who helped spark the Spanish-American War, ran unsuccessfully for governor of New York, owned an opulent mansion stuffed with European art, and helped his untalented mistress become an opera singer. Except for the girlfriend's lack of talent—Hearst's real-life lover, Marion Davies, was an accomplished comic actress—and her chosen medium, the story of Charles Foster Kane mimicked every key aspect of Hearst's life. Hearst understood that *Citizen Kane* depicted a version of himself. He banned mentions of the movie in his papers and pressured the Hollywood moguls who controlled the bookings in most theaters to block its showings, in part by threatening them with exposés of their own private lives and those of their stars. His underlings warned the studio heads that the Hearst papers might launch anti-Semitic investigations of Hollywood.[62]

Although *Citizen Kane* is somewhat sympathetic to its major character, whose youthful egotism comes across as infectious exuberance and whose tragic faults stem from an unhappy childhood, it does portray him as friendly with fascists. The opening sequence, a fake newsreel called *News on the March*, includes a scene in which Kane shares a balcony with the man whose regime, in real life, partnered with Hearst's newsreel company—Adolf Hitler. Kane also symbolizes the blind obstinance of appeasers. In response to a question about the tension in Europe, he assures a fictional reporter, "There will be no war"—shortly before the war begins. The allusions behind the line are layered: Hearst had been quoted as saying, "I don't think there will be a war" in an April 1939 interview; and Frederic Remington, in his famous telegram to the publisher before the Spanish-American War, had allegedly said, "There will be no war," to which Hearst responded, "You furnish the pictures, and I'll furnish the war." Kane's "There will be no war" managed to poke fun simultaneously at Hearst's warmongering past and his recent history as an appeaser.[63]

While films like *Citizen Kane* helped the cause of aiding the Allies, radio could be an even more influential interventionist medium.[64] Radio news and commentary had played a relatively minor role in foreign policy debates before 1938. The three networks—NBC, CBS, and MBS—had found it hard to overcome technical difficulties in broadcasting from overseas, and their listeners seemed uninterested in news from abroad. But the Munich crisis prompted concern about European affairs and thus more coverage of it (though the radio networks still largely ignored Asia until Pearl Harbor).[65]

Franklin Roosevelt understood the power of radio. He had been using it since his first inauguration to circumvent the press lords and communicate directly with the American people. His Fireside Chats showed him to be an expert at this form of political persuasion. As one correspondent explained, "You felt he was there talking to you, not to 50 million others, but to you personally."[66] Some advocates of aid to the Allies wanted the president to talk to them even more frequently. One supporter told press secretary Steve Early that midwesterners, who were "disheartened" by the biased reporting in the Hearst and McCormick newspapers in their region, gained confidence from the president's radio messages. "His fireside chats are always effective," he wrote, "and usually dispel all suspicion and destroy the effect of the unholy propaganda sponsored by Nazi sympathizers and defeatist prophets."[67]

Roosevelt not only mastered the medium of radio, he also had the authority to license radio stations, unlike newspapers. The president made sure broadcasters knew that federal regulators controlled their access to the airwaves and would scrutinize their news reports for accuracy. Early told the National Association of Broadcasters in 1939 that the government was monitoring American radio broadcasts to foreign countries to ensure that they remained "free from false news."[68] The broadcasters seemed to listen. After 1939, when the anti-Semitic Father Charles Coughlin was forced from the air, almost all major radio commentators supported giving aid to Britain.[69]

Radio news stories from Europe also served the interventionist cause by bringing the suffering of Hitler's victims into American living rooms. CBS correspondent Edward R. Murrow, who began his broadcasts with the catchphrase "*This* is London," made the Blitz a horrifying reality for his American listeners. Sometimes reporting from Broadcasting House in the heart of London, sometimes from the rooftops and streets of the city, he let his listeners hear the shrieks of air raid sirens, the roar of anti-aircraft guns, the ominous drone of German planes flying down the Thames, and the hushed footsteps of English citizens rushing to find safety during the black nights of the terror bombing. "You burned the city of London in our houses and we felt the flames that burnt it," Archibald MacLeish, the librarian of Congress and a prominent interventionist, wrote to Murrow.[70]

Because radio seemed unmediated, Americans trusted it as a news source and came to rely on it more over time. From 1937 to 1942, the proportion of Americans who preferred to get their national and foreign news from the radio increased from 40 to 62 percent, while the proportion who favored newspapers declined from 50 to 34 percent.[71]

Isolationists complained bitterly about the power of radio and film in the intervention debate. The *Chicago Tribune* lamented that the Eastern Seaboard had "fallen into a complete state of hysteria" because of the scaremongering of radio commentators.[72] Senate isolationists even launched an investigation in fall 1941 into supposed interventionist propaganda on the air and in the movies.[73] But the inquiry ended quickly, in part because one of the authors of the resolution that prompted the investigation, Senator Gerald Nye, could not stop himself from blaming Hollywood Jews for the push toward war.[74]

The nonprint media—newsreels, feature films, documentaries, and radio shows—helped transform public opinion throughout 1940 and 1941. Radio and newsreels provided more immediate and vivid news about the war, and particularly about the sacrifices of the British people. As Murrow explained, broadcast reports from Europe brought the war "much nearer to the wheat farmer in Kansas than any official communiqué."[75] Perhaps 50 million Americans read the Hearst or Patterson/McCormick press, but 85 million went to the movies every week, and millions more listened to broadcasters like Murrow.[76]

Though most Americans still overwhelmingly opposed joining the war, pollsters noted a shift in their perceptions of the conflict. In May 1940, 64 percent of Americans thought it was more important to stay neutral than to risk war by helping Britain, with 36 percent disagreeing. By November, those numbers had almost flipped, with 60 percent saying it was better to help Britain, no matter the risk.[77] A year later, though most Americans still wanted to avoid entering the conflict, 70 percent reported that it was more important to defeat Germany than to stay out of the war.[78]

■

As interventionists learned to use radio and films to sell Americans on the need to help Britain, they also benefited from a new attitude —or at least a professed new attitude—in British colonial policy. The isolationists had consistently argued that Britain was no different from Germany; it wanted U.S. aid, they said, so that it could continue to rule and oppress the peoples it had colonized. But in the summer of 1941, British officials started to signal—however reluctantly and sometimes unintentionally—that they would consider allowing more self-government and democracy in their colonies after the war. Surprisingly, one of the most persuasive propagandists for Britain's new outlook was a London press lord who had made his name as an enthusiast for empire and isolation.

Max Beaverbrook entered the summer of 1941 holding a new position, minister of supply. His nearly yearlong tenure as minister of aircraft production had ended in spring 1941, when Churchill finally agreed, given the unending bureaucratic warfare between Beaverbrook and the Air Ministry, to accept his latest letter of resignation— by his staff's count, his fourteenth.[79] Beaverbrook stayed in the cabinet as a minister without portfolio for a month until Churchill persuaded him to accept a new remit at the Supply Ministry, coordinating and encouraging the flow of goods from the United States to Britain. After the Nazi invasion of the Soviet Union in June 1941, he also tried to facilitate and increase British and American shipments to Russia. He thus entered a new phase of his career: international diplomat.

Churchill relied on Beaverbrook to charm Americans and Russians. In August 1941, the prime minister asked his Canadian-born supply minister to accompany him to a secret meeting with Roosevelt off the coast of Newfoundland. At the conference, Churchill and Roosevelt signed the Atlantic Charter, a brief document that set out Anglo-American war goals. The leaders vowed to respect "the right of all peoples to choose the form of government under which they will live"; they also called for a lasting peace that would ensure that "all the men in all the lands may live out their lives in freedom from fear and want."[80]

Churchill later tried to play down the importance of this language: it "is not a law—it is a star," he insisted.[81] But Mohandas Gandhi, Nelson Mandela, and other fighters against British imperialism could point to the charter and argue that the embattled British Empire had pledged itself to eventual self-determination for its colonies.[82] Moreover, Roosevelt clearly saw the charter as a prelude to British decolonization.[83] The British need for American help in their darkest hour led to a change in the balance of power in the Anglo-American relationship. In effect, the greatest boosters of the British Empire had knuckled under to American pressure to commit to their colonies' self-governance. Roosevelt had successfully pressured the British government into accepting his anti-imperialist peace aims.

After the Atlantic Conference, Beaverbrook continued to build support for his adopted country by cultivating strategic friendships with American policy makers and journalists. He accompanied Churchill to Washington, D.C., where he lunched with the president, who already regarded him as an "old friend."[84] Beaverbrook also began flattering and manipulating interventionist journalists with the same ardor he had once shown to Joe Patterson. He entertained Henry Luce with such élan that Luce later wrote that Beaverbrook "put the vitamin of zest into the whole business of living."[85]

Beaverbrook turned to wooing the Russians in September 1941, when he traveled to Moscow as the first British minister to

Max Beaverbrook, minister of supply, accompanied Prime Minister
Winston Churchill on board the HMS *Prince of Wales* to the Atlantic
Conference off the coast of Newfoundland in August 1941. Churchill
relied on his Canadian minister to persuade his fellow North Americans
to give more aid to the British. (Fremantle / Alamy Stock Photo)

visit the Soviet Union since Hitler's invasion. Averell Harriman, Roosevelt's personal representative in Europe, headed the American delegation. The two men hoped to encourage Russian resistance to the Nazis by arranging to send a flood of American and British war supplies to the beleaguered Soviet troops. Before they left London, Churchill warned Beaverbrook to look out for British interests. "Your function," the prime minister wrote, "will be not only to aid in the forming of the plans to help Russia, but to make sure we are not bled white in the process."[86]

Beaverbrook got on well with Stalin, who found him an amusing companion, and impressed the Americans with his diplomatic skills. "Beaverbrook has been a great salesman," Harriman recorded. "His personal sincerity was convincing. His genius never worked more effectively."[87] Churchill agreed that the mission helped forge unity among the three nations, and told Beaverbrook, "No one could have done it but you."[88] But one outcome of the trip annoyed him: Beaverbrook's embrace of the Russian position that the British needed to invade Europe to take the pressure off the Soviet Union. Over the next year, Beaverbrook's disagreement with Churchill on the second front would cause friction between them.

■

British concession and salesmanship, along with interventionist propaganda on the radio and the movie screen, helped President Roosevelt win the great debate over intervention. That was the verdict of press monitors and pollsters. Treasury Secretary Henry Morgenthau Jr. directed an assistant to read dozens of newspapers every week and report back on press coverage of the war. The assistant, the journalist Alan Barth, who later became an award-winning editorial writer for the *Washington Post*, was bullish on the chances of more U.S. help to the Allies through much of 1941. In March, right after the passage of Lend-Lease, he predicted that only the "strong-stomached, full-fledged isolationists, the fanatic fringe" would keep fighting aid to the British. The isolationists, he wrote, had been reduced to a "national political alliance of crackpots."[89] By October, he reported that most of the media had been "moved by the logic of events abroad and, perhaps also, by the pressure of public opinion at home toward a steadily increasing interventionism." Across the nation, he said, the majority of newspapers now demanded "a policy of positive and active resistance to Hitlerism."[90]

But the isolationist press would not go along. As millions of Americans gradually turned from isolation to intervention throughout 1941, Joe Patterson, Cissy Patterson, McCormick, and Hearst all kept their faith in isolationism. They believed Roosevelt was dragging an unwilling public into an unnecessary war. They launched slashing attacks on the president and his policies right until—and even after—the Japanese dropped their bombs on Oahu.

The decision by McCormick and Hearst to keep resisting Roosevelt's foreign policy was no surprise; they had despised the president for years and had lost the respect of the rest of the press for their tendency to distort or lie about his policies.[91] But Joe Patterson, "one of the most liberal publishers in the whole country," according to Harold Ickes in 1940, was a different story.[92] His conversion to Roosevelt-hating—even to promoting anti-Roosevelt conspiracy theories—revealed the racist nationalism and anti-Semitism at the core of the right-wing isolationist fight.

Each dramatic event in the European war during the summer of 1941 left the isolationist publishers unmoved, or even more entrenched in their commitment to keep the United States out of the war. The Nazi invasion of the Soviet Union? It proved that the British no longer required American help. "There is no need," the *Tribune* editorialized, "for the American people to sacrifice their freedom in the name of an emergency which does not exist."[93] The Atlantic Charter? It was another sign that the British were manipulating Americans into subsidizing their imperial gains. "It was and is nothing but a statement of the joint philosophy of a dictator made such by the British Parliament and a dictator made such by himself," said the *Daily News*.[94] In another editorial on the Atlantic Conference, the *News* equated Churchill and Roosevelt with the fascist dictators ("Who is the Fuehrer and who is the Duce?"), and suggested that the president might provoke a new American revolution by canceling the 1942 elections.[95] It was the first time that Patterson raised the specter of revolution, but it would not be the last.

In September, the isolationists faced a crisis when their most famous representative, Charles Lindbergh, drew attention to the largely unspoken anti-Semitism within their movement. Lindbergh had already shown that he viewed the war in Europe through the same racial lens as Hearst, McCormick, and Patterson, describing it in one radio broadcast as a quarrel among nations of "the white race."[96] In a magazine article, he called for "a Western Wall of race and arms" to hold back "the infiltration of inferior blood."[97] The Nazis, noticing the similarity of his views to their own, in 1938 had awarded him Germany's highest honor for foreigners, the Service Cross of the German Eagle.

But then Lindbergh made the mistake of going beyond vague invocations of "race" and "blood" to say aloud what isolationists preferred to keep private. In a speech in Des Moines, Iowa, he charged that the three most important groups pushing the country into war were "the British, the Jewish, and the Roosevelt adminis-tration." British people and Jews, he claimed, "for reasons which are not American," were thinking only of their own selfish needs. "We cannot blame them for looking out for what they believe to be their own interests, but we also must look out for ours. We cannot allow the natural passions and prejudices of other peoples to lead our country to destruction." Jews, in his view, were not true Americans but alien forces—"other peoples." Especially menacing was their prominence in powerful institutions: "Their greatest danger to this country lies in their large ownership and influence in our motion pictures, our press, our radio, and our government."[98]

By openly proclaiming the anti-Semitism that some in the anti-interventionist movement had been trying to hide, Lindbergh prompted some soul-searching within the isolationist ranks. He went too far for many, including, most surprisingly, Hearst, who called the speech a "violation of basic Americanism." A Hearst editorial blasted Lindbergh's "intemperate and intolerant address" and denounced it for inciting "racial and religious prejudices."[99] Some members of America First felt betrayed by Hearst's piece and blamed him for heightening the controversy surrounding the speech. Lindbergh's remarks "would have died down as an active issue of controversy," one isolationist complained, "if it had not been for the editorial in the Hearst papers."[100]

By contrast, McCormick, at first, defended Lindbergh. He shared the aviator's feelings about Jews; in fact he had made the same argument—that the British, the New Dealers, and the Jews were pushing America into war—in a letter to Lindbergh months earlier, which may have put the idea in the flier's head, or at least encouraged him to articulate it.[101] The colonel initially responded to the Des Moines speech by warning Jews and other minorities that they might find themselves subject "to the very persecution they fear" unless they began to "think and act as Americans."[102]

But McCormick soon decided to distance himself from the sentiments of Lindbergh's Des Moines speech. The next week the paper published a full-page color photo spread of the medals that many different governments had given Lindbergh for his aviation accomplishments, complete with gushing text ("Never has there been another man ... who has attained quite the popularity of Charles A. Lindbergh"). But McCormick also included a stiff statement that the display should not be regarded as "evidence of approval of the Des Moines speech."[103] The spread showed medals bestowed upon him by Germany's allies, including Japan, but it omitted the Service Cross of the German Eagle.

Patterson took a different tack: he responded to the Des Moines address by gently chiding Lindbergh for misplaced emphasis, but not for deep-seated anti-Semitism. A *News* editorial disputed Lindbergh's contention that the Jews were a "major factor" in the push to war, arguing that they were only a minor one. Rather, Americans should blame the English for drawing them into a war to "preserve the dominance of the British Empire."[104] Patterson disagreed about the relative importance of the three pro-war groups Lindbergh mentioned, but not regarding the assumptions about Americanness at the heart of his argument.

Patterson and McCormick frequently defended themselves from accusations of anti-Semitism by insisting that they distrusted the British at least as much as they distrusted Jewish Americans— without noting the distinction between the actual foreignness of the British and the perceived un-American tendencies of Jews who were their fellow citizens. When they discussed anti-Semitism, the isolationist press lords always defined it narrowly. Jew-haters wore robes and burned crosses, or at least refused to hire Jews or let them in their clubs. They were not "pro-American" newspapers like the *Daily News* or the *Chicago Tribune*. The cousins claimed that their opponents ("warmongers") mistook their genuine hatred of war for anti-Semitism; in effect, their enemies were indulging in a kind of brown-baiting.[105]

Jewish groups, unpersuaded by Patterson's defense, organized a boycott of the *News*. Protesters stationed at strategic street corners passed out cards to New Yorkers that spread the word: "I am doing my bit by not buying the Daily News. They are very unfair to the Jews by their policy. I do not intend to buy their paper until such policy changes." Patterson angrily rebutted the charges. When the managing editor of a Jewish publication tried to interview him about the boycott and the examples of anti-Semitism in the *News*, the publisher penned an indignant retort. "The News is not anti-Semitic," he wrote back, "and never has been. . . . The News is against our entering the war and sending another expeditionary force to Europe, Asia or Africa. That is not anti-Semitism."[106] This explanation did not convince the boycotters, who continued to organize and protest the *News*'s anti-Jewish policies throughout 1941 and the war years.

■

Many interventionists believed that the Lindbergh speech, by revealing the anti-Jewish sentiments fueling America First, actually helped the internationalist cause. Alan Barth, Morgenthau's press monitor, argued that the undisguised anti-Semitism of the speech led to "a fresh winnowing of the fanatic fringe and a swelling of majority pressure for national unity." Some conservative newspaper publishers, he explained, seemed genuinely repulsed by "the dangerous channels into which Lindbergh was directing the isolationist campaign," while others seized on Lindbergh's anti-Semitism "as a convenient pretext for abandoning a position which had become generally untenable."[107] Like other advocates of British aid, he hoped that the widespread condemnation of the speech meant that the president would have an easier time getting more help to the Allies.

But the isolationist press lords still had formidable influence in Congress. In August, anti-interventionists almost defeated a bill that extended the peacetime draft. It ultimately passed the House by a margin of one vote. Roosevelt considered asking Congress to repeal the Neutrality Act, but calculated correctly that he might lose. Instead, he requested that Congress loosen some of its restrictions, and once again he won the battle with few votes to spare.[108]

As Roosevelt struggled to free the U.S. Navy from the fetters of the Neutrality Act, American ships faced increasing danger. The undeclared naval war in the Atlantic turned deadly when German submarines began to sink U.S. ships and kill American sailors. In early September, a German U-boat fired on a navy destroyer, the *Greer*. The ship was not hit, but the incident prompted Roosevelt to instruct the navy to shoot on sight any German submarine spotted in the waters from Canada to Iceland. In mid-October, a German submarine fired a torpedo into a U.S. destroyer, the *Kearny*, with the loss of eleven American lives. At the end of the month, the Germans sank another destroyer, the *Reuben James*, killing more than one hundred American servicemen. Still Roosevelt did not ask Congress for a declaration of war—because he knew he would not get one.

The isolationist press watched the battles in the Atlantic with growing fury—and with increasing conviction that Roosevelt had engineered the incidents. They believed Roosevelt had lied when he failed to explain that the *Greer* had been tracking the German submarine that fired on it (a fact that the chief of naval operations divulged in testimony to Congress later that month). A *Daily News* editorial about the *Greer* incident accused the president of having no respect for truth. It concluded with a list of Roosevelt's antiwar statements from the 1940 election, including the "again and again and again" promise.[109] U.S. Navy secretary Frank Knox protested to Patterson that Roosevelt had not known about the tracking at the time of his speech.[110]

Patterson was correct that Roosevelt wanted to get into the war. By fall 1941 the president could not see any other way to defeat the Nazis.[111] And Roosevelt's first account of the firing on the *Greer* was, as the historian Robert Dallek has concluded, "less than candid."[112] But contrary to the McCormick/Patterson/Hearst allegations, the president was not acting secretly or without democratic sanction. Admiral Harold Stark gave a much fuller story of the *Greer* incident later that month to Congress, with Roosevelt's approval.[113] More important, polls showed that solid majorities of the public supported convoying British ships.[114] Most Americans agreed that helping the British, even at the risk of war, was necessary to rescue democracy in Europe and in the United States.

Yet in Patterson's view, the president was not trying to save democracy by fighting the fascists; he was trying to end democracy in
the United States and make himself dictator. If the United States
entered the war, the *News* concluded, it would be entirely Roosevelt's fault. "Win, lose, or draw, it should be called Roosevelt's
War, because he is the man who got us into it."[115]

That kind of clear, uncompromising rhetoric cheered the beleaguered isolationists. John T. Flynn, a journalist and America First
leader, thanked Patterson for publishing such editorials, which
helped him remain hopeful and confident. "I find that almost all the
people in our organization read them the first thing in the morning,
pretty much as an old monk reads the Following of Christ to buck
up his spirits for the day," he wrote.[116] When the isolationists despaired, fearing that they might be on the losing side of history, the
Daily News assured them that powerful institutions were on their
side.

As the crisis in the Atlantic continued, the nightmarish possibility of a two-ocean war seemed all too plausible. U.S. relations
with Japan deteriorated rapidly through the summer and fall of
1941. In July, as Japanese troops moved further into French Indo-
china, the U.S. government prohibited the sale of oil to Japan,
which crippled Japan's ability to maintain and expand its conquest
of other Asian countries.[117]

Though negotiations continued with the State Department, Japanese leaders grew convinced that compromise was impossible and
secretly drafted plans to attack American and British possessions in
the Pacific.[118] On November 26, six Japanese aircraft carriers—the
core of a strike force—started eastward across the ocean. They
planned to pause near the American naval base at Pearl Harbor,
Oahu, and to bomb the U.S. Pacific fleet in the early morning hours
of December 7.

Throughout the fall of 1941, the isolationist publishers insisted
that there was no reason Japan and the United States could not
reach a mutually satisfactory agreement. The *Daily News*, in a late
November editorial headlined "C'mon, Let's Appease Japan," argued that the United States should never have interfered with
Japan's conquest of Asia and could easily resolve the crisis with a few
concessions (which it did not identify). "It is hard for us to see why a

compromise" could not be reached, the *News* maintained, "and the threat of war with Japan postponed if not erased for good."[119] For his part, Hearst claimed that Americans should let "Japan and China in the Orient attend to their own Oriental business," and compared Japan's conquest of Manchuria with the U.S. invasion of Mexico in 1848. "We did pretty much the same thing," he wrote in his column of December 3.[120] McCormick contended in the *Tribune* that it was a "military impossibility" for Japan to attack the United States. "Even our fleet at Pearl Harbor is beyond the effective striking power of her fleet," the paper argued on October 27.[121]

As the Japanese strike force made its way toward the allegedly impregnable Pearl Harbor, Hearst, McCormick, and Patterson escalated their criticism of "Roosevelt's war" while claiming that the administration was trying to muzzle them. "Mr. Roosevelt seems to have amended his four freedoms," the *Tribune* said, "to the vital extent that freedom of speech and expression shall prevail so long as they do not conflict with his policies."[122]

The *Daily News* defied this purported attempt to intimidate the press and continued its crusade against the president, describing him as a dictator who insisted on starting a war no matter what the cost. On Friday, December 5, the *News* editorial asked why Roosevelt was dragging the country into an unnecessary conflict: "We think the answer is that Mr. Roosevelt has not had his war, as Mr. Churchill has had his and is still having it, and that Mr. Roosevelt is determined to have an even bigger war than Mr. Churchill."[123]

On Saturday, December 6, the *News* predicted that Roosevelt would use the war as an excuse to cancel the 1944 presidential election—and to destroy American democracy. The next day, the *News* editorial repeated a series of antiwar quotes from Roosevelt's 1940 presidential campaign ("I shall say it again and again and again, your boys are not going to be sent into foreign wars"). The headline read: "Why Should We Believe Him?"[124] That was the *Daily News*'s editorial page for Sunday, December 7, 1941.

■

Because the McCormick/Patterson papers viewed Roosevelt as a liar, crook, and would-be dictator, it is not surprising that they chose to ignore federal laws on military secrecy in their fight to expose the president's plots. In December 1941, the *Tribune*'s

Washington bureau obtained a copy of a top-secret military document. An anti-interventionist army officer had stolen a U.S. government contingency plan for war with Germany and passed it to
Senator Burton Wheeler, who leaked it to a *Tribune* correspondent.
McCormick had no doubt about what to do with the scoop: he
would publish it and expose the warmongers in the White House.
On December 4, 1941—the same day as the debut of Marshall
Field's *Chicago Sun*—the *Tribune* announced the story with a huge
front-page headline: "FDR'S WAR PLANS!" The article quoted from
what the reporter called an "astounding document" that included a
"blueprint for total war on a scale unprecedented in at least two
oceans and three continents." The *Daily News* and the *Washington
Times-Herald* also ran the story.[125]

President Roosevelt and his military and policy advisers were
furious about the security breach. At a press conference the next
day, Secretary of War Henry Stimson defended the war planning
process and blasted the *Tribune*. Of course U.S. military leaders
had made plans for war with Germany, he argued; they routinely
investigated "every conceivable type of emergency which may confront this country and every possible method of meeting that
emergency." He questioned the "loyalty and patriotism" of the
publishers who had printed the secret plan and accused them of
giving "gratification" to the nation's enemies.[126]

In private, Stimson urged the president to prosecute McCormick, saying it was the only way to end "this infernal disloyalty" in
the McCormick/Patterson press.[127] Other Roosevelt advisers agreed.
Attorney General Francis Biddle suggested that McCormick could
be charged with espionage; Interior Secretary Harold Ickes thought
he might be guilty of treason.[128]

McCormick maintained that his decision to publish the document was not treasonous but proof of his patriotism. Now the nation could finally debate the real costs of "an adventure in Europe,"
he said in an editorial, without the distractions of the administration's "wishful thinking and downright lying."[129] Privately, McCormick wired his Washington bureau to praise them for "the greatest
scoop in the history of journalism." The bureau chief framed the
colonel's telegram and hung it on his office wall.[130]

It did not stay there for long.

CHAPTER ELEVEN

Which Side Are You On?

T HERE IS A STANDARD mythology about American entry into World War II: the Japanese bombed the U.S. base at Pearl Harbor, and Americans, in unison, rallied to support President Franklin Roosevelt. The American people agreed to back an internationalist foreign policy, and the narrow-minded defeatists of the pre–Pearl Harbor years slunk away in shame. As an article on *PBS*'s American Experience website says, "All debate surrounding U.S. war policy came to an end on December 8, 1941, the day after Japan attacked Pearl Harbor."[1]

But the 50 million Americans who read the newspapers published by the isolationist press lords did not know that the debate had ended. Throughout the war, readers of the McCormick/Patterson papers—and to a lesser extent those of the Hearst chain—learned that America was fighting an unnecessary war against other white people on behalf of the ungrateful British and the un-American Jews. They were told that their president was a woefully incompetent leader of the war effort and that he might have conspired to provoke the Pearl Harbor attack. The Hearst/Patterson/McCormick papers seemed so intent on weakening the government during wartime that some of their critics wondered which side they were on.

■

At 7 a.m. Hawaii time on December 7, 1941, Japanese aviators ended months of diplomatic uncertainty and began an assault on the U.S. Navy base at Pearl Harbor. They killed more than twenty-four hundred Americans, wounded more than eleven hundred, destroyed 188 airplanes, and sank or damaged eighteen ships. The Japanese military also bombed U.S. and British bases in the Philippines, Guam, Wake Island, Thailand, and Malaya. The attacks shocked most Americans, but especially the isolationist publishers, who had maintained until the moment the bombs fell that the Japanese had no intention of going to war with the United States.

William Randolph Hearst heard the news at Wyntoon, his home near Mount Shasta, some two hundred miles north of Sacramento.[2] Remote from urban areas, creditors, and process servers, Wyntoon had been Hearst's refuge since his financial crisis in 1937. Now the estate offered the added advantage of distance from any Japanese raids that might strike the California coast.

Hearst was willing, at first, to support the president in a moment of national crisis. The Hearst papers' editorial on the day after Pearl Harbor, which was framed by images of a ferocious eagle and American flags, pledged "complete unity" during the war.[3] His column promised harmony at home and vengeance against enemies abroad. "Before the war is over," he predicted, "we will have burned up all the paper houses in Japan." But the publisher also staked out his position on war strategy: Japan first, Europe second. "After we have washed up Japan, we can concentrate on Europe and straighten things out there."[4]

This "Pacific first" strategy would be an enduring theme of Hearst's coverage of the war. Because he saw the Pacific war as a "race war" between "the white man's civilization" and the "yellow peril," it seemed obvious to him that the United States should put most of its energy and resources into this existential battle. "It is here in the Pacific," he wrote from California's central valley, "that the two great contending powers and theories of world development have clashed—AND ONLY ONE WILL SURVIVE."[5] If the United States decided instead to "pursue a quarrel" with other white people, the Pacific would no longer be a "white man's ocean" that nurtured and protected the "white man's supremacy" and the "white man's leadership in the progress and possession of the world." A

Europe-first strategy would mean that the "yellow peril would be on our front porch—and even perhaps breaking in our doors."[6]

In fact, the Hearst papers argued that agents of the yellow peril were already on America's front porch and should be sent to concentration camps.[7] Even before Pearl Harbor, Hearst had warned about Japanese saboteurs and spies on the West Coast and encouraged the U.S. Navy secretary to "come to California and see the myriads of little Japs peacefully raising fruit and flowers and vegetables on California farms and basking with oriental satisfaction in the California sunshine, and saying hopefully and wishfully: '*Some day I come with Japanese Army and take all this. Yes sir, thank you.*' "[8] After the United States entered the war, Hearst columnist Henry McLemore published some of the most notorious columns about the "Japanese menace" to California and called for the removal of Japanese Americans from the West Coast. When Attorney General Francis Biddle signaled in early February 1942 that he would force an evacuation by the end of the month, McLemore wrote in fury that Biddle was handling the Japanese "with all the severity of Lord Fauntleroy playing squat tag with his maiden aunt." It was typical of timid liberals, he snarled, to give these saboteurs "time to perfect their time bombs [and] complete their infernal machines."[9]

It was not just the Japanese but America's allies who threatened the nation's safety, in Hearst's view. The U.S. alliance with Britain and Russia did not diminish Hearst's Anglophobia or anti-communism. During the first months of the war, as Britain reeled from the Japanese attacks on its Asian colonies, Hearst described Winston Churchill as a bumbling oaf whose leadership record consisted of nothing but "retreat—and defeat." Why did the British people keep him in power? Because, Hearst explained in a column written two months after Pearl Harbor, the prime minister had finally succeeded at something—at "dragging the United States into England's European entanglements."[10] He trusted the Russians even less than the British. As soon as Germany was defeated, the Hearst papers warned, the Russians "will be busy communizing conquered Europe and trying to communize us."[11]

The Roosevelt administration was bungling the war, Hearst argued, because it cared more about the British, the Soviets, and other foreigners than its own people. Instead of putting America first, he wrote in his column, the administration was neglecting "the interests of our own America and our own Americans in order to be a big shot and a big sap for every foreign country and every alien people in the world."[12] Hearst himself was a hero for alerting the American people to the Roosevelt administration's mistakes and lies. While the New Dealers fed the press propaganda, distortions, and false news, a Hearst editorial insisted, the Hearst newspapers demanded that the government "inspire confidence by truth and honesty" instead of lulling the public into a "false sense of security by stories of victories which are not accurate."[13] Hearst's editorials were so anti-administration that several readers asked the FBI to investigate him for sedition.[14]

Yet unlike other isolationist publishers, Hearst did not, during the war, conflate "New Dealers" and "internationalists" with "Jews." In fact he was surprisingly pro-Zionist. In 1944, he strongly backed Jewish demands to open British Palestine to refugees, even in the face of British resistance. Hearst decided to champion this issue for reasons both noble (sympathy for Jewish victims of Hitler) and base (racism against Palestinians, reflexive opposition to British policy, and fear of increased Jewish immigration to America).[15] Nevertheless, his full-throated support for Zionism led many Jewish leaders to write effusive letters of appreciation. One thanked him for reflecting "the true spirit of American democracy," which was indeed a rare compliment for Hearst.[16]

■

Robert McCormick's truce with Roosevelt and his foreign policy was exceedingly brief and insincere. The day after Pearl Harbor, the *Tribune* ran a short, three-paragraph editorial that called for vengeance against the "insane clique of Japanese militarists" and promised, after a fashion, not to blame the administration for the attack. "Recriminations are useless," the *Tribune* declared, pleased with its noble decision to refrain from them, "and we doubt that they will be indulged in. Certainly not by us. All that matters today is that we are in the war."[17] Maybe that was all that mattered on December 8, but within two weeks the colonel would happily indulge in recriminations.

Like Hearst, McCormick argued that "our single war aim must be the crushing of the Japanese," not battling in Europe—in particular, not fighting for what the *Tribune* saw as the nation's lazy, incompetent, sometimes malevolent allies in Britain and Russia.[18] The *Tribune* portrayed Great Britain as forever tricking the United States into sacrificing lives and treasure to defend its empire. Readers learned that snobbish British aristocrats would never thank the gullible Americans who were fighting and dying for them and that British imperialists had made it a nasty habit to "defame and traduce every other nation" without exempting "the fond friends and allies who are saving her from destruction."[19]

The Soviets, in McCormick's eyes, were even shiftier and more ungrateful than the British. The British wanted Americans to save their empire for them; the Soviets wanted to destroy the republic. The *Tribune* told readers that America's Russian allies plotted to sow "economic confusion and unrest" in the United States as "the prelude to despair and revolution."[20] Because Stalin wanted to take over the world, the Nazis had played a useful and even heroic role in stopping his westward advance. In February 1942, a front-page, full-color *Tribune* editorial cartoon featured an enormous Russian bear chasing a terrified Hitler into the English Channel. "Who will tell him to go back home and settle down?" the caption read.[21]

The *Tribune*'s favorite villains remained the "internationalists," code for Jews and New Dealers. On McCormick's orders, the *Tribune* news stories identified Jews by their original, non-Anglicized names—as in "David K. Niles (whose real name is Nayhus)" or "[Walter] Winchell's real name is Lipschitz."[22] *Tribune* editorial cartoons regularly gave Roosevelt's Jewish advisers hooked noses and swarthy complexions. Treasury Secretary Henry Morgenthau Jr., Supreme Court Justice Felix Frankfurter (the "dwarflike Vienna-born former Harvard law professor"), and adviser Samuel Rosenman, among others, appeared in *Tribune* cartoons whispering secrets behind their hands.[23]

The *Tribune*'s affinity for anti-Semitic tropes offended one of McCormick's Jewish employees, the editorial writer Leon Stolz, who protested privately to the colonel. In a long memo in spring 1944, Stolz objected to the *Tribune*'s frequent use of the term "international bankers" (which, he said, meant "rich and scheming Jews who are determined to destroy their countrymen for the advantage of foreigners") and the paper's tendency to focus on the Jewish origins or names of its opponents. Unaware that McCormick had personally ordered the use of these hoary stereotypes, he suggested that the colonel should tell the Washington bureau to be more sensitive to Jewish concerns.²⁴ Arthur Henning, the *Tribune*'s Washington bureau chief, reacted angrily when McCormick forwarded the memo to him. "I challenge Stolz," he wrote, "to show any anti-Jewish matter originating in this bureau or even any matter that he and other Jews in the most hypercritical moments of an inferiority complex could pronounce anti-Jewish." Stolz had never been a loyal McCormick man, Henning concluded: "I have been wondering for years what he is doing in the Tribune organization."²⁵

McCormick showed his tolerance for anti-Semitism through his choice of friends and employees. He socialized with right-wing activist Merwin K. Hart, even after his cousin Joe warned him that Hart had "a reputation of being a leading or the leading 'Fascist' " in New York.²⁶ He rented space in Tribune Tower to Harry Jung, the head of a prominent anti-Semitic group. Most notably, he retained Donald Day as a foreign correspondent until fall 1942, long after it was clear that Day was a Nazi sympathizer. Over the years Day sent McCormick and his editors many letters laced with anti-Semitic diatribes, noting in October 1941, for example, that Germans had little respect for Americans "so long as our foreign policy is being largely directed by the Red Sea Pedestrians."²⁷ Finally, in August 1942, the U.S. legation in Sweden charged Day with helping the Nazis place their propaganda in American newspapers and took away his passport.²⁸ The *Tribune* ordered him home, but he instead joined the Finnish army to fight against America's wartime ally, the Soviet Union. Two years later, he surfaced as a radio broadcaster of Nazi propaganda in Berlin. In one of his last broadcasts, shortly before the Soviet invasion of Berlin, he said: "It is hard to believe that a Christian people should gang [up] with a barbaric nation to try to exterminate another Christian nation, solely because the victim of this conspiracy expelled the Jews from its country."²⁹

McCormick despised New Dealers for some of the same reasons he distrusted Jews: their alleged "alien notions of social and political organization."³⁰ The *Tribune*'s readers learned that the wild-eyed radicals in the Roosevelt administration treated the war like a "bigger and gaudier WPA project" and a chance to enact their mad schemes.³¹

Their "diabolical conspiracy" would destroy American freedoms and the republic itself.[32] Notably, the *Tribune* frequently worried that alien forces threatened the republican form of government, but rarely expressed concern about the potential loss of American democracy or democratic norms. McCormick and other New Deal opponents believed that when liberals spoke of *democracy* they actually meant *mob rule, collectivism,* and *tyranny.*[33]

In the *Tribune*'s view, the New Dealers had provoked the war and were fighting it with criminal inefficiency. The bureaucrats in Washington—"those who willed the war"—deserved to be "driven from their hiding places and sent to the front where they can share some of the agony they have created."[34] Having started the war, the New Dealers were scheming to use it "to develop a planned state in this country along accepted communist lines."[35] These treacherous government insiders sometimes deliberately put American troops at risk to help the communist cause. In a 1944 speech, McCormick declared that the administration had allowed American soldiers to suffer "untold tortures in Japanese prison camps" because the Reds in Washington wanted to send troops to help the Soviets rather than free the Philippines.[36]

Because McCormick was so convinced that the Roosevelt administration had provoked, and was losing, an unnecessary war, he had little respect for its military secrets. The *Tribune* had already courted an espionage indictment by printing a stolen copy of military contingency plans—"FDR'S WAR PLANS"—on the front page right before Pearl Harbor. It went even further the following spring when it revealed a U.S. code-breaking triumph—and thus endangered American lives.

Before the battle of Midway, American cryptographers had cracked Japan's naval code and learned the locations of Japanese ships. The knowledge gave the U.S. Navy a crucial victory. Understandably, the U.S. military did not want the Japanese to know that it could read their secret messages. Yet on June 7, 1942, the *Tribune* published an article headlined "Navy Had Word of Jap Plan to Strike at Sea." The story, which had a Washington, D.C., dateline and no byline, read: "The strength of the Japanese forces with which the American Navy is battling somewhere west of Midway Island ... was well known in American naval circles, several days before the battle began, reliable sources in the naval intelligence disclosed here tonight."[37] It also ran in the *Daily News* and the *Washington Times-Herald*.

When Chief of Naval Operations Ernest King saw the story in the *Times-Herald*, he ordered an inquiry immediately. King and other navy officers worried that the Japanese would change their codes after reading the article, hiding those messages from U.S. code breakers.[38] Justice Department investigators, who took over the navy's investigation, learned that *Tribune* reporter Stanley Johnston, on board a U.S. transport ship in the Pacific, had obtained a copy of a top-secret cable that summarized the contents of the intercepted Japanese communications. Johnston apparently did not know that the U.S. Navy had secured the information through code breaking. But he did understand that he was not supposed to see or write about the dispatch. He did anyway.

Attorney General Francis Biddle impaneled a grand jury to consider whether the *Tribune* had violated the Espionage Act. The navy, however, refused to cooperate with the inquiry once its intelligence agents realized that the Japanese had not changed their codes in response to Johnston's story, because they, like the *Tribune* and its reporter, failed to grasp the significance of his scoop. The grand jury dismissed the charges.[39]

To McCormick, the espionage investigation was not a sign that his reporter might have endangered national security but rather a transparent attempt to silence the anti-Roosevelt press. "An administration," the *Tribune* announced in a front-page editorial, "which for years has been seeking by one sly means or another, but always with complete futility, to intimidate this newspaper has finally despaired of all other means and is now preparing criminal prosecutions."[40] After the Justice Department dropped the Midway case, the *Tribune* wisely stopped mentioning it, but throughout the war it continued to run news articles about the administration's "smear brigade" and "vilification plot" to "discredit all nationalists as defeatists and traitors."[41] McCormick felt even more persecuted when the Justice Department launched—and ultimately won—an antitrust suit against the Associated Press for refusing, under pressure from McCormick, to sell a membership to the *Tribune*'s rival, Marshall Field's *Chicago Sun*.[42]

McCormick saw himself as the nation's truest patriot, a heroic fighter for real Americanism. In 1944 he would add a new slogan to the *Tribune*'s masthead, "An American Paper for Americans," though he noted, in an editorial, that he hoped Hearst's Chicago paper would "not object to the obvious similarity" (Hearst's motto was "An American Paper for the American People").[43] McCormick's defense of his own patriotism led to one of the most embarrassing incidents of his life: the leak of a letter that revealed the extent of his narcissism. When a former *Tribune* reporter objected to McCormick's relentless criticism of the war effort, the colonel shot back a letter explaining that "this country would be lost" without him. In the colonel's telling, he was personally responsible for many key moments in U.S. military history. No one seemed to appreciate, he wrote, "that I introduced the ROTC into the schools; that I introduced machine guns into the Army; that I introduced mechanization; I introduced automatic rifles. I was the first ground officer to go up in the air and observe artillery fire. Now I have succeeded in making that the regular practice in the Army. I was the first to advocate an alliance with Canada. I forced the acquiring of bases in the Atlantic Ocean." He had not succeeded in everything, of course: "I did get the Marines out of Shanghai," he maintained, "but was unsuccessful in getting the army out of the Philippines."[44]

The letter circulated among incredulous journalists, who found it endlessly amusing. Navy Secretary Frank Knox's paper, the *Chicago Daily News*, published a facsimile under the headline "Whatta Man!" and soon began running a series of cartoons about "Colonel McCosmic," a pompous, fat old man who crowed about his military expertise: "You do not know it, but I crossed the Delaware before Washington did!"[45] At Roosevelt's request, Army Air Forces General Hap Arnold investigated McCormick's boasts and found them untrue. "Perhaps Colonel McCormick had a dream," he concluded.[46] The president noted to Archibald MacLeish of the Office of War Information that McCormick and his cousins "deserve neither hate nor praise—only pity for their unbalanced mentalities."[47]

∎

McCormick faced federal espionage charges, but many interventionists thought his cousins were just as guilty of "inkpot sabotage."[48] The McCormick/Patterson papers blamed the British, the

Soviets, the Jews, and New Dealers more than the Axis for the war. They also questioned whether the war was necessary and whether the Roosevelt administration had lied about its origins.

Cissy Patterson was suspicious about the events surrounding U.S. entry from the start. On the day of the Pearl Harbor attack, she summoned her editors to the *Times-Herald* offices on H Street in Washington. As smoke rose from the Japanese embassy, where diplomats were burning secret papers, and congressional leaders rushed down the streets to meet with the president at the White House, the publisher of the largest paper in the nation's capital asked her editors a shocking question: "Do you think *he* arranged this?"[49] It was clear who "he" was. In Cissy's view, a false flag operation planned by Franklin Roosevelt made more sense than a surprise strike carried out by the Japanese. The *Times-Herald* and its sister papers had been insisting for months that the Japanese posed no danger to the United States.

Some of Cissy's enemies seized the opportunity provided by U.S. entry into the war to taunt her. Clare Boothe Luce, the wife of Henry Luce (and also a renowned actress, playwright, and future member of Congress), sent Cissy a bouquet of roses right after Pearl Harbor with a note: "How do you like everything now? Affectionately, Clare Luce." Cissy got her revenge six months later by publishing a gossipy, nasty piece about the Luces and other interventionist publishers who were all, the headline said, "having a wonderful time" during the war. "By every word and action," the article claimed, "they advanced the idea they would rather see America wrecked, go down to defeat before the Axis than surrender an iota of the new power and influence they suddenly found within easy grasp."[50]

Franklin Roosevelt did not send roses to Joe Patterson, but he did go out of his way to humiliate him. As it happened, thanks to an earnest attempt by a *Daily News* reporter to arrange a rapprochement with the White House, Patterson found himself in Roosevelt's office, in a personal interview with the president, four days after Pearl Harbor. The publisher had come to Washington to consult with his reporters and, at age sixty-two, to ask to reenlist in the army. One of the *News*'s Capitol correspondents, Fred Pasley, decided to try to arrange a reconciliation between his boss and the president. He contacted press secretary Steve Early and suggested that Patterson wanted to see his onetime friend in person as soon as possible to "confess his error" and apologize personally for his isolationist editorials. On that understanding, Early arranged the appointment.[51]

When Patterson stepped into Roosevelt's office at noon on December 11, the president had just learned that Germany and Italy had declared war on the United States and that, in his speech announcing that move, Adolf Hitler had mentioned the December 4 "war plans" scoop in Patterson's family newspapers as one reason for his decision. "A plan prepared by President Roosevelt has been revealed in the United States," the Führer had told the Reichstag, "according to which his intention was to attack Germany by 1943 with all the resources at the disposal of the United States."[52] In truth, Hitler's decision had nothing to do with a newspaper story: according to the historian Richard Evans, he believed it was "vital to strike sooner than later," before the United States had fully mobilized for war.[53] But the "exclusive revelation" in the McCormick/Patterson papers of the U.S. military's contingency war plans gave the Nazi leader a pretext for claiming that the Roosevelt administration had forced his hand.

The meeting between the former friends did not go well. Roosevelt kept Patterson standing throughout the fifteen-minute interview, reading him excerpts from *News* editorials. He was especially incensed by Patterson's predictions that Roosevelt would cancel the 1942 elections—"That would be unconstitutional," the president noted—and by the *Daily News*'s hints that Americans might need to start a revolution to overthrow the administration. He argued, with reason, that the publication of Joe Patterson's editorials in his sister's paper had influenced members of Congress to oppose preparedness efforts and thus set back those efforts by two to three months. Roosevelt told Patterson to revisit all the *Daily News* editorials for 1941: "Read every one and then think over what you have done!" He concluded the meeting by suggesting that Patterson tell his sister to behave herself as well. Press secretary Early, who witnessed the exchange, reported that Patterson began to cry.[54]

Patterson told a different story. He said he stayed impassive throughout the meeting, thinking that the president might be testing his military discipline; but then he realized that Roosevelt just wanted to insult him. Far from feeling repentant, he left the White House inspired to regain the upper hand in their relationship, especially after his request to rejoin the army was turned down.[55] His battle for isolationism and America First would continue through the war years and beyond.

Like Hearst and McCormick, the Pattersons demanded a "Pacific first" strategy against the "yellow peril." The *Daily News* wanted to ensure that the U.S. military was strong enough to stop the "hordes of Asia from spilling over here and helping themselves to our living space, raw materials and women."[56] It was the duty of white men— the "American white man's burden"—to keep "this continent, or, better, this hemisphere, free of invasion from Asia."[57] Despite the banning of poison gas by the Geneva Protocol in 1925, the *News* repeatedly urged the U.S. military to use such weapons against Japanese troops. One headline read, "You Can Cook 'Em Faster with Gas."[58]

The Patterson papers portrayed the British and the Russians, not the Nazis, as America's most insidious enemies. According to the *Daily News,* Stalin was always on the brink of making a separate peace with the Germans or agreeing to divide up Europe, Asia, and the South Pacific with the Japanese.[59] The British were talented manipulators whom the *News* painted as foppish, linen-suited colonialists, "sitting around drinking gin and quinine tonic," as one editorial put it, while oppressed natives did their work and gullible Americans did their fighting for them.[60]

The *Daily News* was most notorious, though, not for its Anglophobia or anti-communist paranoia but for its anti-Semitism. While its editorials seldom used overtly anti-Semitic rhetoric, they often deployed code words like *internationalists* or *foreign-minded* Americans. Its letters to the editor were less discreet. Some observers suspected they were written by *News* staff.[61]

Anti-Semitic tropes also sullied the paper's straight news pages, especially in stories written by the *News's* star Capitol correspondent, John O'Donnell, who wrote a five-day-a-week political column for both Patterson newspapers as well as covering the White House and Congress for them. O'Donnell had earned a reputation among newspapermen as pro-fascist. He once told another journalist that "certain elements needed cleaning up in Germany" and that the Nazis had "done a lot of good things," including creating jobs and restoring "national honor and prestige."[62] Roosevelt so detested O'Donnell that in 1942 he mockingly awarded him a Nazi Iron Cross, which the president had received as a souvenir.[63]

After the war, O'Donnell continued to enhance his reputation for anti-Semitism. A 1945 story falsely claimed that Roosevelt's "foreign-born" friends ("Felix Frankfurter, of Vienna, . . . Dave (Devious Dave) Niles alias Neyhus and the Latvian ex-rabbinical student now known as Sidney Hillman") had forced the removal of General George Patton from his post because he had slapped a Jewish soldier.[64] The article was untrue: the traumatized soldier was, in fact, a member of the Nazarene Church of Indiana. The column prompted protests by many Jewish and progressive groups—"as bitter an attack against the Jews as might have been printed in any German newspaper in 1933," read one typical letter to the editor—but not, in the end, a marked decline in *Daily News* advertising revenue or a change of heart for O'Donnell.[65] In the years to come, he would refer to the Buchenwald death camp as a "jail for murderers, rapists, stick-up boys, Commie spies, etc." and call the postwar trials of Nazi leaders the "Nuremberg lynching."[66]

Because of the coded (and not-so-coded) anti-Semitism in O'Donnell's stories, in the *News* editorials, and in the letters to the editor, the *News's* critics contended that the tabloid routinely published Jew-baiting, Jew-hating, "pro-Nazi poison." One anti-*News* pamphlet featured a drawing of Hitler eagerly reading the paper. "ACH! WHAT A JOB THEY'RE DOING!!" he exclaims. "ALL MY FRIENDS SHOULD BUY IT!"[67] Nazi shortwave radio propagandists read *News* editorials over their networks and portrayed the Patterson/McCormick papers as victims of Roosevelt's dictatorial policies: "These newspapers, being true American papers and representing the majority of American people, are being persecuted by the Roosevelt Administration, even to being accused of saboteurs of the war effort."[68] Interventionist groups reported that seventeen U.S. fascist publications reprinted *Daily News* editorials.[69] The American fascist Gerald L. K. Smith chose the Patterson/McCormick cousins, along with Hearst and Father Coughlin, for his hall of fame of great Americans.[70]

Roosevelt supporters denounced the Pattersons in churches, the halls of Congress, and even elementary school classrooms.

Representative Elmer J. Holland of Pennsylvania infuriated the siblings when spoke on the floor of the House of Representatives in August 1942 to attack "America's number one and number two exponents of the Nazi propaganda line—Cissy and Joe Patterson."[71] ("You're a liar, Congressman Holland," was Joe Patterson's blunt response.)[72] A few months later, when *News* pollsters tried to survey New Yorkers before the 1942 elections, many people throughout the city slammed doors in their faces. Bronx youngsters called out, "There goes the Nazi News." Near the Brighton Beach boardwalk, children surrounded *News* vehicles and condemned the "Fascist and Nazi paper." One student told the pollsters that their schoolteachers told them not to read the *News* because "it is anti-Roosevelt, anti-American and anti-Jewish."[73]

New Yorkers' anger at the *News* prompted Patterson to post a night watchman at his home and engage a public relations expert to assess the potential damage to his business.[74] The consultant, Sidney Wallach, reported that many residents despised and distrusted their city's best-selling paper. "The results show unmistakably," he wrote in December 1942, "that there is a definite feeling in New York City that the Daily News is fascist-minded, anti-Semitic and above all, unfair and extremist in its editorial position. ... A not-negligible portion of the newspaper public is disturbed, distressed and hostile" to the paper. To find out why, Wallach examined twenty-seven editorials in the *News* published during November 1942, and discovered fifteen items that used "unnecessarily irritating, divisive or confusing" language. His survey also found that "an extraordinarily high" number of letters to the editor contained "elements which can be justifiably interpreted as fascistic, anti-Semitic and more than surreptitiously sympathetic to the Axis countries." While these letters and editorials were not *overtly* anti-Semitic, Wallach concluded, they used terms like *internationalist* or other "emotionalized words" that were the "stock in trade of the open and avowed anti-Semite."[75]

Patterson paid Wallach and brusquely told him he had no further need of his services. He then quoted a letter he had sent to an advertiser: "As to my being anti-Semitic, I can only say, as I have said many times before, that I am not so." He based his argument, in part, on the fact that his daughter had married a Jew (the millionaire

Harry Guggenheim) and his conviction that "American citizens of Jewish blood" should have "the same rights and privileges as American citizens of any other blood." Ignoring Wallach's analysis of anti-Semitic tropes in *News* editorials and letters, Patterson insisted that the rumors of his anti-Semitism had been promoted by his competitors to hurt his circulation.[76]

Joe Patterson's fans joined him in scoffing at the charges. "If the *Daily News* . . . is a Fascist newspaper, that makes us, its readers, either fools who cannot distinguish what they read, or traitors who are in sympathy with Fascism," retorted one irate reader. "Are there three million fools and traitors in New York City?"[77] The author of that particular letter was a Russian-Jewish novelist and screenwriter—relatively unknown at the time but soon to become a patron saint of twentieth-century libertarianism—who passionately supported Patterson's crusade against New Dealers. The *News* did not publish the letter, which was sent directly to Patterson; if it had, one wonders if it would have identified her, O'Donnell-style, as "Ayn Rand alias Alisa Rosenbaum."

The *Daily News* warned Americans about another group of internationalists who were just as worrisome as the Jews: the New Dealers, or, as the *News* called them, "dreamers" and "saps" who "infested" the nation's capital. They forced Americans to fight and die in the Pacific to recapture the Far Eastern colonies of decadent European empires. "The Roosevelt policy is to love the world first and ourselves second, to send our boys all over the world, 'from Greenland's icy mountains to India's coral strand,' on freedom crusades," the *News* declared, quoting an old missionary hymn.[78]

These "world-savers," the *News* declared, had turned "America First" into a "term of shame." "Any American who prefers his own country to other countries," read a 1944 editorial, "is smeared by these gentry as a parochial-minded narrowback." The paper promised its readers that it would continue to resist the president's efforts to privilege the rest of the world over the United States. "We're still for America first, aren't ashamed of it, and expect always to be for America first."[79]

The *News* found the New Dealers' postwar plans even more dangerous than their wartime blunders. Roosevelt and his allies, it warned, might try to impoverish Americans after the war "in order

to lift Chinese or Hottentot living standards an inch while drop-
ping our own a yard."[80] Bureaucrats planned to lower or eliminate
immigration limits and tariffs, even though these barriers were the
only things preventing "the world and his wife" from moving into
"our rich and favored country" and destroying wage levels and living standards.[81]

At their most charitable, the *News* editors condemned the internationalists as ridiculously impractical idealists. Other times
they saw something more sinister: a drive to create an international
superstate and make Roosevelt the dictator of the world. The president's bid for a fourth term in 1944 convinced the *News* staff that
he would stop at nothing in his quest to "communize this country"
and seize "all-out power" to "run a one-man show."[82] If he won a
fourth term, the *News* speculated, "it is a cinch bet that he will want
a fifth term, and so on until he dies. He is plainly in love with the
power of the Presidency and determined never to give it up if he
can help it." He would probably try to name one of his sons as his
successor.[83] The threat of a Roosevelt dictatorship was so dire that
the *News* ended nearly every editorial in October 1944 with the
same refrain: "The fourth term is the issue."

In the view of Patterson and his peers, the fourth term imper-
iled the republic precisely because it endangered the *News* and other
Roosevelt critics. The isolationist publishers consistently viewed
themselves as victims—martyrs in the fight against American tyranny. The press was "the last bulwark of freedom—the last forum of
free discussion—in this country," an editorial proclaimed. Yet Roosevelt, the *News* said, equated all criticism with treason; he insisted
that the nation's editors fill their news columns with propaganda
handouts from Washington and that editorial writers "confine their
comment to obsequious yessing of everything the Roosevelt Administration does."[84] By fighting for AP membership for the *Chicago
Sun* and investigating the Midway scoop by the *Chicago Tribune*, the
Roosevelt administration was trying "to curb if not destroy freedom
of expression in this country, while it claims to be waging a war to
bring freedom of expression to the whole world." If the administration succeeded in "gagging" the press, Americans would lose their
right "to talk and write as they please."[85]

The *Daily News* sometimes hinted that violence might be necessary to stop this march toward tyranny. In one editorial on ancient Rome's evolution ("democracy—demagoguery—dictatorship"), the *News* made an extended comparison of Roosevelt and Julius Caesar. The piece began with an account of Caesar's rise to power and subsequent assassination, then segued to Roosevelt and his alleged desire "to become our Julius Caesar." The *News* concluded somewhat obscurely that the voters could not stop Roosevelt from seizing power, and "maybe there is nothing we can do" about his destruction of the republic. At least one reader, who complained to Patterson, interpreted the editorial as an incitement to assassination.[86] Patterson also repeatedly called on returning veterans to start their own nationalist party, an "American party" that would channel their supposed anger at having fought a pointless war. He hinted that internationalist proposals in Washington would provoke a right-wing backlash, perhaps even revolution. "We can assure the talkers and the dreamers," the *News* said, "that when and if they try to bring these dreams into cold, solid reality after the war, they will fan up a fight in this country which will make the recent isolationist-interventionist fight look like a mere warm-up."[87]

■

Patterson's predictions turned out to be wrong, of course. There was no right-wing revolution in the United States. Moreover, the public showed consistently strong support for President Roosevelt and his anti-fascist foreign policy. From American entry into the war until his death, his approval rating never fell below 65 percent. And when Roosevelt did win his fourth term in 1944, only 22 percent of dailies endorsed him, but he bested New York governor Thomas Dewey by more than 7 percentage points in the popular vote and carried thirty-six states.[88]

But New Deal public opinion experts saw some concerning trends in the polls. As early as spring 1942, government propagandists in the Office of Facts and Figures (OFF) noted that about 20 percent of the public continued to "oppose and obstruct" the war effort. At first the OFF proposed calling these right-wing opponents of the war "divisionists," but it soon began using the term "neo-isolationists." These anti–New Deal Americans got much of their information from the Hearst/Patterson/McCormick press. In the words of a government report, these newspapers "consistently impugn the motives of the Government and endeavor to divide the American people from the United Nations."[89] Roosevelt's favorite pollster, Hadley Cantril of Princeton University, found similar results. In August 1942, he reported that isolationism had not died after Pearl Harbor; 35 percent of Americans identified themselves as "non-interventionist," 7 percent *greater* than the percentage just before Pearl Harbor.[90]

Roosevelt understood that ultra-nationalism remained strong. "Anybody who thinks that isolationism is dead in this country is crazy," he said during the war.[91] In response, he organized several government agencies for public opinion polling, press monitoring, and radio, film, and print propaganda.[92] He worked especially hard at crafting and communicating his war goals—the Atlantic Charter, the Four Freedoms, and the survival of democracy—to all people, at home and abroad. In fighting the isolationist press lords, Roosevelt sometimes even appropriated their style. In 1944, he urged one of his publicity experts to adopt the Hearst technique in government propaganda pamphlets. "What would you think of an additional plan—to prepare a series of editorials, based on the Hearst method (Isn't that terrible for me to say)?" he wrote. "In other words, the style of type with a word in large caps every sentence; length to fit into a single page leaflet or handbill, paper of the poorest quality."[93]

The president also wondered if the isolationist publishers served as conduits for Axis propaganda. He asked two government agencies to verify a British intelligence report that the McCormick/Patterson press was parroting Nazi talking points. The agencies reported back that they were not.[94] Indeed, the converse was true: the Nazis were using material put out by the isolationist newspapers. Investigators for the Department of Justice concluded that although the Hearst, Patterson, and McCormick newspapers routinely asserted that Roosevelt was "reprehensible," the U.S. government was corrupt, and its Allies were weak, these papers did not praise the Axis nations or openly attack Jews, and thus failed to disseminate key themes of Nazi propaganda.[95]

It's easy to understand why Roosevelt would question the press lords' loyalty. While the United States was fighting a war for democracy and against fascism, these newspapers were undermining morale by questioning not just strategies but the meaning and purpose of the effort. They also stoked hatred and fear of immigrants and minority groups, revealed national security secrets, and indirectly encouraged a right-wing revolution. Roosevelt fought back—with speeches, propaganda and, in some cases, security investigations—because he thought he must.

■

Like his American counterparts, Max Beaverbrook also attacked his government's war strategies. Yet unlike the right-wing press barons in the United States, Beaverbrook did not see his nation's leaders as enemies of the people. He attacked Churchill's actions, not his patriotism.

As America entered the war, Beaverbrook initially backed Churchill strongly and played a key role in the prime minister's campaign to persuade the United States to do more to help Britain. Just five days after Pearl Harbor, Beaverbrook and Churchill set out to Washington on a British battleship. They aimed to convince Americans to boost their production of tanks, ships, and airplanes, as well as to ignore the calls from the Hearst/Patterson/McCormick press to fight first in Asia and leave the European war to the Europeans.

They succeeded on both counts. The Americans agreed to the Europe-first strategy; Roosevelt had long seen Nazi Germany as America's primary enemy, and he worried that a Pacific first strategy would give the Germans time to beat the Soviet Union, which would make them an even greater threat to the United States.[96] Moreover, it turned out that Beaverbrook, as a North American and successful businessman, was the right person to encourage Americans to produce more war materiel.[97] After hearing his presentations, Roosevelt and his advisers agreed to increase their war production goals in 1942 from 28,600 to 45,000 combat planes, and to more than double the number of tanks, from 20,400 to 45,000.[98]

Beaverbrook spent Christmas 1941 with Churchill and the Roosevelts at the White House and would continue throughout the war to cajole and hector his American friends to do all they could to support their British allies. Churchill was, as usual, impressed with his old friend's performance, cabling back to Clement Attlee, the deputy prime minister, "Max has been magnificent."[99]

Yet Churchill was not always so positive about Beaverbrook's contributions. The press baron's quarrels with Churchill and his repeated petulant threats to resign infuriated many of the prime minister's advisers. Some urged Churchill to let his old friend go. Clementine Churchill accused Beaverbrook of "intrigue & treachery" and begged her husband to "exorcise" him from the government. "Try ridding yourself of this microbe which some people fear is in your blood."[100] Beaverbrook briefly again switched jobs in Churchill's cabinet, from minister of supply to minister of production. Then, in February 1942, he again proffered his resignation, and this time Churchill, exhausted, accepted it.[101]

Once back in private life, Beaverbrook used his newspapers to wage a campaign to force the Churchill government to invade Europe immediately to take the pressure off the Soviet Union. The *Daily Express* organized a large "Attack in Europe!" rally in Trafalgar Square in March 1942 and a "Salute to Russia" demonstration in Birmingham in June. The *Express* publisher personally addressed the Birmingham event, which attracted thirty thousand people. At the speaker's rostrum, draped with a banner consisting of the Union Jack and the Soviet flag stitched together, Beaverbrook announced that the way to "proclaim our faith" in the Soviets was to send forth, without further delay, "our second expeditionary force to fight on the Second Front."[102]

Churchill believed, along with most British military leaders, that a cross-channel invasion in 1942 would be "impossible, disastrous," as an American envoy reported.[103] The Germans were simply too strong to be directly challenged in France. Beaverbrook persisted, however, in using his newspapers to insist that the Russians needed relief, and soon. Churchill's friends were perplexed by the prime minister's refusal to repudiate Beaverbrook even as his newspapers decried his war strategy. Clement Attlee commented that Churchill took the press lord "as a kind of stimulant or drug. He had an undue opinion of his political astuteness but seldom made the mistake of taking his advice."[104]

Yet by fall 1942, after the Americans backed Churchill's plan to delay a second front in Europe, Beaverbrook's papers once again voiced strong support for the prime minister. In September, the *Express* declared "emphatically" that "Mr. Churchill's conduct of the war does not deserve criticism."[105] Its publisher later agreed to rejoin Churchill's cabinet, this time as lord privy seal.

Beaverbrook, in other words, was hardly a cheerleader for all of his government's wartime policies. Yet still he was shocked by the anti-Roosevelt coverage in the American press. He expressed his frustration in a private letter to Joseph Kennedy, the onetime U.S. ambassador to Britain and a prominent anti-interventionist before the war. "As I see it," he wrote Kennedy, "many American newspapers are adopting a deliberate policy of attacking the whole range of the President's policy. He lacks altogether the solid Press backing from which Churchill so greatly profits." Beaverbrook could not understand the U.S. publishers' commitment to "weakening an Administration to which by common consent there is no alternative."[106]

Despite his well-deserved reputation as an intriguer and provocateur, Beaverbrook actually played the role to which the right-wing press in the United States pretended to aspire: that of a skeptical but loyal opposition. He criticized his government's policies and strategies but did not claim that its officials were secretly working to destroy the nation.

The right-wing American press, on the other hand, did not simply accuse Roosevelt of fighting the war with ill-advised strategies; it argued that he was trying to turn the country over to its enemies. The newspapers singled out the "sneaky" Jews, who had changed their names so that they could hide themselves; the crypto-communists, who were biding their time to start a revolution; and the covert supporters of dictatorship, who wanted first Roosevelt, and then his sons, to rule forever. These, in their minds, were America's real enemies, not the Japanese, who had been goaded into war, or the Germans, who shared a common "blood" with real Americans.

∎

In April 1945, the man who had been president for twelve years—through recovery from the Great Depression, and through World War II almost until its end—suddenly died. Many Americans reacted to the news of Roosevelt's fatal stroke with just one word:

"No!" Newspapers around the country recorded the horrified responses of elected officials and ordinary citizens. "It doesn't seem possible," a Detroit woman said. "It seems to me that he will be back on the radio tomorrow, reassuring us all that it was just a mistake."[107]

Most of Roosevelt's enemies in the press managed to report his passing without rancor. Hearst responded with dignity. The news pages of his papers were filled with stories about Roosevelt's historic accomplishments as president, while a full-page editorial described his death as a "calamity" and praised him fulsomely as a leader whose legacy would live "in all the annals of recorded time."[108] McCormick was privately exuberant—he handed $10 bills to elevator operators and pressmen in celebration—but he managed to stifle his jubilation at the death of his enemy long enough to write a brief editorial to "express the deep sorrow which all Americans feel at the passing of their chosen leader."[109]

But Joe Patterson declined to respect the custom of refusing to speak ill of the dead. The day after Roosevelt's passing, the *Daily News* was possibly the only major newspaper not to publish a tribute on its editorial page. Instead, Patterson used the space for a series of Roosevelt's quotations, including his "again and again and again" line, thus managing to accuse the dead president of being a liar without saying so directly.[110] The next day, Patterson did publish an editorial obituary for Roosevelt, and it was vicious. Some of Roosevelt's domestic reforms had been positive, the *News* conceded, but his foreign policy was historically unpopular. "There were grave misgivings in this country over Roosevelt's open sympathy with the Allies from the outbreak of the European war in 1939," the editorial explained. "Furious differences of opinion were aroused by his One World ideas after we got into the war." Future historians might well condemn him, the *News* said. "No one can say now with authority whether the US could have stayed out of it to its own ultimate benefit, whether it will eventually add up on the plus or the minus side as regards human welfare and progress, and so on. The decision on those questions must be left to history."[111]

A month later, in a shockingly tasteless editorial headlined "Three of the Big Ones Dead in a Month," the *News* grouped Roosevelt with the dictators who had ruled the nation's main European enemies: "Each of these three departed headmen—Roosevelt,

Mussolini, Hitler—was touted in his time as the man without whom his country and his people could not get along." It seemed certain that the Germans and the Italians were better off without their late leaders, and Americans might learn the same about Roosevelt, the *News* implied. "As quite a few of us were saying in the 1944 Presidential campaign," the editorial stated, "no man is indispensable."[112] The *New York Post* expressed the disgust of many Roosevelt supporters when it responded that the *News* had failed in its attempt to dishonor the late president; instead, Patterson "dishonored only himself, and the grave in which he will eventually lie."[113]

When the Allies finally defeated the Axis, the McCormick/Patterson press once again stood outside the consensus. To those who had hoped for a total victory over fascism, the end of the war, first in Europe in May, and then in the Pacific in August, was a moment of triumph and self-congratulation. In New York, *Time* publisher Henry Luce cabled Beaverbrook days after the German surrender. "As they say in Oklahoma it's a beautiful morning and few earthly powers had more to do with the suns rising than you my friend. Hail to the victor."[114]

But to the McCormick/Patterson cousins, the end of the war was not just a time for celebration but a long-awaited opportunity to spread more conspiracy theories about its origins. The cousins had, of course, suspected since the moment of the attack on Pearl Harbor that Roosevelt had deliberately provoked it. They assumed two facts not in evidence: first, that the Roosevelt administration must have known that the Japanese would bomb Hawaii. As the *Daily News* said, "Pearl Harbor was one of the most logical of all possible places for the Japs to attack us; we all knew that."[115] Second, they believed Roosevelt had provoked the conflict: that he "kept blowing bellicose blasts at Germany and prodding Japan," the *News* contended, until the United States was "hurled into the war."[116]

Throughout the conflict, McCormick and Patterson hinted frequently at a conspiracy that might or might not ever be exposed. "Some day some historian, digging through the Presidential archives at Hyde Park, may come across some papers which will reveal the full story of Pearl Harbor," the *News* editorialized. "Or he may not. Those papers may not be there, or anywhere, by that time." In a cartoon next to the editorial, Uncle Sam clutched a scroll titled "Pearl Harbor" and looked beseechingly at a beautiful woman wrapped in a sash labeled "history." "The truth is being kept from me now but someday I'll learn it from you," he says to her.[117]

By 1944, Pearl Harbor revisionists, as they called themselves, were networking with other right-wing journalists, academics, and public figures to learn and expose what they termed the truth about December 7. One of the leaders in this campaign was John T. Flynn, an author and journalist best known for his anti-Roosevelt screeds. In fall 1944, just before the presidential election, Flynn persuaded McCormick to publish the results of his massive investigation of the events at Pearl Harbor. The story was a little tentative. It charged Roosevelt with criminal incompetence but not necessarily conspiracy. Flynn also buried his lede; not until the last paragraph of an article of several thousand words did he make his point: that the commanders at Pearl had been "crucified to shield the guilt of the President."[118]

After the war, Flynn felt free to make his argument more explicit, and the Medill grandchildren gave him a platform to spread it. On September 2, 1945, the McCormick/Patterson papers published Flynn's now-it-can-be-told story, which promised to expose the real facts of the war's origins. Flynn accused Roosevelt administration officials of knowing that the Japanese would attack U.S. forces on December 7, 1941 (which they did), and of withholding this information from the Pearl Harbor commanders (which they did not). In fact, as later investigations revealed, top U.S. military and diplomatic leaders knew that the Japanese planned to assault American possessions somewhere in the world on December 7, but they did not know where or when the attack would occur. U.S. intelligence had failed to predict or prevent the Pearl Harbor strike for many complicated reasons, but Flynn and the *Tribune* fixed the blame "squarely upon Franklin D. Roosevelt."[119]

The *Tribune* story prompted a congressional investigation. That inquiry, along with the three investigations that preceded it, all reached the same conclusion: Roosevelt and his aides did not know the place or hour of the Japanese attack, and were in fact surprised that it came at Pearl Harbor.[120]

McCormick was convinced that the evidence proved otherwise. Flynn's investigation, he said, showed that Roosevelt and his advisers had been engaged in a "terrible conspiracy"—the worst conspiracy in American history—to "tempt and force Japan into an attack upon American possessions," including the Philippines, Guam, Wake Island, and Hawaii. The plotters knew when and where the Japanese would strike, yet they "explicitly withheld" this information from military commanders. The anxiety that Knox and Roosevelt felt "that the truth should be known," he surmised, caused their premature deaths.[121]

This was sheer fantasy. To believe this conspiracy theory, one had to think that Knox, Roosevelt, and other national leaders had engaged in a massive, convoluted plot to draw America into war, knowingly killed thousands of Americans in the process, and then hid or faked evidence to conceal their crime. But that's how McCormick and his cousins saw the history of World War II. In their view, neither Japan nor Germany ever posed a real threat to the United States; the American people fought for three and a half years for no purpose except to gratify Franklin Roosevelt's ego. The cousins used their media empire throughout the war to promote these theories. Now they were determined to continue their fight against the New Dealers and their foreign policy into the postwar era.

Epilogue

The end of the war left the isolationist press lords feeling aggrieved and marginalized. Everything they had fought so hard to avoid had come to pass, including the creation of international institutions and widespread support for multilateral diplomacy. With the Allied victory and the revelation of the horrors of the Holocaust, their prewar positions were universally discredited. They had lost the most important foreign policy debate of their time.

In some respects, the press barons' era had passed. But in other ways, they had seeded the ground for a new media landscape.

■

After his confrontation with the president in December 1941, Joe Patterson told his friends that he only wanted to "outlive that bastard Roosevelt."[1] He succeeded, but just by a year. He fell ill from a liver ailment in fall 1945 and died the following May, aged sixty-seven.

On the day after Patterson's death, the *News*'s editorial space was left mostly blank. In its center, framed by black lines, two brief paragraphs announced the publisher's passing and pledged to continue his editorial policy: "Those who are left behind will do their best to keep this page and the paper what we believe he would want them to be."[2] For decades afterward, the *Daily News* would be known for its populist, nationalist coverage.[3] As *Time* magazine said in a remarkably harsh obituary, Joe Patterson had established a *News* tradition of advocating "blind prejudices" in an "adroit, insidious, vindictive" fashion.[4]

After Patterson's death, control of the *News* passed to the five-person board of News Syndicate Inc., which included Cissy Patterson and Robert McCormick.[5] Joe Patterson's sister and cousin did not direct day-to-day operations, but they ensured that the paper hewed to the populist and nationalist editorial line that Joe had found so successful. As late as 1947, the *Daily News* still identified itself as a member of the "isolationist camp."[6]

■

Cissy Patterson lived for another two years after her brother passed. The *Washington Times-Herald*, like the *Daily News*, continued to rail against the United Nations, communists, and Democrats. In November 1946, when the Republicans took back control of Congress for the first time since 1930, she and her cousin took credit for the victory. "Congratulations," McCormick cabled her after the vote. "I wish Joe were here to share our triumph."[7]

She died in the summer of 1948, at age sixty-six, of sudden congestive heart failure.[8] Henry Luce's *Time* magazine took the opportunity to publish another nasty obituary of a Patterson. Cissy had been "vain, shrewd, lonely, and lavishly spoiled" and "perhaps the most hated" woman in the country, though also a great "newspaperman."[9]

Patterson left only part of her estate to her daughter. The newspaper itself she bequeathed to seven top editors (all men). But Franklin Roosevelt's policies of taxing the rich followed her beyond the grave: there was not enough cash to pay the inheritance taxes of 65 percent, or more than $11 million on the $17.9 million estate, without selling some assets. Eugene Meyer, the Republican, Jewish owner of the *Washington Post*—the recipient of Cissy's "pound of flesh" in the early 1930s—offered to buy the *Times-Herald*. To avoid this takeover by a rival who supported international engagement, Robert McCormick swooped in and bought the paper, which he called "an outpost of American principles" in the unfriendly territory of Washington, D.C.[10] Five years later, however, in ill health and tired of the strain of running major papers in two cities, McCormick sold the *Times-Herald* to Meyer for a profit of $2.2 million.[11]

■

William Randolph Hearst lived long enough to see his country join the kind of internationalist institutions he had fought against for decades. But he had the compensating pleasure of living through the Second Red Scare. He assembled a stable of vitriolic anti-communist columnists and reporters and used his front pages to celebrate the inquisitions of allegedly Red artists, actors, directors, and teachers. The Hearst newspapers would become among the greatest champions of Senator Joseph McCarthy and the movement associated with him.

When Hearst died in 1951 at age eighty-eight, not all journalists mourned him. Many obituaries noted his "evil qualities," as the *Manchester Guardian* termed them. "He was essentially a demagogue," the *Guardian* concluded. "He recognised and exploited . . . the tremendous motive power which can be got by giving vent to the grievances of the poor and the unhappy."[12] The editors of the *St. Louis Post-Dispatch*, which was owned by the Pulitzer family, decried Hearst's "jingoism, his imperialism, his isolationism, his nativism" while applauding the American people for declining to elect him to high office.[13] The *Dayton Daily News* noted that he had "outlived his times, and the strictly personal journalism which he embodied is happily not likely to recur."[14]

■

Like the *Dayton Daily News* editors, many newsmen believed after Hearst's death that a historic period in Anglo-American journalism was ending. "Today," reported *Newsweek* in 1952, "the international society of press giants has drawn in its roster until it is one of the most exclusive clubs in the world. There are, in fact, only two men, on either side of the Atlantic, who can claim full, all-privilege membership: Robert Rutherford McCormick, in his Tribune Tower in Chicago, and Lord Beaverbrook."[15]

McCormick's influence continued to grow after the war. Until 1954, he directly controlled the *Tribune* and the *Times-Herald*, which together sold almost 1.2 million copies a day. He also owned and set policy for the *Daily News*, which sold 2.25 million copies a day.[16] With an average of four readers per copy, McCormick addressed almost 14 million Americans every day, and more on Sundays. He was unequaled among American media titans, and he planned to make the most of the time remaining to him.

McCormick saw himself as more than a newspaper publisher. He was also a political activist who excelled in networking with other hard-right intellectuals and politicians. Not only did he use his newspapers to spread his anti–New Deal and isolationist views, he also funded and organized others who wanted to turn back the clock on American domestic and foreign policy.

On the domestic front, McCormick remained convinced that conservatives should oppose any and all movements that aimed to disturb existing social hierarchies. Like his cousins, he demanded stricter immigration controls ("The country is full," he said).[17] He also denounced President Harry Truman's desegregation proposals as "a new form of slavery" and complained that "professional civil rights leaders" were "stirring up racial discord for profit."[18]

The liberation of the Nazi death camps and the revelation of the full extent of what became known as the Holocaust did not prompt McCormick to see World War II as a noble struggle, or to show sympathy to Jews. In 1950 the *Tribune* cemented its reputation for peddling anti-Jewish conspiracy theories when it "revealed" that America was actually governed by a "secret government" consisting of three Jews: New York senator Herbert Lehman, Supreme Court Justice Felix Frankfurter, and former Treasury secretary Henry Morgenthau Jr.[19] When Jews criticized the story, McCormick directed his editor to respond, but not in a manner that seemed "too apologetic." The *Tribune*, he said, did "not intend to stand for censorship in the name of non-discrimination."[20]

As his racial and foreign policy views fell from favor, McCormick felt increasingly victimized by minority groups. Some Jews and Catholics thought that "the majority have no rights that the minority need consider," he wrote in a private letter in 1950. "And what is worse, they seem to be dominating the government today."[21]

As usual, the colonel used his newspaper in 1948 to try to defeat the Democratic nominee for the presidency, ordering vitriolic editorials and news stories that were slanted against President Truman and in favor of the Republican nominee, Governor Thomas Dewey. When Truman responded by criticizing the newspaper, the *Tribune* exulted in its power. "Mr. Truman has added his name to the long list of political crooks and incompetents who have regarded the Tribune as first among their foes," read a front-page

President Harry Truman enjoys his triumph over Robert McCormick's
Chicago Tribune. McCormick's editors were so convinced that Governor
Thomas Dewey, the Republican nominee, would beat the president in
1948 that they printed a definitive, and incorrect, headline in their early
editions. Undeterred by Truman's victory, McCormick would continue
to build the right-wing media and try to create a new far-right political
party. (The Picture Art Collection / Alamy Stock Photo)

editorial. "Thanks in no small measure to the Tribune, the people
of this nation know Mr. Truman for the nincompoop he is."[22] The
Tribune editors' belief in the extent of their power and the righteousness of their cause led them to commit one of the most embarrassing mistakes in American journalism history, the "DEWEY
DEFEATS TRUMAN" headline on early editions of the *Tribune* in November 1948. Truman won by 4.5 percent of the popular vote and
114 electoral votes.

Though he failed to turn Truman out of office, McCormick
found some satisfaction in the investigations and prosecutions of
American communists. Like Hearst, he was thrilled by Senator

McCarthy's crusade to root out communists in the government. "Upon every suitable occasion get back of McCarthy," the colonel instructed his editorial writers in 1953.[23] The paper objected to the ways that liberals maligned the senator and his cause, arguing in one editorial that " 'McCarthyism,' which the senator's enemies deploy as a derogatory term, consists of calling the shots accurately."[24]

McCormick deplored the U.S. government's postwar embrace of international institutions. "What is this United Nations claptrap all about? United to live at the expense of America and American citizens?" he asked in August 1945.[25] Two years later, he concluded that the United Nations was even worse than he had feared. "It is completely unmatched," he told his editorial writer, "as a subversive organization created for the purpose of destroying the liberties that exist only in the United States and to a less [sic] extent in the Latin American countries."[26] Luckily, the colonel had managed to save the country, at least so far. "If those of us who carry the torch of republicanism had been less determined and less willing to sacrifice," he wrote, "Roosevelt and Truman and their gangs would have overthrown the republic before now."[27]

McCormick loathed President Truman almost as passionately as he had Roosevelt, and he battled Truman's international proposals on every front. The president's foreign policy, the *Tribune* claimed, was "not 'foreign' in its effects at all. It is a foreign policy calculated to insure unending domestic dictatorship." Like Stalin, Truman conjured "external threats in order to still domestic disaffection."[28] The creation of the Marshall Plan, the North Atlantic Treaty Organization, and the Central Intelligence Agency; the president's decision to defend South Korea in 1950—all, in McCormick's view, signified executive power run amok.

But McCormick was hardly a libertarian, for his hostility to governmental authority was highly selective. He supported big government and an aggressive foreign policy when they served his interests. McCormick opposed Truman not because the publisher was a farsighted critic of the swelling powers of the executive but because he thought the president was using those powers for the wrong reasons and to benefit the wrong people: immigrants, Blacks, Jews, Europeans, and communists. The *Tribune* embraced expanded state power when it was in the right hands, like Senator

McCarthy's committee or J. Edgar Hoover's Federal Bureau of Investigation.[29]

When postwar Republican leaders accepted internationalism and the welfare state, McCormick wondered whether the party could be saved. He backed the isolationist Robert Taft for the presidency in 1948 and 1952 and was desolate when the Ohio senator lost the Republican nomination, first to Thomas Dewey and then to Dwight Eisenhower. McCormick concluded by 1951 that Dewey was "unfit not only for the presidency but for American citizenship."[30] As for Eisenhower, the *Tribune* reluctantly supported him in the general election of 1952, but only because the Democrats had nominated what the newspaper called a "Europe firster," Illinois governor Adlai Stevenson. "It might seem reasonable to conclude," the *Tribune* wrote in its "endorsement" editorial, "that almost anybody would be preferable to Gen. Eisenhower. Unfortunately, almost anybody is not the opposing candidate, and Adlai Stevenson is."[31]

To stop the nation's drift toward liberalism and interventionism, the colonel decided to form a new "American" party—a right-wing, nationalist alternative to the Democrats and Republicans—and to promote more conservative media outlets. The media activism came first. In Chicago in 1944, he joined a meeting of prewar isolationists hosted by General Robert Wood, the former chairman of the America First Committee, called at the behest of two journalists who shared the colonel's view that America's entry into World War II had been a mistake. The men at the meeting had been active in America First, and all would help to build a far-right movement after the war. They began by creating a newsletter, *Human Events*, that was mostly funded and read by prewar isolationists.[32]

McCormick and the other *Human Events* founders anticipated later conservative criticism of liberal bias in the media.[33] Well before the height of the civil rights movement and the protests against the Vietnam War, the *Tribune* publisher and his right-wing allies argued that the other newspaper chains ignored Roosevelt's and Truman's critics.

Their anger over this alleged media favoritism for Roosevelt's multilateral foreign policy—a "subtle regimentation of public opinion," as one *Human Events* editor explained—inspired these right-wing activists to develop distinctly nationalist and conservative media.[34] As historian Nicole Hemmer has written, "The forge that fashioned postwar media activism was not the New Deal but World War II and the anti-intervention movement."[35] In McCormick's case, the forge was *both* the domestic New Deal and the war; in his view, Roosevelt's foreign and domestic policies were linked, and it was folly to oppose one and not the other.[36]

Even as McCormick and the other *Human Events* co-founders accused the mainstream media of liberal bias, the colonel continued to spread his conservative views in the hugely popular mainstream newspapers that he controlled. He published "the world's greatest newspaper," yet McCormick felt dismissed or silenced by centrist politicians and media outlets. The colonel pointed out to a correspondent in 1946 that though the *Daily News* was far more popular than the internationalist New York newspapers, Republican leaders ignored its message. The *News*, he wrote, "has fifty-five percent coverage in New York where the *New York Times* has eleven percent and the [*New York Herald*] *Tribune* seven percent. I think Republican politicians are largely living in the past journalistically speaking."[37] The future, he believed, would be controlled by the America Firsters who read the McCormick/Patterson papers.

In 1952, after the GOP chose Eisenhower as its presidential nominee, McCormick began to organize a new nationalist conservative party. Like other conservative Republicans, he wanted to build an alliance with Southern Democrats, founded upon their common abhorrence of civil rights, multilateral diplomacy, organized labor, and progressive taxation. But unlike many other Republicans, he had lost faith in the party's ability to reform itself and thought it was time to start anew. "Another party has to come because there are too many of our people not now represented by either the Republican or Democratic nominees," he explained. "They have no place to go."[38] Leaving the Republican Party, even in theory, was a big step for McCormick, whose grandfather had been among its founders. But Eisenhower was far too liberal, in his opinion; the only member of the GOP's internationalist wing who truly understood the dangers of internal subversion was Ike's vice president, Richard Nixon.[39]

In May 1954, McCormick formally set up For America, a radical-right group comprised largely of prewar isolationists, with the goal of promoting nationalist, conservative candidates and policies. The group's declaration of principles inveighed against "super-internationalism and interventionism, one-worldism, and communism."[40]

The members of the new generation of conservative media activists were just beginning to mobilize when McCormick passed from the scene. After his death in 1955 at age seventy-four, For America's leaders reorganized the group as a political action committee co-chaired by two right-wing radio broadcasters, Clarence Manion and Dan Smoot.[41] Political realignment would have to wait until the late 1960s, when Nixon implemented the racist Southern strategy and the Republican Party redefined itself as the uniformly conservative force McCormick had long desired.

■

Max Beaverbrook lived for almost two decades after the war, which gave him time to try to control his historical legacy. His biographers Anne Chisholm and Michael Davie counted more than a dozen books or research projects after the war that he either wrote, commissioned, influenced, or funded.[42] In addition to trying to sculpt the history of his life and times, Beaverbrook worked to bolster his reputation as a philanthropist in the Canadian province where he grew up, giving millions of pounds to the University of New Brunswick and other Canadian universities, public libraries, and parks.[43]

He tried to manage his image in history because he had diminishing power to shape the present. As World War II ended, he was selling 5 million papers every day, more than anyone else in Britain. Yet he no longer influenced the British government or a majority of the electorate. In the election of 1945, his newspapers vociferously supported Winston Churchill's divisive, disastrous campaign, in which the prime minister infamously attacked Labour leaders as incipient totalitarians who would bring "some form of Gestapo" to England.[44] Beaverbrook's newspapers relentlessly assailed Labourites as enemies of freedom and even called them "the National Socialists," despite their service in the coalition government that had defeated the actual National Socialists.[45]

The Beaverbrook papers' biased reporting that year made the press lord himself a campaign issue. Clement Attlee, the Labour

Party leader, pointed to Beaverbrook's "long record of political intrigue and political instability" and his "insatiable appetite for
power" before labeling him the public figure "who is most widely
distrusted by decent men of all parties."[46] The *Manchester Guardian*'s correspondent reminded his readers that Stanley Baldwin
had once denounced Beaverbrook and Rothermere for exercising
"power without responsibility." Now, the reporter explained, in an
ominous turn of events, this power was working in service to the
Tory Party rather than against it.[47]

Beaverbrook responded to the criticism as his isolationist
friends in America had done: by claiming he was maligned. "I make
no complaint of such incursions of animosity into the election," he
wrote in a letter to the *Guardian*. "But I do complain that you
should attempt to make me the guilty man in a matter where, in
fact, I have been the first, and the chief, victim." By using the
phrase "guilty man," Beaverbrook reminded readers that he had not
been included in the famous indictment of the guilty men who had
appeased Hitler and paved the way to war. Far from having power
without responsibility, he said, "now I have responsibility without
power—and apparently without even the right to hit back."[48] The
Express printed Beaverbrook's plaintive note about his powerless-
ness on the front page for his millions of readers.

For the rest of his life, Beaverbrook continued to crusade for
empire and isolation. He campaigned against the Marshall Plan,
the United Nations, and the European Common Market, which
he said aimed to destroy Britain as a sovereign state. He helped extend his imperialist ideals and sensationalist methods to future
generations by mentoring Rupert Murdoch, who worked at the
Express as a young journalist in the mid-1950s.[49] Murdoch, the son
of Keith Murdoch, the Australian editor who had studied and revered Northcliffe's papers, would eventually surpass even Beaverbrook in the size, reach, and influence of his worldwide, right-wing
media kingdom.

Beaverbrook lamented the British public's apparent lack of
interest in the dissolution of their empire. "The greatest and most
promising bond of human brotherhood that the world has ever
known is under heavy fire," he wrote in 1952. "But the public
here and abroad shrug their shoulders and regard this calamitous

spectacle with indifference."[50] When Britain offered to turn over its bases in the Suez Canal Zone to the Egyptian government, the "Empire Crusader" illustration in the *Daily Express*'s nameplate found himself bound with chains. He would remain shackled until after Beaverbrook's death, from cancer, in 1964 at age eighty-five.

Beaverbrook remained a phenomenally successful newspaper publisher, but he failed to diversify his company. After his death, as newsprint and labor costs rose, his papers struggled. His oldest son, Sir Max Aitken, gamely tried to follow in his father's footsteps for more than a decade, though he did renounce his title. "Certainly in my lifetime there will only be one Lord Beaverbrook," he explained.[51] In 1977, he sold the newspapers to an international conglomerate.

Though the *Express* changed hands a few times in the ensuing decades, its foreign policy remained consistent: xenophobic, nationalistic, and intensely anti-European. In 2010 the paper launched a campaign for the British to leave the European Union and "win back their country," proclaiming that "the famous and symbolic Crusader who adorns our masthead" would serve as the "figurehead" of the movement.[52] The paper relentlessly attacked the EU for reaching its "tentacles" into "every aspect of our lives" and "ruining Britain," and it slammed European migrants for allegedly bringing crime and disease.[53] The *Express* was jubilant when Britain left the EU and claimed that its crusade against Brussels—"the fastest growing and ultimately most successful press campaign in history"—was responsible. "We Did It! Decade-Old *Daily Express* Crusade Comes to an End with Brexit Victory" read one headline.[54] The Empire Crusader remains in the paper's masthead to this day.

■

The passing of the press lords marked the end of an era. *Life* magazine called McCormick "the last great bulwark in the U.S. of personal journalism."[55] Beaverbrook was also mourned as the last of his kind. "Fleet Street will never see his like again," said a fellow media entrepreneur, Lord Thomson.[56] In Britain, the newspapers remained right-leaning and partisan, but teams of top editors and managers, rather than one publisher, usually dictated policy. In the United States, as competition from television and later the Internet eroded newspapers' profit margins, corporations bought up papers and consolidated them. Hoping not to offend their readers, the new owners tried to make their products more entertaining and less partisan. The "big losers" in this process, as historian Si Sheppard has said, were the old-style press barons who had ruled "their own empires of opinion."[57]

Yet the press lords' ideas did not die with them. Starting with Northcliffe, they had discovered how to sell suspicion and hatred to a mass audience. They had railed against the liberal elites whose affection for alien ideas and alien peoples would endanger their supposedly racially homogeneous nations. They had met the greatest crisis of the twentieth century not by urging collective action against tyranny but by spinning conspiracy theories, warning of race suicide, or even embracing fascism. They imagined a white nation and then constructed its enemies—not the Nazis, or even the Japanese, but the "warmongers" among their fellow citizens who wanted to resist rather than appease the aggressors.

Far from recoiling in horror at their tactics, their successors would refine them and learn to apply them to different circumstances. Xenophobia, racism, anti-Semitism, and toxic nationalism still influence the debate over Anglo-American foreign policy. The sense of victimhood articulated by the right-wing publishers— their conviction that they, the richest and most powerful people in their countries, were oppressed and marginalized by foreign-minded internationalists—also continues to thrive among British and American conservatives. The publishers and their friends on the right had suffered a relative, not absolute, loss of influence. After the war, when they had to share some of their power with people who were not like them, they could not believe this change would benefit their country.

We can still hear the echoes of their voices today—in the anti-European headlines of the *Daily Express* and the *Daily Mail*, in the angry populism of Fox News and Breitbart, in the nationalist speeches of Boris Johnson and Donald Trump. "From this day forward a new vision will govern our land," President Trump promised in his inaugural address. "From this day forward, it's going to be only America First—America First."[58] The last of the press lords died more than half a century ago, but their heirs continue their crusade for nation, for empire, for the "white race," and for Britain and America First.

Notes

Abbreviations

Archives

AFC	America First Committee Files, Hoover Institution, Stanford, Calif.
AJC	American Jewish Congress Archives, Center for Jewish History, New York, N.Y.
BP	Beaverbrook Papers, Parliamentary Archives, London
CTDP	Chicago Tribune Departmental Papers, consulted at the Colonel Robert R. McCormick Research Center of the First Division Museum at Cantigny Park, Wheaton, Ill. (now moved to Northwestern University, Evanston, Ill.)
DNC	Democratic National Committee Papers, Franklin D. Roosevelt Presidential Library, Hyde Park, N.Y.
DP	Personal papers of Drew Pearson, Lyndon B. Johnson Library, Austin, Tex.
EC	Ernest Cuneo Papers, Franklin D. Roosevelt Presidential Library, Hyde Park, N.Y.
ECP	Edmond Coblentz Papers, Bancroft Library, University of California, Berkeley
EMPP	Eleanor M. Patterson Papers, Syracuse University, Syracuse, N.Y.
FBP	Francis Biddle Papers, Franklin D. Roosevelt Presidential Library, Hyde Park, N.Y.
FDRL	Papers of President Franklin D. Roosevelt, including President's Personal File (PPF), Official File (OF), and President's Secretary's File (PSF), Franklin D. Roosevelt Presidential Library, Hyde Park, N.Y.
FEG	Frank E. Gannett Papers, Cornell University, Ithaca, N.Y.

HCP	Harry Crocker Papers, Academy of Motion Picture Arts and Sciences, Special Collections, Margaret Herrick Library, Fairbanks Center for Motion Picture Study, Beverly Hills, Calif.
HHL	Papers of President Herbert Hoover, including the Post-Presidential Individual File (PPI), Herbert Hoover Presidential Library, West Branch, Iowa
JBP	John Boettiger Papers, Franklin D. Roosevelt Presidential Library, Hyde Park, N.Y.
JMPP	Joseph M. Patterson Papers, Lake Forest College, Ill.
RRMP	Robert Rutherford McCormick Papers, consulted at the Colonel Robert R. McCormick Research Center of the First Division Museum at Cantigny Park, Wheaton, Ill. (now moved to Northwestern University, Evanston, Ill.)
SEP	Stephen Early Papers, Franklin D. Roosevelt Presidential Library, Hyde Park, N.Y.
SHP	Stephanie Hohenlohe Papers, Hoover Institution, Stanford, Calif.
TCA	Tribune Company Archives, consulted at the Colonel Robert R. McCormick Research Center of the First Division Museum at Cantigny Park, Wheaton, Ill. (now moved to Northwestern University, Evanston, Ill.)
TNA	The British National Archives at Kew, United Kingdom
TOHP	Tribune Oral History Project, consulted at the Colonel Robert R. McCormick Research Center of the First Division Museum at Cantigny Park, Wheaton, Ill. (now moved to Northwestern University, Evanston, Ill.)
UCLA	Archive Research & Study Center, UCLA Film and Television Archive, University of California, Los Angeles
WRHP	William Randolph Hearst Papers, Bancroft Library, University of California, Berkeley
WTP	Walter Trohan Papers, Herbert Hoover Presidential Library, West Branch, Iowa

Newspapers

CT	*Chicago Tribune*
DE	London *Daily Express*
DM	London *Daily Mail*
DN	*New York Daily News*
NYT	*New York Times*
SFE	*San Francisco Examiner*
WTH	*Washington Times-Herald*

Introduction

1. Harold Rothermere, "Germany on Her Feet Again," *DM*, December 28, 1934.

2. On the concentration camps, see Nikolaus Wachsmann, *Kl* (New York: Farrar, Straus and Giroux, 2015). On repression in the early years of the Nazi regime, see Richard J. Evans, *The Third Reich in Power, 1933–1939* (New York: Penguin, 2005).

3. For circulation of the *Daily Mail* and *Daily Express*, see Political and Economic Planning, *Report on the British Press* (London: Political and Economic Planning, 1938), 116–17, and table 2.1 in Tom Jeffery and Keith McClelland, "A World Fit to Live In: The *Daily Mail* and the Middle Classes, 1918–39," in *Impacts and Influences: Essays on Media Power in the Twentieth Century*, ed. James Curran, Anthony Smith, and Pauline Wingate (London: Methuen, 1987), 29. For American circulation, see the annual editions of *N. W. Ayer & Son's Directory of Newspapers and Periodicals* (Philadelphia: N. W. Ayer and Son). The circulation figures reflect the number of copies sold. At the time, the newspaper industry assumed four readers per copy.

4. "Fourth Term Smear Tactics," DN, November 10, 1943; "A Vigorous Speech," London *Times*, March 18, 1931.

5. "Mr. Bevin Throws out a Challenge," *Manchester Guardian*, June 13, 1945.

6. "Minutes of Evidence Taken Before the Royal Commission on the Press," in *Royal Commission on the Press* (London: His Majesty's Stationery Office, 1948), 4.

7. W. R. Hearst to Edmond Coblentz, May 1, 1933, "Hearst, Wm. R. Sr., 1933: May–Dec.," box 4, Incoming, ECP.

8. For more on the populist style of mass-market journalism, see Reece Peck, *Fox Populism: Branding Conservatism as Working Class* (Cambridge: Cambridge University Press, 2019), chapter 1; Daniel C. Hallin and Paolo Mancini, *Comparing Media Systems: Three Models of Media and Politics* (Cambridge: Cambridge University Press, 2004), chapter 7; and Adrian Bingham and Martin Conboy, *Tabloid Century: The Popular Press in Britain, 1896 to the Present* (Oxford: Peter Lang, 2015). On the populist style in politics, see Michael Kazin, *The Populist Persuasion: An American History* (New York: Basic, 1995). For a discussion and definition of modern radical-right populism, see Cas Mudde, *Populist Radical Right Parties in Europe* (Cambridge: Cambridge University Press, 2007), especially 11–31, 138–57.

9. "Youth Triumphant," *DM*, July 10, 1933.

10. "Hurrah for the Blackshirts!" *DM*, January 15, 1934.

11. Beaverbrook, "No More War," *DE*, May 25, 1933.

12. "No War This Year," *DE*, August 7, 1939.

13. Ferdinand Lundberg, *Imperial Hearst: A Social Biography* (1936; repr., New York: Modern Library, 1937), 352; George Seldes, "How Hearst Fed Nazi Propaganda to 30,000,000," *In Fact*, March 13, 1944, 4.

14. Letter to Joe Willicombe, published in Edmond D. Coblentz, *William Randolph Hearst: A Portrait in His Own Words* (New York: Simon and Schuster, 1952), 106; "W. R. Hearst Gives His Views on Hitler and Conditions in Europe," *SFE*, September 28, 1934.
15. Quoted in W. A. Swanberg, *Citizen Hearst* (New York: Charles Scribner's Sons, 1961), 430.
16. "In the News," *SFE*, January 29, 1942.
17. "Remember Tarawa," *SFE*, December 7, 1943.
18. "McCormick and His *Tribune*," *Sign*, January 1947, 8.
19. "Invoke Lincoln Spirit in Fight for U.S. Liberty," *CT*, February 13, 1936.
20. "Passing of the Great Race?" *DN*, March 24, 1941.
21. Jeffery and McClelland, "A World Fit to Live In," 29.
22. *Ayer Directory* (1937). For estimates of Hearst's total readership, see David Nasaw, *The Chief: The Life of William Randolph Hearst* (Boston: Mariner Books, 2001), 405; George Seldes, *Lords of the Press* (New York: Julian Messner, 1938), 227; Rodney P. Carlisle, *Hearst and the New Deal: The Progressive as Reactionary* (New York: Garland, 1979), 11; and Ian Mugridge, *The View from Xanadu: William Randolph Hearst and United States Foreign Policy* (Montreal: McGill-Queen's University Press, 1995), 19.
23. For more on the imprecision of the terms *isolationism* and *internationalism*, see Andrew Johnstone, "Isolationism and Internationalism in American Foreign Relations," *Journal of Transatlantic Studies* 9, no. 1 (March 2011): 7–20; and Brooke Blower, "From Isolationism to Neutrality: A New Framework for Understanding American Political Culture, 1919–1941," *Diplomatic History* 38, no. 2 (2014): 345–76. Stephen Wertheim argues that "essentially no one thought of him- or herself" as an isolationist. That may have been true for intellectuals and foreign policy elites, but these press lords—with the exception of McCormick—did use the term to describe themselves. See Stephen Wertheim, *Tomorrow, the World: The Birth of U.S. Global Supremacy* (Cambridge, Mass.: Belknap, 2020), 4. For scholarly studies of noninterventionism in the United States, see Wayne Cole, *Roosevelt and the Isolationists, 1932–45* (Lincoln: University of Nebraska Press, 1983); Justus Doenecke, *Storm on the Horizon: The Challenge to American Intervention, 1939–1941* (Lanham, Md.: Rowman and Littlefield, 2000); Warren Cohen, *The American Revisionists: The Lessons of Intervention in World War I* (Chicago: University of Chicago Press, 1967); Christopher McKnight Nichols, *Promise and Peril: America at the Dawn of a Global Age* (Cambridge, Mass.: Harvard University Press, 2011).
24. "The Madness of Locarno," *DM*, November 18, 1933. See also "Two Voices: Two Policies," *DE*, March 22, 1934; "The Last War Pictures," *DE*, March 24, 1934; Beaverbrook, "Britain Should Make No Alliances Except with U.S.," *SFE*, April 14, 1935; and "Britain Must Keep Out," *DM*, August 24, 1934. For the origins of splendid isolation in Britain, see

Christopher Howard, *Splendid Isolation* (London: Macmillan, 1967); and David F. Krein, *The Last Palmerston Government: Foreign Policy, Domestic Politics, and the Genesis of "Splendid Isolation"* (Ames: Iowa State University Press, 1978).

25. "Splendid Isolation," *DE*, March 27, 1935. See also "Splendid Isolation," *DE*, March 26, 1935; and "Women of Britain!" *DE*, March 22, 1935.

26. See, for example, "Britain Must Keep Out."

27. "Britain Should Make No Alliances Except with U.S."

28. "Medill M'Cormick," *DN*, February 26, 1925.

29. For Patterson's phrase, see Walter Fitzmaurice, "McCormick and His *Tribune*," *Sign*, January 1947, 8. For the *News*'s description of British appeasers as isolationists, see "England's Isolation Party," *DN*, August 15, 1938. The *Tribune/News* reporters began referring to "isolationists" at least as early as 1933. See "Give Up Hope of Immediate Stabilization," *DN*, June 19, 1933.

30. "Alfred Duff Cooper," *DN*, October 5, 1938. See also "What Will Be Happening a Year from Now?" *DN*, September 17, 1938.

31. "Of Course We're for America First," *DN*, October 27, 1944.

32. "In the News," *SFE*, November 17, 1941. For Hearst's argument that the United States had never been isolated, see "The Isolation Myth," *SFE*, February 21, 1935.

33. For McCormick's dislike of the term, see "Independence," *CT*, July 4, 1923; and "Isolation," *CT*, June 25, 1933. McCormick did use the term uncritically at least twice in the 1920s. See "Nearing the End of the Treaty of Versailles and the League," *CT*, March 26, 1925; and "The Frontier against Asia," *CT*, March 3, 1925.

34. Beaverbrook, "Empire Ever: Nazi-ism Never," *DE*, January 14, 1934.

35. Daniel Hucker, *Public Opinion and the End of Appeasement in Britain and France* (Burlington, Vt.: Ashgate, 2011), 20.

36. Tom Harrisson and Charles Madge, *Britain by Mass-Observation* (London: Cresset Library, 1986), 30.

37. Gallup Organization, Gallup Poll #1941-0229: Newspapers/Presidential Election/Lease-Lend Bill/War in Europe, Question 13, USGALLUP.41–229.QKT01 (Gallup Organization, Cornell University, Ithaca, N.Y.: Roper Center for Public Opinion Research, 1941); National Opinion Research Center (NORC), NORC Survey: Attitude toward War in Europe, Question 1, USNORC.41–102.R01A (National Opinion Research Center (NORC), Cornell University, Ithaca, N.Y.: Roper Center for Public Opinion Research, 1941).

38. Hoover liked to invite journalists to the Bohemian Grove, the exclusive men's resort in Northern California. See, among many other examples, Hoover to Roy Howard, May 6, 1942, Hoover to Boake Carter, July 14, 1941, and Hoover to David Lawrence, June 13, 1938, all in Post-Presidential Individual file, HHL.

39. See, for example, 86 Cong. Rec. 12580 (1940) and 87 Cong. Rec. 2698 (1941).

40. Archibald MacLeish, "The Responsibility of the Press" (address delivered before the American Society of Newspaper Editors, April 17, 1942), in MacLeish, *A Time to Act: Selected Addresses* (Boston: Houghton Mifflin, 1943), 10.

41. Samuel I. Rosenman, *Working with Roosevelt* (New York: Harper and Brothers, 1952), 167. See also Robert Dallek, *Franklin D. Roosevelt and American Foreign Policy, 1932–1945* (New York: Oxford University Press, 1979), 152.

42. For more on FDR's mastery of the press and his reliance on opinion polls, see David Greenberg, *Republic of Spin: An Inside History of the American Presidency* (New York: Norton, 2016), chapters 20–27.

43. Grace Tully, *FDR: My Boss* (New York: Charles Scribner's Sons, 1949), 76–77, lists the newspapers Roosevelt read each day. On propaganda agencies, see Richard W. Steele, *Propaganda in an Open Society: The Roosevelt Administration and the Media, 1933–1941* (Westport, Conn.: Greenwood, 1985), 73–94.

44. Fireside Chat, April 28, 1942, The American Presidency Project, https://www.presidency.ucsb.edu/documents/fireside-chat-5.

45. For an astute assessment of the effects of digitization on historical scholarship, see Adrian Bingham, "The Digitization of Newspaper Archives: Opportunities and Challenges for Historians," *Twentieth Century British History* 21, no. 2 (2010): 225–31.

46. Franklin Reid Gannon, *The British Press and Germany, 1936–1939* (Oxford: Oxford University Press, 1971), vii.

47. See Nicole Hemmer, *Messengers of the Right: Conservative Media and the Transformation of American Politics* (Philadelphia: University of Pennsylvania Press, 2016); Heather Hendershot, *What's Fair on the Air: Cold War Right-Wing Broadcasting and the Public Interest* (Chicago: University of Chicago Press, 2011); Heather Hendershot, *Open to Debate: How William F. Buckley Put Liberal America on the Firing Line* (New York: Broadside Books, 2016); and Bryan Hardin Thrift, *Conservative Bias: How Jesse Helms Pioneered the Rise of Right-Wing Media and Realigned the Republican Party* (Gainesville: University Press of Florida, 2016). For a scholarly call for more studies of right-wing media, see Kim Phillips-Fein, "Conservatism: A State of the Field," *Journal of American History* 98, no. 3 (December 2011): 735.

48. See Sam Lebovic, "When the 'Mainstream Media' Was Conservative: Media Criticism in the Age of Reform," in *Media Nation: The Political History of News in Modern America*, ed. Julian Zelizer and Bruce Schulman (Philadelphia: University of Pennsylvania Press, 2017), 63–76.

49. "We're Annoyed with the *N.Y. Times*," *DN*, January 6, 1938.

50. On the history of the term *America First*, see Sarah Churchwell, *Behold, America: A History of America First and the American Dream* (London: Bloomsbury, 2018).

Chapter 1. The Good Haters

1. S. J. Taylor, *The Great Outsiders: Northcliffe, Rothermere and the "Daily Mail"* (London: Weidenfeld and Nicolson, 1996), 73–74; Piers Brendon, *The Life and Death of the Press Barons* (London: Secker and Warburg, 1982), 108–9.

2. Taylor, *Great Outsiders*, 16.

3. Quoted in Collin Brooks, *Devil's Decade: Portrait of the Nineteen-Thirties* (London: MacDonald, 1948), 147.

4. Political and Economic Planning, *Report on the British Press* (London: Political and Economic Planning, 1938), 9.

5. Adrian Bingham, *Gender, Modernity, and the Popular Press in Inter-war Britain* (Oxford: Oxford University Press, 2004), 22.

6. Political and Economic Planning, *Report*, 93.

7. Kennedy Jones, *Fleet Street and Downing Street* (London: Hutchinson, 1920), 202.

8. Key works on the journalism history of this era include Adrian Bingham and Martin Conboy, *Tabloid Century: The Popular Press in Britain, 1896 to the Present* (Oxford: Peter Lang, 2015); John Simpson, *Unreliable Sources: How the 20th Century Was Reported* (London: Macmillan, 2010), chapters 1–12; D. G. Boyce, "Crusaders without Chains: Power and the Press Barons, 1896–1951," in *Impacts and Influences: Essays on Media Power in the Twentieth Century*, ed. James Curran, Anthony Smith, and Pauline Wingate (London: Methuen, 1987), 97–112; Political and Economic Planning, *Report*; James Curran and Jean Seaton, *Power without Responsibility: The Press and Broadcasting in Britain* (London: Routledge, 1991); Stephen Koss, *The Rise and Fall of the Political Press in Britain: The Twentieth Century*, vol. 2 (Chapel Hill: University of North Carolina Press, 1984); and George Boyce, James Curran, and Pauline Wingate, eds., *Newspaper History from the Seventeenth Century to the Present Day* (London: Constable, 1978).

9. Max Pemberton, *Lord Northcliffe: A Memoir* (London: Hodder and Stoughton, 1922), 29–30.

10. Political and Economic Planning, *Report*, 8.

11. Political and Economic Planning, *Report*, 88–89; Adrian Bingham, *Family Newspapers? Sex, Private Life, and the British Popular Press, 1918–1978* (Oxford: Oxford University Press, 2009), 205; "Britain's Beaverbrook," *Time*, November 28, 1938.

12. The quotation is often attributed to Northcliffe. See, for example, Niall Ferguson, *The Rise and Demise of the British World Order and Lessons for a Global Power* (New York: Basic, 2004), 213.

13. Political and Economic Planning, *Report*, 94.

14. "The Great Tragedy," *DM*, July 6, 1900.

15. Jones, *Fleet Street and Downing Street*, 313 ("faked news").

16. Taylor, *Great Outsiders*, 54.

17. Taylor, *Great Outsiders*, 143. See also Bingham and Conboy, *Tabloid Century*, 23–28.

18. Quoted in J. Lee Thompson, *Politicians, The Press, and Propaganda: Lord Northcliffe and the Great War, 1914–1919* (Kent, Ohio: Kent State University Press, 1999), 125.

19. Bingham and Conboy, *Tabloid Century*, 72.

20. George Seldes, *Lords of the Press* (New York: Julian Messner, 1938), 204.

21. Quoted in Taylor, *Great Outsiders*, 205.

22. Michael Kinnear, *The Fall of Lloyd George: The Political Crisis of 1922* (London: Macmillan, 1973), 23.

23. Adrian Addison, *Mail Men: The Unauthorized Story of the "Daily Mail," the Paper That Divided and Conquered Britain* (London: Atlantic Books, 2017), 70.

24. Northcliffe biographer S. J. Taylor investigated the sources of the syphilis rumor and concluded it was untrue. See Taylor, *Great Outsiders*, 219, 363.

25. Quoted in Ruth Dudley Edwards, *Newspapermen: Hugh Cudlipp, Cecil Harmsworth King and the Glory Days of Fleet Street* (London: Secker and Warburg, 2003), 76.

26. Cecil H. King, *Strictly Personal: Some Memoirs of Cecil H. King* (London: Weidenfeld and Nicolson, 1969), 75, 76, 72.

27. Hugh Cudlipp, *The Prerogative of the Harlot: Press Barons and Power* (London: Bodley Head, 1980), 146.

28. King, *Strictly Personal*, 76, 77.

29. Political and Economic Planning, *Report*, 97; Cudlipp, *Prerogative of the Harlot*, 166.

30. King, *Strictly Personal*, 40; Taylor, *Great Outsiders*, 253.

31. Rothermere, *Solvency or Downfall? Squandermania and Its Story* (London: Longmans, Green, 1921), viii, ix.

32. Rothermere, *Solvency or Downfall?* x.

33. Brooks, *Devil's Decade*, 145.

34. For the definitive account, see Gill Bennett, *The Zinoviev Letter: The Conspiracy That Never Dies* (Oxford: Oxford University Press, 2018).

35. "Moscow Orders to Our Reds," *DM*, October 25, 1924.

36. "Moscow's Orders," *DM*, October 25, 1924.

37. Bingham and Conboy, *Tabloid Century*, 74; Adrian Bingham, " 'Stop the Flapper Vote Folly': Lord Rothermere, the *Daily Mail*, and the Equalization of the Franchise, 1927–28," *Twentieth Century British History* 13, no. 1 (2002): 24.

38. "Fatal Flapper-Vote Folly: Viscount Rothermere's Open Letter to Mr. Baldwin," *DM*, November 18, 1927; "A Mad 'Experiment,' " *DM*, November 7, 1927. On Baldwin, see Roy Jenkins, *Baldwin* (London: Collins, 1987).

39. Rothermere to Beaverbrook, May 7, 1934, BBK/C/285b, BP; Beaverbrook to Esmond Rothermere, May 29, 1961, BBK/C/288, BP.

40. See, for example, Beaverbrook, "No More War," *DE*, May 25, 1933.

41. Taylor, *Great Outsiders*, 272–73. On the United Empire Party, see Jerry M. Calton, "Beaverbrook's Split Imperial Personality: Canada, Britain, and the Empire Free Trade Movement of 1929–1931," *Historian* 37, no. 1 (November 1974): 26–45.

42. Rothermere to Beaverbrook, February 2, 1931, BBK/C/287, BP.

43. "A Vigorous Speech," London *Times*, March 18, 1931. Baldwin's cousin, Rudyard Kipling, had coined the phrase several years earlier when feuding with Beaverbrook.

44. Quoted in Ian Colvin, *Vansittart in Office* (London: Victor Gollancz, 1965), 26–27.

45. Quoted in Martin Gilbert and Richard Gott, *The Appeasers* (Boston: Houghton Mifflin, 1963), 14.

46. See Matthew Worley, *Labour inside the Gate: A History of the British Labour Party between the Wars* (London: I. B. Tauris, 2005); and John Callaghan, *The Labour Party and Foreign Policy: A History* (London: Routledge, 2007), chapters 3 and 4.

47. See Viscount Rothermere, *My Campaign for Hungary* (London: Eyre and Spottiswoode, 1939).

48. Stanley Payne, *Fascism, Comparison and Definition* (Madison: University of Wisconsin Press, 1980), 7. See also Robert O. Paxton, *The Anatomy of Fascism* (New York: Knopf, 2004); Federico Finchelstein, *From Fascism to Populism in History* (Oakland: University of California Press, 2017); and Ruth Ben-Ghiat, *Strongmen: Mussolini to the Present* (New York: Norton, 2020).

49. "What Europe Owes to Mussolini," *DM*, September 17, 1923.

50. "What Europe Owes to Mussolini"; "Mussolini's Five Years," *DM*, May 2, 1927.

51. "Mussolini Today," *DM*, March 28, 1928.

52. "Germany and Inevitability," *DM*, September 24, 1930.

53. "My Hitler Article and Its Critics," *DM*, October 2, 1930. For astute analyses of gender and appeasement, see Bingham, *Gender, Modernity, and the Popular Press*, and Julie V. Gottlieb, *"Guilty Women," Foreign Policy, and Appeasement in Inter-war Britain* (New York: Palgrave Macmillan, 2016).

54. "My Hitler Article and Its Critics." On fascist racism and anti-Semitism, see Mark Hayes, *The Ideology of Fascism and the Far Right in Britain* (Ottawa: Red Quill Books, 2014), especially 153–85.

55. Rothermere, "Germany on Her Feet Again," *DM*, December 28, 1934.

56. "Hitler's Special Talk to the *Daily Mail*," *DM*, September 27, 1930.

57. "Hitler's Triumphal Tour of East Prussia," *DM*, July 18, 1932.

58. Quoted in Will Wainewright, *Reporting on Hitler: Rothay Reynolds and the British Press in Nazi Germany* (London: Biteback, 2017), 103.

59. "Our Troubled World," *DM*, March 7, 1933.

60. Wainewright, *Reporting on Hitler,* 101.
61. G. Ward Price, *I Know These Dictators* (New York: Henry Holt, 1938), 165.
62. "Youth Triumphant," *DM,* July 10, 1933.
63. Taylor, *Great Outsiders,* 292.
64. Taylor, *Great Outsiders,* 301.
65. "Germany Must Have Elbow Room," *DM,* March 21, 1934.
66. "Arrested by Hitler," *DM,* July 2, 1934.
67. Martha Schad, *Hitler's Spy Princess: The Extraordinary Life of Stephanie Von Hohenlohe* (Stroud, U.K.: Sutton, 2004), 36–37.
68. Rothermere, "Germany on Her Feet Again."
69. See Robert Skidelsky, *Oswald Mosley* (London: Macmillan, 1975); Martin Pugh, *"Hurrah for the Blackshirts!" Fascists and Fascism in Britain between the Wars* (London: Jonathan Cape, 2005); and Richard Griffiths, *Fellow Travelers of the Right: British Enthusiasts for Nazi Germany, 1933–39* (London: Constable, 1980).
70. Oswald Mosley, *Fascism Explained* (n.p., 1933), 7.
71. Skidelsky, *Oswald Mosley,* 390.
72. Quoted in Pugh, *Hurrah,* 149.
73. "Hurrah for the Blackshirts!" *DM,* January 15, 1934.
74. Pugh, *Hurrah,* 150.
75. Taylor, *Great Outsiders,* 283.
76. Quote from "Oswald Mosley's Circus," *Manchester Guardian,* June 8, 1934. See also "Sir O. Mosley at Olympia" and "Fascists at Olympia," both in London *Times,* June 8, 1934.
77. "Reds' Futile Protests," *DM,* June 8, 1934.
78. Oswald Mosley, *My Life* (London: Thomas Nelson and Sons, 1968), 346–47.
79. Martin Pugh argues that the *Daily Mail* did not promote the BUF "as blatantly as before" the Olympia riot, but still reported on Mosley's speeches. Pugh, "The British Union of Fascists and the Olympia Debate," *Historical Journal* 41, no. 2 (June 1998): 536.
80. Rothermere to Churchill, July 17, 1939, in Martin Gilbert, *Winston S. Churchill,* vol. 5, companion part 3 (London: Heinemann 1982), 1566.
81. Quoted in Taylor, *Great Outsiders,* 300.
82. Rothermere, *My Fight to Rearm Britain* (London: Eyre and Spottiswoode, 1939), 6. For an analysis of Rothermere's views, see Paul Addison, "Patriotism under Pressure: Lord Rothermere and British Foreign Policy," in *The Politics of Reappraisal, 1918–1939,* ed. Gillian Peele and Chris Cook (London: Macmillan, 1975), 189–208.
83. Winston Churchill to Clementine Churchill, August 22, 1934, quoted in Martin Gilbert, *Prophet of Truth: Winston S. Churchill,* vol. 5 (London: Minerva, 1990), 559–60.
84. See Edwards, *Newspapermen,* 77, and Taylor, *Great Outsiders,* chapter 18.

Chapter 2. The Celebrity Strongman

1. James Creelman, *On the Great Highway: The Wanderings and Adventures of a Special Correspondent* (Boston: Lothrop, 1901), 177–78. The story is controversial and no documentary evidence exists to support it. See David Nasaw, *The Chief: The Life of William Randolph Hearst* (Boston: Mariner Books, 2001), 127.

2. Cora Older, *William Randolph Hearst, American* (New York: D. Appleton-Century, 1936), 61. For other biographies of Hearst, see Nasaw, *Chief*; Ben Procter, *William Randolph Hearst: The Later Years, 1911–1951* (New York: Oxford University Press, 2007); and W. A. Swanberg, *Citizen Hearst* (New York: Charles Scribner's Sons, 1961).

3. John D. Stevens, *Sensationalism and the New York Press* (New York: Columbia University Press, 1991), 97; *New York Morning Journal*, May 8, 9, and 10, 1898.

4. Creelman, *Great Highway*, 212.

5. On Hearst's collections, see "$15,000,000 Worth," *Time*, March 14, 1938; and David Nasaw, "Life at San Simeon," *New Yorker*, March 23, 1998.

6. "The Record of the Supine Squander-and-Waste 74th Congress," *SFE*, August 28, 1935.

7. "In Defense of William Randolph Hearst," *University of Washington Daily*, reprinted in the *Seattle Star* as "This Puzzled Us, Too—At First," January 29, 1936, "William Randolph Hearst, 1936–44," OF 846, FDRL.

8. Walter Lippmann, *Liberty and the News* (New York: Harcourt, Brace and Howe, 1920), 67.

9. On the development of the doctrine of objectivity, see Michael Schudson, "The Objectivity Norm in American Journalism," *Journalism* 2, no. 2 (August 2001): 149–70; Schudson, *Discovering the News: Social History of American Newspapers* (New York: Basic Books, 1978); and Richard L. Kaplan, *Politics and the American Press: The Rise of Objectivity, 1865–1920* (Cambridge: Cambridge University Press, 2002). On the newspaper industry and the correspondents of the early twentieth century, see Alfred McClung Lee, *The Daily Newspaper in America: The Evolution of a Social Instrument* (New York: Macmillan, 1947); Quincy Howe, *The News and How to Understand It* (New York: Simon and Schuster, 1940); Leo C. Rosten, *The Washington Correspondents* (New York: Harcourt, Brace, 1937); David Halberstam, *The Powers That Be* (New York: Knopf, 1979); and Donald Ritchie, *Reporting from Washington: The History of the Washington Press Corps* (Oxford: Oxford University Press, 2005).

10. Paul Alfred Pratte, *Gods within the Machine: A History of the American Society of Newspaper Editors, 1923–1993* (Westport, Conn.: Praeger, 1995), 206.

11. Matthew Gentzkow, Edward L. Glaeser, and Claudia Goldin, "The Rise of the Fourth Estate: How Newspapers Became Informative and Why It

Mattered," in *Corruption and Reform: Lessons from America's Economic History*, ed. Edward L. Glaeser and Claudia Goldin (Chicago: University of Chicago Press, March 2006), available at http://www.nber.org/chapters/c9984.

12. Ferdinand Lundberg, *Imperial Hearst: A Social Biography* (New York: Modern Library, 1937). See also Gray Brechin's astute analysis in chapter 5, "The Hearsts," in *Imperial San Francisco: Urban Power, Earthly Ruin* (Berkeley: University of California Press, 2006).

13. Nasaw, *Chief*, 382.

14. "Japanese Entry into Siberia Is Not to Aid the Allies, but to Entrench Japan," *SFE*, March 4, 1918.

15. "Friends Betrayed into the Hands of Enemies," *SFE*, February 12, 1922.

16. Quoted in Nasaw, *Chief*, 271.

17. Older, *William Randolph Hearst*, 415.

18. Cable from Watson, September 8, 1934, "Hearst, Wm. R. Sr., 1934: July–September," box 4, Incoming, ECP.

19. "Hearst for Garner as Party Nominee," *NYT*, January 3, 1932; Nasaw, *Chief*, 453. See also "Whom Did Governor Roosevelt Have in Mind?" January 8, 1932; "John N. Garner and Wall Street," January 10, 1932; and "More History for Senators Dill and Wheeler," January 17, 1932, all in *SFE*.

20. Eric Rauchway, *Winter War: Hoover, Roosevelt, and the First Clash over the New Deal* (New York: Basic, 2018), 53.

21. Robert Dallek, *Franklin D. Roosevelt: A Political Life* (London: Allen Lane, 2017), 120; Nasaw, *Chief*, 456.

22. Frank Luther Mott, "Newspapers in Presidential Campaigns," *Public Opinion Quarterly* 8, no. 3 (Autumn 1944): 357; "60% of Dailies Support Dewey; Roosevelt Backed by 22%," *Editor & Publisher*, November 4, 1944, 9, 68.

23. Harold Ickes, *America's House of Lords: An Inquiry into the Freedom of the Press* (Westport, Conn.: Greenwood, 1939), 8.

24. See letters in PPF 62, FDRL.

25. "All Americans Should Observe 'President's Day,' Sunday, April 30," *SFE*, April 12, 1933.

26. For more on *Gabriel*, see Rauchway, *Winter War*, 190–93.

27. "Back to Democracy," *SFE*, October 31, 1933; "Sinclair Theorist, Hearst Declares," *NYT*, September 2, 1934.

28. "Back to Democracy." On Americans' fears of dictatorship, see Benjamin L. Alpers, *Dictators, Democracy, and American Public Culture: Envisioning the Totalitarian Enemy, 1920s–1950s* (Chapel Hill: University of North Carolina Press, 2003).

29. "Communists Spur Drive in Schools for 'Soviet U.S.,'" *SFE*, March 4, 1934.

30. Willicombe to Coblentz, December 17, 1934, "Hearst, Wm. R. Sr., 1934: July–December," box 4, Incoming, ECP.

31. "Americanism vs. Communism," *SFE*, July 23, 1934.

32. Coblentz to Hearst, March 14, 1935, "Coblentz, Edmond David, 1935," box 1, Outgoing, ECP.

33. "Willie and Bernie: Tory Publishers Seek Comfort in Each Other's Arms as Liberals Turn on Hearst," *Herald Magazine*, March 28, 1936, 6, in "William Randolph Hearst, 1936–44," OF 846, FDRL; see also "Vilest Racketeer of All" in the same file.

34. White to Hearst, January 3, 1936; and Hearst to White, January 11, 1936, folder 37, carton 11, WRHP.

35. Hearst to Coblentz, April 9, 1935, "Hearst, Wm. R. Sr., 1935: January–March," box 4, Incoming, ECP.

36. Harold Ickes, *The Secret Diary of Harold L. Ickes*, vol. 1 (New York: Simon and Schuster, 1953), entry for April 30, 1935, 354–55.

37. Coblentz to Hearst, May 9, 1935, "Coblentz, Edmond David, 1935," box 1, Outgoing, ECP. Edmond D. Coblentz, *William Randolph Hearst: A Portrait in His Own Words* (New York: Simon and Schuster, 1952), 177–78, has slightly different wording.

38. Hearst to Bainbridge Colby and Coblentz, June 19, 1935, "Hearst, Wm. R. Sr., 1935: April–June," box 4, Incoming, ECP.

39. Quoted in Nasaw, *Chief*, 514.

40. Memo to publishers and managing editors of all Hearst papers, June 27, 1935, "Hearst, Wm. R. Sr., 1935: April–June," box 4, Incoming, ECP.

41. See Coblentz to Universal Service bureaus and all Hearst editors, August 7, 1935, PPF 62, FDRL. See also Moley to Early, August 14, 1935, with attachment, box 7, SEP.

42. Statement, August 15, 1935, PPF 62, FDRL.

43. "Soak-Successful Bill Jammed through Senate; Record Peace-time Levies," *SFE*, August 16, 1935.

44. "Awake, American Patriots!" *SFE*, November 24, 1935.

45. George Allen to Mrs. Franklin D. Roosevelt, August 1, 1935, "Publicity 1935," OF 340, FDRL.

46. Roosevelt to General A. F. Lorenzen, July 6, 1935, PPF 2668, FDRL.

47. "Who Will Defeat Mr. Roosevelt? Asks Mr. Hearst," *SFE*, October 6, 1935.

48. On Hearst and the Landon campaign, see George Wolfskill and John A. Hudson, *All but the People: Franklin D. Roosevelt and His Critics, 1933–39* (New York: Macmillan, 1969), 190–94.

49. "Trans-Atlantic Instructions from Mr. W.R. Hearst," date unknown but apparently October 1936, "Hearst, Wm. R. Sr., 1936: Aug–Dec.," box 4, Incoming, ECP.

50. Ickes, *Secret Diary*, vol. 1, entry for November 7, 1936, 702.

51. "The Arms Embargo," *SFE*, April 22, 1933.

52. Hearst to Coblentz, August 22, 1935, "Hearst, Wm. R. Sr., 1935: July–December," box 4, Incoming, ECP.

53. "The Record of the Supine Squander-and-Waste 74th Congress."

54. "Passing Years Add to Mussolini's Power, Says Millicent Hearst," *SFE*, May 11, 1930. On American admiration for Mussolini, see John P. Diggins, *Mussolini and Fascism: The View from America* (Princeton: Princeton University Press, 1972); and Katy Hull, *The Machine Has a Soul: American Sympathy with Italian Fascism* (Princeton: Princeton University Press, 2021).

55. Louis Pizzitola, *Hearst over Hollywood: Power, Passion, and Propaganda in the Movies* (New York: Columbia University Press, 2002), 263; Nasaw, *Chief*, 471. On the fascist leaders contributing to the Hearst papers, see Nasaw, *Chief*, 470–77.

56. General Hermann Wilhelm Goering, "Nazi Germany Stands for Maintenance of Legal Security, Declares Goering," *SFE*, December 2, 1934.

57. Adolf Hitler, "Election Sign of New Peril, Says Hitler," *SFE*, September 28, 1930.

58. "Hearst Is Quoted as Hailing Nazi Vote," *NYT*, August 23, 1934; see also telegram, August 22, 1934, box 4, Incoming, ECP.

59. Hearst did not want to publicize his attendance at such a virulently anti-Semitic event. But historian Louis Pizzitola has found evidence of the Hearst party visit in Nuremberg, including hotel records and newspaper accounts of George Hearst's attendance at the rally. Pizzitola, *Hearst over Hollywood*, 308–10.

60. "W. R. Hearst Discusses a Free Press, Racial Issues, World Peace," *SFE*, September 17, 1934.

61. Harry Crocker, undated, unfinished memoir, "That's Hollywood," folder 26, quotes at XI-13 and XI-14, HCP; Coblentz, *Portrait*, 105. Coblentz prints an account of Hearst's interview with Hitler that Hearst allegedly wrote himself at some unknown date. However, as Louis Pizzitola has pointed out in *Hearst over Hollywood* (311–12), it is written in the third person, and is an almost verbatim copy of Crocker's account.

62. Crocker, "That's Hollywood," XI-15–XI-16.

63. "W. R. Hearst Sees War Threat in Russia's Entry into League," *SFE*, September 30, 1934; "W. R. Hearst Gives His Views on Hitler and Conditions in Europe," *SFE*, September 28, 1934.

64. Pizzitola, *Hearst over Hollywood*, 311–12.

65. Crocker, "That's Hollywood," XI-17.

66. Letter to Willicombe, published in Coblentz, *Portrait*, 106.

67. "Hearst Metrotone News, Inc. vol. 1, UFA Agreement, 1934," Hearst Newsreel Paper Documentation, UCLA, 13.

68. Pizzitola, *Hearst over Hollywood*, 318.

69. Hearst Metrotone News, Inc., Editorial Department Disposition Sheets, weeks ending October 15, 1938; June 3, 1939; and September 29, 1939, UCLA.

70. Lundberg, *Imperial Hearst*, 352; Nasaw, *Chief*, 510; George Seldes, "How Hearst Fed Nazi Propaganda to 30,000,000," *In Fact*, March 13, 1944, 4;

Sigrid Schultz to Robert McCormick, December 14, 1934, folder 9, box 8, RRMP.

71. "Vilest Racketeer of All," undated pamphlet, "William Randolph Hearst, 1936–44," OF 846, FDRL.

Chapter 3. The World's Greatest Publisher

1. Robert Allen, quoted in "The Tales about Lewis and the CIO," *Progressive*, August 28, 1937, 8.
2. Hearst to White, April 25, 1938, in "Hearst, Wm. R. Sr., 1938: April–May," box 5, Incoming, ECP.
3. John Tebbel, *An American Dynasty: The Story of the McCormicks, Medills and Pattersons* (Garden City, N.Y.: Doubleday, 1947), 151.
4. George Seldes, *Lords of the Press* (New York: Julian Messner, 1938), 47. See also Stephen Bates, *An Aristocracy of Critics: Luce, Hutchins, Niebuhr, and the Committee That Redefined Freedom of the Press* (New Haven: Yale University Press, 2020), for a discussion of perceptions of media bias at the time.
5. See, for example, "Dictator Debs Tells of Strike," *CT*, July 6, 1894.
6. The most comprehensive biography of McCormick is Richard Norton Smith, *The Colonel: The Life and Legend of Robert R. McCormick, 1880–1955* (Boston: Houghton Mifflin, 1997). See also Frank C. Waldrop, *McCormick of Chicago: An Unconventional Portrait of a Controversial Figure* (Englewood Cliffs, N.J.: Prentice-Hall, 1966); Tebbel, *American Dynasty*; and Lloyd Wendt, *"Chicago Tribune": The Rise of a Great American Newspaper* (Chicago: Rand McNally, 1979). On McCormick's foreign policy, see Jerome Edwards, *The Foreign Policy of Col. McCormick's "Tribune," 1929–1941* (Reno: University of Nevada Press, 1971).
7. McCormick to Leon Stolz, September 15, 1944, folder 4, box 9, I-61, RRMP.
8. McCormick, "Memoirs," *CT*, January 6, 1952.
9. McCormick, "Memoirs," *CT*, January 6, 1952; Smith, *Colonel*, 48.
10. See, for example, McCormick to Leon Stolz, October 11, 1944, and November 2, 1944, folder 4, box 9, I-61; and McCormick to Joseph Ator, September 8, 1943, folder 8, box 8, I-61, RRMP. On American Anglophobia, see John E. Moser, *Twisting the Lion's Tail: Anglophobia in the United States, 1921–48* (London: Macmillan, 1999).
11. McCormick, "Memoirs: Part II," *CT*, February 3, 1952.
12. McCormick, "Memoirs: Part V," *CT*, May 4, 1952.
13. The first use of "The World's Greatest Newspaper" appeared in a display ad in the *Tribune* on April 6, 1906. The paper started putting the slogan in its nameplate on August 29, 1911.
14. Patterson to McCormick, folder 1, box 51, February 17, 1917, JMPP.
15. McCormick, *With the Russian Army* (New York: Macmillan, 1915), 252.

16. McCormick, "Memoirs, Part XVIII," *CT,* March 1, 1953.

17. McCormick, *The Army of 1918* (New York: Harcourt, Brace and Howe, 1920), 271.

18. McCormick, *Army of 1918,* 276.

19. McCormick, *Army of 1918,* 271.

20. See "The Word Is Coward," *CT,* July 26, 1942.

21. A complete list of the stones appears in *Pictured Encyclopedia of the World's Greatest Newspaper: A Handbook of the Newspaper as Exemplified by the "Chicago Tribune"* (Chicago: Chicago Tribune, 1928), 316–18.

22. Smith, *Colonel,* 253; Walter Trohan, *Political Animals: Memoirs of a Sentimental Cynic* (Garden City, N.Y.: Doubleday, 1975), 19.

23. McCormick to Leon Stolz, June 19, 1944, folder 4, box 9, I-61, RRMP.

24. Seldes, *Lords of the Press,* 64.

25. McCormick to Beck, November 18, 1937, "Great Britain, Newspapers—General, 1927–1951," box 36, I-60, RRMP; "W. G. N. in London," *CT,* November 22, 1937.

26. Trohan, *Political Animals,* 15.

27. Burton Rascoe, *Before I Forget* (New York: Literary Guild of America, 1937), 266.

28. Jack Alexander, "The Duke of Chicago," *Saturday Evening Post,* July 19, 1941, 10–11, 70–75.

29. Edwards, *Foreign Policy,* 138.

30. McCormick to Blake, October 18, 1930, folder 9, box 8, I-61, RRMP.

31. "American Intervention," *CT,* March 20, 1928.

32. "Liberalism and Haiti," *CT,* January 13, 1930.

33. Walter Trohan, "My Life with the Colonel," *Journal of the Illinois State Historical Society* (Winter 1959): 477.

34. McCormick to Blake, January 16, 1930, folder 9, box 8, I-61, RRMP.

35. McCormick to Blake, February 23, 1933, folder 9, box 8, I-61, RRMP.

36. McCormick to Blake, June 30, 1932, folder 9, box 8, I-61, RRMP.

37. McCormick to Blake, March 20, 1932, folder 9, box 8, I-61, RRMP.

38. McCormick to Blake, January 18, 1930, folder 9, box 8, I-61, RRMP.

39. "Text of the President's Final Campaign Address in the Capital of Minnesota," *NYT,* November 6, 1932.

40. "The President in the Campaign," *CT,* November 4, 1932.

41. McCormick to Roosevelt, February 22, 1933, and May 6, 1933; and Roosevelt to McCormick, May 16, 1933, all in PPF 426, FDRL.

42. McCormick to Blake, March 9, 1933, folder 9, box 8, I-61, RRMP.

43. McCormick to Blake, April 9, 1933, folder 9, box 8, I-61, RRMP.

44. McCormick to Blake, May 31, 1933, folder 9, box 8, I-61, RRMP.

45. McCormick to Blake, July 1, 1933, folder 9, box 8, I-61, RRMP.

46. McCormick to Henning, July 3, 1933, folder 16, box 20, I-61, RRMP.

47. McCormick to Blake, August 16, 1934, folder 10, box 8, I-61, RRMP.

48. McCormick to Blake, June 5, 1935, folder 10, box 8, I-61, RRMP.

49. McCormick to Blake, February 16, 1935, folder 10, box 8, I-61, RRMP.

50. "Invoke Lincoln Spirit in Fight for U.S. Liberty," *CT*, February 13, 1936.

51. Seldes, *Lords of the Press*, 56–57; Edwards, *Foreign Policy*, 106. See also Carey McWilliams, *A Mask for Privilege: Anti-Semitism in America* (Boston: Little, Brown, 1948), 184–206; and Donald S. Strong, *Organized Anti-Semitism in America: The Rise of Group Prejudice during the Decade 1930–1940* (Washington, D.C.: American Council on Public Affairs, 1941), 83–106.

52. Stolz to McCormick, no date but apparently 1944, folder 18, box 20, I-61, RRMP.

53. McCormick to Arthur Henning, April 3, 1934, "McCormick, Robert," box 22, JBP.

54. McCormick to John Boettiger, July 5, 1933, "McCormick, Robert," box 22, JBP.

55. McCormick to Jackson Elliott, July 5, 1933, "McCormick, Robert," box 22, JBP.

56. TB to Arthur Henning, June 29, 1934, "McCormick, Robert," box 22, JBP.

57. J. L. Maloney to Boettiger, October 9, 1934, "McCormick, Robert," box 22, JBP.

58. "Hunt Roosevelt Button Takers in Loop Crowds," *CT*, October 14, 1936.

59. George Wolfskill and John A. Hudson, *All but the People: Franklin D. Roosevelt and His Critics, 1933–39* (New York: Macmillan, 1969), 188.

60. "GOP Charges New Deal with Evasion on Tags," *CT*, November 3, 1936.

61. George Seldes, "America's Leading News Faker Joins Fascists," *In Fact* 5, no. 25 (September 1942).

62. "Moscow Orders Reds in U.S. to Back Roosevelt," *CT*, August 9, 1936.

63. McCormick to Landon, August 13, 1936, "Landon, Governor Alfred M., 1936–1949," box 44, I-60, RRMP.

64. W. Cameron Meyers, "The Chicago Newspaper Hoax in the '36 Election Campaign," *Journalism Quarterly* 37, no. 3 (September 1960): 359, 358.

65. "Prove Tribune Story—$5,000!" *Chicago Times*, August 28, 1936.

66. Day to Beck, September 16, 1936, folder 8, box 3, I-62, RRMP.

67. Meyers, "Chicago Newspaper Hoax," 364; "Soviets Take an Active Hand in U.S. Election," *CT*, August 29, 1936.

68. "Soviet Joins in New Deal Drive: Documentary Proof," *SFE*, September 20, 1936.

69. *Chicago Tribune* editorial page of March 11, 1936.

70. E. S. Beck to McCormick, October 21, 1936, "Landon, Governor Alfred M., 1936–1949," box 44, I-60, RRMP.

71. McCormick to Landon, October 28, 1936, "Landon, Governor Alfred M., 1936–1949," box 44, I-60, RRMP; "Landon's Dare Thrills N.Y.," *CT*, October 30, 1936; "Roosevelt Talk Fails to Reply on NRA, AAA," *CT*, November 1, 1936.

72. Meyers, "Chicago Newspaper Hoax," 362.

73. Edwards, *Foreign Policy*, 27.
74. William L. Shirer, *Twentieth Century Journey: A Memoir of a Life and the Times; The Start, 1904–1930* (Boston: Little, Brown, 1976), 349.
75. Lilya Wagner, *Women War Correspondents of World War II* (New York: Greenwood, 1989), 97–99.
76. McCormick to Schultz, September 2, 1932, folder 8, box 8, I-62, RRMP.
77. McCormick to Pat Maloney, May 26, 1939, folder 9, box 8, I-62, RRMP.
78. Schultz to McCormick, February 20, 1933, folder 8, box 8, I-62, RRMP.
79. Schultz to McCormick, March 27, 1933, folder 8, box 8, I-62, RRMP.
80. Gary A. Klein, "The American Press and the Rise of Hitler, 1923–1933" (PhD diss., London School of Economics and Political Science, 1997), 285–86. For an analysis of American perceptions of Nazi Germany, see Michaela Hoenicke Moore, *Know Your Enemy: The American Debate on Nazism, 1933–1945* (Cambridge: Cambridge University Press, 2010).
81. Transcript of Sigrid Schultz interview, April 5 and 6, 1977 (hereafter Schultz oral history), part IV, 10, X-15, TOHP. See also Sigrid Schultz, "Hermann Goring's 'Dragon from Chicago,'" in *How I Got That Story*, ed. David Brown and W. Richard Bruner (New York: E. P. Dutton, 1967), 75–81.
82. Schultz oral history, parts II and III.
83. Robert R. McCormick, "Germany Seen Living under Terror Reign," *CT*, August 12, 1933.
84. Schultz oral history, part III, 6.
85. Edwards, *Foreign Policy*, 94–95.
86. "Versailles Again," *CT*, March 10, 1936.
87. See Klein, "American Press and Rise of Hitler," 290.
88. "Warnings to the American People," *CT*, August 4, 1936.
89. Day to McCormick, December 18, 1933, folder 6, box 3, I-62, RRMP.
90. Day to McCormick, February 26, 1934, folder 7, box 3, I-62, RRMP. On Day, see John Carver Edwards, *Berlin Calling: American Broadcasters in Service to the Third Reich* (New York: Praeger, 1991), chapter 6.
91. McCormick to Schultz, May 5, 1933, folder 8, box 8, I-62, RRMP.
92. McCormick to Tiffany Blake, April 2, 1933, folder 9, box 8, I-61; see also Blake to McCormick, March 31, 1933, in the same folder, RRMP.

Chapter 4. The Ordinary Joe

1. Jack Alexander, "Vox Populi," *New Yorker*, August 6, 1938, 16–17.
2. Patterson to Henry Ozanne, September 11, 1939, folder 6, box 30, JMPP.
3. On Patterson, see John Tebbel, *An American Dynasty: The Story of the McCormicks, Medills and Pattersons* (Garden City, N.Y.: Doubleday, 1947); Jack Alexander, "Vox Populi," *New Yorker*, August 6, 13, and 20, 1938; "1,848,320 of Them," *Time*, July 3, 1939; and George Y. Wells, "Patterson and the *Daily News*," *American Mercury*, December 9, 1944.

4. Joseph Medill Patterson, *The Confessions of a Drone* (Chicago: Charles H. Kerr, 1908), 5.

5. "Mr. Patterson's Novel," *NYT*, August 29, 1908.

6. Jack Alexander, "Vox Populi, II," *New Yorker*, August 13, 1938, 21.

7. McCormick to Patterson, June 5, 1939, folder 2, box 54, JMPP.

8. "1,848,320 of Them."

9. Display ad, *NYT*, June 26, 1919.

10. "Who We Are," *DN*, June 24, 1919.

11. Bruce J. Evensen, *When Dempsey Fought Tunney: Heroes, Hokum, and Storytelling in the Jazz Age* (Knoxville: University of Tennessee Press, 1996), 70.

12. "1,848,320 of Them." For more on how early twentieth-century newspapers helped build communities among their readers, see Julia Guarneri, *Newsprint Metropolis: City Papers and the Making of Modern Americans* (Chicago: University of Chicago Press, 2017).

13. Burton Rascoe, *Before I Forget* (New York: Literary Guild of America, 1937), 277.

14. "1,848,320 of Them."

15. "Dead!" *DN*, January 13, 1928; Tebbel, *American Dynasty*, 257–58.

16. "*N.Y. News*, Now 15, Holds Grip on Masses," *Editor & Publisher*, June 30, 1934.

17. John Chapman, *Tell It to Sweeney: The Informal History of the "New York Daily News"* (Garden City, N.Y.: Doubleday, 1961), 142.

18. John Bainbridge, "Profiles: Editorial Writer" (part 2), *New Yorker*, May 31, 1947.

19. "Fight for France Again??" *DN*, May 23, 1936.

20. Bowles to Patterson, November 1, 1939, folder 4, box 28, JMPP.

21. John Bainbridge, "Profiles: Editorial Writer" (part 1), *New Yorker*, May 24, 1947, 42. See also part 2, May 31, 1947, and part 3, June 7, 1947.

22. Tebbel, *American Dynasty*, 258.

23. "The New President and the New Deal," *DN*, March 4, 1933.

24. Roosevelt to Patterson, March 30, 1933, PPF 245, FDRL.

25. McCormick to William J. Smith, August 17, 1936, "Patterson, Joseph Medill, 1936–1939," box 89, I-60, RRMP.

26. See Sam Lebovic, "When the 'Mainstream Media' Was Conservative: Media Criticism in the Age of Reform," in *Media Nation: The Political History of News in Modern America*, ed. Julian Zelizer and Bruce Schulman (Philadelphia: University of Pennsylvania Press, 2017); and Lebovic, *Free Speech and Unfree News: The Paradox of Press Freedom in America* (Cambridge, Mass.: Harvard University Press, 2016), chapter 2.

27. "The Wayward Press," *New Yorker*, May 14, 1960, 109.

28. Anna Rosenberg to Patterson, December 15, 1936, folder 9, box 26, JMPP.

29. "Is It Revolution? No—Evolution," *DN*, June 21, 1935.

30. "The Gay Reformer," *DN*, July 17, 1936.

31. Patterson to Amon Carter, December 26, 1933, folder 2, box 22, JMPP.

32. At the time, donors had to pay a gift tax—which topped out at 53 percent in 1936—on any contribution over $5,000. The DNC had a plan to allow Patterson to avoid the taxes. The national committee printed souvenir books to commemorate the Democratic convention, arranged for the president to inscribe them, and sold them for $100 apiece, although they cost only $5 each. A DNC official suggested that Patterson buy 250 of these books for $25,000. Doris Fleeson to Patterson, May 14, 1936, folder 6, box 22, JMPP. Though the convention book financing scheme caused a small scandal at the time, it was legal. See Louise Overacker, "Campaign Funds in the Presidential Election of 1936," *American Political Science Review* 31, no. 3 (June 1937): 473–98; Michael J. Webber, *New Deal Fat Cats: Business, Labor, and Campaign Finance in the 1936 Presidential Election* (New York: Fordham University Press, 2000), chapter 5.

33. See table VII in Overacker, "Campaign Funds," 491.

34. "England Had a New Deal, Too," *DN*, October 6, 1936.

35. Stern to Patterson, June 4, 1936, folder 9, box 26, JMPP.

36. Farley to Patterson, February 3, 1936, folder 10, box 22, JMPP.

37. See the letters in PPF 245, FDRL.

38. "Two Ships for One," *DN*, February 4, 1935.

39. "About Staying out of This War," *DN*, August 22, 1935.

40. "Two Ships for One," *DN*, December 10, 1934. For the *News*'s explanation of its campaign, see "Two Ships for One," *DN*, October 21, 1935.

41. "Two Ships for One," *DN*, September 10, 1934.

42. "Two Ships for One," *DN*, January 7, 1935.

43. "Two Ships for One," *DN*, February 11, 1935.

44. "Two Ships for One," *DN*, December 3, 1934; "Two Ships for One," *DN*, January 14, 1935.

45. "West Coast Gold Moved Inland," *DN*, September 3, 1934.

46. E.B., "Yellow Peril," *DN*, March 14, 1936.

47. "Things to Be Thankful For," *DN*, March 9, 1933.

48. "The World Is Full of Nerves," *DN*, August 6, 1935.

49. Original available at FDR Library in Hyde Park, New York. Digitized version available at http://www.fdrlibrary.marist.edu/archives/pdfs/dictatorship.pdf.

50. William E. Kinsella Jr., "The Prescience of a Statesman: FDR's Assessment of Adolf Hitler before the World War, 1933–1941," in *Franklin D. Roosevelt: The Man, the Myth, the Era, 1882–1945*, ed. Herbert D. Rosenbaum and Elizabeth Bartelme (New York: Greenwood, 1987), 73. On FDR and anti-Semitism, see Richard Breitman and Allan J. Lichtman, *FDR and the Jews* (Cambridge, Mass.: Belknap, 2013).

51. "Stay out of It," *DN*, August 20, 1936.

52. "Let's Stay out of It," *DN*, August 1, 1936.

Chapter 5. The Empire Crusader

1. "From across the Atlantic … Comes This Tremendous Message," BBK/F/40, BP. For one reader's description of his surprise at reading the insert, see letter from C. J. Lawrence to Joseph Patterson, May 15, 1935, folder 7, box 21, JMPP.

2. Patterson to Beaverbrook, March 20, 1935, BBK/C/268, BP.

3. "The Glory of Empire: An Empire Day Message from Lord Beaverbrook," *Evening Standard*, May 24, 1934.

4. Beaverbrook, "This Task Awaits Us," *Evening Standard*, July 10, 1936.

5. Glyn Osler to Robert McCormick, October 9, 1922, "Great Britain, Newspapers—Beaverbrook, Lord (London *Daily Express*), 1937–1954," box 36, I-60, RRMP. The most complete biography of Beaverbrook is Anne Chisholm and Michael Davie, *Lord Beaverbrook: A Life* (New York: Knopf, 1993). See also the recent biography by Charles Williams, *Max Beaverbrook: Not Quite a Gentleman* (London: Biteback, 2019), and A. J. P. Taylor's authorized biography, *Beaverbrook* (London: Hamish Hamilton, 1972).

6. Quoted in Robert Blake, *The Unknown Prime Minister: The Life and Times of Andrew Bonar Law, 1858–1923* (London: Eyre and Spottiswoode, 1955), 90.

7. Chisholm and Davie, *Lord Beaverbrook*, 99–100, 135; Taylor, *Beaverbrook*, 74, 99–100.

8. "Britain's Beaverbrook," *Time*, November 28, 1938.

9. "Idealist," *News Review*, August 13, 1936.

10. On Churchill's finances, see David Lough, *No More Champagne: Churchill and His Money* (New York: Picador, 2015).

11. "Little Lord Beaverbrook," *Life*, August 5, 1940.

12. A. J. P. Taylor, *A Personal History* (London: Hamilton, 1983), 221.

13. Arthur Christiansen, *Headlines All My Life* (London: Heinemann, 1961), 144.

14. Political and Economic Planning, *Report on the British Press* (London: Political and Economic Planning, 1938), 231–32.

15. Beaverbrook, "What Wage Earners Tell Me," *DE*, April 24, 1933.

16. "2,126,454 Copies Sold Each Day during June," *DE*, July 6, 1936.

17. "Minutes," *Royal Commission on the Press*, March 18, 1948, 4.

18. Beaverbrook, "Empire Ever: Nazi-ism Never," *DE*, January 14, 1934. See also Beaverbrook, "I Want Peace—with Isolation," *Reynolds*, November 26, 1933, filed in Beaverbrook scrapbooks, BBK/L/61, BP.

19. The first use of the crusader in the masthead that I could find was on March 29, 1930.

20. Beaverbrook, "Newspaper-Making," *Sunday Express*, July 7, 1935.

21. Robert Bruce Lockhart, *The Diaries of Robert Bruce Lockhart*, vol. 1, ed. Kenneth Young (London: Macmillan, 1973), entry for March 6, 1933,

249. For an example of a *DE* editorial rebuking Hitler's critics, see "Hitler's Critics Here," *DE*, April 17, 1933.

22. David Lloyd George, " . . . I Talked to Hitler," *DE*, September 27, 1936.

23. Beaverbrook to Lloyd George, October 6, 1936, BBK/C/218b, BP.

24. "Nazi Footballers," *DE*, November 29, 1935; Beaverbrook to Ribbentrop, November 30, 1935, BBK/C/275, BP.

25. See, among others, Beaverbrook to Ribbentrop, August 4, 1936, August 12, 1936, May 24, 1937, and undated 1938; Ribbentrop to Beaverbrook, June 14, 1936 and March 15, 1939, BBK/C/275, BP.

26. Lockhart, *Diaries*, entry for July 3, 1934, 299.

27. See Martin Ceadel, "The First British Referendum: The Peace Ballot, 1934–5," *English Historical Review* 95, no. 377 (October 1980): 810–39.

28. "Dragging You into War," *DE*, October 25, 1934.

29. "Tear Up the Ballot Paper!" *DE*, November 17, 1934.

30. Beaverbrook to Patterson, March 9, 1935, BBK/C/268, BP.

31. Patterson to Beaverbrook, March 20, 1935, BBK/C/268, BP.

32. Patterson to Beaverbrook, March 20, 1935, BBK/C/268, BP.

33. See Beaverbrook to Patterson, letters dated April 11, 1935, April 29, 1935, and October 25, 1935, all in BBK/C/268, BP.

34. Quentin Reynolds, "Dreams for Sale," *Colliers*, July 2, 1938.

35. "British Income Taxes Go Down," *DN*, April 17, 1935.

36. "More English Views on American-British Peace Co-operation," *DN*, May 27, 1935; "Britons on American-British Co-operation," *DN*, May 4, 1935; "America Hears the Voice of Britain," *DE*, May 5, 1935. See some of the original letters in folders 6 and 7, box 21, JMPP.

37. "Britain Should Make No Alliances Except with U.S.," *SFE*, April 14, 1935.

38. "Splendid Isolation," *DE*, March 27, 1935. See also "Splendid Isolation," March 26, 1935; and "Women of Britain!" *DE*, March 22, 1935.

39. Beaverbrook to Patterson, July 5, 1935, BBK/C/268, BP.

40. Alice Arlen and Michael J. Arlen, *The Huntress: The Adventures, Escapades, and Triumphs of Alicia Patterson* (New York: Pantheon, 2016), 130.

41. Handwritten note, Patterson to Beaverbrook, July 26, 1935, BBK/C/268, BP.

42. "Italy May Win Easily," *DM*, July 15, 1935.

43. Beaverbrook, "We Cannot, We Will Not, We Must Not Police the World Alone," *DE*, September 27, 1935.

44. Beaverbrook, "Let Us Seek Peace," *DE*, September 30, 1935.

45. Beaverbrook, "Are You for Peace?" *DE*, October 18, 1935.

46. "Two Ships for One," *DN*, September 16, 1935.

47. "Whatever It's Called, It's War," *CT*, October 8, 1937; "Mr. Hearst Discusses the Ethiopian War and Crisis in Europe," *SFE*, October 13, 1935. Hearst was influenced by Theodore Roosevelt, who talked about the "waste spaces" of Africa and elsewhere. See, for example, Theodore

Roosevelt, *African Game Trails: An Account of the African Wanderings of an American Hunter-Naturalist* (New York: Charles Scribner's Sons, 1910), xi, 416.

48. Hitler to Rothermere, May 3, 1935, in *Fleet Street, Press Barons and Politics: The Journals of Collin Brooks, 1932–1940*, ed. N. J. Crowson (London: Royal Historical Society, 1998), 282. Two of Hitler's letters to Rothermere are printed in this volume. These two, along with one additional Hitler letter to Rothermere, are also reprinted in the appendices to Martha Schad, *Hitler's Spy Princess: The Extraordinary Life of Stephanie Von Hohenlohe* (Stroud, U.K.: Sutton, 2004), and all the letters are excerpted in S. J. Taylor, *The Great Outsiders: Northcliffe, Rothermere and the "Daily Mail"* (London: Weidenfeld and Nicolson, 1996), 294–97.

49. "As Friend to Friend, John Bull—Stay out of It!" *DN*, August 29, 1935.

50. "About Staying out of This War," *DN*, August 22, 1935.

51. "Is It War?" *DE*, March 9, 1936.

52. "German Soldiers Re-enter the Rhineland," *DN*, March 8, 1936.

53. David Deacon, *British News Media and the Spanish Civil War: Tomorrow May Be Too Late* (Edinburgh: Edinburgh University Press, 2008) 61, 136–37.

54. "Spain: Lay Off," *DE*, August 18, 1936.

55. "Toledo Falls, Alcazar Relieved," *DN*, September 29, 1936.

56. "We're All Americans First," *DN*, November 23, 1936.

Chapter 6. The Lady Newspaperman

1. Beverly Smith, "*Herald* Angel," *American Magazine*, August 1940, 110. Several women served as editors of American newspapers before the twentieth century, but there had been no female editors of big-city dailies for decades before Cissy Patterson took over the *Herald* in 1930. There were a few women who played major management roles in large newspapers in roughly the same era, though none served as editor in chief or publisher until years after Patterson's trailblazing editorship began. Helen Rogers Reid was the advertising director and vice president of the paper owned by her husband, Ogden Mills Reid, the *New York Tribune* (after 1924 the *New York Herald Tribune*). She influenced major policy decisions at the paper, but did not get involved with the day-to-day editorial decisions, and she did not take over the presidency of the paper in her own right until 1947, after her husband's death. Eleanor McClatchy would become president of McClatchy newspapers, headquartered in Sacramento, in 1936, after the illness of her father, the previous president of the chain. Dorothy Schiff would become the majority owner of the *New York Post* in 1939 and its publisher in 1942. See Amanda Smith, *Newspaper Titan: The Infamous Life and Monumental Times of Cissy Patterson* (New York: Knopf, 2011), 318; and Ishbel Ross, *Ladies of the Press: The*

Story of Women in Journalism by an Insider (New York: Harper and Brothers, 1936), 135–41.

2. "Fourth Term Smear Tactics," *DN*, November 10, 1943.

3. There are four biographies of Cissy Patterson. Her great-niece drew on confidential family documents in Alice Albright Hoge, *Cissy Patterson* (New York: Random House, 1966). See also Paul F. Healy, *Cissy: The Biography of Eleanor M. "Cissy" Patterson* (Garden City, N.Y.: Doubleday, 1966); Ralph G. Martin, *Cissy* (New York: Simon and Schuster, 1979); and the most complete biography, Smith, *Titan*.

4. Marguerite Cassini, *Never a Dull Moment: The Memoirs of Countess Marguerite Cassini* (New York: Harper and Brothers, 1956), 201.

5. "Countess Seeks Only to Regain Her Child," *NYT*, June 1, 1908.

6. Healy, *Cissy*, 110.

7. Smith, *Titan*, 234.

8. "Official Washington Satirized in a New Novel," *NYT*, February 21, 1926.

9. Smith, *Titan*, 273.

10. Interview with Maryland McCormick, July 22, 1977, part IV, 1, X-15, TOHP.

11. "*Herald* Angel," 29; David Halberstam, *The Powers That Be* (New York: Knopf, 1979), 182.

12. Smith, *Titan*, 307; Cuneo to Cissy Patterson, July 14, 1941, "Patterson, Eleanor," container 37, EC.

13. Joe Patterson to Cissy Patterson, May 2, 1928, folder 7, box 73, JMPP.

14. Brisbane to Franklin Roosevelt, September 6, 1932, PPF 1405, FDRL.

15. Smith, *Titan*, 317.

16. Hoge, *Cissy Patterson*, 93.

17. "Amazonian War Livens Capital," *Los Angeles Times*, August 5, 1930; "Directs Another Shot at Mrs. Longworth," *NYT*, October 4, 1930; Healy, *Cissy*, 8.

18. "Alicia in Wonderland," *Time*, September 13, 1954, 52.

19. Quoted in Smith, *Titan*, 322.

20. Quoted in Healy, *Cissy*, 272.

21. Hearst to Brisbane, September 26, 1931, "Incoming Correspondence: Hearst, William Randolph, 1930–1935," box 1, EMPP.

22. Patterson to Hearst, October 11, 1931, "Outgoing Correspondence, 1930–1936," box 1, EMPP.

23. *N. W. Ayer & Son's Directory of Newspapers and Periodicals* (Philadelphia: N. W. Ayer and Son, 1937), 142.

24. "*Herald* Angel," 111.

25. Patterson to Hearst, September 11, 1935, "Outgoing Correspondence, 1930–1936," box 1, EMPP.

26. Kathleen Cairns, *Front-Page Women Journalists, 1920–1950* (Lincoln: University of Nebraska Press, 2003), 20, 31, 4.

27. Brisbane to Patterson, August 18, 1931, "Incoming Correspondence—Brisbane, Arthur, 1931," box 1, EMPP.

28. Cairns, *Front-Page Women*, 3. See also Ross, *Ladies of the Press*.

29. "*Herald* Angel," 110.

30. "*Herald* Angel," 110.

31. Martin, *Cissy*, 315–16.

32. Smith, *Titan*, 357–60.

33. Brisbane to Patterson, September 19, 1932, "Incoming Correspondence—Brisbane, Arthur, 1932," box 1, EMPP. For Brisbane's tips, see, for example, Patterson to Brisbane, January 27 and January 30, 1933, "Outgoing Correspondence—1930–1936," box 1, EMPP.

34. Brisbane to Roosevelt, September 6, 1932, PPF 1405, FDRL.

35. Drew Pearson to Felicia Gizycka, September 15, 1932, p. 3, "Family," box 1 of 5 from G (Georgetown Office) 210, DP.

36. "Cissie's Circle," *Town & Country*, April 1, 1935, 33.

37. Harold Ickes, *The Secret Diary of Harold L. Ickes*, vol. 1 (New York: Simon and Schuster, 1953), entry for August 16, 1936, 662.

38. "Ickes Says Nation Is at Crossroads," *NYT*, December 5, 1935.

39. "Ickes Hailed by the Communists!" *SFE*, December 12, 1935.

40. Ickes, *Secret Diary*, vol. 1, entry for December 22, 1935, 492.

41. Ickes, *Secret Diary*, vol. 1, entry for April 21, 1936, 559.

42. Patterson to Hearst, March 25, 1937, "Patterson, Eleanor, 1937," carton 23, WRHP. The timing is somewhat murky. Patterson later told her staff that Meyer made the offer in August 1936 and she immediately borrowed $1 million and leased the *Herald*. Some Patterson biographers have taken her at her word. See Hoge, *Cissy Patterson*, 162; and Smith, *Titan*, 380. However, a memo in the William Randolph Hearst Papers to Tom White dated January 28, 1937 ("Patterson, Eleanor, 1937," carton 23) clearly indicates that Patterson and Hearst had not yet made a deal, and in her March 1937 letter to Hearst, Patterson says that "nothing ever came of" the negotiations. Martin, *Cissy* (378), puts the initial negotiations in January 1937 but indicates that Patterson immediately asked to lease both papers. *Time* ("Two for 'Cissy,'" August 2, 1937) and Healy, *Cissy* (145), say Meyer made an initial offer in January 1937, Patterson leased the *Herald* in April, and she leased the *Times* in July. That timeline seems to fit with the primary sources.

43. "Text of Ickes's Address Alleging a Landon-Hearst Link," *NYT*, August 28, 1936.

44. Ickes, *Secret Diary*, vol. 1, entry for August 25, 1936, 665.

45. Ickes, *Secret Diary*, vol. 1, entry for October 21, 1936, 696.

46. Joe Patterson to Cissy Patterson, April 11, 1938, folder 12, box 73, JMPP.

47. Patterson to Hearst, March 25, 1937, "Patterson, Eleanor, 1937," carton 23, WRHP.

48. Hearst to Patterson, March 28, 1937, "Patterson, Eleanor, 1937," carton 23, WRHP.

49. "Highest Salaries for 1935 Listed," *NYT*, January 7, 1937; Ben Procter, *William Randolph Hearst: The Later Years, 1911–1951* (New York: Oxford University Press, 2007), 213–17.

50. For a thorough summary of Hearst's financial problems, see David Nasaw, *The Chief: The Life of William Randolph Hearst* (Boston: Mariner Books, 2001), 527–42.

51. "Hearst Steps Nos. 2 & 3," *Time*, July 12, 1937.

52. "Hearst to Disperse Vast Art Holdings," *NYT*, March 2, 1938.

53. Nasaw, *Chief*, 536.

54. "American's End," *Time*, July 5, 1937.

55. Hearst to Patterson, June 14, 1937, "Patterson, Eleanor, 1937," carton 23, WRHP.

56. "Morgenthau Hits Tax Ethics as Like Trade Code in '90s," *NYT*, June 18, 1937; "7 Named as Using Devices to Reduce Big Income Taxes," *NYT*, June 19, 1937; "Eleven Are Added to 'Evasion' List; Hearst Is Included," *NYT*, July 14, 1937.

57. Patterson to Hearst, July 19, 1937, "Patterson, Eleanor, 1937," carton 23, WRHP.

58. "Two for 'Cissy.' "

Chapter 7. Undominated

1. "Fate of the Court," *SFE*, March 11, 1937.

2. "Mr. Roosevelt's Assumptions," *CT*, March 9, 1937.

3. Undated Gannett telegram to Roosevelt; and Gannett telegram to Roosevelt, October 22, 1933, folder 1-8, box 1, FEG.

4. Gannett to Josephus Daniels, May 5, 1937, folder 1-28, box 1, FEG. See also Richard Polenberg, "The National Committee to Uphold Constitutional Government, 1937–1941," *Journal of American History* 52, no. 3 (December 1965): 585–86; and Jeff Shesol, *Supreme Power: Franklin Roosevelt vs. the Supreme Court* (New York: Norton, 2010), 358–64.

5. Quoted in Patricia Beard, *Newsmaker: Roy W. Howard, the Mastermind behind the Scripps-Howard News Empire from the Gilded Age to the Atomic Age* (Guilford, Conn.: Rowman and Littlefield, 2016), 198–99.

6. On the court fight, see Laura Kalman, "The Constitution, the Supreme Court, and the New Deal," *American Historical Review* 110, no. 4 (October 2005): 1052–80, and William Leuchtenburg, "Comment on Laura Kalman's Article" in the same issue, 1081–93; see also Leuchtenburg, "The Origins of Franklin D. Roosevelt's 'Court Packing' Plan," *Supreme Court Review* 1966 (1966): 347–400.

7. Gauti Eggertsson, "Great Expectations and the End of the Depression," *American Economic Review* 98, no. 4 (2008): 1477.

8. Christina D. Romer, "What Ended the Great Depression?" *Journal of Economic History* 52, no. 4 (December 1992): 760; Eric Rauchway, *The*

Money Makers: How Roosevelt and Keynes Ended the Depression, Defeated Fascism, and Secured a Prosperous Peace (New York: Basic, 2015), 128–29.

9. James Patterson, *Congressional Conservatism and the New Deal: The Growth of the Conservative Coalition in Congress, 1933–1939* (Lexington: University of Kentucky Press, 1967), 192–93.

10. Harold L. Ickes, *The Secret Diary of Harold L. Ickes*, vol. 2 (New York: Simon and Schuster, 1954), entry for December 6, 1937, 260.

11. Robert Dallek, *Franklin D. Roosevelt and American Foreign Policy, 1932–1945* (New York: Oxford University Press, 1979), 140.

12. The classic account of the United States and the Sino-Japanese conflict is Dorothy Borg, *The United States and the Far Eastern Crisis of 1933–1938* (Cambridge, Mass.: Harvard University Press, 1964).

13. See Dallek, *Franklin D. Roosevelt and American Foreign Policy*, 145–52.

14. Address at Chicago, October 5, 1937, The American Presidency Project, https://www.presidency.ucsb.edu/documents/address-chicago.

15. "Speech on 'War Fears' Stirs Quick Action by League to Curb Japanese," *CT*, October 6, 1937.

16. "He, Too, Would Keep Us out of War," *CT*, October 6, 1937.

17. "Why Can't We Keep out of War," *CT*, November 10, 1937.

18. "Roosevelt's Speech and War Danger," *SFE*, October 6, 1937.

19. Presidential press conference #400, October 6, 1937, 400-20, Press Conferences of President Franklin D. Roosevelt, Franklin D. Roosevelt Presidential Library and Museum, http://www.fdrlibrary.marist.edu/archives/collections/franklin/?p=collections/findingaid&id=508.

20. Roosevelt to Colonel House, October 19, 1937, in *F.D.R.: His Personal Letters, 1928–1945*, vol. 1, ed. Elliott Roosevelt (New York: Duell, Sloan and Pearce, 1950), 719.

21. Quoted in Dallek, *Franklin D. Roosevelt and American Foreign Policy*, 152.

22. "Shall We Take Them Now, or Try It Later?" *DN*, October 7, 1937.

23. " 'Give Me Four Years to Complete Unity,' " *DE*, March 19, 1938.

24. "Hitler's 120-Mile Drive in Triumph," *DM*, March 15, 1938.

25. "520 'Planes Fly Past Hitler," *DM*, March 16, 1938.

26. William L. Shirer, *The Rise and Fall of the Third Reich: A History of Nazi Germany* (New York: Simon and Schuster, 1960), 351.

27. "Vienna Silent as Hitler Speaks," *DE*, March 19, 1938. See also "Thousands Vanish in Vienna; Girls Jump to Death," *DE*, March 22, 1938.

28. "Vienna," *DE*, March 14, 1938.

29. "Splendid Isolation," *DE*, February 16, 1938.

30. "The Taking of Austria," *CT*, March 20, 1938; "Isolation or Participation in Foreign Complications, Which Is It Going to Be?" *SFE*, March 20, 1938.

31. "Can Anything Be Done for the Austrian Jews?" *DN*, March 15, 1938.

32. Frank McDonough, *Neville Chamberlain, Appeasement, and the British Road to War* (Manchester: Manchester University Press, 1998), 53–54; John

Ruggiero, *Hitler's Enabler: Neville Chamberlain and the Origins of the Second World War* (Santa Barbara, Calif.: Praeger, 2015), 66.

33. See his letter to Patterson, July 8, 1936, BBK/C/268, BP.

34. "Half-way to Heaven," *DE*, March 21, 1938.

35. Quoted in A. J. P. Taylor, *Beaverbrook* (London: Hamish Hamilton, 1972), 379. Beaverbrook excluded Andrew Bonar Law from his assessment because he "never got a chance."

36. The phrase "wilderness years" is used frequently by biographer Martin Gilbert and others to describe Churchill's political marginalization in the 1930s. *Life* magazine used the phrase as far back as 1945. "The Lives of Winston Churchill, Part III," *Life*, June 4, 1945, 106.

37. "The Pre-war Attitude of the *Evening Standard* to Germany," undated, unsigned document in BBK/C/275, BP.

38. Entry for March 23, 1938, in Ivan Maisky, *The Maisky Diaries: Red Ambassador to the Court of St. James's, 1932–1943*, ed. Gabriel Gorodetsky (New Haven: Yale University Press, 2015), 110.

39. "Winston Churchill," *DE*, February 25, 1938.

40. House of Commons debate, March 24, 1938, vol. 333, col. 1451.

41. R. J. Thompson to Churchill, March 24, 1938, in Gilbert, *Winston S. Churchill*, vol. 5, companion part 3 (London: Heinemann 1982),957–58.

42. Churchill to Thompson, April 11, 1938, in Gilbert, *Churchill*, vol. 5, companion part 3, 987.

43. Patrick Campbell, *My Life and Easy Times* (London: Pavilion, 1967), 144–45.

44. "Hitler Says He'll Free Sudetens, Defies Britain," *CT*, September 13, 1938.

45. Churchill to Lord Moyne, September 11, 1938, in Gilbert, *Churchill*, vol. 5, companion part 3, 1155.

46. "There Will Be No War," *DE*, September 1, 1938.

47. Beaverbrook to Halifax, November 14, 1938, BBK/C/152, BP.

48. S. J. Taylor, *The Great Outsiders: Northcliffe, Rothermere and the "Daily Mail"* (London: Weidenfeld and Nicolson, 1996), 314; Tom Jeffery and Keith McClelland, "A World Fit to Live In: The *Daily Mail* and the Middle Classes, 1918–39," in *Impacts and Influences: Essays on Media Power in the Twentieth Century*, ed. James Curran, Anthony Smith, and Pauline Wingate (London: Methuen, 1987), figure 2.1, 30.

49. Rothermere, "Further Postscripts: The Real Hitler," *DM*, May 13, 1938.

50. "No Further Obligation: Keep Clear and Arm," *DM*, March 14, 1938.

51. Daniel Hucker, *Public Opinion and the End of Appeasement in Britain and France* (Burlington, Vt.: Ashgate, 2011), 42.

52. Beaverbrook to Halifax, September 16, 1938, BBK/C/152, BP.

53. Beaverbrook to Chamberlain, September 16, 1938, BBK/C/80, BP.

54. Quoted in Richard Cockett, *Twilight of Truth: Chamberlain, Appeasement and the Manipulation of the Press* (London: Weidenfeld and Nicolson, 1989), 94.

55. "This Is the Truth," *DE*, September 22, 1938.

56. Shirer, *Rise and Fall*, 403.

57. Winston Churchill, *The Second World War: The Gathering Storm*, vol. 1 (London: Cassell, 1948), 249.

58. Arthur Christiansen, *Headlines All My Life* (London: Heinemann, 1961), 170–71.

59. "Peace," *DE*, September 30, 1938.

60. "Premier's Wife Mobbed," *DE*, September 30, 1938.

61. "Premier at Palace Hears the Cheering," *DE*, October 1, 1938.

62. "You May Sleep Quietly—It Is Peace for Our Time," *DE*, October 1, 1938.

63. "You May Sleep Quietly—It Is Peace for Our Time."

64. Reinhard Spitzy, *How We Squandered the Reich*, trans. G. T. Waddington (Norwich: Michael Russell, 1997), 254.

65. See W. W. Hadley, *Munich: Before and After* (London: Cassell, 1944), 93–110. Key works on the British press and appeasement include Cockett, *Twilight of Truth;* Franklin Reid Gannon, *The British Press and Germany, 1936–1939* (Oxford: Oxford University Press, 1971); and Benny Morris, *The Roots of Appeasement: The British Weekly Press and Nazi Germany during the 1930s* (London: Frank Cass, 1991).

66. "Chamberlain," *DN*, September 27, 1938.

67. Attlee: House of Commons debate, October 3, 1938, vol. 339, col. 52; Churchill: House of Commons debate, October 5, 1938, vol. 339, col. 360.

68. Quoted in Kenneth Young, *Churchill and Beaverbrook: A Study in Friendship and Politics* (New York: James A. Heineman, 1966), 128.

69. John W. Wheeler-Bennett, *Munich: Prologue to Tragedy* (London: Macmillan, 1948), 171.

70. Virginia Cowles, *Looking for Trouble* (New York: Harper and Brothers, 1941), 180.

71. Will Wainewright, *Reporting on Hitler: Rothay Reynolds and the British Press in Nazi Germany* (London: Biteback, 2017), 228, 230; Geoffrey Cox, *Countdown to War: A Personal Memoir of Europe, 1938–40* (London: William Kimber, 1988), 81–82. See also Cockett, *Twilight of Truth*, 64–65.

72. Anthony Adamthwaite, "The British Government and the Media, 1937–1938," *Journal of Contemporary History* 18, no. 2 (April 1983): 292. On March 5, 1938, during the Anschluss, a poll found that 58 percent opposed Chamberlain's foreign policy. George H. Gallup, *The Gallup International Public Opinion Polls: Great Britain, 1937–1975*, vol. 1 (New York: Random House, 1976), 8.

73. Tom Harrisson and Charles Madge, *Britain by Mass-Observation* (London: Cresset Library, 1986), 75.

74. Robert J. Wybrow, *Britain Speaks Out, 1937–1987: A Social History as Seen through the Gallup Data* (London: Macmillan, 1989), 5.

75. Historians have argued for years over the necessity for and wisdom of the strategy of appeasement. For a comprehensive summary of the evolution of the historiography of appeasement, see Robert J. Caputi, *Neville Chamberlain and Appeasement* (Selinsgrove, Pa.: Susquehanna University Press, 2000). For defenses of the appeasers, see Norrin M. Ripsman and Jack S. Levy, "Wishful Thinking or Buying Time? The Logic of British Appeasement in the 1930s," *International Security* 33, no. 2 (Fall 2008): 148–81; and John Charmley, *Chamberlain and the Lost Peace* (London: Hodder and Stoughton, 1989). For a counter-revisionist thesis, see R. A. C. Parker, *Chamberlain and Appeasement: British Policy and the Coming of the Second World War* (New York: St. Martin's, 1993). For a recent study of appeasement that argues against the revisionist thesis, see Tim Bouverie, *Appeasing Hitler: Chamberlain, Churchill and the Road to War* (London: Bodley Head, 2019).
76. Ian Kershaw, *Hitler 1936–1945: Nemesis* (New York: Norton, 2000), 123.

Chapter 8. "Hitler Agrees with the Daily Express"

1. On Kristallnacht, see Richard J. Evans, *The Third Reich in Power, 1933–1939* (New York: Penguin, 2005), 580–592.
2. "German Press Vents Spleen on U.S.," *CT*, November 18, 1938.
3. Lord Rothermere, "Some More Postscripts," *DM*, May 6, 1938.
4. "The World Protests," *DM*, November 14, 1938. On the *Mail*'s change of view on the Nazis, see Will Wainewright, *Reporting on Hitler: Rothay Reynolds and the British Press in Nazi Ger*many (London: Biteback, 2017), 237–38.
5. "A Black Day for Germany," London *Times*, November 11, 1938.
6. *DE*, November 11, 1938.
7. "Pray for Tolerance," *DE*, November 11, 1938.
8. "Black-out for Jews in Europe," *DE*, November 12, 1938.
9. "A Domestic Issue" and "Each Claims to Be Right," *DE*, November 17, 1938.
10. "Least said—," *DE*, November 21, 1938.
11. Beaverbrook to Gannett, December 9, 1938, folder 1-55, box 1, FEG.
12. Beaverbrook to Patterson, January 25, 1939, BBK/C/268, BP.
13. "What's in the Cards?" *DN*, February 14, 1939.
14. "Diplomatic Incidents," *DN*, November 19, 1938; "Another Refugee Problem," *DN*, November 21, 1938.
15. "Is Hitler Losing His Grip?" *DN*, November 15, 1938.
16. "Diplomatic Incidents."
17. On Americans' failure to grasp the nature of Nazi anti-Semitism, see Deborah E. Lipstadt, *Beyond Belief: The American Press and the Coming of the Holocaust, 1933–1945* (New York: Free Press, 1986).
18. "New Deal Probes Anti-Semitic Drive in New Congress," *DN*, December 15, 1938. For more on Pelley and other anti-Semites in the Depres-

sion, see Leo P. Ribuffo, *The Old Christian Right: The Protestant Far Right from the Great Depression to the Cold War* (Philadelphia: Temple University Press, 1983).

19. "Anti-Semitism Here," *DN*, December 16, 1938.
20. Transcript of conference with Senate Military Affairs Committee, January 31, 1939, in *Franklin D. Roosevelt and Foreign Affairs*, 2nd ser., January 1937–August 1939, vol. 13, ed. Donald B. Schewe (New York: Clearwater, 1979), 203–4.
21. David Reynolds, *From Munich to Pearl Harbor: Roosevelt's America and the Origins of the Second World War* (Chicago: Ivan R. Dee, 2001), 46. See also Michael Sherry, *The Rise of American Air Power: The Creation of Armageddon* (New Haven: Yale University Press, 1987), 79–80.
22. "Roosevelt: 'Nazis Have Shocked Us,'" *DE*, November 16, 1938.
23. Robert E. Herzstein, *Roosevelt and Hitler: Prelude to War* (New York: John Wiley and Sons, 1994), 233.
24. President's Address to Congress, January 4, 1939, The American Presidency Project, https://www.presidency.ucsb.edu/documents/annual-message-congress.
25. Hadley Cantril and Mildred Strunk, *Public Opinion, 1935–1946* (Princeton: Princeton University Press, 1951), 381.
26. See James Q. Whitman, *Hitler's American Model: The United States and the Making of Nazi Race Law* (Princeton: Princeton University Press, 2017), 43–46.
27. Sheldon Neuringer, "Franklin D. Roosevelt and Refuge for Victims of Nazism, 1933–1941," in *Franklin D. Roosevelt: The Man, the Myth, the Era, 1882–1945*, ed. Herbert D. Rosenbaum and Elizabeth Bartelme (New York: Greenwood, 1987), 86.
28. See the chart in Michael Dobbs, *The Unwanted: America, Auschwitz, and a Village Caught in Between* (New York: Knopf, 2019), 296n37.
29. Cantril and Strunk, *Public Opinion*, 1150.
30. Cantril and Strunk, *Public Opinion*, 1081. When the question specified that the children were mostly Jewish, opposition fell slightly, from 66 to 61 percent.
31. Herzstein, *Roosevelt and Hitler*, 237.
32. Richard Breitman and Allan J. Lichtman, *FDR and the Jews* (Cambridge, Mass.: Belknap, 2013), 2.
33. Patterson to Beaverbrook, February 6, 1939, BBK/C/268, BP.
34. "There Is Every Prospect of Peace," *DE*, January 18, 1939.
35. "No War!" *DE*, February 1, 1939. See also "I Believe It Is Peace for a Long Time" and "Jitter-bugs Are on the Run," *DE*, January 31, 1939.
36. Beaverbrook to Patterson, February 23, 1939, BBK/C/268, BP.
37. *Daily Telegraph*, March 16, 1939, quoted in Franklin Reid Gannon, *The British Press and Germany, 1936–1939* (Oxford: Oxford University Press, 1971), 240; "Militarism in Action," London *Times*, March 16, 1939.

38. "Two German Notes," London *Times*, April 29, 1939.
39. "Get on with It!" *DM*, March 11, 1939.
40. "Three New States," *DM*, March 15, 1939; "Arms Alone Count," *DM*, March 16, 1939.
41. "Three New States."
42. "What Next?" *DM*, March 17, 1939.
43. Daniel Hucker, *Public Opinion and the End of Appeasement in Britain and France* (Burlington, Vt.: Ashgate, 2011), 130.
44. "Not Our Concern," *DE*, March 15, 1939.
45. "—But Not Here," *DE*, April 1, 1939.
46. Undated 1938 note in BBK/C/275, BP.
47. Ribbentrop to Beaverbrook, March 15, 1939, and Beaverbrook's response, March 28, 1939, both in BBK/C/275, BP.
48. "Mad Dog Diplomacy," *CT*, May 1, 1939.
49. Coblentz to Hearst editors, June 28, 1939, "Coblentz, Edmond David, 1939," box 1, Outgoing, ECP.
50. "Defeat Anti-Neutrality Bill Now; It Would Lead to War!" *SFE*, June 29, 1939.
51. Hearst to John S. Brookes Jr., June 28, 1939, "Coblentz, Edmond David, 1939," box 1, Outgoing, ECP.
52. "Extension of Remarks of Hon. Hamilton Fish," 85 Cong. Rec. 66 (1939).
53. "F.D.R. Names Names," *DN*, July 6, 1939.
54. "Neutrality Act Change Refused," *DN*, July 20, 1939.
55. Beaverbrook to Halifax, June 22, 1939, BBK/C/152, BP.
56. Beaverbrook to Hoare, June 21, 1939, BBK/C/308a, 1937–1940, BP. See also the *Daily Express* article on Patterson's arrival in Britain, "Best-seller Born on a Farm Heap Back of the Line," *DE*, July 11, 1939; and the correspondence between Patterson and Beaverbrook on arrangements for the trip in BBK/C/268.
57. Patterson, "Hitler's 'Lightning War' Plan Ruined by Chamberlain," *DN*, August 3, 1939.
58. J. M. Patterson, "Reich Unready," *DN*, August 1, 1939.
59. Patterson, "Hitler Holds Self Aloof in Role of Mystic, 'Priest,' " *DN*, August 2, 1939; and Patterson, "Hitler's 'Lightning War' Plan Ruined by Chamberlain."
60. August 1, 1939.
61. "British Have Changed in a Year," *DE*, August 5, 1939.
62. See Tim Bouverie, *Appeasing Hitler: Chamberlain, Churchill and the Road to War* (London: Bodley Head, 2019), 340–41.
63. "Move to Drive Premier out of Office," *Sunday Express*, July 16, 1939.
64. "No War," *DE*, July 18, 1939; "Peace or Destruction," *DE*, July 22, 1939; "Liabilities," *DE*, August 4, 1939.
65. See Ronald Neame with Barbara Roisman Cooper, *Straight from the Horse's Mouth: Ronald Neame: An Autobiography* (Lanham, Md.: Scarecrow, 2003), 62.

66. "No War This Year," August 7, 1939. See also Sian Nicholas, " 'There Will Be No War': The *Daily Express* and the Approach of War, 1938–39," in *Justifying War: Propaganda, Politics and the Modern Age*, ed. David Welch and Jo Fox (New York: Palgrave Macmillan, 2012), 200–217.

67. See, for example, "Beaverbrook Says 'No War,' " *Montreal Gazette*, August 11, 1939.

68. Arthur Christiansen, *Headlines All My Life* (London: Heinemann, 1961), 180.

69. Rothermere to Hitler, June 29, 1939, and Rothermere to Ribbentrop, July 2, 1939, FO 1093/87, TNA; "Effusions": covering note to H.J.W. dated July 6, 1939, in the same file. See also Richard Norton-Taylor, "Months Before War, Rothermere Said Hitler's Work Was Superhuman," *Guardian*, March 31, 2005; and Richard Norton-Taylor, *The State of Secrecy: Spies and the Media in Britain* (London: I. B. Tauris, 2020), 144–45.

70. "Don't Be Misled," *DM*, August 26, 1939. See also "We Still Wait," *DM*, August 30, 1939.

71. "Liabilities."

72. July 22, 1939, BBK/C/286, BP.

73. "Britain Stands by Poland," *DE*, August 23, 1939; "Hitler: 'My Patience Almost Exhausted,' " *DE*, August 26, 1939; "Hitler's Offer Refused," *Sunday Express*, August 27, 1939; " 'I Demand Danzig and the Corridor,' " *DE*, August 28, 1939; "Britain Gives Last Warning," *DE*, September 2, 1939; "Beaverbrook, Cut off from Desk, Begs Interviewer for 'The News,' " *Montreal Gazette*, August 26, 1939.

74. Christiansen, *Headlines All My Life*, 181.

75. *DE*, September 4, 1939.

76. *DE*, September 4, 1939.

Chapter 9. Foreign Wars

1. Memo, May 19, 1938, Hohenlohe MI5 file, KV2/1696, TNA; "Princess Stephanie von Hohenlohe," MI5 document, no date, KV2/1696, TNA. On Hohenlohe, see Martha Schad, *Hitler's Spy Princess: The Extraordinary Life of Stephanie Von Hohenlohe* (Stroud, U.K.: Sutton, 2004); Jim Wilson, *Nazi Princess: Hitler, Lord Rothermere, and Princess Stephanie Von Hohenlohe* (Stroud, U.K.: History Press, 2011); Franz Hohenlohe, *Steph: The Fabulous Princess* (London: New English Library, 1976); and Karina Urbach, *Go-Betweens for Hitler* (Oxford: Oxford University Press, 2015), chapter 5.

2. Letter to Major V. Vivian, August 9, 1939, Hohenlohe MI5 file, KV2/1696, TNA.

3. "Law Report, Nov. 13," London *Times*, November 14, 1939.

4. See memo to MI5, November 18, 1933, Hohenlohe MI5 file, KV2/1696, TNA. See also "When Rothermere Urged Hitler to Invade Romania," *Daily Telegraph*, March 1, 2005.

5. Rothermere to Hohenlohe, January 19, 1938, box 1, SHP.

6. Rothermere to Hitler, January 1, 1938, box 1, SHP.

7. Rothermere to Hitler, April 4, 1938, box 1, SHP.

8. Rothermere to Hitler, July 6, 1938, box 1, SHP.

9. Rothermere to Hitler, October 1, 1938, box 1, SHP.

10. Copy of memorandum, Rothermere to Hohenlohe, no date, and letter, Hitler to Rothermere, May 3, 1935, in box 1, SHP.

11. Undated, unsigned letter to "L.R.," box 1, SHP.

12. Memo, March 7, 1939, re: Wittman, Hohenlohe MI5 file, KV 2/1696; undated memo, re: Stephanie von Hohenlohe, Hohenlohe MI5 file, KV 2/1696, TNA.

13. Confidential memo, September 26, 1939, Hohenlohe MI5 file, KV 2/1697, TNA.

14. "Mystery Woman," *Time*, November 20, 1939, "Lord Rothermere Gets Bill for Boom to Make Him King," *DN*, November 19, 1939.

15. "Mystery Woman."

16. "Congratulations," *DE*, November 16, 1939.

17. Schad, *Hitler's Spy Princess*, 117–20; Wilson, *Nazi Princess*, 145.

18. "Owen, Frank," by Michael Foot, *Oxford Dictionary of National Biography* (published online 2004). Michael Foot later became the leader of the Labour Party.

19. "Abolish This Ministry," *DE*, November 15, 1939.

20. "Craze for Controlling," *DE*, November 22, 1939.

21. "Millions—What For?" *DE*, January 2, 1940.

22. A. J. P. Taylor, *Beaverbrook* (London: Hamish Hamilton, 1972), 398.

23. Hugh Cudlipp, *The Prerogative of the Harlot: Press Barons and Power* (London: Bodley Head, 1980), 284.

24. Anne Chisholm and Michael Davie, *Lord Beaverbrook: A Life* (New York: Knopf, 1993), 371.

25. John McGovern, *Neither Fear nor Favour* (London: Blandford, 1960), chapter 14, quote at 142. Beaverbrook's biographer Taylor judged that McGovern's account of the meeting had the "ring of truth." Taylor, *Beaverbrook*, 405.

26. See the correspondence in PPF 5038, FDRL; and BBK/C/277, BP.

27. Rothermere to Beaverbrook, September 23, 1939, BBK/C/286, BP.

28. Memo attached to letter to Churchill, December 13, 1939, BBK/C/86; Beaverbrook to Halifax, December 11, 1939, BBK/C/152, BP.

29. Halifax to Beaverbrook, December 16, 1939, BBK/C/152, BP.

30. Beaverbrook and Bennett to Halifax, January 23, 1940, BBK/C/152, BP.

31. Franklin Roosevelt Fireside Chat, September 3, 1939, The American Presidency Project, https://www.presidency.ucsb.edu/documents/fireside-chat-13.

32. Roosevelt, "Message to Congress Urging Repeal of the Embargo Provisions of the Neutrality Law," September 21, 1939, The American Presidency Project, https://www.presidency.ucsb.edu/documents/message-congress-urging-repeal-the-embargo-provisions-the-neutrality-law.

33. "Lines Drawn in Fight to End Arms Embargo," *Kokomo Tribune*, September 22, 1939.

34. "500 Phila. Women 'March' at Capitol, Shout at Senators to Keep Embargo," *Philadelphia Inquirer*, September 22, 1939.

35. "Text of Lindbergh's Speech," *Boston Globe*, September 16, 1939.

36. "Arms Embargo Is in the Name of Peace, Neutrality," *SFE*, September 22, 1939.

37. *SFE*, September 22, 1939.

38. "Red Asia Invades Europe," *SFE*, October 9, 1939.

39. Willicombe to the editors of all Hearst newspapers, September 23, 1939, "Hearst, Wm. R. Sr., 1939," box 5, Incoming, EDC.

40. "Repeal Arms Embargo and You Risk War, U.S. Told by Hiram Johnson," *SFE*, October 21, 1939. On the Mothers of America, see "Mothers of America Unite for U.S. Peace," *SFE*, October 21, 1939. On the Hearst papers' sponsorship of the group, see Rodney Carlisle, "The Foreign Policy Views of an Isolationist Press Lord: W. R. Hearst and the International Crisis, 1936–41," *Journal of Contemporary History* 9, no. 3 (July 1974): 224.

41. "We Need No Dictator," *CT*, September 26, 1939.

42. *CT*, October 15, 1939, and October 22, 1939.

43. Taylor to McCormick, December 16, 1939, folder 5, box 3, XI-317, TCA.

44. See flyer "Hear the Truth about Col. McCormick," July 29, 1941, folder 6, box 3, XI-317, TCA.

45. "Why Did Edward Fall? Fascists Deposed Him!" *CT*, August 22, 1937.

46. "Col. M'Cormick Warns America of Red War Plot," *CT*, July 5, 1939.

47. "Mad Dog Diplomacy," *CT*, May 1, 1939.

48. "National Unity against War," *DN*, September 22, 1939.

49. "National Unity against War."

50. "No Use to Get Hysterical," *DN*, September 2, 1939.

51. "War Is as Natural as Peace," *DN*, November 20, 1939.

52. House of Commons debate, May 7, 1940, vol. 360, col. 1150.

53. On the parliamentary debate, see Lynne Olson, *Troublesome Young Men: The Rebels Who Brought Churchill to Power and Helped Save England* (New York: Farrar, Straus and Giroux, 2007), chapter 17.

54. Taylor, *Beaverbrook*, 407.

55. Beaverbrook, "What Is the Damage?" *DE*, May 6, 1940.

56. Chamberlain to Beaverbrook, May 6, 1940, BBK/C/80, BP.

57. Richard Cockett, *Twilight of Truth: Chamberlain, Appeasement and the Manipulation of the Press* (London: Weidenfeld and Nicolson, 1989), 174.

58. Cockett, *Twilight of Truth*, 175.

59. House of Commons debate, May 13, 1940, vol. 360, col. 1502.

60. Quoted in Kenneth Young, *Churchill and Beaverbrook: A Study in Friendship and Politics* (New York: James A. Heineman, 1966), 141.

61. Taylor, *Beaverbrook*, 411.

62. Martin Gilbert, *Finest Hour: Winston S. Churchill*, vol. 6 (Boston: Houghton Mifflin, 1983), 316.

63. Churchill, *The Second World War: Their Finest Hour,* vol. 2 (Boston: Houghton Mifflin, 1949), 13.

64. "The Battle of Britain," London *Times,* June 1, 1945.

65. David Farrer, *The Sky's the Limit: The Story of Beaverbrook at M.A.P.* (London: Hutchinson, 1943), 95.

66. Richard Hough and Denis Richards, *The Battle of Britain: The Jubilee History* (London: Hodder and Stoughton, 1989), 325.

67. See John Terraine, *The Right of the Line: The Royal Air Force in the European War, 1939–1945* (London: Hodder and Stoughton, 1985), 191–92.

68. Quoted in Taylor, *Beaverbrook,* 430. See also Chisholm and Davie, *Lord Beaverbrook,* 395.

69. Terraine, *Right of the Line,* 192.

70. Denis Richards, *The Royal Air Force, 1939–1945,* vol. 1 (London: Her Majesty's Stationery Office, 1974), 154.

71. Cato, *Guilty Men* (London: Victor Gollancz, 1940), 16.

72. Rothermere to Beaverbrook, March 2, 1940, BBK/C/286, BP.

73. Rothermere to Beaverbrook, May 15, 1940, BBK/C/286, BP.

74. Rothermere to Beaverbrook, May 17, 1940, BBK/C/286, BP.

75. Beaverbrook to Rothermere, undated, BBK/C/286, BP.

76. Taylor, *Beaverbrook,* 422.

77. "Report from England," *DN,* August 15, 1940.

78. Taylor, *Beaverbrook,* 422.

79. Beaverbrook to Esmond Rothermere, December 5, 1940, BBK/C/286, BP.

80. See N. J. Crowson, ed., *Fleet Street, Press Barons and Politics: The Journals of Collin Brooks, 1932–1940* (London: Royal Historical Society, 1998), entry for August 4, 1940, 270.

81. Memo, "Editorial Reaction toward Aid for the Allies," June 10, 1940, 3, 4, Division of Press Intelligence, "National Emergency Council 1940," OF 788, FDRL. See also Richard W. Steele, *Propaganda in an Open Society: The Roosevelt Administration and the Media, 1933–1941* (Westport, Conn.: Greenwood, 1985), 100. Historian Susan Dunn argues that many white southerners' British ancestry, their martial traditions, and their concern for the impact of Nazi conquests on their tobacco and cotton sales, as well as their "lingering gratitude to the British for their sympathy toward the Confederacy," help explain their disproportionate support for aid to Britain. Susan Dunn, *Roosevelt's Purge: How FDR Fought to Change the Democratic Party* (Cambridge, Mass.: Belknap, 2010), 221.

82. "Aid for Allies," *Los Angeles Times,* May 31, 1940.

83. "Editorial Reaction toward Aid for the Allies," 14.

84. "Editorial Reaction toward Aid for the Allies," 2.

85. "Uncle Barbara Manville," *DN,* June 8, 1940.

86. "Conscription," *CT,* June 21, 1940.

87. "Republicans and the War," *CT,* June 13, 1940.

88. On the election, see Susan Dunn, *1940: FDR, Willkie, Lindbergh, Hitler —the Election amid the Storm* (New Haven: Yale University Press, 2013).

89. "People's Candidate," *SFE*, June 29, 1940.

90. "In the News," *SFE*, September 10, 1940.

91. "Disloyalty to American Principles," *CT*, May 23, 1940.

92. Ickes, *Freedom of the Press Today* (New York: Vanguard, 1941), 9–10.

93. "Should Draft Roosevelt," *DN*, July 10, 1940.

94. Churchill, *Their Finest Hour*, 404.

95. House of Commons debate, August 20, 1940, vol. 364, col. 1171.

96. "The America First Committee," *CT*, September 7, 1940.

97. Ian Mugridge, *The View from Xanadu: William Randolph Hearst and United States Foreign Policy* (Montreal: McGill-Queen's University Press, 1995), 194n69, notes that the AFC sent Hearst an invitation to join but he seems to have never responded. On the America First Committee, see Wayne S. Cole, *America First: The Battle against Intervention, 1940– 1941* (Madison: University of Wisconsin Press, 1953).

98. "The More We Think of It the Better We Like It," *DN*, September 5, 1940.

99. "We Get the Bases," *CT*, September 4, 1940.

100. "In the News," *SFE*, September 5, 1940.

101. "In the News," *SFE*, September 5, 1940.

102. See David Reynolds, *From Munich to Pearl Harbor: Roosevelt's America and the Origins of the Second World War* (Chicago: Ivan R. Dee, 2001), 87–91, and Waldo Heinrichs, *Threshold of War: Franklin D. Roosevelt and American Entry into World War II* (New York: Oxford University Press, 1988), 10–11.

103. "U.S. Is Called Target of New War Alliance," *CT*, September 28, 1940.

104. For a discussion of the *Daily News*'s sudden change of attitude toward Japan, see "Editorial Writer, Part II," *New Yorker*, May 31, 1947, 37.

105. "Two Ships for One," *DN*, February 4, 1935.

106. "A War on Two Fronts?" *DN*, June 12, 1940.

107. "In the News," *SFE*, October 9, 1940.

108. "Japanese Entry into Siberia Is Not to Aid the Allies, but to Entrench Japan," *SFE*, March 4, 1918.

109. "The Panic's On," *CT*, November 3, 1940; "In the News," *SFE*, November 6, 1940.

110. "One Man!" *SFE*, November 2, 1940.

111. "Texts of President Roosevelt's Addresses in Boston and Hartford," *NYT*, October 31, 1940.

112. Samuel I. Rosenman, *Working with Roosevelt* (New York: Harper and Brothers, 1952), 242.

113. "The Third-Term Candidate vs. the Organized Wealth Candidate," *DN*, November 1, 1940.

114. "Election Balance Sheet," *DN*, November 7, 1940.

Chapter 10. The Dictator Bill

1. "Envoy Flies Here," *NYT,* November 24, 1940.
2. "Envoy Lothian Claims Britain Is Going Broke," *CT,* November 24, 1940.
3. See the account in John W. Wheeler-Bennett, *King George VI: His Life and Reign* (New York: St. Martin's, 1958), 521. But David Reynolds argues that Lothian used different language. See David Reynolds, "Lord Lothian and Anglo-American Relations, 1939–1940," *Transactions of the American Philosophical Society* 73, no. 2 (1983): 48–49.
4. Quoted in David Reynolds, *The Creation of the Anglo-American Alliance, 1937–41: A Study in Competitive Cooperation* (London: Europa Publications Limited, 1981), 152.
5. Churchill, *The Second World War: Their Finest Hour,* vol. 2 (Boston: Houghton Mifflin, 1949), 558.
6. Churchill, *Their Finest Hour,* 567, 566.
7. Press conference, December 17, 1940, The American Presidency Project, https://www.presidency.ucsb.edu/documents/press-conference-3.
8. Fireside Chat, December 29, 1940, The American Presidency Project, https://www.presidency.ucsb.edu/documents/fireside-chat-9.
9. Annual Message to Congress on the State of the Union, January 6, 1941, The American Presidency Project, https://www.presidency.ucsb.edu/documents/annual-message-congress-the-state-the-union.
10. "A Bill to Destroy the Republic," *CT,* January 12, 1941.
11. On the numbering of the bill, see Warren F. Kimball, " '1776': Lend-Lease Gets a Number," *New England Quarterly* 42, no. 2 (June 1969): 260–67.
12. "Lease-Lend Bill Passage Likely in Senate Today," *SFE,* March 8, 1941.
13. "Roosevelt Asks Absolute Power to Give Away U.S. Planes, Guns, Warships," *SFE,* January 11, 1941; "Senate Fight Opened to Beat Dictator Bill," *SFE,* January 14, 1941. See also "President's Stand Stirs Speculation," *SFE,* January 7, 1941, "Bill Up Today Giving FDR 'Blank Check' in Aid for Britain," *SFE,* January 10, 1941.
14. "Senators to Fight F.D.R. Bill," *CT,* January 11, 1941.
15. See, for example, "Dictator Bill's Death in House Appears Likely," *CT,* April 8, 1938; "House Adopts Farm Dictator Bill, 263 to 135," *CT,* February 10, 1938; "Bill Creating War Dictator Looses [*sic*] Steam," *CT,* March 6, 1938.
16. "Radio Talk Exposes Willkie Link to Propaganda," *CT,* January 18, 1941.
17. "Kennedy to Oppose F.D. on Aid Bill," *WTH,* January 17, 1941; "Senate Passes Lend-lease Bill, 60-31," *WTH,* March 9, 1941.
18. *Philadelphia Record* of April 17, 1941, quoted in "O'Donnell's $50,000," *Time,* February 8, 1943.
19. "FDR Hits Wheeler's Criticism as 'Rotten,' " *SFE,* January 15, 1941.
20. See, for example, Warren Kimball, *The Most Unsordid Act: Lend-Lease, 1939–1941* (Baltimore: Johns Hopkins University Press, 1969), 154.

21. "Willkie Okehs Lend-Lease Bill with Revisions; Wheeler Declares Plan Means War," *SFE*, January 13, 1941; "Protests Mount: Wheeler Warns of Dictatorship," *CT*, January 13, 1941. The *Daily News* and *Washington Times-Herald* ran prominent stories on the Wheeler speech but did not use that particular quote.

22. "Speak Up, America, on Lease-Lend Bill!" *SFE*, March 4, 1941.

23. "In the News," *SFE*, February 6, 1941.

24. "Dictatorship thru Conspiracy," *CT*, January 13, 1941; "A Bill to Destroy the Republic," *CT*, January 12, 1941. See also "War and Dictatorship," *CT*, January 17, 1941.

25. "Secretary Hull on the Dictatorship Bill," *DN*, *WTH*, January 17, 1941.

26. *DN*, *WTH*, January 23, 1941.

27. *DN*, *WTH*, February 11, 1941.

28. Reynolds to Patterson, April 28, 1941, folder 3, box 32, JMPP.

29. "Unhappy New Year," *WTH*, January 1, 1941.

30. "If We Invade Europe Again," *DN*, February 4, 1941.

31. "We're Not Anti-British," *WTH*, February 23, 1941.

32. "New Deal Probes Anti-Semitic Drive on New Congress," *DN*, December 15, 1938; "Brief of the American Jewish Congress on Exceptions to Record, Proposed Decision and Memorandum Opinion," June 19, 1947, folder 7, *Daily News American Jewish Congress Brief*, box 584, I-77, AJC.

33. "The Big Bomb Plot," *DN*, January 16, 1940.

34. "H.R. 1776 Becomes Law," *DN*, *WTH*, March 13, 1941. See also "What is Anti-Semitism?" *DN*, September 10, 1941.

35. "Wealth and the War Bill," *CT*, February 17, 1941.

36. "Trying, with Some Effort, to Be Philosophical," *DN*, February 15, 1941.

37. "Passing of the Great Race?" *DN*, March 24, 1941.

38. Patterson to Wood, January 14, 1941, folder 2, box 28, JMPP; Richard Norton Smith, *The Colonel: The Life and Legend of Robert R. McCormick, 1880–1955* (Boston: Houghton Mifflin, 1997), 407.

39. Wood to McCormick, March 20, 1941, "Wood, Robert E., 1930–1942," box 138, I-60, RRMP; Wood to Patterson, October 31, 1941, folder 2, box 28, JMPP.

40. Edwin S. Webster Jr. to Patterson, October 23, 1941, folder 2, box 28, JMPP.

41. "Radio Talk Exposes Willkie Link to Propaganda."

42. Richard W. Steele, *Propaganda in an Open Society: The Roosevelt Administration and the Media, 1933–1941* (Westport, Conn.: Greenwood, 1985), 73–94. See also Linda Lotridge Levin, *The Making of FDR: The Story of Stephen T. Early, America's First Modern Press Secretary* (Amherst, N.Y.: Prometheus Books, 2008).

43. See Michael Leigh, *Mobilizing Consent: Public Opinion and American Foreign Policy, 1937–1947* (Westport, Conn.: Greenwood, 1976), 62–65; and Steele, *Propaganda*, 85–95, for debates over the creation of a central propaganda agency.

44. For more on the CDAAA and other interventionist groups, see Andrew Johnstone, *Against Immediate Evil: American Internationalists and the Four Freedoms on the Eve of World War II* (Ithaca: Cornell University Press, 2014).

45. "The America First Committee," *CT*, September 7, 1940; Steele, *Propaganda*, 77.

46. Nicholas John Cull, *Selling War: The British Propaganda Campaign against American "Neutrality" in World War II* (Oxford: Oxford University Press, 1995), 4.

47. In addition to Cull, *Selling War*, see Susan Brewer, *To Win the Peace: British Propaganda in the United States during World War II* (Ithaca: Cornell University Press, 1997).

48. Bradley W. Hart, *Hitler's American Friends: The Third Reich's Supporters in the United States* (New York: Thomas Dunne Books / St. Martin's, 2018), chapter 4. See also Francis MacDonnell, *Insidious Foes: The Axis Fifth Column and the American Home Front* (New York: Oxford University Press, 1995).

49. "Marshall Field: The Native's Return," *New Republic*, November 3, 1941, 581–83.

50. "The American Century," *Life*, February 17, 1941, 63, 64. On Luce, see Alan Brinkley, *The Publisher: Henry Luce and His American Century* (New York: Knopf, 2010).

51. *N. W. Ayer & Son's Directory of Newspapers and Periodicals* (Philadelphia: N. W. Ayer and Son, 1940), 212, 219, 636; Raymond Fielding, *The March of Time, 1935–1951* (New York: Oxford University Press, 1978), 239.

52. Fielding, *March of Time*, 192–93, 195.

53. Fielding, *March of Time*, 268.

54. John Elliot Bradshaw Jr., "Projections of the Fatherland: Representations of Germany in the Hearst Newsreels, 1929–1939" (MA thesis, University of Southern California, 2005), 55, 56, 120, 186, 188. See also Kenneth Hough, "Home Invasions: Hearst Newsreels, American Preparedness, and the Coming of World War II," in *Rediscovering U.S. Newsfilm: Cinema, Television, and the Archive*, ed. Mark Garrett Cooper, Sara Beth Levavy, Ross Melnick, and Mark Williams (New York: Routledge, 2018), 58–60; and the thirty-four-hour compilation of selected *Hearst Metrotone News* and *News of the Day* films on videocassette, *The 1930s: Prelude to War* (Los Angeles: UCLA Film and Television Archives, 1998).

55. Ben Urwand terms Hollywood's failure to criticize Hitler before 1939 "collaboration." See Urwand, *The Collaboration: Hollywood's Pact with Hitler* (Cambridge, Mass.: Harvard University Press, 2013). Thomas Doherty, in *Hollywood and Hitler, 1933–1939* (New York: Columbia University Press, 2013), agrees that the studios avoided direct criticism of the Nazi regime but also places blame on domestic groups and regulators.

56. Goldwyn is often credited with the line, but the earliest published source attributes it to Moss Hart. See Fred R. Shapiro, ed., *The Yale Book of Quotations* (New Haven: Yale University Press, 2006), 343.

57. M. Todd Bennett, "The Celluloid War: State and Studio in Anglo-American Propaganda Film-making, 1939–1941," *International History Review* 24, no. 1 (March 2002): 78, 76.

58. Bennett, "Celluloid War," 75.

59. M. Todd Bennett, *One World, Big Screen: Hollywood, the Allies, and World War II* (Chapel Hill: University of North Carolina Press, 2012), chapter 2.

60. Raymond Gram Swing, *Forerunners of American Fascism* (New York: Julian Messner, 1935).

61. Patrick McGilligan, *Young Orson: The Years of Luck and Genius on the Path to Citizen Kane* (New York: Harper, 2015), 621–23.

62. Richard Meryman, *Mank: The Wit, World, and Life of Herman Mankiewicz* (New York: William Morrow, 1978), 268.

63. " 'Let America Set a World Example,' Urges W. R. Hearst," *SFE*, April 30, 1939; James Creelman, *On the Great Highway: The Wanderings and Adventures of a Special Correspondent* (Boston: Lothrop, 1901), 177–78.

64. On the role of radio in the intervention debate, see David Holbrook Culbert, *News for Everyman: Radio and Foreign Affairs in Thirties America* (Westport, Conn.: Greenwood, 1976), 6; Betty Houchin Winfield, *FDR and the News Media* (Urbana: University of Illinois Press, 1990), 103–11; Gerd Horten, *Radio Goes to War: The Cultural Politics of Propaganda during World War II* (Berkeley: University of California Press, 2002), 33; Steele, *Propaganda*, 136–46.

65. Culbert, *News for Everyman*, 4–5, 20.

66. Quoted in Winfield, *FDR and the News Media*, 104.

67. S. L. Brenner to Stephen Early, February 28, 1941, "Newspapers 1941–1942 Jan–July," OF 144, FDRL.

68. Culbert, *News for Everyman*, 25; "Credits America with Sound Sense," *Logan* (Utah) *Herald-Journal*, July 11, 1939.

69. Horten, *Radio Goes to War*, 34.

70. Quoted in Cull, *Selling War*, 109.

71. Hadley Cantril and Mildred Strunk, *Public Opinion, 1935–1946* (Princeton: Princeton University Press, 1951), 523.

72. "Look at the Actualities," *CT*, June 8, 1940.

73. U.S. Senate, 77th Cong., 1st sess., Subcommittee of the Committee on Interstate Commerce, *Propaganda in Motion Pictures*, hearings (September 9–26, 1941). On the hearings, see John E. Moser, " 'Gigantic Engines of Propaganda': The 1941 Senate Investigation of Hollywood," *Historian* 63, no. 4 (Summer 2001): 731–51; Bennett, *One World, Big Screen*, 83–88; and Clayton R. Koppes and Gregory D. Black, *Hollywood Goes to War: How Politics, Profits, and Propaganda Shaped World War II Movies* (New York: Free Press, 1987), 40–45.

74. U.S. Senate, *Propaganda in Motion Pictures*, 11, 17–18.

75. Quoted in Horten, *Radio Goes to War*, 37.

76. For movie attendance for 1941, see table Dh388–391, *Historical Statistics of the United States, Earliest Times to the Present: Millennial Edition*, ed.

Susan B. Carter et al., vol. 4, *Part D: Economic Sectors* (Cambridge: Cambridge University Press, 2006), 1123.

77. Cantril and Strunk, *Public Opinion*, 973.

78. Cantril and Strunk, *Public Opinion*, 973, 975.

79. Anne Chisholm and Michael Davie, *Lord Beaverbrook: A Life* (New York: Knopf, 1993), 397.

80. Atlantic Charter, August 14, 1941, Franklin D. Roosevelt Presidential Library and Museum, https://www.fdrlibrary.org/documents/356632/390886/atlantic_charter.pdf/30b3c906-e448-4192-8657-7bbb9e0fdd38.

81. Quoted in Elizabeth Borgwardt, *A New Deal for the World: America's Vision for Human Rights* (Cambridge, Mass.: Belknap, 2005), 45.

82. Borgwardt, *New Deal for the World*, 34, 44.

83. Reynolds, *Creation of the Anglo-American Alliance*, 259.

84. Note, October 11, 1939, PPF 5038, FDRL.

85. Luce to Beaverbrook, July 13, 1943, BBK/C/22, BP.

86. Quoted in Martin Gilbert, *Finest Hour: Winston S. Churchill*, vol. 6 (Boston: Houghton Mifflin, 1983), 1178.

87. Quoted in A. J. P. Taylor, *Beaverbrook* (London: Hamish Hamilton, 1972), 490.

88. Quoted in Kenneth Young, *Churchill and Beaverbrook: A Study in Friendship and Politics* (New York: James A. Heineman, 1966), 209.

89. "Evolution of the Minority," March 14, 1941, PSF (Subject): Lend-Lease, box 141, FDRL; "Alan Barth, Retired Post Writer, Dies," *Washington Post*, November 21, 1979.

90. Barth to Ferdinand Kuhn Jr., October 10, 1941, PSF (Departmental): Treasury: Morgenthau, Henry: Editorial Opinion, box 80, FDRL.

91. On other reporters' views of Hearst and McCormick, see Leo C. Rosten, *The Washington Correspondents* (New York: Harcourt, Brace, 1937), 357.

92. Ickes, *The Secret Diary of Harold L. Ickes*, vol. 3 (New York: Simon and Schuster, 1954), entry for June 2, 1940, 199.

93. "The Heat Is Off," *CT*, June 23, 1941.

94. " 'I Am the State,' " *DN*, November 10, 1941.

95. "Who's Fuehrer Now?" *DN*, August 9, 1941.

96. "Text of Lindbergh's Speech," *Boston Globe*, September 16, 1939.

97. Charles Lindbergh, "Aviation, Geography, and Race," *Reader's Digest*, November 1939, 66. For a vivid account of Lindbergh, Roosevelt, and the debate over intervention, see Lynne Olson, *Those Angry Days: Roosevelt, Lindbergh, and America's Fight over World War II, 1939–1941* (New York: Random House, 2013).

98. "The Text of Lindbergh's Address in Des Moines Coliseum," *Des Moines Register*, September 12, 1941.

99. "Tolerance and Religious Freedom Must Be Preserved in U.S.," *SFE*, September 16, 1941.

100. John L. Wheeler to R. Douglas Stuart, September 16, 1941, "Chapter Reactions to C. A. Lindbergh's Des Moines Speech," box 5, AFC.

101. McCormick to Lindbergh, March 7, 1941, "Lindbergh, Charles A., 1927–1953," box 50, I-60, RRMP.

102. "Lindbergh, Willkie, and the Jews," *CT*, September 13, 1941.

103. "Lindbergh's World Honors," *CT*, September 21, 1941; "The Circumstances Require This Explanation," *CT*, September 20, 1941; "World Honors Conferred on Lindbergh," *CT*, September 21, 1941.

104. "Conversation Piece," *DN*, September 18, 1941.

105. "What Is Anti-Semitism?" *DN*, September 10, 1941.

106. Patterson to Louis Harap, October 29, 1941, with boycott card attached, folder 6, box 29, JMPP.

107. Barth to Ferdinand Kuhn Jr., October 10, 1941, PSF (Departmental): Treasury: Morgenthau, Henry: Editorial Opinion, box 80, FDRL.

108. David Reynolds, *From Munich to Pearl Harbor: Roosevelt's America and the Origins of the Second World War* (Chicago: Ivan R. Dee, 2001), 155–56.

109. "More about the USS *Greer*," *DN*, October 29, 1941. On the *Greer* incident, see Robert Dallek, *Franklin D. Roosevelt and American Foreign Policy, 1932–1945* (New York: Oxford University Press, 1979), 287–89.

110. Knox to Patterson, November 1941 (exact date uncertain), "Navy—Knox, Frank, 1939–1941," box 62, PSF, FDRL.

111. See Dallek, *Franklin D. Roosevelt and American Foreign Policy*, 286; and Churchill's briefing to the war cabinet, August 19, 1941, 104–5, National Archives reference CAB 65-19-20, TNA.

112. Dallek, *Franklin D. Roosevelt and American Foreign Policy*, 587n24.

113. See Roosevelt's comments on Stark's proposed testimony: Roosevelt to Stark, September 18, 1941, "Navy—Knox, Frank, 1939–1941," box 62, PSF, FDRL.

114. Cantril and Strunk, *Public Opinion*, 1128. In October 1941, 58 percent supported convoys, with 35 percent opposed.

115. "Roosevelt's War," *DN*, October 21, 1941.

116. Flynn to Patterson, October 6, 1941, folder 2, box 28, JMPP.

117. See Waldo Heinrichs, *Threshold of War: Franklin D. Roosevelt and American Entry into World War II* (New York: Oxford University Press, 1988), 133–42.

118. Gerhard L. Weinberg, *A World at Arms: A Global History of World War II*, 2nd ed. (Cambridge: Cambridge University Press, 2005), 252–60.

119. "C'mon, Let's Appease Japan," *DN*, November 24, 1941.

120. "In the News," *SFE*, December 3, 1941.

121. "Mr. Knox Spies a War," *CT*, October 27, 1941.

122. "Mr. Roosevelt and Time," *CT*, November 29, 1941.

123. " 'Blood, Toil, Tears and Sweat'—and Poverty," *DN*, December 5, 1941.

124. "We Hope We're Proved Liars, but We're Afraid Not," *DN*, December 6, 1941; "Why Should We Believe Him?" *DN*, December 7, 1941.

125. Some secondary sources say that the *Daily News* did not publish the story, but in fact it did. See " 'War Plan' Asks AEF of 5 Million," *DN*, December 4, 1941; and "Ask Congress Probe Plan for Giant AEF," *DN*, December 5, 1941. For the best summaries of the incident, see Douglas M. Charles, *J. Edgar Hoover and the Anti-interventionists: FBI Political Surveillance and the Rise of the Domestic Security State, 1939–1945* (Columbus: Ohio State University Press, 2007), chapter 5; and Jerome Edwards, *The Foreign Policy of Col. McCormick's "Tribune," 1929–1941* (Reno: University of Nevada Press, 1971), 176–80.

126. "Stimson Assails Telling War Plan," *NYT*, December 6, 1941.

127. Quoted in Charles, *J. Edgar Hoover*, 123.

128. Charles, *J. Edgar Hoover*, 123; Ickes, *Secret Diary*, vol. 3, entry for December 7, 1941, 660.

129. "The Real War Plan," *CT*, December 4, 1941.

130. Smith, *Colonel*, 417, 419.

Chapter 11. Which Side Are You On?

1. "Fallen Hero," American Experience, accessed January 25, 2021, https://www.pbs.org/wgbh/americanexperience/features/lindbergh-fallen-hero/.

2. For a detailed discussion of Hearst's whereabouts on December 7, see Taylor Coffman, "Hearst and Pearl Harbor: A Memoir in 41 Parts," 15, accessed January 25, 2021, http://www.coffmanbooks.com/HPHpdfs/HearstPH-v7.pdf.

3. "United Nation Marches to Victory," *SFE*, December 8, 1941.

4. "In the News," *SFE*, December 8, 1941.

5. "In the News," *SFE*, January 29, 1942.

6. "In the News," *SFE*, January 25, January 6, February 17, and January 29, 1942.

7. Roosevelt used the term "concentration camp" at the time. See press conference #853, October 20, 1942, 157, Press Conferences of President Franklin D. Roosevelt, Franklin D. Roosevelt Presidential Library and Museum, http://www.fdrlibrary.marist.edu/_resources/images/pc/pco139.pdf.

8. "In the News," *SFE*, February 21, 1941.

9. Henry McLemore, "The Japs Stay until Feb. 24!" *SFE*, February 5, 1942.

10. "In the News," *SFE*, February 17, 1942.

11. "Editorial," *SFE*, November 8, 1942.

12. "In the News," *SFE*, March 10, 1942.

13. "Editorial," *SFE*, October 25, 1942.

14. See, for example, the letters dated December 24, 1941, January 26, 1942, and April 29, 1942, in part 1 of Hearst's FBI file, FBI Records: The Vault, https://vault.fbi.gov/reading-room-index.

15. "Open Doors of Palestine," *SFE*, April 20, 1944. See also "Keep Palestine Open," *SFE*, April 2, 1944. On the Hearst press and Palestine, see Deborah E. Lipstadt, *Beyond Belief: The American Press and the Coming of the Holocaust, 1933–1945* (New York: Free Press, 1986), 224–27.

16. "Jewish Leaders Thank Hearst Papers for Efforts to Keep Palestine Open," *SFE*, April 10, 1944.

17. "We All Have Only One Task," *CT*, December 8, 1941.

18. "Our Principal Enemy," *CT*, January 14, 1942.

19. "Poisoned News," *CT*, July 15, 1944.

20. "America and France," *CT*, November 30, 1942.

21. "If Stalin Conquers Europe," *CT*, February 15, 1942.

22. "Fascist! That's New Deal Tag for Its Critics," *CT*, March 31, 1944; "Smear Brigade Sets Stage to Keep FDR In," *CT*, February 21, 1944.

23. "Fascist! That's New Deal Tag for Its Critics." For anti-Semitic stereotypes, see the *Chicago Tribune* cartoons of January 11, 1943, February 9, 1943, March 23, 1943, August 5, 1943, August 14, 1943, December 27, 1943, and February 9, 1944.

24. Stolz to McCormick, no date but apparently 1944, folder 18, box 20, I-61, RRMP.

25. Henning to McCormick, April 12, 1944, folder 18, box 20, I-61, RRMP.

26. Patterson to McCormick, April 5, 1944, folder 6, box 54, JMPP.

27. Day to Maloney, October 28, 1941, "Editor's Office, Misc., 1942–1972, Day, Donald," XI-125, CTDP.

28. Cable to Mr. Maxwell, August 26, 1942, "Editor's Office, Misc., 1942–1972, Day, Donald," XI-125, CTDP; Maloney to Manly, September 7, 1942, XI-125, CTDP.

29. Quoted in Mark Weber, foreword to Donald Day, *Onward Christian Soldiers: An American Journalist's Dissident Look at World War II* (Newport Beach, Calif.: Noontide, 2002), vii. Day was interned for nine months by the U.S. military after the war. Eventually he got his U.S. passport back. He freelanced for the *Daily Mail* and the *Tribune* and received a pension from the *Tribune* until his death in 1966. For more on Day, see John Carver Edwards, *Berlin Calling: American Broadcasters in Service to the Third Reich* (New York: Praeger, 1991), chapter 6.

30. "The Dies Committee," *CT*, March 13, 1942.

31. "Farewell to the Power of the Purse," *CT*, March 19, 1942; " 'Wild' New Deal Schemes Ripped in House Debate," *CT*, March 4, 1942.

32. "Col. McCormick Warns of Plot to Betray U.S.," *CT*, August 7, 1943.

33. John Tebbel, *An American Dynasty: The Story of the McCormicks, Medills and Pattersons* (Garden City, N.Y.: Doubleday, 1947), 239.

34. "Pvt. Richard Graff," *CT*, February 9, 1942.

35. "Probers Blast REA for Waste of War Metals," *CT*, March 6, 1942.

36. "Col. M'Cormick Says Reds Balk Arms to Pacific," *CT*, February 16, 1944.

37. "Navy Had Word of Jap Plan to Strike at Sea," *CT*, June 7, 1942.

38. Trohan to McCormick, folder 7, box 4, XI-317, TCA.

39. On the *Tribune*'s Midway story, see Richard Norton Smith, *The Colonel: The Life and Legend of Robert R. McCormick, 1880–1955* (Boston: Houghton Mifflin, 1997), 429–40; Dina Goren, "Communication Intelligence and the Freedom of the Press: The *Chicago Tribune*'s Battle of Midway Dispatch and the Breaking of the Japanese Naval Code," *Journal of Contemporary History* 16, no. 4 (October 1981): 663–90; and David Kahn, *The Codebreakers: The Story of Secret Writing* (London: Weidenfeld and Nicolson, 1967), 603.

40. "In the Open," *CT*, August 9, 1942.

41. "Smear Brigade Sets Stage to Keep FDR In: Vilification Plot Unfolds Again," *CT*, February 21, 1944; "Willkie or FDR, It's All One to Superstaters," *CT*, February 28, 1944.

42. On the AP antitrust suit, see Sam Lebovic, *Free Speech and Unfree News: The Paradox of Press Freedom in America* (Cambridge, Mass.: Harvard University Press, 2016), 76–84.

43. "On Slogans," *CT*, August 10, 1944.

44. "Whatta Man!" *Chicago Daily News*, March 19, 1942, PPF 426, FDRL.

45. "The Adventures of Colonel McCosmic," *Chicago Daily News*, March 25, 1942.

46. Memo for the president, April 4, 1942, PPF 426, FDRL.

47. Roosevelt to MacLeish, July 13, 1942, PPF 6295, FDRL.

48. L. M. Birkhead, *The Case against the McCormick-Patterson Press* (Girard, Kans.: Haldeman-Julius, 1945), 6.

49. Chalmers M. Roberts, " . . . And When We Heard," *Washington Post*, December 7, 1991.

50. "Having a Wonderful Time," *WTH*, June 21, 1942.

51. Memo, Early to Watson, December 10, 1941, PPF 245, FDRL.

52. "Textual Excerpts from the War Speech," *NYT*, December 12, 1941.

53. Richard J. Evans, *The Third Reich at War* (New York: Penguin, 2009), 243.

54. Grace Tully, *FDR: My Boss* (New York: Charles Scribner's Sons, 1949), 291–93, quote at 293; John Chapman, *Tell It to Sweeney: The Informal History of the "New York Daily News"* (Garden City, N.Y.: Doubleday, 1961), 186.

55. Chapman, *Tell It to Sweeney*, 181–86.

56. "Good-by Wasp," *DN*, October 28, 1942.

57. "The White Man's Burden," *DN*, November 1, 1942.

58. October 30, 1944. See also "Give Our Boys a Break—Gas the Japs," *DN*, March 6, 1945; and "We Should Gas Japan," *DN*, November 30, 1943.

59. "Russia First??" *DN*, February 6, 1942.

60. "The White Man's Burden."

61. "Antidote for Venom," *Camden* (N.J.) *Courier-Post*, May 27, 1942. For more on anti-Semitism in the war years, see Stephen H. Norwood, "American

Anti-Semitism during World War II," in *A Companion to World War II*, ed. Thomas Zeiler (Malden, Mass.: Wiley-Blackwell, 2013), 909–25.

62. Deposition of Robert S. Allen, quoted in "Early Testifies F.R. Termed Convoys Story 'Deliberate Lie,'" *Camden (N.J.) Morning Post*, October 23, 1941.

63. See Betty Houchin Winfield, *FDR and the News Media* (Urbana: University of Illinois Press, 1990), 68; Graham J. White, *FDR and the Press* (Chicago: University of Chicago Press, 1979), 44–45; Carolyn Sayler, *Doris Fleeson: Incomparably the First Political Journalist of Her Time* (Santa Fe: Sunstone, 2011), 51–53; Chapman, *Tell It to Sweeney*, 207–09.

64. John O'Donnell, "Capitol Stuff," *DN*, October 3, 1945.

65. Mildred Beetman et al. to Patterson, October 3, 1945, folder 8, box 36, JMPP. Other letters of protest are in the same folder. On Patterson's unfounded fears of an advertising boycott because of O'Donnell's column, see Patterson to McCormick, October 18, 1945, and October 22, 1945, both in folder 8, box 54, JMPP.

66. Robert E. Segal, "As We Were Saying," *American Israelite*, December 14, 1950; O'Donnell, "Capitol Stuff," *DN*, February 2 and October 27, 1948.

67. Non-Sectarian Anti-Nazi League, "You Are Reading Pro-Nazi Poison," undated, folder 1, box 29, JMPP.

68. Quoted in Tebbel, *American Dynasty*, 265; Birkhead, *McCormick-Patterson Press*, 19.

69. Birkhead, *McCormick-Patterson Press*, 16–17.

70. "Journalettes," *McComb* (Miss.) *Daily Journal*, May 28, 1942.

71. "House Member Raps at Two Newspapers as Aids to Fascists," *Cincinnati Enquirer*, August 4, 1942.

72. "You're a Liar, Congressman Holland," *DN*, August 5, 1942.

73. Robert Conway to Mr. Fritzinger, memo on anti-*News* sentiment, November 5, 1942, folder 1, box 29, JMPP.

74. Night watchman: Patterson to W. B. Denhart, April 30, 1942, folder 7, box 28, JMPP.

75. Memo, Wallach to Patterson, December 8, 1942, folder 5, box 32, JMPP. For an example, see the letter about "alien-minded elements" headlined "Us and Our Public," *DN*, November 12, 1942.

76. Patterson to Wallach, December 9, 1942, folder 5, box 32, JMPP.

77. Ayn Rand to Patterson, August 5, 1942, folder 3, box 32, JMPP.

78. "Our Asiatic Crusade," *DN*, October 29, 1944.

79. "Of Course We're for America First," *DN*, October 27, 1944.

80. "What Are Our War Aims?" *DN*, June 13, 1943.

81. "Brave New World," *DN*, June 7, 1942.

82. "Dewey on Taxes," *DN*, October 6, 1944; "Capitol Stuff," *DN*, November 13, 1944.

83. "The Fourth Term Is the Issue," *DN*, October 14, 1944.

84. "President Petulant at Pearson," *DN*, September 2, 1943.

85. "Freedom on the Air," *DN*, February 17, 1943.

86. "A Fourth Term for Caesar?" *DN*, August 9, 1942; Morris Ernst to Patterson, August 7, 1942, folder 9, box 28, JMPP. The date on the letter appears to be incorrect, for the editorial in question appeared August 9. Patterson's reply is dated August 11.

87. "Brave New World."

88. "60% of Dailies Support Dewey; Roosevelt Backed by 22%," *Editor & Publisher*, November 4, 1944, 9, 68.

89. "Survey of Intelligence Materials No. 19," April 15, 1942, Office of War Information: Survey of Intelligence: April 1942, 3, 12, box 155, PSF, FDRL.

90. Hadley Cantril, "Pre–Pearl Harbor Interventionists and Non-interventionists," August 3, 1942, "Interventionist Report (pre–Pearl Harbor), Office of Public Opinion Research," box 583, DNC. On the role of isolationism in the 1942 midterms, see Richard E. Darilek, *A Loyal Opposition in Time of War: The Republican Party and the Politics of Foreign Policy from Pearl Harbor to Yalta* (Westport, Conn.: Greenwood, 1976), 54–55.

91. Arthur M. Schlesinger Jr., "Franklin Delano Roosevelt," *Time*, April 13, 1998.

92. On the Roosevelt administration's propaganda efforts during the war, see Steven Casey, *Cautious Crusade: Franklin D. Roosevelt, American Public Opinion, and the War against Nazi Germany* (New York: Oxford University Press, 2001); Michael Leigh, *Mobilizing Consent: Public Opinion and American Foreign Policy, 1937–1947* (Westport, Conn.: Greenwood, 1976), chapter 3; and Winfield, *FDR and the News Media*, chapter 8.

93. FDR to Lowell Mellett, January 18, 1944, box 142, PSF Subject file: Mellett, Lowell, FDRL.

94. Richard W. Steele, "Franklin D. Roosevelt and His Foreign Policy Critics," *Political Science Quarterly* 94, no. 1 (Spring 1979): 30; Steele, *Free Speech in the Good War* (New York: St. Martin's, 1999), 167–68.

95. Department of Justice, memorandum, content analysis of the *Chicago Daily Tribune;* the *New York Journal American;* and the *New York Daily News*, all dated May 19, 1942, "Propaganda, Domestic," FBP.

96. See Mark A. Stoler, *The Politics of the Second Front: American Military Planning and Diplomacy in Coalition Warfare, 1941–1943* (Westport, Conn.: Greenwood, 1977), 22–23; and Casey, *Cautious Crusade*, 83–84.

97. Tom Driberg, *Beaverbrook: A Study in Power and Frustration* (London: Weidenfeld and Nicolson, 1956), 273.

98. Anne Chisholm and Michael Davie, *Lord Beaverbrook: A Life* (New York: Knopf, 1993), 425. See also Bureau of Demobilization, *Industrial Mobilization for War: History of the War Production Board and Its Predecessor Agencies, 1940–1945, Production and Administration*, vol. 1 (Washington, D.C.: U.S. Government Printing Office, 1947), 278–79; and Franklin Roosevelt, State of the Union Address, January 6, 1942, The American Presidency Project, https://www.presidency.ucsb.edu/documents/state-the-union-address-1.

99. Winston Churchill, *The Second World War: The Grand Alliance*, vol. 3 (Boston: Houghton Mifflin, 1948–53), 690.

100. Richard Toye, *Winston Churchill: A Life in the News* (Oxford: Oxford University Press, 2020), 199; Clementine Churchill to Winston Churchill, probably February 12, 1942, in *Speaking for Themselves: The Personal Letters of Winston and Clementine Churchill*, ed. Mary Soames (London: Doubleday, 1998), 463–64.

101. Chisholm and Davie, *Lord Beaverbrook*, 428–29.

102. Beaverbrook, "To the Battlefield Let Us Go Forth . . . ," *DE*, June 22, 1942.

103. Chisholm and Davie, *Lord Beaverbrook*, 433; Averell Harriman and Elie Abel, *Special Envoy to Churchill and Stalin, 1941–1946* (New York: Random House, 1975), 133.

104. Quoted in Kenneth Young, *Churchill and Beaverbrook: A Study in Friendship and Politics* (New York: James A. Heineman, 1966), 232.

105. "Mr. Churchill," *DE*, September 21, 1942. On Churchill's relationship with the press during the war, see Toye, *Winston Churchill*, chapters 6 and 7.

106. Beaverbrook to Kennedy, September 8, 1942, BBK/C/193, BP.

107. Harold Orlansky, "Reactions to the Death of President Roosevelt," *Journal of Social Psychology* 26, no. 2 (November 1947): 239.

108. "President Roosevelt," *SFE*, April 13, 1945.

109. Smith, *Colonel*, 454; "A Nation Mourns," *CT*, April 13, 1945.

110. "Famous Sayings of Franklin D. Roosevelt," *DN*, April 13, 1945.

111. "Roosevelt in History," *DN*, April 14, 1945.

112. "Three of the Big Ones Dead in a Month," *DN*, May 5, 1945.

113. Quoted in Tebbel, *American Dynasty*, 270.

114. Luce to Beaverbrook, May 10, 1945, BBK/C/227, BP.

115. "More Silence about Pearl Harbor," *DN*, October 22, 1944.

116. "Of Course We're for America First."

117. "Three Years Ago Today," *DN*, December 7, 1944.

118. John T. Flynn, "Records Bare Truth about Pearl Harbor," *CT*, October 22, 1944.

119. John T. Flynn, "Exposes More Secrets of Pearl Harbor Scandal," *CT*, September 2, 1945.

120. See David Kahn, "The Intelligence Failure of Pearl Harbor," *Foreign Affairs* 70, no. 5 (Winter 1991): 138–53. On Pearl Harbor conspiracy theories, see Kathryn S. Olmsted, *Real Enemies: Conspiracy Theories and American Democracy, World War I to 9/11* (New York: Oxford University Press, 2009), chapter 2.

121. McCormick to Ator, September 9, 1945, and November 7, 1945, folder 5, box 9, I-61, RRMP.

Epilogue

1. Alice Albright Hoge, *Cissy Patterson* (New York: Random House, 1966), 185.
2. "Joseph Medill Patterson," *DN*, May 27, 1946.
3. Matthew Pressman astutely analyzes the right-wing populism of the *Daily News* from the 1940s to the 1960s in his unpublished conference paper, "Tabloid Journalism and Right-Wing Populism: The *New York Daily News* in the Mid-20th Century" (paper delivered at the annual conference of the Association for Education in Journalism and Mass Communication, Toronto, August 2019).
4. "Passing of a Giant," *Time*, June 3, 1946.
5. "*News* Elects New Officers," *DN*, September 2, 1946.
6. "Strange Bedfellows, Etc.," *DN*, March 30, 1947.
7. McCormick to Cissy Patterson, November 6, 1946, "Patterson Family: Eleanor Medill Patterson, 1941–1948," box 90, I-60, RRMP.
8. See Walter Trohan to McCormick, September 1, 1948, "Patterson Family: Eleanor Medill Patterson, Death and Estate, 1948–1954," box 90, I-60, RRMP.
9. "Cissie," *Time*, August 2, 1948.
10. "Outpost," *Time*, April 11, 1949.
11. Richard Norton Smith, *The Colonel: The Life and Legend of Robert R. McCormick, 1880–1955* (Boston: Houghton Mifflin, 1997), 517–18.
12. "W. R. Hearst," *Manchester Guardian*, August 15, 1951.
13. "William Randolph Hearst," *St. Louis Post-Dispatch*, August 15, 1951.
14. "William Randolph Hearst," *Dayton Daily News*, August 15, 1951.
15. "In the Beaver's News Kingdom Empire Propaganda Comes First," *Newsweek*, April 28, 1952, 48.
16. "In the Beaver's News Kingdom Empire Propaganda Comes First."
17. McCormick to Ator, August 15, 1946, folder 8, box 8, I-61, RRMP.
18. "Flying Carpet," *Time*, March 20, 1950; McCormick to Ator, August 21, 1948, folder 8, box 8, I-61, RRMP.
19. "3 Men Called a Government in Themselves," *CT*, May 29, 1950.
20. McCormick to Maloney, June 10, 1950, "Lehman, Frankfurter and Morgenthau," box 44, I-60, RRMP.
21. McCormick to Wheeler, June 5, 1950, "Jewry, 1929–1950," box 44, I-60, RRMP. On conservatives' use of the discourse of victimhood, see Lee Bebout, "Weaponizing Victimhood: Discourses of Oppression and the Maintenance of Supremacy on the Right," in *News on the Right: Studying Conservative News Cultures*, ed. Anthony Nadler and A. J. Bauer (New York: Oxford University Press, 2020), 64–83.
22. "How We Earned His Hate," *CT*, June 11, 1948.
23. McCormick to Ator, May 26, 1953, folder 8, box 8, I-61, RRMP.
24. "Rip Van Winkle Wakes Up," *CT*, October 4, 1952.
25. McCormick to Ator, August 28, 1945, folder 8, box 8, I-61, RRMP.

26. McCormick to Ator, June 27, 1947, folder 8, box 8, I-61, RRMP.

27. McCormick to Ator, October 7, 1947, folder 8, box 8, I-61, RRMP.

28. "Why Change Jackasses in Midstream?" *CT*, November 13, 1949.

29. See, for example, the *Tribune*'s suggestion that all foreign and domestic intelligence be placed under Hoover's control: "Intelligence Flops," *CT*, July 1, 1955.

30. McCormick to Ator, August 31, 1951, folder 8, box 8, I-61, RRMP.

31. "Eisenhower or Stevenson?" *CT*, October 26, 1952.

32. See the correspondence between Herbert Hoover and Henry Regnery regarding Hoover's efforts to raise money for *Human Events*, folder "Regnery, Henry, 1945–1960," box 183, PPI, HHL. On the founding of *Human Events*, see "*Human Events*, 1944–," in *The Conservative Press in Twentieth-Century America*, ed. Ronald Lora and William Henry Longton (Westport, Conn.: Greenwood, 1999), 449–59. On the old isolationists after World War II, see Justus D. Doenecke, *Not to the Swift: The Old Isolationists in the Cold War Era* (Lewisburg: Bucknell University Press, 1979).

33. On changes in the media after World War II, see Matthew Pressman, *On Press: The Liberal Values That Shaped the News* (Cambridge, Mass.: Harvard University Press, 2018). For more on conservatives' attacks on the allegedly liberal media, see Eric Alterman, *What Liberal Media? The Truth about Bias and the News* (New York: Basic, 2003).

34. Felix Morley, "An Adventure in Journalism," in *A Year of Human Events* (Washington, D.C.: Human Events, 1945), vii.

35. Nicole Hemmer, *Messengers of the Right: Conservative Media and the Transformation of American Politics* (Philadelphia: University of Pennsylvania Press, 2016), 17.

36. For other scholars who find the origins of modern conservatism in the 1930s, see Joseph E. Lowndes, *From the New Deal to the New Right: Race and the Southern Origins of Modern Conservatism* (New Haven: Yale University Press, 2008); Kim Phillips-Fein, *Invisible Hands: The Businessmen's Crusade against the New Deal* (New York: Norton, 2010); Elliot A. Rosen, *The Republican Party in the Age of Roosevelt: Sources of Anti-Government Conservatism in the United States* (Charlottesville: University of Virginia Press, 2014); Clyde P. Weed, *The Nemesis of Reform: The Republican Party during the New Deal* (New York: Columbia University Press, 1994); and Jefferson Cowie, *The Great Exception: The New Deal and the Limits of American Politics* (Princeton: Princeton University Press, 2017).

37. McCormick to Walter Trohan, November 14, 1946, "*Chicago Tribune*—McCormick, Robert R., 1944–47," box 10, WTP.

38. "Col. McCormick Sees New Party With '56 Slate," *CT*, September 5, 1952.

39. "The Real Platform," *CT*, August 20, 1952.

40. " 'For America' Group Formed by 14 Leaders," *CT*, May 8, 1954.

41. Hemmer, *Messengers*, 133.

42. Anne Chisholm and Michael Davie, *Lord Beaverbrook: A Life* (New York: Knopf, 1993), 509–11.

43. Chisholm and Davie, *Lord Beaverbrook*, 462–66; "In the Beaver's News Kingdom Empire Propaganda Comes First," *Newsweek*, April 28, 1952, 48–51.

44. " 'Gestapo in Britain if Socialists Win,' " *DE*, June 5, 1945.

45. "What Attlee Said: The National Socialists," *DE*, June 6, 1945.

46. "Tories Will Regret Beaverbrook," *Manchester Guardian*, June 21, 1945.

47. "Heavy Poll Foreshadowed by Party Organisers," *Manchester Guardian*, June 22, 1945.

48. "Who Are the Guilty Men?" *DE*, June 23, 1945.

49. Michael Wolff, *The Man Who Owns the News: Inside the Secret World of Rupert Murdoch* (New York: Broadway Books, 2010), 71–72.

50. Beaverbrook, "Do You Care if We Lose the Empire?" *Sunday Express*, January 27, 1952, in Beaverbrook scrapbooks, BBK/L/64, BP.

51. "Beaverbrook's Title Is Renounced by Son," *NYT*, June 12, 1964.

52. "Get Britain out of Europe," *DE*, November 25, 2010.

53. "From Ferrets to Fish … New EU Laws That Are Ruining Britain," *DE*, June 24, 2014; United Nations Human Rights, Office of the High Commissioner, press release, "UN Human Rights Chief Urges U.K. to Tackle Tabloid Hate Speech," April 24, 2015, https://www.ohchr.org/EN/NewsEvents/Pages/DisplayNews.aspx?NewsID=15885.

54. "We Did It! Decade-Old *Daily Express* Crusade Comes to an End with Brexit Victory," *DE*, January 10, 2020. For a discussion of the British press and Brexit, see Angela Phillips, "The British Right-Wing Mainstream and the European Referendum," in Nadler and Bauer, *News on the Right*, 141–56.

55. "The *Tribune's* Colonel Dies," *Life*, April 11, 1955, 47.

56. "Sir Winston's Tribute," *Guardian*, June 10, 1964.

57. Si Sheppard, *The Partisan Press: A History of Media Bias in the United States* (Jefferson, N.C.: McFarland, 2008), 260. On the postwar British press, see Jeremy Tunstall, *Newspaper Power: The New National Press in Britain* (Oxford: Clarendon, 1996).

58. "Trump's Full Inauguration Speech," January 20, 2017, *New York Times*, https://www.nytimes.com/video/us/politics/100000004863342/donald-trump-full-inaugural-address-2017.html.

Index

Illustrations are indicated by italicized page numbers.